revelations

an anthology of expository essays by and about blacks

Fifth Edition

Teresa M. Redd
Carolyn E. Shuttlesworth

Learning Solutions

New York Boston San Francisco
London Toronto Sydney Tokyo Singapore Madrid
Mexico City Munich Paris Cape Town Hong Kong Montreal

Pearson Learning Solutions, 501 Boylston Street, Suite 900, Boston, MA 02116
A Pearson Education Company
www.pearsoned.com

Printed in the United States of America

2 3 4 5 6 7 8 9 10 XXXX 15 14 13 12 11 10

000200010270641859

CG/CA

ISBN 10: 0-558-74853-8
ISBN 13: 978-0-558-74853-1

Copyright Acknowledgments

Contents

Rhetorical Index

Acknowledgments

In many ways this anthology is a product of the Department of English at Howard University. My colleagues in the Department made me think of creating such an anthology, they urged me to undertake the project, and then they wholeheartedly supported my efforts. Thus, I thank *all* of my colleagues in the Department—past and present.

—Teresa M. Redd, Ph.D.

This edition of the anthology is a result of the Writing Faculty's commitment to revising Freshman English 002. We listened to our students, and we assessed the trends and best practices in expository writing and crafted a model to suit the specific needs of a wonderfully brilliant population of students. Professor's Edward Preston, Patricia Elam, Patricia Noone, Wade Harrell, Joyce Camper and Ada Vilageliu-Diaz made specific recommendations for additions to this edition. The entire faculty's enthusiasm for this contemporary edition will undoubtedly enhance teaching and learning.

—Carolyn E. Shuttlesworth, Ph.D.

Preface for Students

The fifth edition of *Revelations* offers a chronological approach to the subjects considered, beginning with the Egyptian civilization and ending with the present. Works have been chosen to display good writing and to reflect the temporal context of the ideas of outstanding individuals. A broad approach to the African Diaspora, including Africa and the Caribbean as well as consideration of Black Indian and Afro-Latino culture, has been taken. Readers will find works from several disciplines that foster interdisciplinary discourse. The expository essays convey information and concepts to prepare writers to express ideas clearly and to develop skills of critical thinking and logic.

All of the writers in this book have a great deal to say about the things that matter most to us. They write about landmark events such as African scientific discoveries, the enslavement of Africans in the United States, the Civil Rights Movement, and the Black Power Movement. They also write about Black culture—our language, our literature, our music, and our art. These writers explain themselves, their community and the world. They explain by illustrating, comparing, contrasting, classifying, defining terms, analyzing processes, identifying causes and describing effects. These are the strategies of expository writing. Used appropriately, expository strategies can help writers generate ideas and organize thoughts in a logical and meaningful way. As you read this anthology, notice how the writers employ theses strategies to develop their essays. Do they *contrast* two subjects, highlighting the differences point by point or subject by subject? Do they identify discrete stages of a *process*? Do they divide a group into categories according to a principle of *classification?*

In addition to the expository patterns, notice each writer's sentence structure, word choice, and punctuation. Do you prefer the clean, simple prose of Haki Madhubuti or the long, rhythmic sentences of Ralph Ellison? What do you think of the mixture of Black English and academic English in Geneva Smitherman's essay or the distinctive diction in Eleanor Traylor's? Do you agree with the ideas about hip hop culture expressed by Imani Perry?

Finally, think critically about the content of the essays. Compare your experiences and observations to those described here. At first, you might respond to these essays by recalling your own experience in a journal entry or by writing a summary. After carefully examining an essay, you might compose a critique to question or support one of the author's statements. Later, after consulting related readings, you might compose a synthesis of the opinions, facts, and examples from many sources.

Regardless of the approach you choose, take advantage of the opportunity to write about issues raised in this book. They are important and can be clarified by writing, for writing is a means of exploring ideas, of turning them inside out and looking at them slowly, carefully, thoughtfully. In other words, when you write about these issues, write in order to communicate with readers, but also—as author Terry McMillan advises—"write in order to *know.*"

Ancient Egyptians:
Innovators of the Past
Richard O'Bryant

Art, science and engineering have a history that is deep in human existence. Often, people have little knowledge of the origins of the techniques and ideas in use today. Many of the techniques and innovations in use today originate from the times of ancient Egypt. These contributions are often overlooked by historians. The Egyptians contributed many things to the arts, sciences and engineering. These contributions include many of the building, mathematical and creative arts techniques we use today. Many people are aware of the great pyramids and ancient artifacts of Ancient Egypt. However, they are unaware that this African civilization may have provided the basic building blocks for civilizations to follow, such as the Greek and Roman civilizations. Dr. Aziz Batran, Associate Professor of History here at Howard University, shared his knowledge on a few of the many Egyptian contributions to fine art, science and engineering.

To understand the Egyptian contribution to these fields, one must understand the time in which [the Egyptians] lived. About 4000 B.C. the Kingdoms of Upper Egypt and Lower Egypt were born. These Kingdoms grew very quickly. During this period, buildings began to be made of bricks, the 365 day calendar was invented, architecture styles developed and a writing system, hieroglyphics, was developed.

The unification of Egypt occurred in 3200 B.C. after a long period of intense growth. Throughout the Nile Valley, new and improved methods of agriculture, domestication of animals and food production were developed. The potential of the rich and fertile Nile Valley was being tapped. Thus village life developed rapidly along the Nile River.

For about 3000 years, the black people of Ancient Egypt, heirs to the Neolithic Revolution in the Nile Valley, built a civilization that surpassed in its splendor any other civilization of that time. It predated the civilizations of the

Middle East, Greece and Rome. It may have provided the foundation on which these civilizations were developed. Ancient Egypt was an authentic African civilization, developed by Africans on African soil.

Fine Art

"skill acquired by experience, study or observation: the conscious use of skill and creative imagination esp. in the production of aesthetic objects; also: works so produced"

The Egyptians made a great deal of contributions to the field of arts and crafts. They explored and utilized the various natural resources of their country as well as neighboring countries to create their art. The Egyptians mastered the techniques of metal working such as forging, hammering, casting, stamping, soldering and riveting. They built factories where gold and silver were fashioned into jewelry, and copper into weapons and large statues. They also mastered wood-working. Egyptian carpenters used saws, pliers, hammers and drills to manufacture many kinds of beautiful furniture. The carpenters who had the most significant effect on the Egyptian lifestyles were those who specialized in boat making. The boats were used all along the Nile to transport food, people, and stone blocks weighing between 8 and 10 tons each. These blocks were used for building temples, statues and pyramids. The boats were also used in trading expeditions to Syria, Palestine and down the Red Sea to Somalia.

The Egyptians were among the first to perfect the techniques of spinning and linen making, which were used in the textile industries. Spinning was done by the women, who produced a variety of fine fabrics. The finest cloth of all, byssus, was woven in the temples. It was sold abroad and brought huge revenues to the Egyptian Kingdom. In addition to textiles, Egyptians are credited with the invention of glass making techniques for both transparent and non-transparent glass. They manufactured vases, beads, mirrors and, later, colored glass.

Another of their great contributions was the making of Papyrus, from which the word paper is derived. The fibers of this plant were used for boat making, wicks for oil lamps, mats, baskets and ropes. Papyrus or paper was made by placing crosswise layers of fine strips taken from the stem of the Papyrus plant. After pressing and drying, the woven strips formed a large sheet of paper. Ancient Egypt was the source of many of the materials and methods that are used today in the field of fine arts.

Science

"knowledge covering general truths or the operation of general laws esp. as obtained and tested through scientific method: such knowledge concerned with the physical world and its phenomena"

In the field of science perhaps the most outstanding contribution of the Ancient Egyptians is mummification. Their perfection of mummification shows their precise knowledge of the sciences, including physics, chemistry, medicine and surgery. Mummification involves soaking the body of a deceased person in a chemical called Natron. This chemical was found in certain areas in Egypt, particularly in the Wadi el Natron (Wadi means Valley). The compounds of Natron are a mixture of sodium carbonate, sodium bicarbonate, salt and sodium sulphate. After having soaked the body in Natron for 70 days, [the Egyptians] drew the brain out through the nostrils and removed the intestines through an incision made in the side of the body. Operations as delicate as these necessitated an accurate knowledge of anatomy and surgery.

The Egyptians' medical knowledge can be considered as one of the most important early contributions of the Ancient Egyptians to the history of man. One of the most significant personalities in the history of medicine was Imhotep, the prime minister, architect and physician of King Zoser of the Third Dynasty. Imhotep was adopted by the Greeks. They called him Askelepios, the God of Medicine.

[The Egyptians] also had a vast knowledge of herbs, minerals and various chemical substances. The Egyptian doctor, like modern doctors, examined his patient and determined the symptoms of his ailment. Among the ailments identified and treated by the doctors were gastric disorders, stomach swelling, skin cancer, laryngitis, diabetes, bilharzia, opthalmia, bronchitis, and constipation. Doctors would treat their patients with ointments, syrups, potions, oils and inhalants.

Egyptian surgeons developed their surgical techniques at a very early period in their history. From the surgical pamphlets which survived from the old kingdom, historians have come to learn about the Egyptians' mastery of bone surgery, external pathology, dentistry and medicine.

Engineering

"the application of science and mathematics by which the properties of matter and the sources of energy in nature are made useful to man in structures, machines, products, systems and processes"

Engineering is a technical activity that specifies means for altering the physical environment to create utility. The genius of the Egyptians in the field of engineering can be seen today in the magnificent statues, obelisks, pyramids, sphinxes and temples which they constructed. The Egyptians were also very proficient in math. Their method of numeration is based on the decimal system. They did not use zero but used fractions such as ½, ⅓, ¼, etc. Egyptian administrative organization required the knowledge of arithmetic and the need to survey the area of land eroded or added each year by the flooding of the Nile. This led them to invent geometry. The Egyptians knew perfectly well how to calculate the area and volume of several geometric shapes. Their greatest mathematical success was the calculation of the area of a circle. They have been credited with approximating the value of pi to be 3.1605.

The Egyptians applied their mathematical knowledge to the extraction, transportation and positioning of the huge blocks of stone used in their massive architectural projects. They had a long tradition in using mudbricks and various kinds of stone from very early times. Their first use of heavy granite was during the period of the First Dynasty at which time it was used for flooring the tombs belonging to Al-Abydos. In the Second Dynasty, they used limestone to construct the walls of tombs.

The Egyptians used their mechanical engineering abilities in the construction of boats, vehicles and ramps, which were used to build pyramids, sphinxes and temples. They applied the principle of leverage to transport the large pieces of stone for very long distances.

The Egyptian architectural triumphs are among the best known. The most vital development in Egyptian architecture took place during the Third Dynasty. It was during this time [the Egyptians] constructed the first complete building of stone, the step pyramid of King Zoser.

The greatest of all pyramids was erected by Pharoah Khufu and remains number one on the list of the seven wonders of the ancient world. Its great proportions and longevity stand today as proof of the engineering, architectural and administrative expertise of the Egyptians. The exact proportions, measurements and orientation of the chambers and corridors of the Giza pyramid, not to mention the cutting and erection of giant obelisks in solid stone, indicate their great technical skills.

The pyramids built for the dead pharaohs were considered to be houses where they spent their immortal life. By their great height, the pyramids were meant to join earth with the heavens.

Khufu's pyramid stands 481 feet high; each of its square sides is 175 feet in length; 2,300,000 blocks of granite, each weighing between 8 and 10 tons, were used in its construction.

The cutting of stone and construction of the pyramids were accomplished solely through the strength of human hands. Every year, after the harvest season, some 100,000 peasants worked on the construction of the pyramids. Contrary to what many European historians believe, no slave labor was used. The labor was provided willingly and freely by the Egyptian peasants to immortalize the pharaohs who were thought to embody and symbolize the whole nation.

In addition to pyramids, the Egyptians built numerous Sphinxes out of solid rock. Sphinxes have the head of a man and body of a lion and symbolize power and strength. The Great Sphinx of Giza is believed to be the image of Khufu. The Sphinx, which was meant to commemorate Pharaoh Chephren, is believed to have been shot at and damaged as ordered by Napoleon because of its distinct black male features.

The Ancient [Egyptians were] ahead of their time. Their contributions, to what many consider to be European advancements, are innumerable. Only a few of their many developments were discussed by Dr. Batran. This cursory introduction to Ancient Egyptian advancements does not do justice to the greatness of their civilization. Their civilization warrants study by all people. For although their contributions are often overlooked, it is clear that their great civilization was an incubator for many of the techniques we use to this day.

They Came Before Columbus: The African Presence in Ancient America
Ivan Van Sertima

A study of the Olmec civilization reveals elements that so closely parallel ritual traits and techniques in the Egypto-Nubian world of the same period that it is difficult to maintain all these are due to mere coincidence. While it is possible to find a cultural trait or a technique in one place which is similar to that in another, *without any contact having taken place*, there is a method by which we can examine a parallel or a series of parallels to determine with relative certainty when something is purely coincidental or whether it is strongly suggestive of contact with, and influence from outsiders.

Let us first look at the monarchic traits, that is, the royal and priestly dress and emblems of power among the Olmecs and Egyptians. We can point to a cluster of half a dozen royal traits shared by ruling circles in both civilizations that are functionally related and appear in a combination too arbitrary and unique to be independently duplicated.

The double crown. This grew out of special historical circumstances in Egypt, the joining of the "two lands," Lower and Upper Egypt, by the African Pharoah Menes. The Nubian pharoahs donned the double crown of the two lands in the 8th century B.C. when they regained their power over the north. The double crown appears on an Olmec dignitary at Cerro de la Piedra. He is seen offering a glyph (symbolic object) with the Egyptian cross motif to a seated figure that has African features and African-type hair.

The royal flail. This was part of the ceremonial regalia of the pharoah. It has one or more pendants hanging from a staff and is usually represented resting on the king's shoulder. In an Olmec painting at Oxtotitlan, the Olmec personage seated on the throne has this type of flail, and it is in the same position behind the head.

The sacred boat or ceremonial bark of kings. This not only appears in both civilizations with the same function and curved shape but it also carries the same name (Mexican *cipac*; Egyptian *sibak*).

The use of purple. The religious value of purple and its use to distinguish priests and people of high risk had its origin among the Egyptians. Sanctity was attached to shell purple because the murex shell, from which it was extracted, revealed, by the sequence of colors through which it moved before acquiring its final fixed purple, a parallel to color changes of the Nile in flood. The Egyptians, therefore, considered purple a noble and sacred color, and, through the Phoenicians, who adopted the purple industry, the association of purple with royalty, the priesthood and the high-born spread throughout the Mediterranean.

We find purple having the same value in the Olmec world. Professor Zenil Medellin has noted that a patch of purple dye appears on one of the African monumental heads at San Lorenzo. He claims that these stone heads were originally painted but that the paint faded over time. In the *Nuttall Codex* (one of the few surviving documents of ancient America), Zelia Nuttall, the discoverer of the codex, notes "pictures of no fewer than 13 Mexican women of rank wearing purple skirts and five capes and jackets of the same color. In addition, 45 chieftains are figured with short, fringed round, purple waistcloths, and there are also three examples of the use of a close fitting purple cap."

The artificial beard. Another sign of royal or priestly office is the beard. A study of Olmec sculptures, carvings on stelae and paintings seems to suggest that the beard is alien to the usually hairless American chin. When it does appear on the native American chin, it looks like an appendage, artificially tapered and attached. When found on men with the air and poise of authority, it also functions as a badge of high rank. The use of highly stylized chin stubs as a mark of distinction is a custom of the Egyptian pharoahs.

Feathered fans or sunshades. The Egyptian pharoahs bore feathered fans that are almost identical in shape, style and color to those found in ancient Mexican paintings in the pyramid of Las Higueras. These fans were painted in an Olmec area and in a culture influenced by the Olmec, even though this culture (Totonac) is of a slightly later period. The fans are made of feathers arranged in concentric circles of blue, red and green. In Mexico they are blue, red and light blue. The Mexican light blue is the nearest equivalent on the color spectrum to the Egyptian green.

The parasol or ceremonial umbrella is another emblem of royalty in the two cultures. Today, the umbrella is so common and has such a utilitarian function (protection from sunburn or the occasional shower), that its unique ritual use and value as an index of rank has been forgotten. Professor A. Varron has demonstrated the use of the umbrella or parasol as an emblem of dignity and power in ancient times. The parasol is one of the items mentioned as being brought into Mexico by foreigners in an oral tradition recorded in the *Titulo Coyoi*. This is a major document of the Quiche' Maya. They were touched by the earlier Olmec and their tradition harks back to ancestral visitors of that time. "These things came from the east," goes the tradition, "from the other side of the water and the sea: they came here, they had their throne, their little benches and stools, they had their *parasols* and bone flutes."

It is important to understand what a great burden of proof is required to establish a cultural influence, even when there is a sound case for a physical presence and contact. Any one of the above traits, standing by itself as a single parallel, can be dismissed as coincidence. When such traits appear as an interconnected cluster, performing a single function duplicated nowhere else in the world, except where the Egyptians traveled or left their influence, then only a dogmatic conservative or a bigot can deny the possibility of both a physical contact and a cultural influence.

Gikuyu Industries: Hut-Building

Jomo Kenyatta

It is a common ambition of every Gikuyu young man to own a hut or huts, which means implicitly to have a wife or wives. The establishment of a homestead gives a man special status in the community; he is referred to as *muthuri* (an elder), and is considered capable of holding a responsible position in tribal affairs. Thus, it is the desire of every Gikuyu man to work hard and accumulate property which will enable him to build a homestead of his own. There is a proverb in Gikuyu which says: "*Wega uumaga na mocie*," that is, the quality of a man is judged by his homestead. With these few remarks we will proceed to describe how a hut is built.

Gikuyu huts are of the round type, with wooden walls and grass thatched roofs. The actual building of a hut takes only one day; and as soon as it is completed, a new fire is drilled from sacred fire-sticks, "*githegethi na Geka kia Igong-ona.*" But in case of rebuilding, the fire from the old hut is preserved to be transferred to the new hut. The fire is ritually lit in the new hut, and after a short ceremony of communing with the ancestral spirits the owner moves into the new homestead. Sometimes two or more huts are built simultaneously, as in the case of a man having more than one wife or a large family which could not be housed in one hut. But general custom requires that even a man with one wife should have two huts, one for his wife's private use and one for himself for general use. The woman's hut is called *nyomba*. Here it is taboo for a mere stranger to enter, because *nyomba* is considered as the traditional sacred abode of the family and the proper place to hold communion with their ancestral spirits. All aspects of religious and magical ceremonies and sacrifices which concern the family are centered around the *nyomba*. It is for fear of defilement and ill-luck that strangers are not allowed to cross this sacred threshold. The man's hut is called *thingira;* in this, friends and casual visitors are entertained.

Nowadays the system of having two huts for a man with only one wife is dying out, owing to the heavy burden of hut taxes imposed on the people by the British Government. The result has been congestion, whole families being crowded in one hut, for many such families can hardly maintain their livelihood and at the same time afford to find money for hut taxation.

We have mentioned that a hut is built and occupied in the same day; this statement may puzzle those who are not acquainted with the Gikuyu method of building. To avoid this, let us at once explain how the work that expedites the putting up of a hut is organized. Most important of all is the Gikuyu collective method of working. A few days before the erection of a hut or huts the building materials are collected. In doing this the division of labour according to sex plays an important role. The work of cutting wood necessary for building falls on men; women take the responsibility of providing thatching grass and other materials.

When a family is engaged in the work of building a hut or huts, the help of neighbours and friends is necessary in order to expedite the work. A man goes round asking his friends to help him, and at the same time telling them what kind of building materials he would like them to supply him with. In the same manner the wife visits her women friends, requesting them to help in various ways. Those who cannot take part in collecting building materials are asked to help in providing food and drink for the builders' feast, which is called *"iruga ria mwako."* On the day appointed many of these friends will turn up, bringing with them the required materials for building. The man and his wife or wives receive their helpers joyfully and bid them to sit down and rest. After all have arrived a feast is provided, consisting of a variety of food and drink. During the feasting this group of men and women entertain themselves with traditional songs relating to teamwork. Before they part, a day is appointed when the actual building of a hut or huts will take place.

It is obvious that without this system of teamwork it would take a man a long time to complete the work, especially in a community where the system of paid labour is traditionally unknown. In its place, mutual help guided by the rules of give and take plays a significant part. In every branch of work reciprocity is the fundamental principle governing the relationship between a man and his neighbours, and also between various groups or clans and the tribe. If a man, after having been asked to give his service, absents himself without a good reason, especially when his neighbour has urgent work, such as building a hut or a cattle kraal, which has to be completed in one day (for it is feared that should a hut or a kraal be left unfinished and unoccupied, evil spirits might dwell therein and, therefore, cause constant misfortune to the future occupants and their herd), the result will be that the defaulter will find himself socially boycotted for his individualistic attitude. When a man has thus been ostracised, *"kohingwo,"* he will have to pay a fine of one sheep or a he-goat to his neighbours for his bad behaviour. When the fine is paid, the animal is slaughtered for a feast, and then, after a short ceremony of reunion, the man's status as a good and helpful neighbour is reacknowledged.

After the building materials have been collected, the head of the family selects a plot where he wishes to establish his new homestead. In selecting the plot care is taken to see that the land is not associated with any ancestral curse or taboo. The plot must also be one that has been lawfully acquired. The homestead must not be built on or near a graveyard, or on a place where a fierce battle has taken place, resulting in loss of lives. Such places are considered as the resting homes for the departed spirits, and to disturb them would mean to invoke their anger.

When these preliminary arrangements have been made, the man prepares sugar-cane or honey beer for the foundation ceremony. Early in the morning, on the day of building a hut or huts, a small quantity of the beer is taken to the selected plot and, in communion with the ancestral spirits, it is sprinkled on the ground where the new home is to be built. Sometimes milk or uncooked gruel, "*gethambio*," is preferred for this ceremony, according to the custom of the clan to which the individual belongs. After the ancestral spirits have been summoned to join in the work of building, the friends who have gathered to help their neighbour start to clear and to level the ground. Then the foundation is marked according to the size of the hut which a man wants. To make a good circle a kind of string compass is employed. A stick is put in the centre of the circle and a string tied to it, then a man holds one end of the string and, after measuring the required paces, he holds the string tight and then goes round, marking the ground until the circle lines meet. This is called "*gokurura kiea*." When this is done the builders start digging holes in the ground for the outer wall. The holes are about one foot deep and about six inches in diameter. After this the inner circle is marked, which divides the hut into several apartments. Immediately the wall is erected and the roof put on. This completes the men's work in building, leaving the thatching to the womenfolk.

While the women are engaged in thatching, the men retire to a feast which has been awaiting them. During the feasting the men sing songs relating to the art of building; those who are clever and hard workers are highly praised in these songs; at the same time contemptuous phrases are uttered for laziness. In some of the phrases men call on the women in teasing tones, saying: "Look on those lazy-bones who are working like chameleons, the sun is going down; do you want us to make torches for you? Do hurry up and join us in feasting, and let us utter blessings for the homestead before the sun is completely gone down." To this the women answer in chorus, saying: "You men, you lack the most important art in building, namely, thatching. A wall and an empty roof cannot protect you from heavy rain, nor from burning sun. It is our careful thatching that makes a hut worth living in. We are not chameleons, but we do thatch our huts like '*nyoni ya nyagathanga*' (this is the name of a small bird in Gikuyu which is well known by its sweet songs and the neatness of its nest)."

In many of the Gikuyu cradle stories and legends *nyoni ya nyagathanga* and its work is highly praised. This acts as an encouragement to both boys and girls to become industrious in their future activities in life. It is characteristic of the Gikuyu people to sing inspiring songs while performing a task, for it is said: "to work in a happy mood is to make the task easier, and to relieve the heart from fatigue." ("*Koruta wera na ngoro theru ni kohothia wera na konyihia minoga.*")

When the women have finally finished thatching they join the men in feasting. Before the party comes to a close the owner of the homestead brings the remainder of the beer or the milk which has been sprinkled on the foundation; he hands it to a ceremonial elder, who after pouring the liquid into a ritual horn, calls upon those present to stand up. Then the ceremonial elder, with his hands raised holding the horn, turns towards Kere-Nyaga (Mount Kenya). In this position he chants a prayer, calling for a blessing for the homestead and its future prosperity. The following is the form of the prayer used for such an occasion:

> "*Wee Githuri oikaraga Kere-Nyaga; kerathimo geaku nikeo getomaga mecie ethegee. Namo marakara maku, nemo mahukagia mecie. Togogo-thaitha tweturaneire ohamwe na ngoma cia aciari aito. Togokoria ate orinderere mocie oyo na otome wethegee. Reke atumia ona mahio mathathare. Thaaai, thathayai Ngai, thaaai.*"

The following is the translation of the above prayer: "You, the Great Elder, who dwells on the Kere-Nyaga, your blessing allows homesteads to spread. Your anger destroys homesteads. We beseech You, and in this we are in harmony with the spirits of our ancestors: we ask You to guard this homestead and let it spread. Let the women, herd, and flock be prolific. (Chorus) Peace, praise, or beseech ye, Ngai (God), peace be with us."

After this the homestead is declared open. The next thing is to light the fire which we have mentioned in our earlier description. Two children, male and female, are selected for this ritual; they are looked upon as a symbol of peace and prosperity for the homestead. The ceremonial elder hands the fire to the children and instructs them how to light it; at the same time he gives them the ritual words to be used in this connection. The children enter the hut, with the elder following behind them, to see that the ritual is correctly carried out. Behind this small procession the owner of the homestead and his wife follow carrying firewood to kindle the fire, for it is considered as a bad omen for such a fire to go out. After the fire has been properly lit, things are moved in without any further ceremony.

Some African Cultural Concepts
Steve Biko

One of the most difficult things to do these days is to talk with authority on anything to do with African culture. Somehow Africans are not expected to have any deep understanding of their own culture or even of themselves. Other people have become authorities on all aspects of the African life or to be more accurate on BANTU life. Thus we have the thickest of volumes on some of the strangest subjects—even "the feeding habits of the Urban Africans," a publication by a fairly "liberal" group, Institute of Race Relations.

In my opinion it is not necessary to talk with Africans about African culture. However, in the light of the above statements one realises that there is so much confusion sown, not only amongst casual non-African readers, but even amongst Africans themselves, that perhaps a sincere attempt should be made at emphasising the authentic cultural aspects of the African people by Africans themselves.

Since that unfortunate date—1652—we have been experiencing a process of acculturation. It is perhaps presumptuous to call it "acculturation" because this term implies a fusion of different cultures. In our case this fusion has been extremely one-sided. The two major cultures that met and "fused" were the African Culture and the Anglo-Boer Culture. Whereas the African culture was unsophisticated and simple, the Anglo-Boer culture had all the trappings of a colonialist culture and therefore was heavily equipped for conquest. Where they could, they conquered by persuasion, using a highly exclusive religion that denounced all other Gods and demanded a strict code of behaviour with respect to clothing, education, ritual and custom. Where it was impossible to convert, fire-arms were readily available and used to advantage. Hence the Anglo-Boer culture was the more powerful culture in almost all facets. This is where the African began to lose a grip on himself and his surroundings.

Thus in taking a look at cultural aspects of the African people one inevitably finds himself having to compare. This is primarily because of the contempt that the "superior" culture shows towards the indigenous culture. To justify its exploitative basis, the Anglo-Boer culture has at all times been directed at bestowing an inferior status to all cultural aspects of the indigenous people.

I am against the belief that African culture is time-bound, the notion that with the conquest of the African all his culture was obliterated. I am also against the belief that when one talks of African culture one is necessarily talking of the pre-Van Riebeeck culture. Obviously the African culture has had to sustain severe blows and may have been battered nearly out of shape by the belligerent cultures it collided with, yet in essence even today one can easily find the fundamental aspects of the pure African culture in the present day African. Hence in taking a look at African culture I am going to refer as well to what I have termed the modern African culture.

One of the most fundamental aspects of our culture is the importance we attach to Man. Ours has always been a Man-centred society. Westerners have on many occasions been surprised at the capacity we have for talking to each other—not for the sake of arriving at a particular conclusion but merely to enjoy the communication for its own sake. Intimacy is a term not exclusive for particular friends but applying to a whole group of people who find themselves together either through work or through residential requirements.

In fact in the traditional African culture, there is no such thing as two friends. Conversation groups were more or less naturally determined by age and division of labour. Thus one would find all boys whose job was to look after cattle periodically meeting at popular spots to engage in conversation about their cattle, girlfriends, parents, heroes etc. All commonly shared their secrets, joys and woes. No one felt unnecessarily an intruder into someone else's business. The curiosity manifested was welcome. It came out of a desire to share. This pattern one would find in all age groups. House visiting was always a feature of the elderly folk's way of life. No reason was needed as a basis for visits. It was all part of our deep concern for each other.

These are things never done in the Westerner's culture. A visitor to someone's house, with the exception of friends, is always met with the question "what can I do for you?". This attitude to see people not as themselves but as agents for some particular function either to one's disadvantage or advantage is foreign to us. We are not a suspicious race. We believe in the inherent goodness of man. We enjoy man for himself. We regard our living together not as an unfortunate mishap warranting endless competition among us, but as a deliberate act of God to make us a community of brothers and sisters jointly involved in the quest for a composite answer to the varied problems of life. Hence in all we do we always place Man first, and hence all our action is usually joint community oriented action rather than the individualism which is the hallmark of the capitalist approach. We always refrain from using people as stepping stones. Instead we are prepared to have a much slower progress in an effort to make sure that all of us are marching to the same tune.

Nothing dramatises the eagerness of the African to communicate with each other more than their love for song and rhythm. Music in the African culture features in all emotional states. When we go to work, we share the burdens and pleasures of the work we are doing through music. This particular facet strangely enough has filtered through to the present day. Tourists always watch with amazement the synchrony of music and action as Africans working at a road side use their picks and shovels with well-timed precision to the accompaniment of a background song. Battle songs were a feature of the long march to war in the olden days. Girls and boys never played any game without using music and rhythm as its basis. In other words with Africans, music and rhythm were not luxuries but part and parcel of our way of communication. Any suffering we experienced was made much more real by song and rhythm. There is no doubt that the so called "Negro spirituals" sung by Black slaves in the States as they toiled under oppression were indicative of their African heritage.

The major thing to note about our songs is that they never were songs for individuals. All African songs are group songs. Though many have words, this is not the most important thing about them. Tunes were adapted to suit the occasion and had the wonderful effect of making everybody read the same things from the common experience. In war the songs reassured those who were scared, highlighted the determination of the regiment to win a particular encounter and made much more urgent the need to settle the score; in suffering, as in the case of the Black slaves, they derived sustenance out of a feeling of togetherness, at work the binding rhythm makes everybody brush off the burden and hence Africans can continue for hours on end because of this added energy.

Attitudes of Africans to property again show just how unindividualistic the African is. As everybody here knows, African society had the village community as its basis. Africans always believed in having many villages with a controllable number of people in each rather than the reverse. This obviously was a requirement to suit the needs of a community-based and man-centred society. Hence most things were jointly owned by the group, for instance there was no such thing as individual land ownership. The land belonged to the people and was merely under the control of the local chief on behalf of the people. When cattle went to graze it was on an open field and not on anybody's specific farm.

Farming and agriculture, though on individual family basis, had many characteristics of joint efforts. Each person could by a simple request and holding of a special ceremony, invite neighbours to come and work on his plots. This service was returned in kind and no remuneration was ever given.

Poverty was a foreign concept. This could only be really brought about to the entire community by an adverse climate during a particular season. It never was considered repugnant to ask one's neighbors for help if one was struggling. In almost all instances there was help between individuals, tribe and tribe, chief and chief etc. even in spite of war.

Another important aspect of the African culture is our mental attitude to problems presented by life in general. Whereas the Westerner is geared to use a problem-solving approach following very trenchant analyses, our approach is that of situation-experiencing. I will quote from Dr. Kaunda to illustrate this point:

> The Westerner has an aggressive mentality. When he sees a problem he will not rest until he has formulated some solution to it. He cannot live with contradictory ideas in his mind; he must settle for one or the other or else evolve a third idea in his mind which harmonises or reconciles the other two. And he is vigorously scientific in rejecting solutions for which there is no basis in logic. He draws a sharp line between the natural and the supernatural, the rational and non-rational, and more often than not, he dismisses the supernatural and non-rational as superstition. . . .
>
> Africans being a prescientific people do not recognize any conceptual cleavage between the natural and supernatural. They experience a situation rather than face a problem. By this I mean they allow both the rational and non-rational elements to make an impact upon them, and any action they may take could be described more as a response of the total personality to the situation than the result of some mental exercise.

This I find a most apt analysis of the essential difference in the approach to life of these two groups. We as a community are prepared to accept that nature will have its enigmas which are beyond our powers to solve. Many people have interpreted this attitude as lack of initiative and drive, yet in spite of my belief in the strong need for scientific experimentation, I cannot help feeling that more time also should be spent in teaching man and man to live together, and that perhaps the African personality with its attitude of laying less stress on power and more stress on man is well on the way to solving our confrontation problems.

All people are agreed that Africans are a deeply religious race. In the various forms of worship that one found throughout the Southern part of our Continent there was at least a common basis. We all accepted without any doubt the existence of a God. We had our own community of saints. We believed— and this was consistent with our views of life—that all people who died had a special place next to God. We felt that a communication with God could only be through these people. We never knew anything about hell—we do not believe that God can create people only to punish them eternally after a short period on earth.

Another aspect of religious practices was the occasion of worship. Again we did not believe that religion could be featured as a separate part of our existence on earth. It was manifest in our daily lives. We thanked God through our ancestors before we drank beer, married, worked etc. We would obviously find it artificial to create special occasions for worship. Neither did we see it logical to have a particular building in which all worship would be conducted. We believed that God was always in communication with us and therefore merited attention everywhere and anywhere.

It was the missionaries who confused our people with their new religion. By some strange logic, they argued that theirs was a scientific religion and ours was mere superstition in spite of the biological discrepancies so obvious in the basis of their religion. They further went on to preach a theology of the existence of hell, scaring our fathers and mothers with stories about burning in eternal flames and gnashing of teeth and grinding of bone. This cold cruel religion was strange to us, but our forefathers were sufficiently scared of the unknown impending anger to believe that it was worth a try. Down went our cultural values!

Yet it is difficult to kill the African heritage. There remains, in spite of the superficial cultural similarities between the detribalised and the Westerner, a number of cultural characteristics that mark out the detribalised as an African. I am not here making a case for separation on the basis of cultural differences. I am sufficiently proud to believe that under a normal situation, Africans can comfortably stay with people of other cultures and be able to contribute to the joint cultures of the communities they have joined. However, what I want to illustrate here is that even in a pluralistic society like ours, there are still some cultural traits that we can boast of which have been able to withstand the process of deliberate bastardisation. These are aspects of the modern African culture—a culture that has used concepts from the white world to expand on inherent cultural characteristics.

Thus we see that in the area of music, the African still expresses himself with conviction. The craze about jazz arises out of a conversion by the African artists of mere notes to meaningful music, expressive of real feelings. The Monkey Jive, Soul etc. are all aspects of modern type African culture that expresses the same original feelings. Solos like those of Pat Boone and Elvis Presley could never really find expression within the African culture because it is not in us to listen passively to pure musical notes. Yet when soul struck with its all-engulfing rhythm it immediately caught on and set hundreds of millions of black bodies in gyration throughout the world. These were people reading in soul the real meaning—the defiant message "say it loud! I'm black and I'm proud". This is fast becoming our modern culture. A culture of defiance, self-assertion and group pride and solidarity. This is a culture that emanates from a situation of common experience of oppression. Just as it now finds expression in our music and our dress, it will spread to other aspects. This is the new and modern black culture to which we have given a major contribution. This is the modern black culture that is responsible for the restoration of our faith in ourselves and therefore offers a hope in the direction we are taking from here.

Thus in its entirety the African Culture spells us out as people particularly close to nature. As Kaunda puts it, our people may be unlettered and their physical horizons may be limited yet "they inhabit a larger world than the sophisticated Westerner who has magnified his physical senses through inverted gadgets at the price all too often of cutting out the dimension of the spiritual." This close proximity to Nature enables the emotional component in us to be so much richer in that it makes it possible for us, without any apparent difficulty to feel for people and to easily identify with them in any emotional situation arising out of suffering.

The advent of the Western Culture has changed our outlook almost drastically. No more could we run our own affairs. We were required to fit in as people tolerated with great restraint in a western type society. We were tolerated simply because our cheap labour is needed. Hence we are judged in terms of standards we are not responsible for. Whenever colonisation sets in with its dominant culture it devours the native culture and leaves behind a bastardised culture that can only thrive at the rate and pace allowed it by the dominant culture. This is what has happened to the African culture. It is called a sub-culture purely because the African people in the urban complexes are mimicking the white man rather unashamedly.

In rejecting Western values, therefore, we are rejecting those things that are not only foreign to us but that seek to destroy the most cherished of our beliefs—that the cornerstone of society is man himself—not just his welfare, not his material well being but just man himself with all his ramifications. We reject the power-based society of the Westerner that seems to be ever concerned with perfecting their technological know-how while losing out on their spiritual dimension. We believe that in the long run the special contribution to the world by Africa will be in this field of human relationship. The great powers of the world may have done wonders in giving the world an industrial and military look, but the great gift still has to come from Africa—giving the world a more human face.

The Black Founding Fathers
Lerone Bennett

Institutions are mirrors, sounding boards, communication channels, and deposits of energy. They are mediations between man and man, between man and things, between man and the past, between man and the unknown. Without institutions, men cannot see themselves or be themselves. Without institutions, without rituals, without structures of relationship and meaning, men cannot communicate with their dead or pass on their experiences to the unborn. In order to be and in order to become, men must have institutions.

It was in obedience to that primal law that the white founding fathers gathered in Independence Hall to create a structure and an order. And it was in obedience to that same law that the excluded came together in the same year to create an order of another kind. Perhaps the key move in the second ingathering was made in Philadelphia in the same year of the Constitutional Convention. In that year Richard Allen and Absalom Jones, two former slaves, withdrew from the St. George's Methodist Episcopal Church and created a germinal black institution. The immediate cause of the withdrawal was the rising tide of racism in the church. But there were other and deeper causes. Richard Allen and Absalom Jones and their followers already had a new sense of themselves and of what they wanted and of what they would accept. In their minds, in a larval state, was the idea of an African-American personality. They felt, they said, *cramped* in the exclusionist and whitened atmosphere of white institutions. They did not want, they said, to be *under* the government of whites but an integral part of that government. An admirable formulation, as you can see, and one which would form the dominant thrust of the African-American personality for years to come.

When whites transgressed the line Allen and his colleagues had defined as inviolable, they marched out of St. George's Methodist Episcopal Church in the first mass demonstration in black American history. Richard Allen was there. Let him speak:

"A number of us usually attended St. George's church in Fourth street; and when the colored people began to get numerous in attending the church, they moved us from the seats we usually sat on, and placed us around the wall, and on Sabbath morning we went to church and the sexton stood at the door, and told us to go in the gallery. . . . We expected to take the seats over the ones we formerly occupied below, not knowing any better. . . . Meeting had begun and they were nearly done singing and just as we got to the seats, the elder said, 'Let us pray.' We had not been long upon our knees before I heard considerable scuffling and low talking. I raised my head up and saw one of the trustees . . . having hold of the Rev. Absalom Jones, pulling him up off his knees, and saying, 'You must get up—you must not kneel here.' Mr. Jones replied, 'Wait until the prayer is over.' [The trustee] said, 'No, you must get up now, or I will call for aid and force you away.' Mr. Jones said, 'Wait until prayer is over, and I will get up and trouble you no more.' With that [the trustee] beckoned to one of the other trustees. . . . to come to his assistance. He came, and went to William White to pull him up. By this time prayer was over, and we all went out of the church in a body, and they were no more plagued with us in the church."

They were no more plagued with black people in a great many places. The Philadelphia demonstration was the focal point of a spontaneous movement that erupted in city after city. Without premeditation or plan or design, blacks in Boston, New York, and other Northern centers walked out of white institutions and created counter-institutions. Here again the key move was made in Philadelphia, where, on April 12, 1787, Richard Allen and Absalom Jones created the Free African Society, which DuBois called "the first wavering step of a people toward a more organized social life." The society was a mutual aid society, an embryonic church, and a political structure. It also contained the germ of a major black business, the insurance company.

Similar societies were formed in New York City, Boston, and Newport, Rhode Island. In the formation and rapid spread of these societies we have irrefutable proof of the growth of an independent black consciousness. The product of a new consciousness, the free African societies engendered an even higher level of consciousness, creating links between the isolated free Northern colonies. Through the medium of these societies, free blacks exchanged information, ideas, and programs.

The formation of the African societies was a crucial and formative educational experience for the pioneer leaders. In these organizations pioneer leaders learned how to resolve and how to bring collective pressure to bear. They learned to see their lives in a time-line which extended from Africa to the Day of Judgment they believed would vindicate them.

From this fount concentric circles of commitment spread to all of the communities of the North, leading to the creation of a second level of organization, the independent Black Church. Out of the Free African Society of Philadelphia came two of the first black churches; the First African Church of St. Thomas, the first black Episcopal church, and Bethel AME Church, the mother church of the African Methodist Episcopal Church. In 1796 the first congregation of the AME Zion Church was organized in New York City. Around 1809 black Baptist churches were organized in Boston, Philadelphia, and New York. By the War of 1812, there were black churches of every conceivable description, including a black Dutch Reformed church in New York City.

A further development of these organizational acts was the founding of national church bodies. In 1816, sixteen ministers met in Philadelphia and formed the African Methodist Episcopal Church. Five years later nineteen ministers representing six churches formed the African Methodist Episcopal Zion Church.

A third level of organization consisted of lodges and fraternal orders. In 1787 Prince Hall, the Revolutionary War veteran and Methodist minister, organized African [Masonic] Lodge No. 459 in Boston. Five years later a Grand Lodge, the first black interstate organization, was launched with Hall as the Grand Master.

Less dramatic but no less relevant was the fourth level of educational and cultural institutions. In 1787 Boston leaders, led by Prince Hall, sounded one of the dominant themes of black concern by petitioning the state legislature for equal educational facilities. The plea was denied; and in 1798 the black parents of Boston opened a school in Prince Hall's home. The school was transferred later to the African Meeting House and was operated for some twenty-nine years. A similar course of development was roughly characteristic of other Northern centers, including Philadelphia, where Richard Allen opened a day school for black children and a night school for black adults.

Substantial help came from white organizations, in particular the New York Manumission Society, which was largely responsible for the organization of the famous African Free Schools of New York City. According to some authorities, the opening of the first African Free School in November, 1787, marked the beginning of free secular education in New York. James Weldon Johnson called the school, which received aid from the city and state, the "precursor of the New York Public School System."

The Free African Schools were run with dispatch and efficacy. Males were taught "reading, writing, arithmetic, English grammar, composition, geography, astronomy, use of the globe, and map and linear drawing." Females were taught reading, writing, arithmetic, grammar, geography, sewing, and knitting.

According to contemporary accounts, the black students were models of industriousness and seriousness. In its issue of May 12, 1824, the *Commercial Advertiser* commented:

> We had the pleasure on Friday of attending the annual examination of the scholars of the New York African Free School, and we are free to confess that we never derived more satisfaction, or felt a deeper interest, in any school exhibition in our life. The male and female schools. . . . were united on this occasion, and the whole number present was about six hundred. . . . The whole scene was highly interesting and gratifying. We never beheld a white school of the same age (of and under the age of fifteen) in which, without exception, there was more order, and neatness of dress, and cleanliness of person. And the exercises were performed with a degree of promptness and accuracy which was surprising. . . . We were particularly struck with the appearance of the female school. . . . There was a neatness of dress and person, a propriety of manner, and an ease of carriage, which reflected great credit upon themselves and their teacher.

The work of the schools for children and adults was supplemented by study circles, reading groups, and benevolent organizations. By 1831 there were more than forty-three benevolent organizations in Philadelphia alone. Among the groups listed were the African Friendly Society of St. Thomas, Sons of Africa, United Brethren, Humane Mechanics, African Female Band Benevolent Society of Bethel, Female African Benevolent, and the Daughters of Ethiopia.

Perhaps the best known of the black cultural institutions was the African Theater of New York City, which presented performances of *Othello, Richard III*, and other European fare. One observes with interest that the theater, at the African Grove, corner of Bleecker and Mercer streets, had a partitioned section in the back for white patrons. The managers said whites were segregated because they "do not know how to conduct themselves at entertainments for ladies and gentlemen of color."

With the organization of the first newspapers and magazines, the different organizations and colonies of black America began to coexist in the same time zone. The first edition of the first black newspaper, *Freedom's Journal,* was published on Friday, March 16, 1827, under the editorship of Samuel E. Cornish, a minister and writer, and John B. Russwurm, the first black college graduate (Bowdoin). Russwurm later withdrew from the editorship and settled in Liberia, where he edited the *Liberia Herald,* a pioneer newspaper, and served as governor of the colony of Maryland. Cornish continued to edit the paper under a new name, *Rights for All.* He later edited another newspaper, the *Colored American.* David Ruggles, another pioneer New York leader and one of the most radical men of his times, was editor of the first black magazine, *Mirror of Liberty,* which appeared in August, 1838, one month before the publication of William Whipper's *National Reformer.*

The appearance of the first newspapers and magazines brought the black community closer together and focused its thinking.

Slave Resistance
John Hope Franklin

It cannot be denied that as old as the institution of slavery was, human beings had not, by the nineteenth century, brought themselves to the point where they could be subjected to it without protest and resistance. Resistance could be found wherever slavery existed, and slavery in the United States was no exception. Too frequently, misunderstanding, suspicion, and hatred were mutually shared by master and slave. Indeed, they were natural enemies, and on many occasions they conducted themselves as such. There are, of course, numerous examples of kindness and understanding on the part of owners as well as docility—which may be more accurately described as accommodation—and tractability on the part of slaves. But this master-slave relationship was an unnatural relationship and was not, by the nature of things, inherent in the system.

The brutality that apparently was inherent in a system of human exploitation existed in every community in which slavery was established. The wastefulness and extravagance of the plantation system made no exception of human resources. Slaves were for economic gain, and if beating them would increase their efficiency—which was generally believed—then the rod and lash should not be spared. Far from being a civilizing force, moreover, the plantation bred indecency in human relations, and the slave was the immediate victim of the barbarity of a system that commonly exploited the sex of the women and the work of everyone. Finally, the psychological situation that was created by the master-slave relationship stimulated terrorism and brutality because masters felt secure in their position and interpreted their role as calling for that type of conduct. Many masters as well as slaves got the reputation of being "bad," which contributed to the tension that seemed to be mounting everywhere as the institution developed.

Laws for the purpose of protecting slaves were few and were seldom enforced. It was almost impossible to secure the conviction of a master who mistreated a slave. Knowing that, the owner was inclined to take the law into his or her own hands. Overseers were generally notorious for their brutality, and the accounts of abuse and mistreatment on their part as well as on the part of those who hired slaves are numerous. Masters and mistresses were perhaps almost as guilty. In 1827 a Georgia grand jury brought in a true bill of manslaughter against a slave owner for beating his slave to death, but he was acquitted. Several years later Thomas Sorrell of the same state was found guilty of killing one of his slaves with an axe, but the jury recommended him to the mercy of the court. In Kentucky a Mrs. Maxwell had a wide reputation for beating her slaves, both men and women, on the face as well as the body. There is also the shocking account of Mrs. Alpheus Lewis, who burned her slave girl around the neck with hot tongs. Drunken masters had little regard for their slaves; the most sensational example of which is a Kentucky man who dismembered his slave and threw him piece by piece into the fire. One Mississippi master dragged from the bed a slave whom he suspected of theft and inflicted more than 1,000 lashes. Repeated descriptions of runaways contained phrases such as "large scar on hip," "no marks except those on his back," "much scarred with the whip," and "will no doubt show the marks of a recent whipping." They suggest a type of brutality that doubtless contributed to the slave's decision to abscond.

To the demonstrations of brutality as well as to the very institution of slavery itself, slaves reacted in various ways. Thanks to the religion of their masters they could be philosophical about the whole situation and escape through ritual and song. The emphasis on otherworldliness in slave songs certainly suggested grim dissatisfaction with their worldly status. "Dere's a Great Camp Meetin' in de Promised Land," "Look Away in de Heaven, Lord," "Fo' My Soul's Goin' to Heaven Jes' Sho's You Born," and "Heaven, Heaven, Everybody Talkin' 'Bout Heaven Ain't Goin' There" are only a few of the songs that slaves sang in the hope that their burdens would be relieved in the next world. As long as they were in this world they had to make the most of a bad situation by loafing on the job, feigning illness in the fields and on the auction block, and engaging in an elaborate program of sabotage. Slaves were so hard on farming tools that special ones were developed for them. They drove the animals with a cruelty that suggested revenge, and they could be so ruthless in destruction of the fields that the most careful supervision was necessary to ensure survival of the crops until harvest time. Forests, barns, and homes were burned to the extent that members of the patrol were frequently fearful of leaving home lest they be visited with revenge in the form of destruction of their property by fire.

Self-mutilation and suicide were popular forms of resistance to slavery. Slaves cut off their toes and hands and mutilated themselves in other ways so as to render themselves ineffective as workers. One Kentucky slave carpenter, for example, cut off one of his hands and the fingers of the other when he learned that he was to be sold down the river. There were several instances of slaves having shot themselves in the hand or foot, especially upon being recovered from running away. The number of suicides seems relatively high, and certainly the practice was widespread. Slaves fresh from Africa committed suicide in great numbers. In 1807 two boatloads of Africans newly arrived in Charleston starved themselves to death. When his slave woman was found dead by her own hanging in 1829, a Georgia planter was amazed since he saw no reason why she should want to take her own life. When two Louisiana slaves were returned to their owner after having been stolen in 1858, they drowned themselves in the bayou. One of the South's wealthiest planters, Charles Manigault, lost a slave by a similar act when the overseer threatened him with punishment. Sometimes slave mothers killed their own children to prevent them from growing up in slavery.

Much more disturbing to the whites of the South were the numerous instances of slaves doing violence to the master class. Poisoning was always feared, and perhaps some planters felt a real need for an official taster. As early as 1761 the Charleston *Gazette* remarked that the "Negroes have begun the hellish act of poisoning." Arsenic and other similar compounds were used. Where they were not available, slaves are known to have resorted to mixing ground glass in the gravy for their owners' tables. Numerous slaves were convicted of murdering their owners and overseers, but some escaped. In 1797 a Screven County, Georgia, planter was killed by his newly imported African slave. Another Georgia master was killed by a slave who stabbed him sixteen times. The slave was later burned alive. The slave of William Pearce of Florida killed his owner with an axe when Pearce sought to punish him. Carolina Turner of Kentucky was choked to death by a slave whom she was flogging. Though the citizenry had long complained of the woman's merciless brutality in dealing with her slaves, her killer was summarily hanged for his deed. The times that overseers and owners were killed by slaves in the woods or fields were exceedingly numerous, as the careful reading of almost any Southern newspaper will reveal.

Every Southern community raised its annual crop of runaway slaves. Both federal and state legislation aided in their recovery, but many slaves escaped forever. The practice of running away became so widespread that every state sought to strengthen its patrol and other safeguards to little avail. Hardly a newspaper went to press without several advertisements listing runaways, and sometimes there were several columns of such advertisements. The following is typical:

> Absconded from the Forest Plantation of the late William Dunbar, on Sunday the 7th instant, a very handsome Mulattress called Harriet, about 13 years old, with straight back hair and dark eyes. This girl was lately in New Orleans, and is known to have seen there a man whom she claims as her father and who does now or did lately live on the Mississippi, a little above the mouth of the Caffalaya. It is highly probable some plan has been concocted for the girl's escape.

Long before the Underground Railroad was an effective antislavery device slaves were running away: men, women, and children, singly, in pairs, or in groups. At times they went so far as to organize themselves into groups called Maroons and to live in communities, on the order of Palmares in Brazil. The forests, mountains, and swamps of the Southern states were their favorite locations, and they proved to be troublesome to the owners who sought to maintain strict order on their plantations.

Some slaves disguised themselves or armed themselves with free passes in their effort to escape. Others simply walked off, apparently hoping that fate would be kind and assist in their permanent escape. Some were inveterate runaways, such as the North Carolina woman who fled from her owner's plantation no less than sixteen times. Others were not as daring and gave up after one unsuccessful attempt. While there is no way of even approximating the number of runaways, it is obvious that fleeing from the institution was one of the slaves' most effective means of resistance. It represented the continuous fight that slaves carried on against their masters.

The most sensational and desperate reaction of slaves to their status was the conspiracy to revolt. Those slaves who could summon the nerve to strike for their freedom in a group, that is, who could engage in "carrying the fight to the enemy," hoped that insurrection would end, once and for all, the degradation of human enslavement. To whites rebellion was a mad, sinister act of desperate savages, in league with the devil, who could not appreciate the benign influences of the institution and who would dare shed the blood of their benefactors. Inherent in revolts was bloodshed on both sides. Blacks accepted this as the price of liberty, while whites were panic-stricken at the very thought of it. Even rumors of insurrections struck terror in the hearts of slaveholders and called forth the vigorous efforts to guard against the dreaded eventuality.

Revolts, or conspiracies to revolt, persisted until 1865. They began with the institution and did not end until slavery was abolished. It can, therefore, be said that they were a part of the institution, a kind of bitterness that whites had to take along with the sweetness of slavery. As the country was turning to Jeffersonian Republicanism at the beginning of the nineteenth century, many people believed that a new day had arrived for the common person. Some blacks, however, felt that they would have to force their new day by breaking away from slavery. In Henrico County, Virginia, they resolved to revolt against the institution under the leadership of Gabriel Prosser and Jack Bowler. For months they planned the desperate move, gathering clubs, swords, and the like for the appointed day. On August 30, 1800, more than 1,000 slaves met six miles outside of Richmond and began to march on the city, but a violent storm almost routed the insurgents. Two slaves had already informed the whites, and Governor Monroe, acting promptly, called out more than 600 troops and notified every militia commander in the state. In due time scores of slaves were arrested, and 35 were executed. Gabriel Prosser was captured in late September, and after he refused to talk to anyone he too was executed.

Whites speculated extravagantly over the number of slaves involved in this major uprising. The estimates ran all the way from 2,000 to 50,000. The large numbers, together with the total disregard slaves seemed to have for their own lives, caused the whites to shudder. The high ground that slaves took in maintaining silence added to the stark terror of the whole situation. When one was asked what he had to say, he calmly replied:

> I have nothing more to offer than what General Washington would have had to offer, had he been taken by the British officers and put to trial by them. I have ventured my life in endeavouring to obtain the liberty of my countrymen, and am a willing sacrifice to their cause; and I beg, as a favour, that I may be immediately led to execution. I know that you have predetermined to shed my blood, why then all this mockery of a trial?

The unrest among slaves, even in Virginia, continued into the following year, and plots were reported in Petersburg and Norfolk and in various places in North Carolina. The latter state became so alarmed that many slaves were lashed, branded, and cropped, and at least 15 were hanged for alleged implication in conspiracies. In the subsequent years, before the war with England, there were reports of insurrection up and down the Atlantic seaboard. Conspiracy had crossed the mountains, for in 1810 a plot was uncovered in Lexington, Kentucky. The following year, more than 400 rebellious slaves in Louisiana had to be put down by federal and state troops. At least 75 slaves lost their lives in the encounter and in the trials that ensued. There was another uprising in New Orleans in the following year.

Following the War of 1812 the efforts of slaves to revolt continued. In Virginia in 1815 a white man, George Boxley, decided to attempt to free the slaves. He made elaborate plans, but a slave woman betrayed him and his conspirators. Although Boxley himself escaped, six slaves were hanged and another six were banished. When the revolutions of Latin America and Europe broke out, Americans could not restrain themselves in their praise and support of the fighters for liberty. The South joined in the loud hosannas, while slaves watched the movements for the emancipation of the slaves in Latin America and the Caribbean. Perhaps all these developments had something to do with what was the most elaborate, though not the most effective, conspiracy of the period: the Denmark Vesey insurrection.

Vesey had purchased his freedom in 1800 and for a score of years had made a respectable living as a carpenter in Charleston, South Carolina. He was a sensitive, liberty-loving person and was not satisfied in the enjoyment of his own relatively comfortable existence. He believed in equality for everyone and resolved to do something for his slave brothers and sisters. Over a period of several years he carefully plotted his revolt and chose his assistants. Together they made and collected their weapons: 250 pike heads and bayonets and 300 daggers. Vesey also sought assistance from Haiti. He set the second Sunday in July 1822 for the day of the revolt; and when the word leaked out, he moved it up one month, but his assistants, who were scattered for miles around Charleston, did not all get the word. Meanwhile, the whites were well aware of what was going on and began to round up suspects. At least 139 blacks were arrested, 47 of whom were condemned. Even 4 white men were fined and imprisoned for encouraging the revolt. Estimates of the number of blacks involved in the plot ran as high as 9,000.

The following decade saw the entire South apprehensive over possible uprisings. The revival of the antislavery movement and the publication of such incendiary material as David Walker's *Appeal* put the South's nerves on edge. Several revolts were reported on Louisiana plantations in 1829, and in 1830 a number of citizens of North Carolina asked their legislature for aid because their slaves had become "almost uncountroulable." The panic of the 1820s culminated in 1831 with the insurrection of Nat Turner. This slave from Southampton County, Virginia, was a mystical, rebellious person who had on one occasion run away and then decided to return to his owner. Perhaps he had already begun to feel that he had been selected by some divine power to deliver his people from slavery.

Upon the occasion of the solar eclipse in February 1831, Turner decided that the time had come for him to lead his people out of bondage. He selected the Fourth of July as the day, but when he became ill he postponed the revolt until he saw another sign. On August 13, when the sun turned a "peculiar greenish blue," he called the revolt for August 21. He and his followers began by killing Turner's master, Joseph Travis, and his family. In rapid succession other families fell before the blows of the blacks. Within twenty-four hours 60 whites had been killed. The revolt was spreading rapidly when the main group of blacks was met and overpowered by state and federal troops. More than 100 slaves were killed in the encounter, and 13 slaves and 3 free Negroes were immediately hanged. Turner was captured on October 30, and in less than two weeks, on November 11, he was executed.

The South was completely dazed by the Southampton uprising. The situation was grossly exaggerated in many communities. Some reports were that whites had been murdered by the hundreds in Virginia. Small wonder that several states felt it necessary to call special sessions of the legislature to consider the emergency. Most states strengthened their Slave Codes, and citizens literally remained awake nights waiting for slaves to make another break. The uprisings continued. In 1835 several slaves in Monroe County, Georgia, were hanged or whipped to death because of implication in a conspiracy. In the following decade there were several uprisings in Alabama, Louisiana, and Mississippi. In 1853 a serious revolt in New Orleans involving 2,500 slaves was aborted by the informing of a free black. In 1856 the Maroons in Bladen and Robeson counties, North Carolina, "went on the warpath" and terrorized the countryside. Up until and throughout the Civil War, slaves demonstrated their violent antipathy for slavery by continuing to rise against it.

The Meaning of July Fourth for the Negro

Frederick Douglass

What, to the American slave, is your 4th of July? I answer; a day that reveals to him, more than all other days in the year, the gross injustice and cruelty to which he is the constant victim. To him, your celebration is a sham; your boasted liberty, an unholy license; your national greatness, swelling vanity; your sounds of rejoicing are empty and heartless; your denunciation of tyrants, brass fronted impudence; your shouts of liberty and equality, hollow mockery; your prayers and hymns, your sermons and thanksgivings, with all your religious parade and solemnity, are, to Him, mere bombast, fraud, deception, impiety, and hypocrisy—a thin veil to cover up crimes which would disgrace a nation of savages. There is not a nation on the earth guilty of practices more shocking and bloody than are the people of the United States, at this very hour.

Go where you may, search where you will, roam through all the monarchies and despotisms of the Old World, travel through South America, search out every abuse, and when you have found the last, lay your facts by the side of the everyday practices of this nation, and you will say with me, that, for revolting barbarity and shameless hypocrisy, America reigns without a rival.

Take the American slave-trade, which we are told by the papers, is especially prosperous just now. Ex-Senator Benton tells us that the price of men was never higher than now. He mentions the fact to show that slavery is in no danger. This trade is one of the peculiarities of American institutions. It is carried on in all the large towns and cities in one-half of this confederacy; and millions are pocketed every year by dealers in this horrid traffic. In several states this trade is a chief source of wealth. It is called (in contradistinction to the foreign slave-trade) *"the internal slave-trade."* It is, probably, called so, too, in order to divert from it the horror with which the foreign slave-trade is contemplated. That trade has long since been denounced by this government as piracy. It has been denounced with burning words from the high places of the nation as an execrable traffic. To arrest it, to put an end to it, this nation keeps a squadron, at immense cost, on the coast of Africa. Everywhere, in this country, it is safe to speak of this foreign slave-trade as a most inhuman traffic, opposed alike to the laws of God and of man. The duty to extirpate and destroy it, is admitted even by our doctors of divinity. In order to put an end to it, some of these last have consented that their colored brethren (nominally free) should leave this country, and establish themselves on the western coast of Africa! It is, however, a notable fact that, while so much execration is poured out by Americans upon all those engaged in the foreign slave-trade, the men engaged in the slave-trade between the states pass without condemnation, and their business is deemed honorable.

Behold the practical operation of this internal slave-trade, the American slave-trade, sustained by American politics and American religion. Here you will see men and women reared like swine for the market. You know what is a swine-drover? I will show you a man-drover. They inhabit all our Southern States. They perambulate the country, and crowd the highways of the nation, with droves of human stock. You will see one of these human flesh jobbers, armed with pistol, whip, and bowie-knife, driving a company of a hundred men, women, and children, from the Potomac to the slave market at New Orleans. These wretched people are to be sold singly, or in lots, to suit purchasers. They are food for the cotton-field and the deadly sugar-mill. Mark the sad procession, as it moves wearily along, and the inhuman wretch who drives them. Hear his savage yells and his blood-curdling oaths, as he hurries on his affrighted captives! There, see the old man with locks thinned and gray. Cast one glance, if you please, upon that young mother, whose shoulders are bare to the scorching sun, her briny tears falling on the brow of the babe in her arms. See, too, that girl of thirteen, weeping, *yes!* weeping, as she thinks of the mother from whom she has been torn! The drove moves tardily. Heat and sorrow have nearly consumed their strength; suddenly you hear a quick snap, like the discharge of a rifle; the fetters clank, and the chain rattles simultaneously; your ears are saluted with a scream, that seems to have torn its way to the centre of your soul! The crack you heard was the sound of the slave-whip; the scream you heard was from the woman you saw with the babe. Her speed had faltered under the weight of her child and her chains! That gash on her shoulder tells her to move on. Follow this drove to New Orleans. Attend the auction; see men examined like horses; see the forms of women rudely and brutally exposed to the shocking gaze of American slave-buyers. See this drove sold and separated forever; and never forget the deep, sad sobs that arose from that scattered multitude. Tell me, citizens, where, under the sun, you can witness a spectacle more fiendish and shocking. Yet this is but a glance at the American slave-trade, as it exists, at this moment, in the ruling part of the United States.

I was born amid such sights and scenes. To me the American slave-trade is a terrible reality. When a child, my soul was often pierced with a sense of its horrors. I lived on Philpot Street, Fell's Point, Baltimore, and have watched from the wharves the slave ships in the Basin, anchored from the shore, with their cargoes of human flesh, waiting for favorable winds to waft them down the Chesapeake. There was, at that time, a grand slave mart kept at the head of Pratt Street, by Austin Woldfolk. His agents were sent into every town and county in Maryland, announcing their arrival, through the papers, and on flaming *"hand-bills,"* headed cash for Negroes. These men were generally well dressed men, and very captivating in their manners; ever ready to drink, to treat, and to gamble. The fate of many a slave has depended upon the turn of a single card; and many a child has been snatched from the arms of its mother by bargains arranged in a state of brutal drunkenness.

The flesh-mongers gather up their victims by dozens, and drive them, chained, to the general depot at Baltimore. When a sufficient number has been collected here, a ship is chartered for the purpose of conveying the forlorn crew to Mobile, or to New Orleans. From the slave prison to the ship, they are usually driven in the darkness of night; for since the antislavery agitation, a certain caution is observed.

In the deep, still darkness of midnight, I have been often aroused by the dead, heavy footsteps, and the piteous cries of the chained gangs that passed our door. The anguish of my boyish heart was intense; and I was often consoled, when speaking to my mistress in the morning, to hear her say that the custom was very wicked; that she hated to hear the rattle of the chains and the heart-rending cries. I was glad to find one who sympathized with me in my horror.

Fellow-citizens, this murderous traffic is, to-day, in active operation in this boasted republic. In the solitude of my spirit I see clouds of dust raised on the highways of the South; I see the bleeding footsteps; I hear the doleful wail of fettered humanity on the way to the slave-markets, where the victims are to be sold like *horses, sheep,* and *swine,* knocked off to the highest bidder. There I see the tenderest ties ruthlessly broken, to gratify the lust, caprice and rapacity of the buyers and sellers of men. My soul sickens at the sight.

> *Is this the land your Fathers loved,*
> *The freedom which they toiled to win?*
> *Is this the earth whereon they moved?*
> *Are these the graves they slumber in?*

Niagra Movement Resolution at Harpers Ferry, 1906

W.E.B. DuBois and W.M. Trotter

The men of the Niagara Movement, coming from the toil of the year's hard work, and pausing a moment from the earning of their daily bread, turn toward the nation and again ask in the name of ten million the privilege of a hearing. In the past year the work of the Negro hater has flourished in the land. Step by step the defenders of the rights of American citizens have retreated. The work of stealing the black man's ballot has progressed and the fifty and more representatives of stolen votes still sit in the nation's capital. Discrimination in travel and public accommodation has so spread that some of our weaker brethren are actually afraid to thunder against color discrimination as such and are simply whispering for ordinary decencies.

Against this the Niagara Movement eternally protests. We will not be satisfied to take one jot or tittle less than our full manhood rights. We claim for ourselves every single right that belongs to a freeborn American, political, civil and social; and until we get these rights we will never cease to protest and assail the ears of America. The battle we wage is not for ourselves alone, but for all true Americans. It is a fight for ideals, lest this, our common fatherland, false to its founding, become in truth the land of the Thief and the home of the Slave—a by-word and a hissing among the nations for its sounding pretensions and pitiful accomplishment.

Never before in the modern age has a great and civilized folk threatened to adopt so cowardly a creed in the treatment of its fellow-citizens, born and bred on its soil. Stripped of verbiage and subterfuge and in its naked nastiness, the new American creed says: fear to let black men even try to rise lest they become the equals of the white. And this is the land that professes to follow Jesus Christ. The blasphemy of such a course is only matched by its cowardice.

In detail our demands are clear and unequivocal.

First. We would vote; with the right to vote goes everything: freedom, manhood, the honor of your wives, the chastity of your daughters, the right to work, and the chance to rise; let no man listen to those who deny this.

We want full manhood suffrage, and we want it now, henceforth and forever.

Second. We want discrimination in public accommodation to cease. Separation in railway and street cars, based simply on race and color, is un-American, undemocratic, and silly. We protest against all such discrimination.

Third. We claim the right of freemen to walk, talk and be with them that wish to be with us. No man has the right to choose another man's friends, and to attempt to do so is an impudent interference with the most fundamental human privilege.

Fourth. We want the laws enforced against rich as well as poor; against Capitalist as well as Laborer; against white as well as black. We are not more lawless than the white race, we are more often arrested, convicted and mobbed. We want justice even for criminals and outlaws. We want the Constitution of the country enforced. We want Congress to take charge of the Congressional elections. We want the Fourteenth Amendment carried out to the letter and every State disfranchised in Congress which attempts to disfranchise its rightful voters. We want the Fifteenth Amendment enforced and no State allowed to base its franchise simply on color.

The failure of the Republican Party in Congress at the session just closed to redeem its pledge of 1904 with reference to suffrage conditions at the South seems a plain, deliberate, and premeditated breach of promise, and stamps that party as guilty of obtaining votes under false pretense.

Fifth. We want our children educated. The school system in the country districts of the South is a disgrace and in few towns and cities are the Negro schools what they ought to be. We want the national government to step in and wipe out illiteracy in the South. Either the United States will destroy ignorance or ignorance will destroy the United States.

And when we call for education, we mean real education. We believe in work. We ourselves are workers, but work is not necessarily education. Education is the development of power and ideal. We want our children trained as intelligent human beings should be, and we will fight for all time against any proposal to educate black boys and girls simply as servants and underlings, or simply for the use of other people. They have a right to know, to think, to aspire.

These are some of the chief things which we want. How shall we get them? By voting where we may vote; by persistent, unceasing agitation; by hammering at the truth; by sacrifice and work.

We do not believe in violence, neither in the despised violence of the raid nor the lauded violence of the soldier, nor the barbarous violence of the mob; but we do believe in John Brown, in that incarnate spirit of justice, that hatred of a lie, that willingness to sacrifice money, reputation, and life itself on the altar of right. And here on the scene of John Brown's martyrdom, we reconsecrate ourselves, our honor, our property to the final emancipation of the race for whose freedom John Brown died.

The Migration of the Talented Tenth

Carter G. Woodson

What classes then have migrated? In the first place, the Negro politicians, who, after the restoration of Bourbon rule in the South, found themselves thrown out of office and often humiliated and impoverished, had to find some way out of the difficulty. Some few have been relieved by sympathetic leaders of the Republican party, who secured for them federal appointments in Washington. These appointments when sometimes paying lucrative salaries have been given as a reward to those Negroes who, although dethroned in the South, remain in touch with the remnant of the Republican party there and control the delegates to the national conventions nominating candidates for President. Many Negroes of this class have settled in Washington. In some cases, the observer witnesses the pitiable scene of a man once a prominent public functionary in the South now serving in Washington as a messenger or a clerk.

The well-established blacks, however, have not been so easily induced to go. The Negroes in business in the South have usually been loath to leave their people among whom they can acquire property, whereas, if they go to the North, they have merely political freedom with no assurance of an opportunity in the economic world. But not a few of these have given themselves up to unrelenting toil with a view to accumulating sufficient wealth to move North and live thereafter on the income from their investments. Many of this class now spend some of their time in the North to educate their children. But they do not like to have these children who have been under refining influences return to the South to suffer the humiliation which during the last generation has been growing more and more aggravating. Endeavoring to carry out their policy of keeping the Negro down, southerners too often carefully plan to humiliate the progressive and intelligent blacks and in some cases form mobs to drive them out, as they are bad examples for that class of Negroes whom they desire to keep as menials.

There are also the migrating educated Negroes. They have studied history, law and economics and well understand what it is to get the rights guaranteed them by the constitution. The more they know the more discontented they become. They cannot speak out for what they want. No one is likely to second such a protest, not even the Negroes themselves, so generally have they been intimidated. The more outspoken they become, moreover, the more necessary is it for them to leave, for they thereby destroy their chances to earn a livelihood. White men in control of the public schools of the South see to it that the subserviency of the Negro teachers employed be certified beforehand. They dare not complain too much about equipment and salaries even if the per capita appropriation for the education of the Negroes be one fourth of that for the whites.

In the higher institutions of learning, especially the State schools, it is exceptional to find a principal who has the confidence of the Negroes. The Negroes will openly assert that he is in the pay of the reactionary whites, whose purpose is to keep the Negro down; and the incumbent himself will tell his board of regents how much he is opposed by the Negroes because he labors for the interests of the white race. Out of such sycophancy it is easily explained why our State schools have been so ineffective as to necessitate the sending of the Negro youth to private institutions maintained by northern philanthropy. Yet if an outspoken Negro happens to be an instructor in a private school conducted by educators from the North, he has to be careful about contending for a square deal; for, if the head of his institution does not suggest to him to proceed conservatively, the mob will dispose of the complainant. Physicians, lawyers and preachers who are not so economically dependent as teachers can exercise no more freedom of speech in the midst of this triumphant rule of the lawless.

A large number of educated Negroes, therefore, have on account of these conditions been compelled to leave the South. Finding in the North, however, practically nothing in their line to do, because of the proscription by race prejudice and trades unions, many of them lead the life of menials, serving as waiters, porters, butlers and chauffeurs. While in Chicago, not long ago, the writer was in the office of a graduate of a colored southern college, who was showing his former teacher the picture of his class. In accounting for his classmates in the various walks of life, he reported that more than one third of them were settled to the occupation of Pullman porters.

The largest number of Negroes who have gone North during this period, however, belong to the intelligent laboring class. Some of them have become discontented for the very same reasons that the higher classes have tired of oppression in the South, but the larger number of them have gone North to improve their economic condition. Most of these have migrated to the large cities in the East and Northwest, such as Philadelphia, New York, Indianapolis, Pittsburgh, Cleveland, Columbus, Detroit and Chicago. To understand this problem in its urban aspects the accompanying diagram showing the increase in the Negro population of northern cities during the first decade of this century will be helpful.

Some of these Negroes have migrated after careful consideration; others have just happened to go north as wanderers; and a still larger number on the many excursions to the cities conducted by railroads during the summer months. Sometimes one excursion brings to Chicago two or three thousand Negroes, two thirds of whom never go back. They do not often follow the higher pursuits of labor in the North but they earn more money than they have been accustomed to earn in the South. They are attracted also by the liberal attitude of some whites, which, although not that of social equality, gives the Negroes a liberty in northern centers which leads them to think that they are citizens of the country.

This shifting in the population has had an unusually significant effect on the black belt. Frederick Douglass advised the Negroes in 1879 to remain in the South where they would be in sufficiently large numbers to have political power, but they have gradually scattered from the black belt so as to diminish greatly their chances ever to become the political force they formerly were in this country. The Negroes once had this possibility in South Carolina, Georgia, Alabama, Mississippi and Louisiana and, had the process of Africanization prior to the Civil War had a few decades longer to do its work, there would not have been any doubt as to the ultimate preponderance of the Negroes in those commonwealths. The tendencies of the black population according to the censuses of the United States and especially that of 1910, however, show that the chances for the control of these State governments by Negroes no longer exist except in South Carolina and Mississippi. It has been predicted, therefore, that, if the same tendencies continue for the next fifty years, there will be even few counties in which the Negroes will be in a majority. All of the Southern States except Arkansas showed a proportionate increase of the white population over that of the black between 1900 and 1910, while West Virginia and Oklahoma with relatively small numbers of blacks showed, for reasons stated elsewhere, an increase in the Negro population. Thus we see coming to pass something like the proposed plan of Jefferson and other statesmen who a hundred years ago advocated the expansion of slavery to lessen the evil of the institution by distributing its burdens.

The migration of intelligent blacks, however, has been attended with several handicaps to the race. The large part of the black population is in the South and there it will stay for decades to come. The southern Negroes, therefore, have been robbed of their due part of the talented tenth. The educated blacks have had no constituency in the North and, consequently, have been unable to realize their sweetest dreams of the land of the free. In their new home the enlightened Negro must live with his light under a bushel. Those left behind in the South soon despair of seeing a brighter day and yield to the yoke. In the places of the leaders who were wont to speak for their people, the whites have raised up Negroes who accept favors offered them on the condition that their lips be sealed up forever on the rights of the Negro.

This emigration too has left the Negro subject to other evils. There are many first-class Negro business men in the South, but although there were once progressive men of color, who endeavored to protect the blacks from being plundered by white sharks and harpies there have arisen numerous unscrupulous Negroes who have for a part of the proceeds from such jobbery associated themselves with ill-designing white men to dupe illiterate Negroes. This trickery is brought into play in marketing their crops, selling them supplies, or purchasing their property. To carry out this iniquitous plan the persons concerned have the protection of the law, for while Negroes in general are imposed upon, those engaged in robbing them have no cause to fear.

Ida B. Wells: "Free Speech" and Black Struggle
Rosemarie Freeney-Harding

By the end of the 1880s it was clear that writing—especially advocacy journalism—was Ida Wells' central vocation and public school teaching was simply her way of earning a respectable living. Her writing continued to focus on problems within the local community, but her reputation went beyond the city limits of Memphis and even the Mason-Dixon line. But Memphis was home, and in order to find means to express the growing interest she held for Black journalism, Miss Ida joined the local Black newspaper called the *Free Speech and Headlight* in the year 1890. From the outset, Ida's writings for the *Free Speech* were often sharply critical and created controversy. For instance, her criticism of her co-worker, Rev. Nightengale, who actually served as publisher (he was a minister of one of the leading Black Baptist churches and it was his church which housed the press from which the *Free Speech* came), for infidelity and suppression of her articles, finally resulted in his withdrawal from the paper.

Her writings in the local paper also began to reflect the dangerous disdain she held for the local board of education. She regularly criticized its treatment of Black schools, and then, in 1891, she implied in one editorial that there were white male members on the board who hired Black teachers for sexual favors that such teachers gave them, rather than for the ability these teachers possessed for teaching Black children.

That was the beginning of the end. For it was one thing to write about Black ministers in a Black journal, or even to send articles outside the South criticizing brutal lynchings there, but it was another very threatening thing for a Black journalist to publicly criticize leading white men about their relations to Black women in the very community in which all parties resided. Because she was now clearly a threat, obviously the foremost public spokesperson for the Black community of Memphis, Ida B. Wells could no longer be ignored. Official notice of white attention came shortly after the critical editorial, and the outspoken journalist was told that her teaching contract would not be renewed.

The loss of her job was a release—a gift of freedom to give full time to her first love. Teaching was never the challenge that Ida needed, although she was confident that her work proved more than adequate. But even at that time, when her teacher's salary had been most inadequate to meet her responsibilities for her younger brothers and sisters and her need to buy her reading and writing materials, not to mention the paying of rent, Ida knew that if she remained in a white controlled structure, even with a higher salary, she would never be free to write the things that needed to be said.

For Ida Wells, nothing stood higher on the list of topics to be dealt with than lynching—the ruthless public murder of Black people. In the decades before the turn of the twentieth century, lynching, for all practical purposes, was a national pastime of torture, murder and destruction against the Black communities, especially in the South. This was usually done by young white males, although the crowd of lynchers (usually called "mobs" or "rioters" or "the lower element of the whites") might have women and children of all ages present to encourage the murder of the victims, who might also be men, women or children. Although primarily based in the southern portions of the United States, the sympathy and understanding of the lynching mania, indeed the subtle and sometimes not so subtle encouragement of the "justified passions of an outraged people" prevailed throughout the United States and its territories. Blacks were being hung from trees, riddled with bullets, mutilated with knives, burned in village squares and in isolated fields.

Except for a few brave editorials that raged from the Black press in the South and the North, national news coverage of anti-lynching protest was not consistently reaching nor influencing the public. There was no local or national legislation attempting to protect Black people and their property from the mobs. It was a common practice after lynching one or more Black citizens for the group of white lynchers, joined by an ever larger number of persons, to visit other Black sections of the county and burn, loot and murder people, until such passions had waned and until the reality of white supremacy went unquestioned.

In the closing winter days of 1892, all these matters became forcibly personal to Ida. While traveling in the lower Mississippi Valley, Wells received word that lynching had reached the city limits of Memphis when three Black men were taken from jail, tortured and shot in the early morning hours on March 9. This time the victims were all known personally to Ida B. Wells, and one, Tom Moss, a letter carrier, was a close friend. Tom Moss' young daughter was Ida B. Wells' godchild. Moss and the other two men had owned a store, the People's Grocery, in a suburban area just outside the city limits, in a section called the "Curve." Before the three men had set up their clean and efficient establishment, a white grocer had had a monopoly on the trade of the largely Black population surrounding the "Curve."

When the three friends began their store and won customers away, the white merchant's hostile feelings were set in motion. One event led to another, with threats of destroying the People's Store coming from the white grocer.

After the three grocers sought legal counsel as to their right to arm themselves against intrusion, they set up groups of Black men to guard their store in the evenings. One evening early in March a group of policemen in plain clothes and in the company of other white men broke into the store under the pretense of looking for a criminal. They found instead a barrage of shots from Black men, and three policemen were seriously wounded.

In the confusion and terror that followed the shooting nearly thirty-five Black men were arrested in the area. Houses in the Black section were searched for weapons, while the Black militia's guns were confiscated by official decree. For three days, the Black prisoners were held in jail and beaten without the right of legal counsel or other visitors. Any contact with relatives or friends was denied the men while they underwent all forms of punishment, leaving some permanently scarred and crippled.

On the Tuesday following the shooting of the officers, the papers announced that the three white men were out of danger and the Black community rested with the knowledge and expectation that no further violence would take place. Instead, that same night, the three Black grocery store owners, Tom Moss, Calvin McDowell and Will Stewart, were taken from their cells in prison by "... the mob, in obedience to a plan known to every prominent white man in the city ..." The three men were put on a "yard engine" in the railway yard that took them a short distance from the city. Here, they were beaten and tortured once again, but not without their resisting. Finally, they were killed.

When the white newspaper reported the lynching the next day, a graphic description described the way in which the men fought. Ida B. Wells' friend, Tom Moss, was reported to have told the sea of white faces surrounding the three of them, "If you will kill us, turn our faces to the West."

When Ida B. Wells received news of the lynching, she did not know the surrounding circumstances. However, she returned to the city and pieced together as much of the story as possible, including the detailed report of the lynching in the white owned paper the day following the murders. After accusing the white journal of having had a reporter on the death scene, she began a series of articles that carried the theme taken from the last words of Tom Moss, "If you will kill us, turn our faces to the West."

And so they turned, first by the hundreds and then by the thousands. Ida B. Wells took up the call with a fierce passion. The angry, distressed Black woman urged Memphis' Black community to migrate to the West, especially to Oklahoma where large numbers of Blacks had gone as early as 1875–1876. Her editorials in the *Free Speech and Headlight* blamed the white power structure for the murders and reminded her Black readers that they had every right to leave "... a community whose laws did not protect them."

More than six thousand Black persons left Memphis within a space of two months. Whole blocks were left vacant. At least two church congregations departed en masse for the West, settling in both Kansas and California. Stores and shops were closed as their paying customers either stopped patronizing them or sent word to close their accounts. Black folk slowly began to walk to their jobs rather than ride the city trolleys. Soon there were so few riders that officials from the trolley lines were sent to the *Free Speech* offices to ask that the paper attempt to encourage Black people to ride the trolleys once again.

Ida B. Wells listened as these emissaries claimed that the owners were northerners who had no feelings of hostility to the Black riders, and although service had been not the best for Blacks in the past, all such acts of insult and rudeness would be promptly settled if only the editors would promise to tell the riders to use the public conveyance again. When Ida B. Wells asked the men why they came to the offices of the *Free Speech*, they responded that revenue to keep the trolleys in operation came from her people. She then asked why they thought Black people were no longer riding the trolleys, and they answered that maybe Blacks were afraid of the electricity that moved the car along the tracks. Could it not be that exactly six weeks ago when they stopped riding the cars was the same time that the murder of the three Black grocers took place? When she raised the possibility that there might be a relation to the murders and the trolley boycott the white men went away with no hope that the *Free Speech* might end the boycott. Instead, Ida B. Wells continued to encourage the men and women to walk rather than ride.

Many Blacks were leaving the city and quitting their places of work in order to join the swelling throng of migrants to the West. To combat the serious economic effects of the migration, a local white newspaper ran a series of articles on the horrible, fearful fate that awaited the new arrivals to the "wild" West. In response to these articles and the fears they engendered, Ida B. Wells decided to follow the migration. Using her press card she visited parts of Oklahoma to ascertain for herself the state of the resettlement of the thousands of migrants from Memphis, Tennessee. What she found was that there were many hardships. The ferry across the Mississippi from Memphis to the eastern shore of Arkansas could hardly carry the large number of fleeing Blacks. And the wagon trains on the other side of the river were loaded with families and friends, ready to brave the "wild" West. In this move away from the constant threat of death, the Black citizens of Memphis were reaching toward independence.

On May 21, 1892, Wells wrote another editorial. This time she reported lynchings in other parts of the South as more and more Black persons were being killed by mobs under the accusation of rape, usually without the benefit of facing their accusers, and always without trial by jury. She wrote:

> Eight negroes lynched in one week. Since last issue of *Free Speech* one was lynched at Little Rock, Ark., where the citizens broke into the penitentiary and got their man; three near Anniston, Ala., and one in New Orleans, all on the same charge, the new alarm of assaulting white women—and three near Clarksville, Ga., for killing a white

man. The same program of hanging—then
shooting bullets into the lifeless bodies was
carried out to the letter. Nobody in this section of the country believes the old thread-
bare lie that negro men rape white women. If
Southern white men are not careful they will
overreach themselves, and public sentiment
will have reaction. A conclusion will then be
reached which will be very damaging to the
moral reputation of their women.

By this time, white business leaders were in conference almost daily about
the Black "uprising" in Memphis. The exodus of the many thousand Black
workers with the combination of brave and fearless words coming from the
Free Speech raised additional concerns among the white power structure of the
city. The main problem was how to stop the writing of Ida B. Wells in the *Free
Speech*. It is not clear if these white leaders knew that she did the actual writing.
As far as the white men were concerned, everyone connected with the paper
was responsible for the writings. With Wells, there was J. L. Fleming, the business manager of the *Free Speech*. Another partner, Rev. Nightengale, was no
longer associated with the paper when Ida B. Wells wrote her May 21 article.

So on the following Wednesday, after Ida B. Wells' article appeared on the
streets of Memphis, the *Daily Commercial Appeal* wrote: "Those negroes who are
attempting to make lynching of individuals of their race a means of arousing the
worst passions of their kind, are playing with a dangerous sentiment. The
negroes may as well understand that there is no mercy for the negro rapist and
little patience with his defenders. A negro organ (the *Free Speech*) printed in this
city a recent issue publishes *(sic)* the following atrocious paragraph:—." That
"atrocious" paragraph was Ida B. Wells' statement on the reaction of the public to
the reputation of white women. The *Commercial Appeal* editorial concluded with:
"The fact that a black scoundrel is allowed to live and utter such loathsome and
repulsive calumnies is a volume of evidence as to the wonderful patience of
Southern whites. There are some things the Southern white man will not tolerate,
and the obscene intimation of the foregoing has brought the writer to the very
uttermost limit of public patience. We hope we have said enough."

The evening journal, *The Evening Scimitar*, another white paper, thought
there was more to say to the Black writer. "Patience under such circumstances
is not a virtue. If the negroes themselves do not apply the remedy without
delay, it will be the duty of those he has attacked, to tie the wretch who utters
these calumnies to a stake at the intersection of Main and Madison streets
(and) brand him in the forehead ..." The message was clear to the white leaders in the city: obviously, the *Free Speech* had to go.

When all of these events were taking place, Ida B. Wells was in the North.
The Friday before her article appeared, she had left the written copy to be
printed and distributed in their weekly Tuesday edition and that afternoon or

early evening had taken the train to Philadelphia to attend the A.M.E. Church conference. She had plans to travel on to New York, to meet with T. Thomas Fortune of the *New York Age*, and then return home after a few days. By the time she reached New York in the afternoon of May 25, 1892, word of the destruction of the *Free Speech* and the beating and humiliation of Rev. Nightengale had preceded her arrival. J. L. Fleming had already fled the city, after being warned by a white Republican that his life was in danger.

By this time the white leaders of Memphis knew that the writer of the infamous editorial was none other than Ida B. Wells, a Black woman—not a man. The threats that emanated from white Memphis were just as fierce against her as they would have been for anyone else. She was warned never to return South and that if she did, she would be stripped and whipped to death. Even in the face of such danger, Ida considered returning to Memphis. Indeed a message from Black men there, promising to fight to the death to protect her, was both encouragement and deterrence. She knew that both the Black and white forces would keep their promises to her and the superior firepower and political power of the whites would lead to a terrible bloodletting. She decided she should not return to precipitate that further tragedy.

Nevertheless, if the white Memphis leaders thought that the Black crusader would for a moment halt her campaign against lynching, they were wrong. For Ida B. Wells continued to send anti-lynching press releases to the nation and the world from her new headquarters at the *New York Age*. Moreover, T. Thomas Fortune, the publisher and editor of the *Age*, was instrumental in assisting Wells in setting up speaking engagements and putting her in touch with persons throughout the North who could give financial and moral support to her activities. In exchange for Ida B. Wells' list of subscribers to the *Free Speech*, Fortune offered her a position with his paper and encouraged her to continue writing on the horrors of lynching. Frederick Douglass came to the *New York Age* offices to see for himself this writer of such brave and critical attacks on a South that he was all too familiar with. They shared the growing fear of what the lynching mania was doing to their people.

Meanwhile, the support and encouragement that she got from women in Brooklyn and New York meant a great deal to Ida B. Wells, for it was her first experience of coming together with Black women around political and social issues. While still working with the *Age*, she went to their meetings and gave such a moving account of the current state of Black people in the South that the women determined to organize around the struggle for justice much more fully than ever before. Eventually, these contacts by Wells led to a new source of life for the women's club movement in the Black community.

For instance, the gathering in Brooklyn of these sisters, who gave moral and financial support to Ida B. Wells, was inspiration and strength for her soul. To this young newspaper woman who only a few months ago was writing in Memphis about the need for Blacks to support one another in the migration West and in the boycotting within the area of Memphis, this reception and encouragement was a balm that both soothed and strengthened her for the yet unknown and difficult times ahead. And it was significant that such support came from that group of humans who were ordinarily assumed to be too weak, uninterested or, by "nature," unqualified to persist in demonstrating such solidarity and commitment about public issues.

There was no fireside at this gathering in Brooklyn, no sewing needles and small talk on the exploits of persons far and unrelated to the lives of these women. Instead, before them stood a woman who had defied the very foundations of racism by daring to challenge the myths of white supremacy and standing upon a platform, speaking with tears of the cost of such a challenge.

Actually, what was taking place in the life of Ida B. Wells was that for the first time she was coming into intimate contact with Black women who were in a tradition of social club work and she was also meeting Northern-based Black writers and spokespersons. From this beginning, she went to other parts of the northeast, speaking and describing the events that took place in Memphis and those that were taking place throughout the South within the Black communities.

For the next four decades she continued to carry out this dangerous vocation all over America and across the Atlantic, insisting that the world awaken to the conditions of her people, determined that the spotlight of truth would remain focused on the darkness of white America, hoping always that the light would eventually prevail.

James Madison Nabrit, Jr.
Michael R. Winston

One standard of greatness in a law school is its impact on law and society. By that measure the Howard law school holds special distinction in its leading role in the destruction of statutory segregation in the United States, arguably the most significant social reform of the twentieth century. Of the constellation of brilliant lawyers who participated in that remarkable effort, one of the brightest stars was James M. Nabrit, Jr., who was appointed to the law faculty in 1936 and served as Dean from 1958 until 1960, when he became President of Howard University.

James M. Nabrit Jr. was born in, Atlanta, Georgia on September 24, 1900, the eldest of eight children of the Reverend James M. Nabrit and Gertrude West Nabrit.[1] The turn of the century was the high tide of the white supremacy movement in the South, when the legal status of Black Americans was at its lowest point since the Emancipation. When James Nabrit, Jr. was about ten years old he saw a black man beaten and burned to death by a white mob in Americus, Georgia because he had cheered too heartily when Jack Johnson, the famous prizefighter, defeated a white opponent, Jim Jeffries, at that time called "The Great White Hope". Not surprisingly, this made a deep impression on him.[2] When his father had a pastorate in Augusta, the young James Nabrit saw that whites had three public high schools, and blacks had none (which the Supreme Court of the United States had held did *not* "violate any of the privileges belonging to [Negroes] as citizens of the United States" in its decision in *Cumming* v. *Richmond County Board of Education*, 1899).

He entered the Academy of Morehouse College in 1915 to pursue his high school education. While there he was inspired by the school's impressive President, John Hope, its legendary Dean, Samuel H. "Big Boy" Archer, and by some of the outstanding teachers, including John W. Davis, Mordecai W. Johnson, and Benjamin Brawley. Continuing his education at Morehouse, he entered the College in 1919. An end on the football team and short stop on the baseball team, Nabrit was undefeated as a debater. Coached in debate by Benjamin Mays, he was also greatly influenced by E. Franklin Frazier, whose uninhibited thinking and sharp attacks on segregation were unusual, particularly in the South. While he was a Morehouse student Nabrit was arrested in down-town Atlanta for getting off a streetcar at the white exit rather than the colored exit. More and more, he saw that "something was wrong with the law."

During the summers he worked in a number of the northern and mid-western industrial plants opened for the first time to black employees by the manpower shortage of World War I, including the Jones and Laughlin Steel Mills in Pittsburgh and the Riggs Body Company in Detroit. In Washington and Chicago he also had the opportunity to meet a number of young black attorneys—George E. C. Hayes and Charles H. Houston in Washington, and J. Alston Atkins and Carter Wesley in Chicago. As a result of these associa-tions, and his own ideas about his experiences in the South, he decided to pursue a career in law as a way to change things. "As soon as I found out what the law was, then I knew that was what I wanted. That was all I could think of, that's all I ever thought of studying."

After graduating from Morehouse with honors in 1923, James Nabrit entered the Northwestern University School of Law. There he was free of Atlanta's style of racial domination, but not from the common idea that the pro-fession of law was for whites. When he first arrived at Northwestern, the white students drummed their feet to drown out his voice whenever he started to recite in class. In response, characteristically, he moved to the front row, and as he recalled later, "I would hold my hand up. The professor would be right there and he wouldn't pay any attention, but I kept on and after several days he stopped and said 'Yes?' I asked my question. And he said, 'As I was saying' and went on." Not long thereafter, the Dean, John H. Wigmore, gave all of the first year students an examination of 200 questions based on required reading. For the first time a student had 200 correct answers—James M. Nabrit. After that result was posted, the heckling of Nabrit ceased. This result is all the more remarkable in light of the fact that he had no financial assistance and was work-ing his way through law school. He went to law classes until three in the after-noon, then from 4 to 10 P.M. Nabrit worked as a red cap at the railroad station, then studied much of the night for the next day's classes.[3] After two years of law school he went to teach English for a year at Leland College in Baker, Louisiana (1925–1926), then returned to Northwestern. Elected to the Order of the Coif because of his outstanding academic record, he graduated with hon-ors, but unlike his white classmates, he received no offers for employment in the law. He returned to Leland to teach, 1927–1928, then was appointed Profes-sor of English and Dean at Arkansas A.M. & N. College, Pine Bluff, Arkansas, 1928–1930.

Finally, in 1930 he was able to pursue his dream of a legal career by moving to Houston, Texas, where he joined J. Alston Atkins, a Yale Law graduate and Carter W. Wesley, a Northwestern Law graduate, to form the firm of Nabrit, Atkins and Wesley. Atkins and Wesley had practiced earlier in Oklahoma, suc-cessfully representing Indians and Negroes who had oil interests, and as a result had the means to start in Houston a newspaper, an insurance company and a real estate business. Atkins and Wesley handled the business and political side of the firm, and Nabrit was the principal litigator and manager of the firm's legal portfolio. Handling all sorts of cases, including many criminal cases, Nabrit developed a very broad and thriving practice, including representation of clients defending their rights to oil properties. As he later said, practicing in Houston at that time was in a "wild west" atmosphere, with large sums of money at stake, ruthlessness the norm, and whites as well as blacks heavily armed. Despite the business and legal success of the firm, Nabrit was dissatisfied. From his first days in Texas he was seeking ways to attack the various forms of segregation imposed on Negroes. He believed the key to removing many of the civic disabilities of the black population was access to the power of the ballot. In Texas, the "white primary" system was in force, in which no blacks could vote in the primary, but only in the general election, which was meaningless since the Democratic candidates selected in the primary would win overwhelmingly in the general election. While in Houston Nabrit began his relentless assault on the disfranchisement of blacks in Texas, starting with the case *Nixon* v. *Condon*, (1932).[4]

Meanwhile, Dean Charles H. Houston of the Howard Law School, William H. Hastie of the Howard faculty and the NAACP, and President Mordecai W. Johnson had written to him and talked with him for several years about leaving his Houston practice to join the Howard law faculty. Despite the success of his law practice, Nabrit was dissatisfied with the prospects for making headway on his most cherished projects in the civil rights field if he stayed in Texas. He had no access to the library of the Texas Bar Association, restricted to its white members, and no access to any other law libraries in the state. There was also the practical reality that his Houston law firm could only take on civil rights cases as a sideline. At Howard there was developing a unique mobilization of legal talent focused on attacking legally required and enforced racial domination in all of the former slave states.

Nabrit joined the Howard Law faculty in 1936, but his razor-sharp mind and administrative ability caused the University's President to appoint him Administrative Assistant to the President (1938–1939) in addition to his law school duties, and a year later, Secretary of Howard University, one of the top three administrative positions in the University at that time. What for others might have been a fatal distraction from professional objectives was simply a parallel responsibility for Nabrit. For the entire period 1938 to 1960, when he became President, he carried multiple responsibilities, teaching in the law school, serving as Director of Public Relations (1940–1950), Dean of the Law School (1958–1960) and full-time Secretary of the Board of Trustees and the University (1939–1960).

Upon his arrival at the Howard Law School, Professor Nabrit proposed to the faculty the adoption of a course in Civil Rights. Approved and offered for the first time in 1937, it was the first such formal course in any law school in the United States. The purpose of the course was to "discover what the law was in respect to minorities in this area of civil rights; second, to develop techniques for raising constitutional questions in respect to disabilities affecting minorities . . . and third, to separate those disabilities for which legislative action would be required for their elimination."[5]

While many brilliant civil rights lawyers taught for a time at the Howard Law School, one of the striking things about Nabrit's career was that he remained at the core of the faculty for a quarter of a century, with a single-minded focus on destroying the legal foundations of segregation in the United States. As he later described the Howard Law School in the 1930's and 1940's, it was the intellectual anchor for an emerging system that he has called the "Howard Law School—NAACP Nexus." At that time the NAACP was under-staffed, with Thurgood Marshall working with little direct legal assistance, and a network of cooperating attorneys in various jurisdictions. The Law School provided a reservoir of talent for legal research. Outstanding students, such as Spottswood Robinson, III, Oliver Hill, Joseph Waddy and Robert L. Carter, were fully involved during their student years in cutting-edge legal research on constitutional issues. This connection with the NAACP's effort also gave the law faculty the opportunity to test new ideas in litigation. The Howard Law School was transformed by this new emphasis. "Our students," Nabrit later said, "who had formerly been just reciting and listening to the professor lecture, were now made to start drafting documents, drafting pleadings and procedure." The law school, he added "was focusing on the mechanism of pleading, trying cases and appealing cases."[6] As is now well known, a crucial part of this new system was the massive preparation for Supreme Court cases, in which the highlight was the Howard Law School Moot Court, on the Saturday before oral argument, in which Howard faculty, students, and alumni, along with invited members of the Washington Bar, would critique the arguments and propound questions that might be asked by the Justices of the Supreme Court.

The whole process created a new environment in the Howard Law School, embodying Charles Hamilton Houston's concept of the school as "The West Point of the Civil Rights Movement." According to Nabrit, an unsung hero of this whole development was President Mordecai W. Johnson, who not only "took in the significance of the law for us as a people," but put the resources of the University behind the effort. Considering the politically volatile potential of such cases as Nabrit's *Lane* v. *Wilson* (Oklahoma, 1939) and *Terry* v. *Adams*, (Texas, 1953), voting rights cases affecting the jurisdictions of Members of Congress involved in Howard's annual federal appropriation, the courage required to support the battalion of Howard civil rights lawyers, year after year, was formidable. The stimulus of working on civil rights cases, and the intense pressures of high level appellate litigation "was the centralizing factor in the development of the Howard Law School."[7] In those years Professor Nabrit not only participated in the major voting rights and education cases, but developed a set of theories in constitutional law that were more aggressive than the consensus views of the National Legal Committee of the NAACP and the NAACP Legal Defense Fund. He was, for example, an early advocate of the class-action suit as a strategy to leapfrog over Houston's earlier, protracted case-by-case approach. Most importantly, he was the boldest advocate of an attack on the constitutionality of segregation *per se*. Nabrit argued that in the so-called "equalization cases" attacking public school segregation, judicial relief tended to be temporary, since within a relatively short time southern jurisdictions created new inequalities, forcing the civil rights forces to be on an endless treadmill of litigation about unequal teachers' salaries, facilities, per-pupil expenditures, and so forth. Moreover, the Houston-Marshall equalization strategy left *Plessy* v. *Ferguson* intact as constitutional doctrine.

In what is perhaps his greatest case, *Bolling* v. *Sharpe*, (the District of Columbia school desegregation case decided along with *Brown* v. *Board of Education*, 1954) argued with his Howard colleague and friend, George E. C. Hayes. Nabrit did not maintain that segregated public schools in the District of Columbia were unconstitutional because they were unequal, but that racial segregation itself was unconstitutional. The system of segregated schools constituted, he said, a bill of attainder, since it deprived, as a class, black citizens of rights without due process of law. The prevailing view among civil rights lawyers at the time was that an attack on segregation *per se* was too risky because the Supreme Court might re-affirm *Plessy*, destroying in the eyes of many lawyers the gains made in the twenty years of litigation attacking inequality on the premises of the *Plessy* doctrine. Nabrit thought that any temporizing was playing into the hands of the segregationists.

To those who said it was foolish to put the white South's back to the wall, which might provoke widespread violence, Nabrit replied with his characteristic toughness: "Suppose it does? Shall the Negro child be required to wait for his constitutional rights until the white South is educated, industrialized, and ready to confer these rights on his children's children?" No concessions were to be made to "southern custom" and the Supreme Court's habit of deferring issues that might be politically and socially explosive: "Wherever the Negro is laboring under constitutional disabilities in the South, there is the best place to attack. The attack should be waged with the most devastating forces at hand. . . . The Supreme Court will have to worry over community attitudes. Let us worry over the problem of pressing for our civil rights. . . . Let the Supreme Court take the blame if it dares say to the entire world, 'Yes, democracy [in the United States] rests on a legalized caste system. Segregation of races is legal.' Make the Court choose. . . ."[8] In 1952 Nabrit closed his oral argument in *Bolling* v. *Sharpe*, with an eloquent statement of his position. The attorney for the defendants, Nabrit said, had "dwelt in the past upon the white man's burden, and he has seemed to feel that for some reason that exists today."

"It would appear to me," Nabrit continued, "that in 1952 the Negro should not be viewed as anybody's burden." Furthermore:

He is a citizen. He is performing his duties in peace and in war, and today, on the bloody hills of Korea, he is serving in an unsegregated war.

All we ask of this Court is that it say under the Constitution he is entitled to live and send his children to school in the District of Columbia unsegregated, with the children of his war comrades. That is simple. The Constitution gives him that right.

The basic argument here is one of liberty, and under liberty, under the due process clause, you cannot deal with it as you deal with equal protection of laws, because there you deal with it as a quantum of treatment, substantially equal.

You either have liberty or you do not. When liberty is interfered with by the state, it has to be justified, and you cannot justify it by saying that we only took a little liberty. You justify it by the reasonableness of the taking.

We submit that in this case, in the heart of the nation's capital, in the capital of democracy, in the capital of the free world, there is no place for a segregated school system. This country cannot afford it, and the Constitution does not permit it and the statutes of Congress do not authorize it.[9]

Although he was best known in the legal profession for his brilliant work as a civil rights lawyer in such landmark cases as *Lane* v. *Wilson, Sweatt* v. *Painter,* and *Bolling* v. *Sharpe,* for many Howard Law students Professor Nabrit was simply the best teacher they had ever encountered. Genial, easy to talk to, he was also demanding, skeptical, and breath-takingly analytical. He could cut through a case, an issue, or student filibuster with awesome speed and precision. "With Nabrit," one law student said, "you don't simply learn law, you argue it."[10] Students were also impressed by Nabrit's great versatility. He was a member of the President's Committee on Government Contracts during the Eisenhower administration, a participant in the International Labor Conferences in Geneva, Switzerland, and Legal Adviser to the Governor of the Virgin Islands on the Reorganization of the Executive Branch.

By the time Dr. Nabrit became Dean of the Law School in 1958, many thought of him as embodying the best in the legal profession. He had also shown how intellect, harnessed to firm purpose and disciplined inquiry could reshape the law, and through it the operation of society itself. In 1960, at the end of his deanship, the graduating seniors of the law school dedicated their section of the yearbook to James M. Nabrit, Jr. The students wrote that just as he was an "indispensable leader of society," his qualities of "humility, good humour, sincerity, competence, and friendliness" had made him "just as indispensable" to his students.

Dean Nabrit's elevation to the Presidency of Howard University opened a new era at Howard. He was President during one of the most turbulent periods of United States history. Swept into the multiplying tensions generated by white backlash against the civil rights, black identity and black power movements, colleges and universities had to cope also with the growing anti-war and women's rights movements. Always a place where controversies could thrive because of its many national and international constituencies, Howard also became during Dr. Nabrit's Presidency a national center of protest thought and student upheaval. With his usual aplomb and frankness, he met the roughest days of his career. Students and faculty alike saw once again his courage under fire. During the time he served as U.S. Permanent Deputy Representative to the United Nations, he gave the commencement address at Howard, June 3, 1966. Despite the enormous pressures generated by the sudden popularity of anti-integration leaders such as Malcolm X, President Nabrit insisted on holding to his lifelong faith in the United States Constitution and the ideals of democracy. To the rising voices of the black nationalists and those who would abandon the goal of achieving an integrated society based on the Constitution, he said:

Frustrated and bitter, disillusioned and skeptical men do foolish and violent things. But having fought all my life for the rights and privileges of an American citizen, which I am, and for the rights to which all are entitled under the Constitution of the United States, which they are, I would not give up hope for their achievement at the very time when the first clear hopeful view of their attainment comes into sight—I would not at the very moment when integration begins to appear on the horizon, turn my back on this revolutionary struggle and steep myself in racial hatred and loneliness and misery in a chauvinistic embrace of black nationalism. . . . Let us not apologize either for uniformed or ill-advised Negroes who do feel hatred, or frustration or pursue black nationalistic myths—for if the white man who is richer, better educated, with more political power—who enjoys to the limits all of his constitutional rights can produce Ku Klux Klansmen, John Birchites, and Rockwell Nazis, why cannot we be permitted to have our share of the lunatic fringe and of aberrant groups too? As for me, I not only will not apologize for them, but I do not even intend to engage in any more criticism of them than I do with respect to any group with which I personally do not agree.

When he retired as President of the University on June 30, 1969, James Madison Nabrit, Jr., ended a brilliant career of service to his country. Lawyer, dean, diplomat, and university president, he has been one of the shapers of a new American society in the twentieth century. He continues to this day, at the age of 94, to watch with enthusiasm the work of Howard University, and especially his beloved Law School, where he was able to pursue his dream of Equal Justice Under Law for all Americans.

Notes

[1] Basic biographical data for this article was drawn from the James M. Nabrit, Jr. biographical file, Moorland-Spingarn Research Center, Howard University. For assistance in the University Archives, I am indebted to Dr. Clifford L. Muse, Jr., University Archivist, and for assistance in the Library Division of the Research Center, Mrs. Avril Madison, Reference Librarian.

[2] Richard Kluger, *Simple Justice: The History of Brown v. Board of Education and Black America's Struggle for Equality* (New York: Alfred A. Knopf, 1976), p. 518.

[3] James M. Nabrit, Jr., Interview with Michael R. Winston, Washington, D.C., September 25, 1979.

[4] For the significant role of the Nabrit, Atkins and Wesley firm in the Texas disfranchisement cases, see August Meier and Elliott Rudwick, "Attorneys in Black and White: A Case Study of Race Relations with the NAACP" in Meier and Rudwick, *Along the Color Line: Explorations in the Black Experience* (Urbana: University of Illinois Press, 1976), pp. 147–154.

[5] James M. Nabrit, Jr., *Cases and Materials on Civil Rights*, quoted in J. Clay Smith, Jr., *Emancipation: The Making of the Black Lawyer, 1844–1944* (Philadelphia: University of Pennsylvania Press, 1993), p. 51.

[6] James M. Nabrit, Jr., Interview with Michael R. Winston, October 11, 1979.

[7] *Ibid.*

[8] James M. Nabrit, Jr., quoted in Kluger, *op. cit.*, pp. 536–537.

[9] James M. Nabrit, Jr., Oral Argument, *Spottswood Thomas Bolling, et al., vs. C. Melvin Sharpe et al.* before the Supreme Court of the United States, December 10, 1952, in *Argument: The Oral Argument Before the Supreme Court in Brown v. Board of Education of Topeka, 1952–55*, edited by Leon Friedman (New York: Chelsea House Publishers, 1969), p. 142.

[10] "James M. Nabrit, Jr." in "Six Howard Professors" [Nabrit, Charles Drew, Sterling Brown, E. Franklin Frazier, Rayford W. Logan and Alain Locke] in *Our World* (January, 1950), p. 29.

"Introduction" to In the Castle of My Skin by George Lamming
Richard Wright

Accounting for one of the aspects of the complex social and political drama in which most of the subject people of our time are caught, I once wrote: "... to a greater or less degree, almost all of human life on earth today *can* be described as moving away from traditional, agrarian, simple handicraft ways of living toward modern industrialization."

These words deal with vast, cold, impersonal social forces which are somewhat difficult to grasp unless one has had the dubious fortune of having had one's own life shaped by the reality of those forces. The act of ripping the sensitive human personality from one culture and the planting of that personality in another culture is a tortured, convoluted process that must, before it can appeal to peoples' hearts, be projected either in terms of vivid drama or highly sensual poetry.

It has been through the medium of the latter—a charged and poetic prose— that George Lamming, a young West Indian Negro of Barbados, has presented his autobiographical summation of a tropical island childhood that, though steeped in the luminous images of sea, earth, sky, and wind, drifts slowly toward the edge of the realms of political and industrial strife. Notwithstanding the fact that Lamming's story, as such, is his own, it is, at the same time, a symbolic repetition of the story of millions of simple folk who, sprawled over half of the world's surface and involving more than half of the human race, are today being catapulted out of their peaceful, indigenously earthy lives and into the turbulence and anxiety of the twentieth century.

I, too, have been long crying these stern tidings; and, when I catch the echo of yet another voice declaiming in alien accents a description of this same reality, I react with pride and excitement, and I want to urge others to listen to that voice. One feels not so much alone when, from a distant witness, supporting evidence comes to buttress one's own testimony. And the voice that I now bid you hear is sounding in Lamming's *In the Castle of My Skin*. What, then, is this story that Lamming tells?

Without adequate preparation, the Negro of the Western world lives, in *one* life, *many* lifetimes. Most whites' lives are couched in norms more or less traditional: born of stable family groups, a white boy emerges from adolescence, enters high school, finishes college, studies a profession, marries, builds a home, raises children, etc. The Negro, though born in the Western world, is not quite of it; due to policies of racial exclusion, his is the story of *two* cultures: the dying culture in which he happens to be born, and the culture into which he is trying to enter—a culture which has, for him, not quite yet come into being; and it is up the shaky ladder of all the intervening stages between these two cultures that Negro life must climb. Such a story is, above all, a record of shifting, troubled feelings groping their way toward a future that frightens as much as it beckons.

Lamming's quietly melodious prose is faithful not only to social detail, but renders with fidelity the myth-content of folk minds; paints lovingly the personalities of boyhood friends; sketches authentically the characters of schoolmasters and village merchants; and depicts the moods of an adolescent boy in an adolescent society. ... Lamming rehearses the rituals of matriarchal families so common to people upon whom the strident blessings of an industrial world are falling—families whose men have been either killed, carted off to war, or hired to work in distant lands, leaving behind nervous mothers to rule with anxious hysteria over a brood of children who grow up restless, rebellious, and disdainful of authority.

Lamming recounts, in terms of anecdote, the sex mores of his people, their religious attitudes, their drinking habits, their brawls in the sunlit marketplaces, the fear of the little people for the overseers, and the fear of the overseers for the big white boss in the faraway house on the hill. (Unlike the population ratio in the United States, the English in these tiny islands comprise a minority surrounded by a majority of blacks; hence, that chronic, grinding, racial hatred and fear, which have so long been the hallmark of both white and black attitudes in our own Southland, are largely absent from these pages.)

Lamming objectifies the conscience of his village in those superbly drawn character portraits of Pa and Ma, those folk Negroes of yesteryear whose personalities, bearing the contours of Old Testament, Biblical heroes, have left their stamp upon so many young Lammings of the Western world. I feel that Lamming, in accounting for himself and his generation, was particularly fortunate in creating this device of a symbolic Pa and Ma whose lineaments evoke in our minds images of simple, peasant parents musing uncomprehendingly upon the social changes that disrupt their lives and threaten the destinies of their children. ...

The clash of this dying culture with the emerging new world is not without its humor, both ribald and pathetic: the impact of the concept of marriage upon the naive, paganlike minds is amusingly related by Lamming in his story of Bots, Bambi, and Bambina. The superstitions of his boyhood friends are laid engagingly before us. And there's a kind of poetry suggested even in the outlandish names of his boyhood playmates: Trumper, Boy Blue, Big Bam, Cutsie, Botsie, Knucker Hand, Po King, Puss-in-Boots, and Suck Me Toe. ...

Just as young Lamming is ready to leave Barbados Island for Trinidad, Trumper, who has gone to America and has been influenced by mass racial and political agitation, returns and, in a garbled manner, tells of the frenzied gospel of racial self-assertion—that strange soul-food of the rootless outsiders of the twentieth century. The magnetic symbol of Paul Robeson (shown here purely in racial and *not* political terms!) attracts as much as disturbs young Lamming as he hears Robeson sing over a tiny recording device: *Let My People Go!*

Even before Lamming leaves his island home, that home is already dying in his heart; and what happens to Lamming after that is something that we all know, for we have but to lift our eyes and look into the streets and we see countless young, dark-skinned Lammings of the soil marching in picket lines, attending political rallies, impulsively, frantically seeking a new identity. ...

Filtered through a poetic temperament like Lamming's, this story of change from folk life to the borders of the industrial world adds a new and poignant dimension to a reality that is already global in its meaning.

Lamming's is a true gift; as an artist, he possesses a quiet and stubborn courage; and in him a new writer takes his place in the literary world.

Paris, 1953   *Richard Wright*

Pilgrimage to Nonviolence
Martin Luther King, Jr.

When I went to Montgomery as a pastor, I had not the slightest idea that I would later become involved in a crisis in which nonviolent resistance would be applicable. I neither started the protest nor suggested it. I simply responded to the call of the people for a spokesman. When the protest began, my mind, consciously or unconsciously, was driven back to the Sermon on the Mount, with its sublime teachings on love, and the Gandhian method of nonviolent resistance. As the days unfolded, I came to see the power of nonviolence more and more. Living through the actual experience of the protest, nonviolence became more than a method to which I gave intellectual assent; it became a commitment to a way of life. Many of the things that I had not cleared up intellectually concerning nonviolence were now solved in the sphere of practical action.

Since the philosophy of nonviolence played such a positive role in the Montgomery Movement, it may be wise to turn to a brief discussion of some basic aspects of this philosophy.

First, it must be emphasized that nonviolent resistance is not a method for cowards; it does resist. If one uses this method because he is afraid or merely because he lacks the instruments of violence, he is not truly nonviolent. This is why Gandhi often said that if cowardice is the only alternative to violence, it is better to fight. He made this statement conscious of the fact that there is always another alternative: no individual or group need submit to any wrong, nor need they use violence to right the wrong; there is the way of nonviolent resistance. This is ultimately the way of the strong man. It is not a method of stagnant passivity. The phrase "passive resistance" often gives the false impression that this is a sort of "do-nothing method" in which the resister quietly and passively accepts evil. But nothing is further from the truth. For while the nonviolent resister is passive in the sense that he is not physically aggressive toward his opponent, his mind and emotions are always active, constantly seeking to persuade his opponent that he is wrong. The method is passive physically, but strongly active spiritually. It is not passive nonresistance to evil, it is active nonviolent resistance to evil.

A second basic fact that characterizes nonviolence is that it does not seek to defeat or humiliate the opponent, but to win his friendship and understanding. The nonviolent resister must often express his protest through noncooperation or boycotts, but he realizes that these are not ends themselves; they are merely means to awaken a sense of moral shame in the opponent. The end is redemption and reconciliation. The aftermath of nonviolence is the creation of the beloved community, while the aftermath of violence is tragic bitterness.

A third characteristic of this method is that the attack is directed against forces of evil rather than against persons who happen to be doing the evil. It is evil that the nonviolent resister seeks to defeat, not the persons victimized by evil. If he is opposing racial injustice, the nonviolent resister has the vision to say that the basic tension is not between races. As I like to say to the people in Montgomery: "The tension in this city is not between white people and Negro people. The tension is, at bottom, between justice and injustice, between the forces of light and the forces of darkness. And if there is a victory, it will be a victory not merely for fifty thousand Negroes, but a victory for justice and the forces of light. We are out to defeat injustice and not white persons who may be unjust."

A fourth point that characterizes nonviolent resistance is a willingness to accept suffering without retaliation, to accept blows from the opponent without striking back. "Rivers of blood may have to flow before we gain our freedom, but it must be our blood," Gandhi said to his countrymen. The nonviolent resister is willing to accept violence if necessary, but never to inflict it. He does not seek to dodge jail. If going to jail is necessary, he enters it "as a bridegroom enters the bride's chamber."

One may well ask: "What is the nonviolent resister's justification for this ordeal to which he invites men, for this mass political application of the ancient doctrine of turning the other cheek?" The answer is found in the realization that unearned suffering is redemptive. Suffering, the nonviolent resister realizes, has tremendous educational and transforming possibilities. "Things of fundamental importance to people are not secured by reason alone, but have to be purchased with their suffering," said Gandhi. He continues: "Suffering is infinitely more powerful than the law of the jungle for converting the opponent and opening his ears which are otherwise shut to the voice of reason."

A fifth point concerning nonviolent resistance is that it avoids not only external physical violence but also internal violence of spirit. The nonviolent resister not only refuses to shoot his opponent but he also refuses to hate him. At the center of nonviolence stands the principle of love. The nonviolent resister would contend that in the struggle for human dignity, the oppressed people of the world must not succumb to the temptation of becoming bitter or indulging in hate campaigns. To retaliate in kind would do nothing but intensify the existence of hate in the universe. Along the way of life, someone must have sense enough and morality enough to cut off the chain of hate. This can only be done by projecting the ethic of love to the center of our lives.

In speaking of love at this point, we are not referring to some sentimental or affectionate emotion. It would be nonsense to urge men to love their oppressors in an affectionate sense. Love in this connection means understanding, redemptive good will. Here the Greek language comes to our aid. There are three words for love in the Greek New Testament. First, there is *eros*. In Platonic philosophy *eros* meant the yearning of the soul for the realm of the divine. It has come now to mean a sort of aesthetic or romantic love. Second, there is *philia*, which means intimate affection between personal friends. *Philia* denotes a sort of reciprocal love; the person loves because he is loved. When we speak of loving those who oppose us, we refer to neither *eros* nor *philia*; we speak of a love which is expressed in the Greek word *agape*. *Agape* means understanding, redeeming good will for all men. It is an overflowing love which is purely spontaneous, unmotivated, groundless, and creative. It is not set in motion by any quality or function of its object. It is the love of God operating in the human heart.

Agape is disinterested love. It is a love in which the individual seeks not his own good, but the good of his neighbor (I Cor. 10:24). *Agape* does not begin by discriminating between worthy and unworthy people, or any qualities people possess. It begins by loving others *for their sakes*. It is entirely "neighbor-regarding concern for others," which discovers the neighbor in every man it meets. There, *agape* makes no distinction between friend and enemy; it is directed toward both. If one loves an individual merely on account of friendliness, he loves him for the sake of the benefits to be gained from the friendship, rather than for the friend's own sake. Consequently, the best way to assure oneself that Love is disinterested is to have love for the enemy-neighbor from whom you can expect no good in return, but only hostility and persecution.

Another basic point about *agape* is that it springs from the *need* of the other person—his need for belonging to the best in the human family. The Samaritan who helped the Jew on the Jericho Road was "good" because he responded to the human need that he was presented with. God's love is eternal and fails not because man needs his love. St. Paul assures us that the loving act of redemption was done "while we were yet sinners"—that is, at the point of our greatest need for love. Since the white man's personality is greatly distorted by segregation, and his soul is greatly scarred, he needs the love of the Negro. The Negro must love the white man, because the white man needs his love to remove his tensions, insecurities, and fears.

Agape is not a weak, passive love. It is love in action. *Agape* is love seeking to preserve and create community. It is insistence on community even when one seeks to break it. *Agape* is a willingness to sacrifice in the interest of mutuality. *Agape* is a willingness to go to any length to restore community. It doesn't stop at the first mile, but it goes the second mile to restore community. It is a willingness to forgive, not seven times, but seventy times seven to restore community. The cross is the eternal expression of the length to which God will go in order to restore broken community. The resurrection is a symbol of God's triumph over all the forces that seek to block community. The Holy Spirit is the continuing community creating reality that moves through history. He who works against community is working against the whole of creation. Therefore, if I respond to hate with a reciprocal hate I do nothing but intensify cleavage in broken community. I can only close the gap in broken community by meeting hate with love. If I meet hate with hate, I become depersonalized, because creation is so designed that my personality can only be fulfilled in the context of community. Booker T. Washington was right: "Let no man pull you so low as to make you hate him." When he pulls you that low he brings you to the point of working against community; he drags you to the point of defying creation, and thereby becoming depersonalized.

In the final analysis, *agape* means a recognition of the fact that all life is interrelated. All humanity is involved in a single process, and all men are brothers. To the degree that I harm my brother, no matter what he is doing to me, to that extent I am harming myself. For example, white men often refuse federal aid to education in order to avoid giving the Negro his rights; but because all men are brothers they cannot deny Negro children without harming their own. They end, all efforts to the contrary, by hurting themselves. Why is this? Because men are brothers. If you harm me, you harm yourself.

Love, *agape*, is the only cement that can hold this broken community together. When I am commanded to love, I am commanded to restore community, to resist injustice, and to meet the needs of my brothers.

A sixth basic fact about nonviolent resistance is that it is based on the conviction that the universe is on the side of justice. Consequently, the believer in nonviolence has deep faith in the future. This faith is another reason why the nonviolent resister can accept suffering without retaliation. For he knows that in his struggle for justice he has cosmic companionship. It is true that there are devout believers in nonviolence who find it difficult to believe in a personal God. But even these persons believe in the existence of some creative force that works for universal wholeness. Whether we call it an unconscious process, an impersonal Brahman, or a Personal Being of matchless power and infinite love, there is a creative force in this universe that works to bring the disconnected aspects of reality into a harmonious whole.

Message to the Grass Roots
Malcolm X

If you're afraid of black nationalism, you're afraid of revolution. And if you love revolution, you love black nationalism.

To understand this, you have to go back to what the young brother here referred to as the house Negro and the field Negro back during slavery. There were two kinds of slaves, the house Negro and the field Negro. The house Negroes—they lived in the house with master, they dressed pretty good, they ate good because they ate his food—what he left. They lived in the attic or the basement, but still they lived near the master; and they loved the master more than the master loved himself. They would give their life to save the master's house—quicker than the master would. If the master said, "We got a good house here," the house Negro would say, "Yeah, we got a good house here." Whenever the master said "we," he said "we." That's how you can tell a house Negro.

If the master's house caught on fire, the house Negro would fight harder to put the blaze out than the master would. If the master got sick, the house Negro would say, "What's the matter, boss, *we* sick?" *We* sick! He identified himself with his master, more than his master identified with himself. And if you came to the house Negro and said, "Let's run away, let's escape, let's separate," the house Negro would look at you and say, "Man, you crazy. What you mean, separate? Where is there a better house than this? Where can I wear better clothes than this? Where can I eat better food than this?" That was that house Negro. In those days he was called a "house nigger." And that's what we call them today, because we've still got some house niggers running around here.

This modern house Negro loves his master. He wants to live near him. He'll pay three times as much as the house is worth just to live near his master, and then brag about "I'm the only Negro out here." "I'm the only one on my job." "I'm the only one in this school." You're nothing but a house Negro. And if someone comes to you right now and says, "Let's separate," you say the same thing that the house Negro said on the plantation. "What you mean, separate? From America, this good white man? Where you going to get a better job than you get here?" I mean, this is what you say, "I ain't left nothing in Africa," that's what you say. Why, you left your mind in Africa.

On that same plantation, there was the field Negro. The field Negroes—those were the masses. There were always more Negroes in the field than there were Negroes in the house. The Negro in the field caught hell. He ate leftovers. In the house they ate high up on the hog. The Negro in the field didn't get anything but what was left of the insides of the hog. They call it "chitt'lings" nowadays. In those days they called them what they were—guts. That's what you were—gut-eaters. And some of you are still gut-eaters.

The field Negro was beaten from morning to night; he lived in a shack, in a hut; he wore old, castoff clothes. He hated his master. I say he hated his master. He was intelligent. That house Negro loved his master, but that field Negro—remember, they were in the majority, and they hated the master. When the house caught on fire, he didn't try to put it out; that field Negro prayed for a wind, for a breeze. When the master got sick, the field Negro prayed that he'd die. If someone came to the field Negro and said, "Let's separate, let's run," he didn't say "Where we going?" He'd say, "Any place is better than here." You've got field Negroes in America today. I'm a field Negro. The masses are the field Negroes. When they see this man's house on fire, you don't hear the little Negroes talking about "*our* government is in trouble." They say, "*The* government is in trouble." Imagine a Negro: "*Our* government"! I even heard one say "*our* astronauts." They won't even let him near the plant—and "*our* astronauts"! "*Our* Navy"—that's a Negro that is out of his mind, a Negro that is out of his mind.

Just as the slavemaster of that day used Tom, the house Negro, to keep the field Negroes in check, the same old slavemaster today has Negroes who are nothing but modern Uncle Toms, twentieth-century Uncle Toms, to keep you and me in check, to keep us under control, keep us passive and peaceful and nonviolent. That's Tom making you nonviolent. It's like when you go to the dentist, and the man's going to take your tooth. You're going to fight him when he starts pulling. So he squirts some stuff in your jaw called novocaine, to make you think they're not doing anything to you. So you sit there and because you've got all of that novocaine in your jaw, you suffer—peacefully. Blood running all down your jaw, and you don't know what's happening. Because someone has taught you to suffer—peacefully.

The white man does the same thing to you in the street, when he wants to put knots on your head and take advantage of you and not have to be afraid of your fighting back. To keep you from fighting back, he gets these old religious Uncle Toms to teach you and me, just like novocaine, to suffer peacefully. Don't stop suffering—just suffer peacefully. As Rev. Cleage pointed out, they say you should let your blood flow in the streets. This is a shame. You know he's a Christian preacher. If it's a shame to him, you know what it is to me.

There is nothing in our book, the Koran, that teaches us to suffer peacefully. Our religion teaches us to be intelligent. Be peaceful, be courteous, obey the law, respect everyone; but if someone puts his hand on you, send him to the cemetery. That's a good religion. In fact, that's old-time religion. That's the one that Ma and Pa used to talk about: an eye for an eye, and a tooth for a tooth, and a head for a head; and a life for a life. That's a good religion. And nobody resents that kind of religion being taught but a wolf, who intends to make you his meal.

This is the way it is with the white man in America. He's a wolf—and you're sheep. Any time a shepherd, a pastor, teaches you and me not to run from the white man and, at the same time, teaches us not to fight the white man, he's a traitor to you and me. Don't lay down a life all by itself. No, preserve your life, it's the best thing you've got. And if you've got to give it up, let it be even-steven.

Black Music in Our Hands
Bernice Reagon

In the early 1960s, I was in college at Albany State. My major interests were music and biology. In music I was a contralto soloist with the choir, studying Italian arias and German lieder. The black music I sang was of three types:

1) Spirituals sung by the college choir. These were arranged by such people as Nathaniel Dett and William Dawson and had major injections of European musical harmony and composition. 2) Rhythm'n'Blues, music done by and for Blacks in social settings. This included the music of bands at proms, juke boxes, and football game songs. 3) Church music; gospel was a major part of Black church music by the time I was in college. I was a soloist with the gospel choir.

Prior to the gospel choir, introduced in my church when I was twelve, was many years' experience with unaccompanied music—Black choral singing, hymns, lined out by strong song leaders with full, powerful, richly ornate congregational responses. These hymns were offset by upbeat, clapping call-and-response songs.

I saw people in church sing and pray until they shouted. I knew *that* music as a part of a cultural expression that was powerful enough to take people from their conscious selves to a place where the physical and intellectual being worked in harmony with the spirit. I enjoyed and needed that experience. The music of the church was an integral part of the cultural world into which I was born.

Outside of church, I saw music as good, powerful sounds you made or listened to. Rhythm and blues—you danced to; music of the college choir—you clapped after the number was finished.

The Civil Rights Movement changed my view of music. It was after my first march. I began to sing a song and in the course of singing changed the song so that it made sense for that particular moment. Although I was not consciously aware of it, this was one of my earliest experiences with how my music was supposed to *function*. This music was to be integrative of and consistent with everything I was doing at that time; it was to be tied to activities that went beyond artistic affairs such as concerts, dances, and church meetings.

The next level of awareness came while in jail. I had grown up in a rural area outside the city limits, riding a bus to public school or driving to college. My life had been a pretty consistent, balanced blend of church, school, and proper upbringing. I was aware of a Black educated class that taught me in high school and college, of taxi cabs I never rode in, and of people who used buses I never boarded. I went to school with their children.

In jail with me were all these people. All ages. In my section were women from about thirteen to eighty years old. Ministers' wives and teachers and teachers' wives who had only nodded at me or clapped at a concert or spoken to my mother. A few people from my classes. A large number of people who rode segregated city buses. One or two women who had been drinking along the two-block stretch of Little Harlem as the march went by. Very quickly, clashes arose: around age, who would have authority, what was proper behavior?

The Albany Movement was already a singing movement, and we took the songs to jail. There the songs I had sung because they made me feel good or because they said what I thought about a specific issue did something. I would start a song and everybody would join in. After the song, the differences among us would not be as great. Somehow, making a song required an expression of that which was common to us all. The songs did not feel like the same songs I had sung in college. This music was like an instrument, like holding a tool in your hand.

I found that although I was younger than many of the women in my section of the jail, I was asked to take on leadership roles. First as a song leader and then in most other matters concerning the group, especially in discussions, or when speaking with prison officials.

I fell in love with that kind of music. I saw that to define music as something you listen to, something that pleases you, is very different from defining it as an instrument with which you can drive a point. In both instances, you can have the same song. But using it as an instrument makes it a different kind of music.

The next level of awareness occurred during the first mass meeting after my release from jail. I was asked to lead the song that I had changed after the first march. When I opened my mouth and began to sing, there was a force and power within myself I had never heard before. Somehow this music—music I could use as an instrument to do things with, music that was mine to shape and change so that it made the statement I needed to make—released a kind of power and required a level of concentrated energy I did not know I had. I liked the feeling.

For several years, I worked with the Movement eventually doing Civil Rights songs with the Freedom Singers. The Freedom Singers used the songs, interspersed with narrative, to convey the story of the Civil Rights Movement's struggles. The songs were more powerful than spoken conversation. They became a major way of making people who were not on the scene feel the intensity of what was happening in the south. Hopefully, they would move the people to take a stand, to organize support groups or participate in various projects.

The Georgia Sea Island Singers, whom I first heard at the Newport Festival, were a major link. Bessie Jones, coming from within twenty miles of Albany, Georgia, had a repertoire and song-leading style I recognized from the churches I had grown up in. She, along with John Davis, would talk about songs that Black people had sung as slaves and what those songs meant in terms of their struggle to be free. The songs did not sound like the spirituals I had sung in college choirs; they sounded like the songs I had grown up with in church. There I had been told the songs had to do with worship of Jesus Christ.

The next few years I spent focusing on three components: 1) The music I had found in the Civil Rights Movement. 2) Songs of the Georgia Sea Island Singers and other traditional groups, and the ways in which those songs were linked to the struggles of Black peoples at earlier times. 3) Songs of the church that now sounded like those traditional songs and came close to having, for many people, the same kind of freeing power.

There was another experience that helped to shape my present-day use of music. After getting out of jail, the mother of the church my father pastored was at the mass meeting. She prayed, a prayer I had heard hundreds of times. I had focused on its sound, tune, rhythm chant, whether the moans came at the proper pace and intensity. That morning I heard every word that she said. She did not have to change one word of prayer she had been praying for much of her Christian life for me to know she was addressing the issues we were facing at that moment. More than her personal prayer, it felt like an analysis of the Albany, Georgia Black community.

My collection, study, and creation of Black music has been, to a large extent, about freeing the sounds and the words and the messages from casings in which they have been put, about hearing clearly what the music has to say about Black people and their struggle.

When I first began to search, I looked for what was then being called folk music, rather than for other Black forms, such as jazz, rhythm and blues, or gospel. It slowly dawned on me that during the Movement we had used all those forms. When we were relaxing in the office, we made up songs using popular rhythm and blues tunes; songs based in rhythm and blues also came out of jails, especially from the sit-in movement and the march to Selma, Alabama. "Oh Wallace, You Never Can Jail Us All" is an example from Selma. "You Better Leave Segregation Alone" came out of the Nashville Freedom Rides and was based on a bit by Little Willie John, "You Better Leave My Kitten Alone." Gospel choirs became the major musical vehicle in the urban center of Birmingham, with the choir led by Carlton Reese. There was also a gospel choir in the Chicago work, as well as an instrumental ensemble led by Ben Branch.

Jazz had not been a strong part of my musical life. I began to hear it as I traveled north. Thelonious Monk and Charlie Mingus played on the first SNCC benefit at Carnegie Hall. I heard of and then heard Coltrane. Then I began to pick up the pieces that had been laid by Charlie Parker and Coleman Hawkins and whole lifetimes of music. This music had no words. But, it had power, intensity, and movement under various degrees of pressure; it had vocal texture and color. I could feel that the music knew how it felt to be Black and Angry. Black and Down, Black and Loved, Black and Fighting.

I now believe that Black music exists in every place where Black people run, every corner where they live, every level on which they struggle. We have been here a long while, in many situations. It takes all that we have created to sing our song. I believe that Black musicians/artists have a responsibility to be conscious of their world and to let their consciousness be heard in their songs.

And we need it all—blues, gospel, ballads, children's games, dance, rhythm, jazz, lovesongs, topical songs—doing what it has always done. We need Black music that functions in relation to the people and community who provide the nurturing compost that makes its creation and continuation possible.

The English Language
Is My Enemy

Ossie Davis

A superficial examination of Roget's *Thesaurus of the English Language* reveals the following facts: the word WHITENESS has 134 synonyms, 44 of which are favorable and pleasing to contemplate, i.e., purity, cleanness, immaculateness, bright, shining, ivory, fair, blonde, stainless, clean, clear, chaste, unblemished, unsullied, innocent, honorable, upright, just, straightforward, fair, genuine, trustworthy (a white man's colloquialism). Only ten synonyms for WHITENESS appear to me to have negative implications—and these only in the mildest sense: gloss over, whitewash, gray, wan, pale, ashen, etc.

The word BLACKNESS has 120 synonyms, 60 of which are distinctly unfavorable, and none of them even mildly positive. Among the offending 60 were such words as: blot, blotch, smut, smudge, sully, begrime, soot, becloud, obscure, dingy, murky, low-toned, threatening, frowning, foreboding, forbidden, sinister, baneful, dismal, thundery, evil, wicked, malignant, deadly, unclean, dirty, unwashed, foul, etc. . . . not to mention 20 synonyms directly related to race, such as: Negro, Negress, nigger, darky, blackamoor, etc.

When you consider the fact that *thinking* itself is sub-vocal speech—in other words, one must use *words* in order to think at all—you will appreciate the enormous heritage of racial prejudgment that lies in wait for any child born into the English Language. Any teacher good or bad, white or black, Jew or Gentile, who uses the English Language as a medium of communication is forced, willy-nilly, to teach the Negro child 60 ways to despise himself, and the white child 60 ways to aid and abet him in the crime.

Who speaks to me in my Mother Tongue damns me indeed! . . . the English Language—in which I cannot conceive my self as a black man without, at the same time, debasing myself . . . my enemy, with which to survive at all I must continually be at war.

Pan-Africanism
Kwame Ture

Whether we want it or not, there are divisions among black Africans living in the United States, the Caribbean and on the African continent, divisions which have been imposed on us by Europeans. There are geographical divisions, countries such as Senegal and Mauritania, Mozambique and Guinea, created by Europeans as they struggled for the wealth of Africa. Then there are political divisions and economic divisions, again imposed on us by Europeans.

Now they are planning to impose on us grave cultural divisions and, most of all, to divide us by naming us different things. If you are in San Francisco, for example, and you see a Japanese or a Chinese walking down the street you do not say that there goes an American Japanese or a Japanese American. You say simply that there goes a Japanese—period. Yet probably that Japanese cannot speak Japanese at all; he may be the third or fourth generation in America. But no one calls him a Japanese American. The first thing you call him is a Japanese, because a person is defined, really, at first by his physical presence, or in terms of his ancestral stock. Whether he is Chinese, Japanese or African. The same is true of the Indians. Even in America, when you see a red Indian, you do not say he is an American; you say he is an Indian. The same is true for East Indians; the same for Filipinos. Wherever you see them, in any part of the world, you call them Chinese or what not.

The same is not true for Africans.

Let's ask ourselves why.

If you see an African in Europe, you do not say that he is an African. If you see him in America you do not call him an African. He may be Negro; he may be West Indian; he may be everything else but African. That is because Europe took its time to divide us carefully, quite carefully. And they gave us different names so that we would never, always never, refer to ourselves by the same name; which helped ensure that there would always be differences. If you say you are West Indian, it is fairly obvious that you are something different to be set apart from an African. An American Negro and an African also obviously are not the same thing.

One of the most important things we must now begin to do is to call our-selves "African." No matter where we may be from, we are first of all and finally Africans. Africans. Africans. Africans. The same also happens to be true of North Africa. When they say "Algerians" or "Egyptians" they are talking about Africans, because Africa happens to be one solid continent. Among Africans there will and must be no divisions. They are just Africans—period.

What America Would Be Like Without Blacks

Ralph Ellison

The fantasy of an America free of blacks is at least as old as the dream of creating a truly democratic society. While we are aware that there is something inescapably tragic about the cost of achieving our democratic ideals, we keep such tragic awareness segregated to the rear of our minds. We allow it to come to the fore only during moments of great national crisis.

On the other hand, there is something so embarrassingly absurd about the notion of purging the nation of blacks that it seems hardly a product of thought at all. It is more like a primitive reflex, a throwback to the dim past of tribal experience which we rationalize and try to make respectable by dressing it up in the gaudy and highly questionable trappings of what we call the "concept of race." Yet, despite its absurdity, the fantasy of a blackless America continues to turn up. It is a fantasy born not merely of racism but of petulance, of exasperation, of moral fatigue. It is like a boil bursting forth from impurities in the bloodstream of democracy.

In its benign manifestations, it can be outrageously comic—in the picturesque adventures of Percival Brownlee who appears in William Faulkner's story "The Bear." Exasperating to his white masters because his aspirations and talents are for preaching and conducting choirs rather than for farming, Brownlee is "freed" after much resistance and ends up as the prosperous proprietor of a New Orleans brothel. In Faulkner's hands, the uncomprehending drive of Brownlee's owners to "get shut" of him is comically instructive. Indeed, the story resonates certain abiding, tragic themes of American history with which it is interwoven, and which are causing great turbulence in the social atmosphere today. I refer to the exasperation and bemusement of the white American with the black, the black American's ceaseless (and swiftly accelerating) struggle to escape the misconceptions of whites, and the continual confusing of the black American's racial background with his individual culture. Most of all, I refer to the recurring fantasy of solving one basic problem of American democracy by "getting shut" of the blacks through various wishful schemes that would banish them from the nation's bloodstream, from its social structure, and from its conscience and historical consciousness.

This fantastic vision of a lily-white America appeared as early as 1713, with the suggestion of a white "native American," thought to be from New Jersey, that all the Negroes be given their freedom and returned to Africa. In 1777, Thomas Jefferson, while serving in the Virginia legislature, began drafting a plan for the gradual emancipation and exportation of the slaves. Nor were Negroes themselves immune to the fantasy. In 1815, Paul Cuffe, a wealthy merchant, shipbuilder, and landowner from the New Bedford area, shipped and settled at his own expense thirty-eight of his fellow Negroes in Africa. It was perhaps his example that led in the following year to the creation of the American Colonization Society, which was to establish in 1821 the colony of Liberia. Great amounts of cash and a perplexing mixture of motives went into the venture. The slaveowners and many Border-state politicians wanted to use it as a scheme to rid the country not of slaves but of the militant free Negroes who were agitating against the "peculiar institution." The abolitionists, until they took a lead from free Negro leaders and began attacking the scheme, also participated as a means of righting a great historical injustice. Many blacks went along with it simply because they were sick of the black and white American mess and hoped to prosper in the quiet peace of the old ancestral home.

Such conflicting motives doomed the Colonization Society to failure, but what amazes one even more than the notion that anyone could have believed in its success is the fact that it was attempted during a period when the blacks, slave and free, made up eighteen percent of the total population. When we consider how long blacks had been in the New World and had been transforming it and being Americanized by it, the scheme appears not only fantastic, but the product of a free-floating irrationality. Indeed, a national pathology.

Nevertheless, some of the noblest of Americans were bemused. Not only Jefferson but later Abraham Lincoln was to give the scheme credence. According to historian John Hope Franklin, Negro colonization seemed as important to Lincoln as emancipation. In 1862, Franklin notes, Lincoln called a group of prominent free Negroes to the White House and urged them to support colonization, telling them, "Your race suffers greatly, many of them by living among us, while ours suffers from your presence. If this is admitted, it affords a reason why we should be separated."

In spite of his unquestioned greatness, Abraham Lincoln was a man of his times and limited by some of the less worthy thinking of his times. This is demonstrated both by his reliance upon the concept of race in his analysis of the American dilemma and by his involvement in a plan of purging the nation of blacks as a means of healing the badly shattered ideals of democratic federalism. Although benign, his motive was no less a product of fantasy. It envisaged an attempt to relieve an inevitable suffering that marked the growing pains of the youthful body politic by an operation which would have amounted to the severing of a healthy and indispensable member.

Yet, like its twin, the illusion of secession, the fantasy of a benign amputation that would rid the country of black men to the benefit of a nation's health not only persists; today, in the form of neo-Garveyism, it fascinates black men no less than it once hypnotized whites. Both fantasies become operative whenever the nation grows weary of the struggle toward the ideal of American democratic equality. Both would use the black man as a scapegoat to achieve a national catharsis, and both would, by way of curing the patient, destroy him.

What is ultimately intriguing about the fantasy of "getting shut" of the Negro American is the fact that no one who entertains it seems ever to have considered what the nation would have become had Africans *not* been brought to the New World, and had their descendants not played such a complex and confounding role in the creation of American history and culture. Nor do they appear to have considered with any seriousness the effect upon the nation of having any of the schemes for exporting blacks succeed beyond settling some fifteen thousand or so in Liberia.

We are reminded that Daniel Patrick Moynihan, who has recently aggravated our social confusion over the racial issue while allegedly attempting to clarify it, is coauthor of a work which insists that the American melting pot didn't melt because our white ethnic groups have resisted all assimilative forces that appear to threaten their identities. The problem here is that few Americans know who and what they really are. That is why few of these groups—or at least few of the children of these groups—have been able to resist the movies, television, baseball, jazz, football, drum-majoretting, rock, comic strips, radio commercials, soap operas, book clubs, slang, or any of a thousand other expressions and carriers of our pluralistic and easily available popular culture. And it is here precisely that ethnic resistance is least effective. On this level the melting pot did indeed melt, creating such deceptive metamorphoses and blending of identities, values, and lifestyles that most American whites are culturally part Negro American without even realizing it.

If we can resist for a moment the temptation to view everything having to do with Negro Americans in terms of their racially imposed status, we become aware of the fact that for all the harsh reality of the social and economic injustices visited upon them, these injustices have failed to keep Negroes clear of the cultural mainstream; Negro Americans are in fact one of its major tributaries. If we can cease approaching American social reality in terms of such false concepts as white and nonwhite, black culture and white culture, and think of these apparently unthinkable matters in the realistic manner of Western pioneers confronting the unknown prairie, perhaps we can begin to imagine what the United States would have been, or not been, had there been no blacks to give it—if I may be so bold as to say—color.

For one thing, the American nation is in a sense the product of the American language, a colloquial speech that began emerging long before the British colonials and Africans were transformed into Americans. It is a language that evolved from the king's English but, basing itself upon the realities of the

American land and colonial institutions—or lack of institutions, began quite early as a vernacular revolt against the signs, symbols, manners, and authority of the mother country. It is a language that began by merging the sounds of many tongues, brought together in the struggle of diverse regions. And whether it is admitted or not, much of the sound of that language is derived from the timbre of the African voice and the listening habits of the African ear. So there is a *de'z* and *do'z* of slave speech sounding beneath our most polished Harvard accents, and if there is such a thing as a Yale accent, there is a Negro wail in it—doubtlessly introduced there by Old Yalie John C. Calhoun, who probably got it from his mammy.

Whitman viewed the spoken idiom of Negro Americans as a source for a native grand opera. Its flexibility, its musicality, its rhythms, freewheeling diction, and metaphors, as projected in Negro American folklore, were absorbed by the creators of our great nineteenth-century literature even when the majority of blacks were still enslaved. Mark Twain celebrated it in the prose of *Huckleberry Finn*; without the presence of blacks, the book could not have been written. No Huck and Jim, no American novel as we know it. For not only is the black man a co-creator of the language that Mark Twain raised to the level of literary eloquence, but Jim's condition as American and Huck's commitment to freedom are at the moral center of the novel.

In other words, had there been no blacks, certain creative tensions arising from the cross-purposes of whites and blacks would also not have existed. Not only would there have been no Faulkner; there would have been no Stephen Crane, who found certain basic themes of his writing in the Civil War. Thus, also, there would have been no Hemingway, who took Crane as a source and guide. Without the presence of Negro American style, our jokes, our tall tales, even our sports would be lacking in the sudden turns, the shocks, the swift changes of pace (all jazz-shaped) that serve to remind us that the world is ever unexplored, and that while a complete mastery of life is mere illusion, the real secret of the game is to make life swing. It is its ability to articulate this tragic-comic attitude toward life that explains much of the mysterious power and attractiveness of that quality of Negro American style known as "soul." An expression of American diversity within unity, of blackness with whiteness, soul announces the presence of a creative struggle against the realities of existence.

Without the presence of blacks, our political history would have been otherwise. No slave economy, no Civil War; no violent destruction of the Reconstruction, no K.K.K. and no Jim Crow system. And without the disenfranchisement of black Americans and the manipulation of racial fears and prejudices, the disproportionate impact of white Southern politicians upon our domestic and foreign policies would have been impossible. Indeed, it is almost impossible to conceive of what our political system would have become without the snarl of forces—cultural, racial, religious—that make our nation what it is today.

Absent, too, would be the need for that tragic knowledge which we try ceaselessly to evade: that the true subject of democracy is not simply material

well-being but the extension of the democratic process in the direction of perfecting itself. And that the most obvious test and clue to that perfection is the
inclusion—*not* assimilation—of the black man.

Since the beginning of the nation, white Americans have suffered from a
deep inner uncertainty as to who they really are. One of the ways that has been
used to simplify the answer has been to seize upon the presence of black
Americans and use them as a marker, a symbol of limits, a metaphor for the
"outsider." Many whites could look at the social position of blacks and feel
that color formed an easy and reliable gauge for determining to what extent
one was or was not American. Perhaps that is why one of the first epithets that
many European immigrants learned when they got off the boat was the term
"nigger"—it made them feel instantly American. But this is tricky magic.
Despite his racial difference and social status, something indisputably American about Negroes not only raised doubts about the white man's value system
but aroused the troubling suspicion that whatever else the true American is,
he is also somehow black.

Materially, psychologically, and culturally, part of the nation's heritage is
Negro American, and whatever it becomes will be shaped in part by the
Negro's presence. Which is fortunate, for today it is the black American who
puts pressure upon the nation to live up to its ideals. It is he who gives creative
tension to our struggle for justice and for the elimination of those factors,
social and psychological, which make for slums and shaky suburban communities. It is he who insists that we purify the American language by demanding that there be a closer correlation between the meaning of words and reality,
between ideal and conduct, our assertions and our actions. Without the black
American, something irrepressibly hopeful and creative would go out of the
American spirit, and the nation might well succumb to the moral slobbism
that has ever threatened its existence from within.

When we look objectively at how the dry bones of the nation were hung
together, it seems obvious that some one of the many groups that compose the
United States had to suffer the fate of being allowed no easy escape from experiencing the harsh realities of the human condition as they were to exist under
even so fortunate a democracy as ours. It would seem that some one group
had to be stripped of the possibility of escaping such tragic knowledge by taking sanctuary in moral equivocation, racial chauvinism, or the advantage of
superior social status. There is no point in complaining over the past or apolo-
gizing for one's fate. But for blacks, there are no hiding places down here, not
in suburbia or in penthouse, neither in country nor in city. They are an American people who are geared to what is and who yet are driven by a sense of
what it is possible for human life to be in this society. The nation could not survive being deprived of their presence because, by the irony implicit in the
dynamics of American democracy, they symbolize both its most stringent testing and the possibility of its greatest human freedom.

Tomorrow's Tomorrow:
The Black Woman
Joyce Ladner

I have attempted to depict the intricacy of Black womanhood as a sociohistorical phenomenon and as it relates to largely low-income adolescent Black girls growing up in the large metropolitan centers. It is difficult to capture the *essence* of this complex period of psychosocial development because of the peculiar historical backdrop against which this process occurs. Therefore, I have endeavored to analyze their present lives as they emerge out of these historical forces, for they have been involved in a strong reciprocal relationship in that they have been shaped by the forces of oppression but have also exerted their influence so as to alter certain of these patterns.

What has come to be popularly referred to as *institutional racism* has exerted the strongest impact upon all facets of the Black woman's life. Institutional racism has been defined as:

> . . . the operating policies, priorities, and functions of an ongoing system of normative patterns which serve to subjugate, oppress, and force dependence of individuals or groups by: (1) establishing and sanctioning unequal goals; and (2) sanctioning inequality in status as well as in access to goods and services.[1]

The dynamics of institutional racism have been responsible for both the strengths and weaknesses of Black womanhood. The weaknesses are obvious and have been almost exclusively focused on in the social science and popular literature. The work of E. Franklin Frazier[2] and the infamous Moynihan Report[3] are representative of the "disorganization perspective" although they appeared twenty-five years apart. The dominant intellectual perspective on the Black family and the Black woman is still one which views them as pathological and an aberrant of the white middle-class model. However, it has been the overt and covert malignancy of institutional racism which has produced the alleged deviance and pathology. The behavioral characteristics of Black women which assumed these negative dimensions (when judged by the larger

society) emerged as adaptations to a pathological society. It was the institu-
tionalized structures and processes of racism which caused the so-called family disorganization, matriarchal society, high rates of juvenile delinquency,
"illegitimacy," violence and homicide.

One of the peculiar aspects of racism in this country is that it has structured
the *dominant* and *subordinate* roles and relationships between Blacks and
whites, and placed Blacks within a relatively closed system; yet it has blamed
the alleged *deviant* behavioral adaptations on its victims. In this kind of social
system the most pervasive form of neo-colonialism with all its subtle manifestations becomes apparent and destructive. The most destructive of these manifestations is the ability of the oppressing class to indoctrinate the oppressed to
believe in their alleged inferiority. Carter G. Woodson addresses this effective
psychological tool in his work *The Miseducation of the Negro.*

> No systematic effort toward change has been
> possible, for taught the same economics, his-
> tory, philosophy, literature, and religion
> which have established the present code of
> morals, the Negro's mind has been brought
> under the control of his oppressor. The prob-
> lem of holding the Negro down therefore is
> easily solved. When you control a man's
> thinking you do not have to tell him not to
> stand here or go yonder. He will find his
> "proper place" and will stay in it. You do not
> need to send him to the back door. He will go
> without being told. In fact, if there is no back
> door, he will cut one for his special benefit.
> His education makes it necessary.[4]

The serious problem which Woodson addresses is one which requires an
alternative system of formal and informal socialization. This socialization
process is referred to by some scholars as "decolonization," or the refusal to
allow the oppressor to define the problems and solutions of the oppressed.[5]

The normative patterns that exist in the white middle-class society are considered by its adherents as rational, justifiable and an *ideal* model. If one
accepts the legitimacy of this model, any deviations from it would be considered within the realm of aberrant behavior. However, if the model is considered illegitimate, there should be no concern that one is obligated to conform
to it because the value and behavioral system which undergirds it would be
considered irrelevant. This seems to be the core of the white versus Black culture thesis. It is simply a question of whether or not the values, attitudes,
behavior and systems of belief which govern the dominant white middle class
should be the criteria by which Black people, most of whom have never been
allowed to assimilate into the American mainstream, should be evaluated.

This raises another fundamental question relating to the validity of the
middle-class model. The structure of American institutions is, inherently,

closed to Black participation except on the most minimal level. The blatant discriminatory practices have been historically documented through unemployment statistics, deteriorated housing conditions, inferior educational standards, minimal political participation, police repression, etc. But at the same time that these oppressive conditions exist (and seem to be worsening in the 1970s), the demands are being made by middle-class whites that Blacks conform to the same ethic which allegedly guides their lives. Two things seem apparent in this regard. First, even if Blacks wanted to conform to the white middle-class life-style it would be very difficult because of their inability to garner the necessary resources to accomplish these goals. Second, one must question the validity of the white middle-class life-style from its very foundation because it has already proven itself to be decadent and unworthy of emulation. The obvious symbols of this bankruptcy are to be observed in the "generation gap"; the problems of drug abuse among white youth; the "tuning out" by thousands of young whites into hippie communes instead of actively engaging in the struggle to initiate social change in the larger society; suburban "swingers" (sex clubs); the absent father who spends so much time away from his home that it, according to the classic definition, becomes a "matriarchal" society; the inability of many whites to accept the very basic humanist value that is attached to having children—in or out of wedlock; liberalized abortion laws; the destruction of the natural resources through the pollution of the rivers and the destruction of the land; the creation of ignorance, poverty and disease manifested by the callous disregard for the preservation of life in its fullest extension. This includes a refusal to become involved in eliminating readily preventable diseases and combating hunger among the poor, a refusal to use the full resources of the middle class to destroy every vestige of neo-colonialism that exists within American society and abroad.

If this model is felt to be the ideal by which the values and behavior of Black people ought to be judged, we must seek other alternatives and more viable standards because that which purports to be the exemplary one is in the process of internal destruction, and there is little within it which seems worthy of being salvaged. The very fact that white society could produce and perpetuate institutional racism for over three centuries raises a serious concern for its validity, even for its adherents. The Black writer James Baldwin has prophetically analyzed the problem:

> If we, who can scarcely be considered a white nation, persist in thinking ourselves as one, we condemn ourselves, with the truly white nations, to sterility and decay, whereas if we could accept ourselves *as we are*, we might bring new life to the Western achievements, and transform them. . . . Hence the question: Do I really *want* to be integrated into a burning house? . . . there is certainly little enough in the white man's public or private life that one should desire to imitate.[6]

His observation raises a fundamental question about the basic values of the dominant society and their relevance to the needs of Black people. Also, the question should be raised as to whether or not the dominant middle class should continue to adhere to a system of values which is in a rapid process of deterioration. Perhaps they too should seek to devise a value system which can save the entire society from ruination. On this point, we again turn to Baldwin:

> White people cannot . . . be taken as models of how to live. Rather, the white man is himself in sore need of new standards which will release him from his confusion and place him once again in fruitful communion with the depths of his own being.[7]

Black people should reject these values and work toward strengthening those which have emerged out of the Black experience.

I raised the controversy over the existence of a distinct Black culture in Chapter One, and pinpointed some of the specific arguments *for* and *against*. I am proposing now that there does exist a strong Black culture that is separate from that of the dominant white middle class, and it is comprised of primarily two elements: (1) it is a result of certain Africanisms which survived slavery; and (2) it grew out of the adaptive responses which Blacks were forced to make to the slavery system and the systematic discrimination after slavery. Black culture has been referred to as a subculture, subsociety, the Black experience, "soul," etc. Regardless of the name which has been applied, it exists as a fairly autonomous entity within the larger social system and functions to meet the needs of Black people. As this relates to the lower class, Rainwater has suggested that:

> . . . lower-class groups have a relatively high degree of functional autonomy vis-à-vis the total social system because that system does little to meet their needs. In general the fewer the rewards a society offers members of a particular group in the society, the more autonomous will that group prove to be with reference to the norms of the society. Only by constructing an elaborate repressive machinery, as in concentration camps, can the effect be otherwise.[8]

The functional autonomy which characterizes much of the Black community allows for the sustenance and strengthening of Black culture. Black music, dance, art and spirituality are generally recognized to have strong African roots. It is not difficult to imagine how these cultural elements could be transmitted throughout the generations when one takes into consideration the fact that assimilation of Blacks into the mainstream has rarely been possible. As Hannerz notes:

> Black people are not moving into main-
> stream society as individuals *and* as a
> group—they are only trickling into it one by
> one on white people's terms, while most of
> them remain in the ghettos.[9]

All of this is changing as Blacks demand the recognition of the validity of a
highly functional culture which is not to be measured against the standards of
the middle-class norm. The Black nationalist movements are advocating the
rejection of the American value system, and pointing out the dangers of "integrating into" the society on terms already dictated by the oppressing group.
Indeed, some reject integration altogether, while others only view it as a goal
which should be accomplished only when Blacks are able to negotiate their
demands from a basis of power. It is assumed that once the power base has
been established, Blacks can set their own terms for *integration* or *equality*. Of
equal importance, however, is the fact that the various repressive measures
which seem to be forecast for Blacks during the decade of the seventies will
make the "trickling" of individuals into the mainstream even more difficult.

The concept "soul" symbolizes the foundation of Black culture. Black culture can be viewed as a non-material culture, and can be more clearly
observed in the emotive responses of Black people than in their artifacts; more
poignantly in their spirituals and jazz than in their craftsmanship; more
lucidly in the strong bond between mother and child than in the ability to provide that child with all of the *material* luxuries life can afford. Indeed, the ultimate nature of this culture can be made with a simple distinction between
Aretha Franklin singing the blues, and her imitator the late Janis Joplin. Aretha
Franklin has lived the oppressed life—the blues—and Janis Joplin had not.
Hence, Miss Joplin *never* comprehended this highest form of reality. Our gift to
American society has been spiritual and cultural and has, at various times in
our history, acted to forge basic humanistic values which this society greatly
needed. Lerone Bennett, historian, articulates the meaning of soul and its
implications for Black culture in his essay "Ethos: Voices from the Cave":

> The whole corpus of the tradition . . . is com-
> pressed into the folk myth of *Soul*, the Amer-
> ican counterpart of the African *Negritude*, a
> distinct quality of Negro-ness growing out of
> the Negro's experience and not his genes.
> *Soul* is a metaphorical evocation of Negro
> being as expressed in the Negro tradition. It
> is the feeling with which an artist invests his
> creation, the style with which a man lives his
> life. It is, above all, the spirit rather than the
> letter: a certain way of feeling, a certain way
> of expressing oneself, a certain way of being.

> From the womb of this non-Puritan, non-machine, nonexploitative tradition have come insights, values, and attitudes that have changed the face of America. The tradition is very definitely nonmachine, but it is not anti-machine; it simply recognizes that machines are generative power and not soul, instruments and not ends.[10]

It is this spiritual, aesthetic quality of Black culture that offers this society the basic humanistic values which have disappeared through the process of neo-colonialism and its rapid technological advancements. These mechanized processes came to value efficiency over the basic spiritual qualities of life. Perhaps this Black humanism has the capacity to counteract the prevailing destructive forces within the society, if it is given the opportunity to do so. This already seems to be a realization among some middle-class whites who tend to view the "soul ideology" as their personal salvation and seek to emulate the Black life-style whenever possible.

It must be emphasized that, although there are very positive qualities within Black culture, one must not romanticize these to the extent that they become an opiate and an end unto themselves. No matter how much we celebrate our culture and its heroes, we must still do the necessary *activist* work to eliminate oppression. Cultural nationalism can never be a total substitute for direct political involvement.

In spite of the observations made by Baldwin and other Black thinkers about the devaluation of American middle-class culture, and the definitions which have been provided for an authentic Black culture, the fact is that Black people have been strongly influenced by the dominant society. Growing up in America, and being exposed to the normative patterns of the dominant group, one could expect to be shaped by what W. E. B. DuBois has referred to as a "double consciousness."

In 1903 he wrote in *The Souls of Black Folk* that:

> The Negro is a sort of seventh son, born with a veil, and gifted with second-sight in this American world,—in a world which yields him no true self-consciousness; but only lets him see himself through the revelation of the other world. It is a peculiar sensation, this double-consciousness, this sense of always looking at one's self through the eyes of others, of measuring one's soul by the tape of a world that looks on in amused contempt and pity. One ever feels his twoness,—an American and a

Negro; two souls; two thoughts, two unreconciled strivings, two warring ideals in one dark
body whose dogged strength alone keeps it
from being torn asunder.[11]

This twoness to which DuBois refers characterizes the majority of Blacks, who find the influences of the dominant culture inescapable. Thus, it is strongly reflected in the lives of the girls in this study through their ambivalence, guilt and general tensions and struggles to define their lives as Black women. Although they were very realistic about their opportunities, statuses and goals, they never-theless lived from day to day with this "double-consciousness." The "dogged strength" to which DuBois refers is the same as the "inner resourcefulness" which I described to be a major component of their lives, and which accounted for their highly creative ability not only to devise the most ingenious ways to adapt to oppression, but also to develop immense creativity within this process. Perhaps it is through oppression and bountiful suffering that one's creative abilities reach their zenith.

The nature of this dualism—"double consciousness"—has had a major imprint upon Black women throughout our history, and in recent years has reached a new peak because of the current revolution in women's rights in the larger society. Many Black women who have traditionally accepted the white models of femininity are now rejecting them for the same general reasons that I have proposed we should reject the white middle-class life-style. Black women in this society are the only ethnic or racial group which has had the opportunity *to be women*. By this I simply mean that much of the current focus on being liberated from the constraints and protectiveness of the society which is proposed by Women's Liberation groups has never applied to Black women, and in that sense, we have always been "free," and able to develop as individuals even under the most harsh circumstances. This freedom, as well as the tremendous hardships from which Black women suffered, allowed for the development of a female personality that is rarely described in the scholarly journals for its obstinate strength and ability to survive. Neither is its peculiar humanistic character and quiet courage viewed as the epitome of what the American model of femininity should be.

American white women were never allowed the opportunity to develop and become the socially mature beings many of them must have viewed as desirable. The highly pristine image which they were forced to develop during slavery has manifested itself in the most subtle forms even today. During slavery they were protected from Black men at all costs, placed on a pedestal and even protected from their spouses. Sexual relations were ide-ally confined to the marital relationship, and according to one author, to the act of procreation itself.[12] As part of the white man's creation of the myth of sacred white womanhood and as the perpetuator of racial supremacy, an illusionary world surrounding her chastity came into being. This chastity was manifested not only in the sexual sense, but it pervaded all areas of her life. Hemton notes that:

> Not only did the southern white woman push sex out of her life as a shameful thing never to be mentioned; not only did she silently give up her husband to illicit, backyard love affairs— she also gave up her children to "black mammies" to suckle and nurture, because, according to the myth of sacred white womanhood, the white woman was above such "nasty" things as attending to the biological functions and needs of child-rearing. And in time these poor abandoned white "ladies" lived to witness their sons and daughters turning away from them in times of stress and strain toward the Negro mammies for affection, solace, and human understanding.[13]

The tragedy of this situation is manifested today by the pathological hang-ups which almost inevitably emerge within Black male-white female relationships. It is also reflected in the myths which surround the racist assumptions regarding the alleged animalistic sexual tendencies of the Black female. One must note that very often it is the white woman who makes the sexual advances toward Black men. Many Black men have been lynched because they refused to engage in intimate relations with white women who cried "rape" because they could not bear the idea of being refused by a Black man. When Black men violated the "sacred" laws governing white womanhood they were punished severely, oftentimes with lynching. Even today severe penalties are imposed on Black men who are accused of raping white women. At the same time, however, Black women became the objects of the most debased sexual passions of white men. They were raped, forced to bear children by their masters, denied the right to keep their offspring if the master wanted to sell the child, and most importantly, their very *femininity* and *humanity* were denied them because they were considered to be neither feminine nor human. In all of this suffering, Black women bore a remarkable and perhaps unprecedented courage, not to be paralleled in human history. They adjusted to all of these conditions, fought them with vigor and emerged with fewer scars than seems normal. All of these devastating influences actually caused them to become stronger, and to transmit the art of survival to subsequent generations. This is why I feel that the most viable model of womanhood in the United States is the one which Black women symbolize. At the same time, certain features in this model pose problems and should be given serious re-evaluation and alteration. (These will be dealt with more fully below.)

One of the major characteristics which define the Black woman is her stark realism as this relates to her resources. Instead of becoming resigned to her fate, she has always sought creative solutions to her problems. The ability to utilize her existing resources and yet maintain a forthright determination to struggle against the racist society in whatever overt and subtle ways necessary is one of her major attributes. Perhaps more than in any other way, the Black woman has suffered from the institutional racist impact upon her role in, and relationship to, her family. It has been within the family that much of her strength has developed because it was here that she was forced to accept obligations and responsibilities for not only the care and protection of her own life, but for that of her offspring as well. Still, under the most rugged conditions she has managed to survive and to offer substantial contributions to the society as well.

The Black woman suffers from the twin burden of being *Black* and *female.* Her life is shaped by the subjugated statuses which are assigned to being a woman and being Black, both of which carry with them a double jeopardy. On the surface this would imply that Black women should be at the forefront of the Women's Liberation movement. Yet the problems to which members of Women's Liberation groups are addressing themselves are far less relevant to Black women. The movement is led largely by white middle-class women whose problems are basically different from those of Black women, regardless of class. The protective shelters which the society has imposed on white women have never been problematic to Black women because the society has refused to offer them the same protectiveness. One of the most blatant symbols of institutional racism has historically been the society's refusal to allow Black men to protect their women. As a result, Black women have always been "liberated."

Another major difference is that the "battle between the sexes" which characterizes the Women's Liberation groups—struggles over equalization of power in interpersonal relations—is the kind of luxury which Black people as a race can ill afford. Black women do not perceive their enemy to be Black men, but rather the enemy is considered to be the oppressive forces in the larger society which subjugate Black *men, women and children.* A preoccupation with the equalization of roles between Black men and women is almost irrelevant when one places it within the context of total priorities related to the survival of the race. All of the energies and resources of males and females are necessary to obliterate institutional racism.

Many of the tensions and conflicts which the girls in this study experienced are reflected more profoundly in the interpersonal relations between adult males and females. The advent of the civil rights movement brought into being an assertion of Black masculinity that could be felt in practically all walks of life. Their demands for the right to provide for and protect their families, to compete equally with men of other races in the job market, in politics and in education were expressions of their refusal to continue to abide by the illegitimate laws governing their lives. Thus, the urban rebellions, the rise of revolutionary and cultural nationalism and the other outward signs of revolt against the American system are manifestations of this adamant rejection. The bold assertion of Black masculinity has required that Black women redefine their roles, especially as these relate to Black men.

The strong roles which Black women have traditionally played are now coming into sharp focus amid the controversy over whether or not she should basically be a *passive supporter* of Black men or should continue to *assert her individuality* and make the contributions to the Black community that she has always proved capable of making. Many Blacks have already redefined the woman's role to be that of the *passive*, non-assertive individual, whose major function is to be supportive of her spouse (defined in this context as husband or boyfriend). The justification for this position is that manhood is defined in terms of strength and it is assumed that Black men cannot find their places at the top of the family hierarchy if women continue to maintain the aggressive roles which many of them fulfill. Some base this on the African polygynous model, in which women assume the more passive roles. Others maintain that all of the Black institutions will eventually have to change if they are to remain relevant to its people and this redefinition of the male-female relationship is only one such change to anticipate. The counter-position is that Black men must assert their masculinity in spite of the traditional role Black women have played. The assumption is also made that the full resources of both sexes are vitally needed and women must not, unfairly, be asked calculatedly to submit themselves to all the demands of Black men. The proponents of this viewpoint state that manhood will not be gained at the calculated expense of woman-hood, but that men must discover their assertiveness through their own inner resourcefulness, with the compassionate *support* of Black women.

What is clear, however, is that an alteration of roles between Black males and females must occur. The traditional "strong" Black woman has probably outlived her usefulness because this role has been challenged by the Black man, who has demanded that the white society acknowledge his manhood and deal directly with him instead of using his woman—considered the weaker sex—as a buffer. The cowardice which characterized the relationship between the larger society and Black women has come to an abrupt end. I am not suggesting that the distinctive positive character of Black womanhood forged by centuries of oppression should be abolished. Obviously there is much to be preserved from this model because of its highly functional as well as humanistic value. I am proposing, however, that the stereotyped "Sap-phire" ("Sapphire" is the name applied to the typical *strong* Black woman) cannot continue to operate in the traditional manner but must make the nec-essary adjustments that will allow for the full development of *male and female*. Black women must utilize those survival techniques in the larger struggle for the liberation of Black people. Even the middle-class Black woman must rede-fine her role. No longer must she view herself as an independent professional woman devoid of the burdens of race prejudice and discrimination, simply because she had the opportunity to be socially mobile. Her destiny is intri-cately related to those of poor women, and her commitment to survival must also be the same.

Black women must join all Black people in the process of defining who they are, what their goals are to be, who their prophets and heroes—past and present—are and what the strategies of survival will be; whether we will allow ourselves to become assimilated into the mainstream on the oppressor's terms or whether we will fight the ominous extermination that is already taking a toll on the lives of college students, political activists and anyone else who defies the social system in ways which have been forbidden.

The decade of the seventies will be a period when the priorities of Blacks— adequate living wage, standard housing facilities, elimination of poverty, disease and ignorance, political participation—will be reordered. The current trend will be for the issues relating to ecology, population control, the creation of an elitist corps, Women's Liberation (white middle-class) and a variety of issues that are secondary to the survival of Black people. This calculated reordering of priorities is manifested in the United States Government's appropriating more resources to combat the pollution of the land and rivers than to eliminate hunger.

Many of the gains which were realized through massive protest demonstrations, the loss of lives, jailings and other forms of brutal assaults on individuals who sought to make the United States Constitution a reality are now becoming nullified. This is evidenced by the attacks by governmental officials on intellectuals, students and Blacks; in the refusal of the government to enforce school desegregation guidelines which were based on the 1954 Supreme Court Decision (Brown *vs.* Topeka Board of Education); in the police repressive tactics which are granting them *legal* rights to arrest, fingerprint and detain "suspects" for long periods of time; and in the wholesale slaughter of innocent students and Blacks throughout the country. There is also a design to incarcerate "political" prisoners so that they will not be free to disturb the equilibrium of the society. The confiscation of these fundamental rights forecasts a bleak era, and can only be counteracted by the most aggressive assertion of unified power by Blacks against these forces.

In many ways the Black woman is the "carrier of culture" because it has been she who has epitomized what it meant to be Black, oppressed and yet given some small opportunity to negotiate the different demands which the society placed upon all Black people. Thus, she can be considered an amalgam of the diverse components which comprise Black culture: the pains and sorrows as well as the joys and successes. Most of all, it was she who survived in a country where survival was not always considered possible. As we return to the lives of the adolescent girls presented in this study, we must be aware that their lives cannot be viewed in an isolated context—in the context of a slum area in St. Louis, Missouri—but rather within the national and international context of neocolonialism and its disastrous effects upon oppressed peoples. Their conditions and life chances are necessarily interwoven with the status of the oppressed all over the world. As this broader context changes, so will their lives. It is no accident that when I revisited the same community in the spring of 1970 (the community in which they lived from 1964 to 1968, during the period when most of the data was collected), the environmental conditions had actually worsened. The unemployment rates were higher; the public housing project in which the majority of them lived had a vacancy rate of over 60 per cent, owing primarily to the unsuitable living conditions; and very few positive changes were apparent. This revisit only mirrored the worsening conditions that are occurring in every metropolitan center in the United States, and unfortunately, Blacks are the most severely affected by these.

These girls, like Black girls throughout America, will enter womanhood in an era when the demands for commitment to the fight for survival will be more necessary than at any other time in recent history. They will be forced to engage themselves in those serious tasks which will ensure the survival of Black people against extermination. Unfortunately, they will not have the luxury of living the carefree life of many of their middle-class counterparts. Perhaps it will be the strength of their forebears which will allow them to triumph!

Notes

1. Walter Stafford and Joyce Ladner, "Comprehensive Planning and Racism," *Journal of the American Institute of Planning*, Vol. 35, No. 2, March 1969, p. 70.

2. *The Negro Family in the United States*, Chicago, University of Chicago Press, 1939.

3. *The Negro Family: The Case for National Action*, Government Printing Office, March 1965.

4. Carter G. Woodson, *The Miseducation of the Negro:* Washington, D.C., Association Publishers Inc., 1969 edition, p. xxxiii.

5. This concept has been used as it relates to the problems of social research among minority groups. See Robert Blauner and David Wellman, "Towards the Decolonization of Social Research," Paper delivered at the "Workshops on Problems of Research with Low Income and Minority Groups in the United States," sponsored by the National Institute of Child Health and Human Development, March 8–10, 1970. It has also assumed popular usage by progressive Black scholars and activists.

6. James Baldwin, *The Fire Next Time,* New York, Dial Press, 1963, pp. 108–9.

7. Ibid., pp. 110–11.

8. Lee Rainwater, "Crucible of Identity: The Negro Lower-class Family," *The Negro American*, Talcott Parsons and Kenneth Clark (eds.), Boston, Houghton Mifflin Company, 1966, p. 200.

9. Ulf Hannerz, *Soulside: Inquiries into Ghetto Life and Community*, New York, Columbia University Press, 1969, p. 197.

10. Lerone Bennett, *The Negro Mood*, New York, Ballantine Books, 1964, p. 89.

11. W. E. B. DuBois, *Souls of Black Folk,* New York, Fawcett World Library, 6th Premier printing, August 1968, p. 16.

12. See Oscar Handlin, *Race and Nationality in American Life,* New York, Doubleday Anchor Books, 1957 edition, p. 122.

13. Calvin Hernton, *Sex and Racism in America,* New York, Grove Press, 1965, p. 18.

Bibliography

Alkalimat, Abd-L Hakimu Ibn, "The Ideology of Black Social Science," *Black Scholar*, December 1969.

Anonymous, *God Struck Me Dead: Religious Conversion Experiences and Autobiographies of Negro Ex-Slaves.* Nashville: Fisk University Social Science Institute, 1945.

Aries, Philippe, *Centuries of Childhood: A Social History of Family Life.* New York: Random House, 1962.

Baldwin, James, *The Fire Next Time.* New York: Dial Press, 1963.

Barbour. Floyd. *The Black Power Revolt.* Boston: Porter Sargent Publishers, 1968.

Becker, Howard S., *The Outsiders.* New York: Free Press, 1963.

Bennett, Lerone, "The Challenge of Blackness," *Black Paper Series,* Institute of the Black World Publishers, April 1970.

——, *The Negro Mood.* New York: Ballantine Books, 1964.

Bernard, Jessie, *Marriage and Family Among Negroes.* Englewood Cliffs, N.J.: Prentice-Hall, 1966.

Billingsley, Andrew, *Black Families in White America.* Englewood Cliffs, N.J.: Prentice-Hall. 1968.

Blauner, Robert, "Internal Colonialism and Ghetto Revolt," *Social Problems,* Vol. 16, No. 4, Spring 1969.

——, "Negro Culture: Myth or Reality," in *Black Experience: The Transformation of Activism,* Trans-action publication, 1970.

Blauner, Robert and David Wellman, "Towards the Decolonization of Social Research," paper delivered at the "Workshops on Problems of Research with Low Income and Minority in the United States of America.

Black History's Diversified Clientele
Benjamin Quarles

Along with many other denials since he arrived on these shores, the Black American has until recently been denied a past. The consequent damage to his psyche can hardly be imagined. In a poem entitled "Negro History," appearing in the volume *From the Ashes: Voices of Watts* (Budd Schulberg, editor), young Jimmie Sherman depicts the past as his grandfather viewed it:

A ship
A chain
A distant land
A whip
A pain
A white man's hand
A sack
A field
of cotton balls—
The only things
Grandpa recalls.

Such an outlook on the past has a stultifying effect, making for apathy and despair. Hence Black leaders since the birth of the republic have been advocates of Negro history, obviously envisioning a far broader coverage of it than Jimmie Sherman's grandpa had come to know. Black scholars, led by Carter G. Woodson in 1915, began to remove the layers of ignorance and distortion that had encrusted the Afro-American past. One of these scholars, W. E. B. Du Bois, in the closing line of his autobiography, written during his last months, bespoke anew his lifelong devotion to history: "Teach us, Forever Dead, there is no Dream but Deed, there is no Deed but Memory." A quarter of a century earlier Du Bois fired back a sharp rejoinder to a magazine editor who had rejected a Du Bois essay because it had touched upon the past. "Don't you understand," Du Bois wrote, "that the past is present; that without what was, nothing is."

During the past decade the cry for Black history has been stronger than ever before. Numbered among the proponents of such history are the newer Black militants. "We Blacks," writes Imamu Amiri Baraka (LeRoi Jones), "must learn our collective past in order to design a collective destiny." Of his period of confinement at the Norfolk (Massachusetts) Prison Colony, Malcolm X wrote: "I began first telling my Black brother inmates about the glorious history of the Black man—things they had never dreamed." On another occasion he referred to history as "a people's memory" without which "man is demoted to the lower animals." In his assessment of the past, Malcolm X did not ignore the less glorious aspects of the Black pilgrimage in America. Speaking to a ghetto audience in Detroit in 1953 he evoked a deep response with the words: "We didn't land on Plymouth Rock, my brothers and sisters—Plymouth Rock landed on us!"

Eldridge Cleaver, who, like Malcolm X, became a serious student of history while serving time in prison, spoke its praises. In his essay "To All Black Women, From All Black Men," in *Soul on Ice,* he writes:

> Be convinced, Sable Sister, that the past is no forbidden vista upon which we dare not look, out of a phantom fear of being, as the wife of Lot, turned into pillars of salt. Rather the past is an omniscient mirror: we gaze and see reflected there ourselves and each other— what we used to be and what we are today, how we got this way, and what we are becoming. To decline to look into the Mirror of Then, my heart, is to refuse to view the face of Now.

One of the sable sisters who has needed no convincing about history's role is poet Sarah Webster Fabio, who writes:

> Now at all costs, we must heal our history.
> Or else our future rots in the disease of our past.

Although Black history is now coming into its own as never before, not all of its proponents are in pursuit of the same goal. Indeed, today Black history is being called upon to serve an increasing variety of publics, four of whom we may scrutinize briefly. These are the Black rank and file, the Black revolutionary nationalists, the Black academicians, and the white world, both scholarly and lay. Not mutually exclusive, these groups often overlap. But this fourfold typology enables us to illustrate the major contemporary uses of Black history. We may take these in turn, first describing their aims and then noting their general content and style.

For the Black rank and file, the man in the street, the laity, Black history's main objective is to create a sense of racial pride and personal worth. To the rank and file the new Black history is good therapy, its end result an improved self-image. In a world that has traditionally equated blackness with inferiority, Black history serves as a balm to make the wounded whole. In a world that has traditionally equated blackness with low aim, Black history serves as a stimulus to success. To a Black person seeking to resolve an identity crisis, Black history is ego-soothing; it places one in the thick of things, thereby diminishing his sense of alienation, of rootlessness. Black history is a search for the values and the strengths imbedded in the Black subculture. Black history strikes at the Black American's legacy of self-rejection, the burden of shame that he had been taught was his to bear going back to the curse of Cain. "I always wanted to be somebody," runs the title of the autobiography of a Black tennis champion. Black history tells the Black reader that he is somebody, however vicariously.

In its content Black history for the masses reflects somewhat "the great man" theory of history. White or Black, the typical American, himself individualistic, conceives of his country's past as the achievements of a group of outstanding characters, pushing on against Herculean odds. History is a tableau of heroes set in bold relief. To the generality of blacks their men of mark constitute their history, the bulk of their attention falling upon individual achievers—an underground railroad conductor like Harriet Tubman, a dedicated bishop like Daniel E. Payne, an educator like Mary McLeod Bethune, a sports celebrity like prize fighter Peter Jackson or jockey Isaac Murphy, and a singer like Elizabeth Taylor Greenfield (the "Black Swan") or Bessie Smith. The list is endless, ranging from an early African king to a present-day ghetto leader.

Upbeat and achievement-oriented, Black history for the rank and file stresses victories—the peak that was scaled, the foe that was vanquished, the deep river that was crossed. Moreover, to the masses, youth makes a special appeal, the younger Frederick Douglass arousing more interest than the Sage of Anacostia. Local Black historical figures likewise meet with a readier response than out-of-staters, however more nationally important the latter may be. Moreover, history designed for the laity will of necessity devote as much attention to popular culture and the lively arts as to the more traditional staples, politics and economics, particularly since the Black stamp on the former is more readily discernible.

The emphasis on the lively arts and popular culture lends itself to the mass media. Hence Black history for laymen has found a natural ally in television, commercial as well as educational, but obviously of far greater proportions in the latter. Radio, too, especially in the Folkways recordings, lends itself to Black cultural history. Other mass media such as newspapers and magazines are increasingly carrying Black history articles, biographical sketches, and pictorial materials. Sensing the growing interest in Black history, commercial firms have brought out coloring books, alphabet books, Black history games, and Black history in comic-book format.

History as hero worship is hardly the kind of history espoused by the second Black group under survey—the Black revolutionary nationalists. This group focuses upon exploiters and oppressors, a case study in man's inhumanity to man. This group views history as grievance collecting, a looking back in anger. Black nationalist history is essentially the story of a powerful white majority imposing its will upon a defenseless Black minority. Black nationalists hold that American society needs to be reconstructed and that Black history is, or should be, a means of ideological indoctrination in the revolutionary cause of Black liberation.

Black nationalist history is not without its traces of paranoid thinking, one which holds that the forces of evil are banded in an eternal conspiracy to maintain their oppressive sway. Of very ancient origin, this devil theory of history is deeply rooted in the human psyche and hence should occasion no surprise when met in any of its multiple guises.

Like so much else in American life, Black nationalism has, as it has always had, a variety of forms—cultural, religious, and economic, among others. Revolutionary nationalism moves a step beyond the others in its goals and does not rule out violence in achieving them. Revolutionary Black nationalists, having carefully examined the almost unbelievable pervasiveness of color prejudice in our society, have, in essence, given up on America. Estranged from the land of their birth, they ponder its dismantlement.

As to content, revolutionary Black history is not as interested in historical spadework as in providing new interpretations of that which is already known. Black nationalist history emphasizes racial contrast, physical and cultural. It propounds a Black aesthetic and implies a Black mystique. It bespeaks the essential kinship of Black people on whatever continent they be located or in whatever walk of life. Its central theme is oppression, slavery in one guise or another. Rebelliousness against the oppressor likewise looms large in nationalist lore.

A compound of Black rage and white guilt, revolutionary Black history makes much of the analogy of colonialism, holding that Black Americans live in a state of vassalage to white Americans. Black America is a semicolony of white America.

Going further, the revolutionary school of thought stresses separatism, insisting that Black Americans have always constituted a nation. To those who hold these views, Black history has one overriding purpose, namely, to promote nation-building.

In tone, Black revolutionary history is judgmental, with overtones of recrimination, moral condemnation, and prophetic warning. Apocalyptic and polemical in temper, it scorns objectivity, which it equates with a defense of the status quo. Revolutionary Black history may, on occasion, read like social commentary, sometimes taking on a man-the-barricades urgency.

Selective in content, Black revolutionary history ignores as irrelevant those aspects of the past which do not relate to its philosophy. As will be noted in just a moment, however, this tendency to pick and choose is nothing new in the historical profession.

The third group under survey are the Black academicians—the intellectually sophisticated, the college and university trained, the well-read. Like the revolutionary nationalists, they operate on a more studious level. They would concur with the revolutionary nationalists in holding that history is a weapon in the warfare. But to the academically oriented mind the basic foe is ignorance, be it willful or otherwise. It hardly need be added that ignorance is a somewhat impersonal foe and hence less easily pinpointed, less starkly isolated.

To the Black academician, history is a discipline, an attempt to recapture and mirror the past as accurately as possible. Admittedly this is a tall order, considering the nature of the evidence and the unreliability of so many of the witnesses. Black academicians hardly need to be reminded that history, as we know it, is not neutral, not value-free. Who can tell the Black academician anything new about the insensitivity of past generations of white scholars, of their neglect or distortion of the role of Black peoples? But the Black academician would question the viewpoint that prejudiced history must be met with prejudiced history; he would doubt that the best way to strike at the mythmakers of history is to imitate them. In *The Fire Next Time,* James Baldwin has observed that "an invented past can never be used; it cracks and crumbles under the pressures of life like clay in a season of drought." As we have noted, however, white Americans have made some use of an invented past. But Black Americans must realize that a powerful majority may for a time be able to afford the luxury of fantasy. Such indulgence on the part of a minority is a species of living beyond its means, a minority having to husband carefully its limited resources.

Like the layman and the nationalist, the Black academician finds in Black history a deepening sense of racial worth and of peoplehood. He, too, reads Black history with pride. The Black academician views America as a civilization upon which his ancestors have left their stamp. Hence he does not regard America as a white civilization exclusively; to him it also has its Black, red, and yellow components. The Black academician holds that his forebears helped to build America, and this being the case no one should sensibly expect him to pack his belongings and leave for other shores.

In addition to personal and racial gratification the Black academician reads Black history because he feels that it will contribute to his knowledge and understanding of mankind, of his fellow travelers in time and space.

For academicians, the content of Black history would be more selective than for the laymen, in an attempt to avoid the obvious or the well known. Black history for the academician would deal less with persons and more with processes, less with general Black history than with selected topics in Black history. It would include comparative studies and pose methodological problems. On the grounds that academicians do not shy away from the unpleasant,

Black history for them would not ignore the less glorious aspects of the Black past—the African tribesmen who engaged in the slave trade, the slave drivers on the Southern plantations, the Black informers who divulged the slave conspiracies or those who revealed the hiding place of a runaway slave. History has its share of those blacks who turned out to be all too human.

The academician would grant that, more often than not, the truth makes one sick. But he believes the New Testament adage about truth also making one free. The academician holds that truth, including the search for it, has a liberating effect. To be truly free is to be free first and foremost in the great franchise of the mind. To a group like Black Americans, who have been subjected to so much falsehood by others, it would seem that the quest for truth should be held in high favor, having a relevance never failing.

Black history written for the academic fraternity will in the main take on a reflective, judicial tone, taking its cue from the careful winnowing and sifting that preceded it. The style will be sober, the rhetoric restrained. Passionate and deeply emotional language is highly necessary and desirable in human affairs, but such expression is more the province of the poet, the orator, and the charismatic leader than of the professional historian. An orator may give full vent to his innermost feelings, and to the innermost feelings of his audience, but a social scientist works in a discipline which has imperatives of its own, imperatives which may point to conclusions that run counter to his private wishes.

The codes of his discipline bring the Black academician face to face with one of the major problems confronting every social scientist, namely, whether his citizen role should overshadow his professional role, whether he should give priority to social action or to scientific inquiry. Should an academician strive for competence in his discipline or should he seek primarily to become personally involved and relevant? To the Black academician this dilemma takes on an unusual urgency inasmuch as he is fully aware of the long-standing discrimination against Black people in the American social order. Addressing himself to this question of citizenship role versus professional role, sociologist Ernest Q. Campbell comes to the conclusion that "there is no intrinsic reason why the roles of scientific inquirer and staunch advocate are incompatible" ("Negroes, Education, and the Southern States," *Social Forces,* March 1969). But to play these two roles simultaneously would seem to require unusual abilities and energies. In their absence each Black academician must come to some hard choices as to his own major commitment.

To the final audience under survey, the white community—academic and lay—Black history has an important message. Black history should not be confined to blacks alone—this would be like confining the Gospel to those already converted, to use a familiar figure. Black history, like other phases of Black studies, is no longer a matter of limited concern. Whites need to know Black history. As Theodore Draper points out in *The Rediscovery of Black Nationalism* (New York, 1970), "In the interest of the entire society, white students need Black Studies as much or even more than Black students." At a meeting of the Organization of American Historians in 1969, C. Vann Woodward voiced much the same sentiment in his presidential address, "Clio with Soul." Woodward spoke of Black history as being "too important to be left entirely to Negro historians."

To begin with, whites should realize that the major reason for the long neglect of Black history falls upon the historical guild itself. As Carl Becker has pointed out, "The historian selects from a number of particular facts certain facts which he considers most important to be known." Historians, continues Becker, "unconsciously read the objective facts of the past in the light of their own purposes, or the preoccupations of their own age." To point out that written history has a subjective element is certainly nothing new—Becker's observations were made in 1910. But to mention this matter at the outset makes for the open-mindedness so essential to a proper perspective on the Black American. Whites who read history should know by now that white historians have until recently dealt with the American past in such a way as to ignore the Black presence or to minimize its importance in the making of America.

The aim of Black history for white readers is twofold: first, to eliminate the myth that our country's past was rosy and romantic, a new Eden "with liberty and justice for all," and second, to illustrate the centrality of the Black American in our national experience. White historians have until recently tended to play down the somber aspects of Black-white relationships in America—the deeply ingrained sense of white superiority dating back to Jamestown and Plymouth, the brutality of slavery, the mockery of post-Reconstruction, and the twentieth-century offshoots of these persistent pathologies. The American past has a tragic component which cannot be brushed away. White Americans must take a second thought as they sing the familiar lines, "Thine alabaster cities gleam,/Undimmed by human tears."

Black history would enable whites to more realistically appraise some of our country's boasted achievements and some of its acclaimed public figures. For example, whites generally view the age of Andrew Jackson as one in which the right to vote was extended to the common man. But whites need to know that it was during this period that states like North Carolina and Pennsylvania were explicitly prohibiting blacks from exercising this privilege. White readers of American history have thought highly of Woodrow Wilson for his espousal of the "New Freedom" and for his doctrine of "making the world safe for democracy." But white readers need to know that during Wilson's presidency, and with his acquiescence, Black federal workers in the District of Columbia were systematically segregated and were given inferior working conditions and restroom facilities such as had not existed up to this time in the federal government.

Black history would be remiss if it did not call attention to these sobering aspects of the American past. But Black history does not consist solely of white denial and discrimination. Hence Black history for whites would indicate the myriad ways in which this country's history and culture would have been different without the presence of the Black man. Many of these ways—economic, political, constitutional, and military—are more quickly spotted than others. In some fields—art, literature, music, the dance, and popular culture in general—the Black contribution centers in the common core, making its stamp more difficult to isolate. But whether obvious or subtle, the Black man's gifts to America have been freely received if slowly acknowledged. To this extent all Americans are part Black in their cultural patrimony. Blacks in general would concur in the sentiment expressed by a stanza from James Weldon Johnson ("Fifty Years, 1863–1913," in his *Fifty Years and Other Poems*, Boston, 1921):

> This land is ours by right of birth,
>   This land is ours by right of toil;
> We helped to turn its virgin earth,
>   Our sweat is in its fruitful soil.

The acceptance of Black history by whites has been greatly facilitated by the current emphasis on social history. "It is a good moment to be a social historian" writes E. J. Hobsbawn (*Daedalus*, Winter 1971), history professor at the University of London. This branch of history pays particular attention to the anonymous common man and to the manners and customs of everyday life. And even more importantly for a Black orientation, this branch of history emphasizes social movements and the phenomena of social protest.

For the white reader of Black history the content would, at least initially, suggest the centrality of the Negro American and his identification with this country's great, professed goals. Therefore such history would comprise a general presentation of the American past with the Black component interwoven throughout, appearing at its proper chronological juncture and not separately, somewhat like a disjointed subtheme for the curious, Clio's underworld.

In style and technique Black history for whites would differentiate between the white layman and the white intellectual. For the white layman the approach would be much the same as for his Black counterpart, that is, an emphasis on biographical sketches and on the lively arts and popular culture, including sports. Again, as for the Black layman, books would be greatly supplemented by the mass media. Indeed, of course, the mass media outlets used to reach Black people will inevitably reach many whites.

For the white academician the approach to Black history might be broader than the biographical and less fearful of the recipient's short attention span. Black studies for white intellectuals would back assertion with documentation, presenting proof and citing authorities. A footnote is not an end unto itself. But those of an academic bent have been trained to look for the hard evidence; to them a statement must be intellectually tenable, its sources as trustworthy as possible. For the open-minded scholar—the seeker after truth—the will to believe is not an acceptable substitute for the data that corroborates.

We have dealt with Black history for four different audiences. But in written history the use of different approaches and viewpoints need come as no surprise. No one category of events, no single interpretation, can furnish the cloth for that seamless garment we call history. There is no single compass by which to unravel the course of historical causation. Written history, in form and content, is many-sided, however much this may disconcert the doctrinaire types.

This short excursion into Black history has taken note of varying viewpoints as to its function. Although varied, these approaches are often complementary rather than contradictory. More than anything else they demonstrate that there are alternate ways of looking at the past. The viewpoints of the revolutionary nationalist and the academic historian are not necessarily antagonistic. The academician, for example, may disavow an activist role and say that he is dealing with ideas for their own sake. But ideas are weapons and, as a rule, action is germinated by ideas.

In the formation of the new Black history the academician—the traditionalist—will continue to be of major importance. But if Black history is to come of age, revolutionary Black nationalists will also have much to contribute. The nationalist historians will force a reexamination of the historic patterns of color prejudice in America, not only in its grosser, more obvious manifestations, but in its manifold subtle forms, its protective coloration, one might say. The nationalists will bring into purview the blacks of the so-called Third World, comparing and contrasting them with their counterparts in America. The tone of moral outrage that characterizes the nationalist school has its value, too, a healthy anger often acting as a social catalyst.

And finally the revolutionary Black nationalist has made it clear that to properly assess the Black past we need newer, nontraditional techniques. A multidisciplinary approach is called for, one not relying so largely on written records. Historical inquiry is already profiting from the methodology of the behavioral sciences—sociology, anthropology, and psychology. Interdisciplinary history opens vistas across and beyond the traditional chronological and geographic boundaries. These widening approaches to appraising the past have led to such newer periodicals as the *Journal of Interdisciplinary History*, its first issue appearing in the autumn of 1970 and its avowed purpose to "stimulate historians to examine their own subjects in a new light, whether they be derived from psychology, physics, or paleontology."

This is the age of ideological cross-fertilization. It is to be noted, for example, that today in the study of early man on this planet no fewer than twelve different special skills are necessary—six field skills and six laboratory skills. In properly assessing the Black role in American history a comparable if less numerous list of skills is needed. Without the use of these newer tools the past will remain an incomplete past. In fine, historians of the Black past must take into consideration "the changing character of historical evidence, the development of new techniques and concepts in related disciplines, and the growing body of research by non-historians into historical problems," to borrow a phrase from David S. Landes and Charles Tilly ("History as Social Science," in Social Science Research Council *Items,* March 1971).

The newer Black history, looking afresh down the corridors of time, has a revolutionary potential of its own. For blacks it is a new way to see themselves. For whites it furnishes a new version of American history, one that especially challenges our national sense of smugness and self-righteousness and our avowal of fair play. Beyond this the new Black history summons the entire historical guild—writers, teachers, and learners—to higher levels of expectation and performance. History, as all of its disciples know, is both continuity and change. Change stems from our readiness to challenge the current order, using the best tools of our trade. A new Black history would revitalize education, quickening whatever it touches.

In 1925 in the foreword to his pathbreaking volume *The New Negro*, Alain Locke, one of the many illustrious Howard University scholar-humanists, said many things that have a contemporary ring: "Negro life is not only establishing new contacts and founding new centers, it is finding a new soul. There is a fresh spiritual and cultural focusing. . . . There is a renewed race-spirit that consciously and proudly sets itself apart." Locke, of course, was speaking primarily of creative expression in the arts, but his words aptly characterize the current Black thrust in history. In its work of restoring history's lost boundaries, the Black history of today is establishing new contacts and finding a new soul.

The Supreme Court
and the Negro
Rayford W. Logan

Practically all the relevant decisions of the United States Supreme Court during Reconstruction and to the end of the century nullified or curtailed those rights of Negroes which the Reconstruction "Radicals" thought they had written into laws and into the Constitution. Some of these decisions are still generally accepted—even though two of the most important were decided by a five to four vote. Another, Plessy v. Ferguson which laid down the doctrine of "separate but equal accommodations," is being challenged in the Supreme Court as this book goes to press. The rulings in the jury cases have been largely reversed. This fairly good record of the Supreme Court is, however, somewhat vitiated by expressions of social philosophy in some of the cases.*

The decisions of the Court were largely the handiwork of Northerners and Republicans. The first Southerner appointed to the Court since 1852 was William B. Woods, a Republican from Georgia, in 1880. John Marshall Harlan, appointed in 1881, came from the ex-slave state of Kentucky, but he had fought in the Union Army. The first Democrat after Stephen J. Field of California, appointed in 1862, was Lamar of Mississippi, appointed in 1888. There were thus only two Southerners, both of them Republicans, and one Democrat, from California, on the bench when it handed down the devastating Civil Rights decision in 1883. In 1896 when the Court wrote the more controversial decision, Plessy v. Ferguson, there was only one Southerner, Edward Douglass White of Louisiana (Woods and Lamar had died). There were only two Democrats, Field and White. An Ohio Republican, Morrison R. Waite, was Chief Justice from 1874 to 1888. Chief Justice Melville W. Fuller (1888–1910), was a graduate of

---

*Supreme Court decisions since 1941, the Civil Rights laws of 1957, 1960, 1964, and state laws now give evidence of attempts to apply these basic principles to almost 12 million American Negroes.

Bowdoin College, Maine; he had attended Harvard Law School and practiced law in Illinois. Field, the California Democrat, and Joseph Bradley, the New Jersey Republican—who served from 1863 to 1897 and 1870 to 1892, respectively—were probably the most conservative. The most notable dissenter was the Kentucky Republican Unionist, Harlan, 1877–1911. His dissenting opinions in the Civil Rights Cases and in Plessy *v.* Ferguson are still cited by lawyers and laymen who reject the validity of these decisions.*

In order to obtain a complete picture of the loopholes that the Supreme Court found in the efforts of the Reconstruction "Radicals" to protect the rights of Negroes, an examination of decisions from 1873 to 1877 is necessary. To some degree, the decisions against Negroes after 1877 followed the general pattern of the reaction against nationalism that had become evident, 1870–1873, under Chief Justice Salmon P. Chase. During the eighty-one years from 1789 to 1869 only four Acts of Congress had been declared invalid, but from 1870 to 1873 six such Acts were held unconstitutional. Since none of these six cases involved the rights of Negroes, it may be argued that subsequent decisions affecting Negro rights merely reflected the continued reaction of the Court against federal power. It can not be gainsaid, however, that some of these subsequent decisions also reflected the changing attitude in the nation at large with respect to the Negro.

It was during this early period of judicial reaction against nationalism that the Supreme Court first interpreted the Fourteenth Amendment. While the Slaughter-House Cases, 1873, did not directly involve the rights of Negroes, the Court frequently referred to these cases in later interpretations of those rights. The legislature of Louisiana had passed a statute which granted a monopoly of the slaughterhouse business within certain parishes of New Orleans in favor of one corporation, and thus deprived over one thousand persons of the right to engage in that business. Opponents of the monopoly contended that this state law created an involuntary servitude, abridged the privileges and immunities of citizens of the United States, denied them equal protection of the laws, and deprived them of their property without due process of law. By a majority of five to four the Court upheld the state law on all counts. The decision scoffed at the idea that the involuntary servitude forbidden by the Thirteenth Amendment could possibly refer to a servitude attached to property. But the real significance of the case involved the interpretation of the Fourteenth Amendment.

The five majority justices pointed out: "We do not deny that no one else but the negro can share in this protection." But, they declared, if the right to be

---

*The doctrine of "separate but equal" was reversed by the Supreme Court decision of May 17, 1954. This decision stated: "We conclude that in the field of public education the doctrine of 'separate but equal' has no place." Subsequent decisions expanded the thrust of this decision.

freed from monopoly existed, it was not as a privilege or immunity of a citizen of the United States. The majority opinion did not attempt to give a complete list of the privileges and immunities that inhered in state citizenship. The former, however, could all be comprehended under the following general heads: "protection by the government, with the right to acquire and possess property of every kind, and to pursue and obtain happiness and safety, subject, nevertheless, to such restraints as the government may prescribe for the general good of the whole." Having concluded that the privileges and immunities relied on in the argument belonged to citizens of states, as such, the Court held that it was excused from defining those privileges and immunities of citizens of the United States which no state can abridge, until some case involving those privileges and immunities made it necessary for the Court to define them. The Court, did, none the less, enumerate certain privileges and immunities that inhered in United States citizenship. Among these were the rights secured by the Thirteenth and Fifteenth Amendments and the clauses in the Fourteenth Amendment which the Court then considered.

The due process clause had been a part of the Constitution since the adoption of the Fifth Amendment which placed a restraint upon the federal government. But, under no construction of cases involving that Amendment could the Court find that the butchers in the Slaughter-House Cases had been deprived by Louisiana of their property without due process of law. The history of the Fourteenth Amendment showed clearly that the equal protection clause was clearly designed to forbid laws "which discriminated with gross injustice against them [the newly emancipated Negroes] as a class." The Court doubted whether any action of a state that did not fall within this category would ever be held to come within the purview of the equal protection provision. (In fact, however, between 1890 and 1910 only 19 of the 528 cases before the Court involving the Fourteenth Amendment applied to Negro rights; 288 of these cases referred to corporations which were considered "persons" within the language of the Fourteenth Amendment.) No such case was before the Court in this instance, the majority held.

The four dissenting judges, including Chief Justice Chase, pointed out that the majority opinion rendered the privileges and immunities clause a practical nullity. For, "with privileges and immunities pertaining only to citizens of the United States *as such*, no State ever could have interfered by its laws," and hence no new constitutional provision was necessary to prohibit such interference. The dissenting opinions added that, even before the Fourteenth Amendment, the supremacy of the Constitution and laws of the United States always controlled any legislation of that character. The clear purpose of the relevant clause was to prevent states from abridging the privileges and immunities which citizens enjoyed as citizens of states.

One of the most intriguing aspects of this case is the fact that the principal attorney for the plaintiffs argued frequently that the Fourteenth Amendment was intended to secure the rights of the recently emancipated slaves against their former masters. This attorney was John A. Campbell of Alabama, a former member of the United States Supreme Court who had concurred with the majority in the Dred Scott Case and who had resigned when Alabama seceded from the Union. Against a background of frequent references to the purpose of the amendment, he insisted that it "brought the federal government into immediate contact with every person and gave to every citizen a claim upon its protecting power." The Amendment, he continued, placed the privileges and immunities of national citizenship beyond the power of the state government. National citizenship and state citizenship were the same.

Campbell later declared that the decision was "probably best for the country." Had he deliberately portrayed the fulsome potentialities of the Fourteenth Amendment in protecting rights of Negroes in order to evoke a decision curtailing those potentialities? Whatever his purpose may have been, consideration of the privileges and immunities of national citizenship virtually disappeared from constitutional law until a tax case in 1935. A five to four decision nullified the aim of the Reconstruction "Radicals"—if Campbell was right—to protect, through the privileges and immunities clause, the freedmen against hostile state laws. One wonders how Campbell would have voted had he still been a member of the Court.

Three years later, in 1876, the Supreme Court found loopholes in the Civil Rights Enforcement Act of May 31, 1870. In United States *v.* Reese, the Court held that under the Fifteenth Amendment, congressional action was limited to that which prevented discrimination in the right to vote on account of race, color or previous condition of servitude. Since sections three and four of the Act were not confined to such a limited class of discrimination, those sections were unconstitutional. The sections of the Act of May 31, 1870, dealing with the right to vote were repealed by the Act of Congress of February 8, 1894.*

In the same year the Court held that section six of the Act of May 31, 1870, was constitutional, subject to a vital restriction of its scope. That section forbade two or more persons to "injure, oppress, threaten, or intimidate any citizen with intent to prevent or hinder his free exercise and enjoyment of any right or privilege granted or secured to him by the Constitution or laws of the United States, or because of his having exercised the same." The penalty for violation of this section was a fine of not more than $5,000, imprisonment for not more than ten years, and ineligibility "to any office, or place of honor, or trust created by the Constitution and laws of the United States." The defendants were charged with conspiring to prevent two Negro citizens of the United States

---

*Title I of the Civil Rights Acts of 1957, 1960, and 1964 included provisions designed to protect the rights of Negroes to vote. The language can be construed as being based upon both the Fourteenth and Fifteenth Amendments.

from the enjoyment of their rights peaceably to assemble with others, to petition for redress of grievances, to bear arms and to vote. They were further charged with conspiring falsely to imprison and murder the two Negroes and thus to deprive them of their lives and liberty without due process of law. The Court, in United States *v.* Cruikshank, with one dissenting opinion, rejected all the charges as not having been indictable under any act of Congress.*

In order for the case to be brought under the operation of the statute, the Court held that it would have to be demonstrated that the right in question was one granted or secured by the Constitution or laws of the United States. Since the rights peaceably to assemble and to bear arms had existed prior to the Constitution, they were therefore not derived from it. If the right to petition Congress had been involved, the case would have come within the statute, and within the scope of the sovereignty of the United States. The offense, as stated in the indictment, would have been established if it had been shown that the object of the conspiracy was to prevent a meeting for *any* lawful purpose. The United States had no more power to punish for a conspiracy falsely to imprison and to murder than to punish for false imprisonment or murder itself. This power was vested in the states. The Court also laid down the doctrine which is generally accepted, namely, that the due process clause in the Fourteenth Amendment did not add anything to the rights of one citizen against another. The due process clause merely furnished an additional procedural guarantee against any encroachment by the states upon the fundamental rights which belong to every citizen as a member of society. The counts in the indictment did not call for the exercise of any of the powers conferred by the due process clause of the Fourteenth Amendment.

The judgment of the Court with respect to equal protection of the laws is especially revealing. The Court pointed out that there was no allegation that the conspiracy under this count was because of the race or color of the persons conspired against. It then gave this interpretation of the meaning of the equal protection clause:

> The fourteenth amendment prohibits a State
> from denying to any person within its juris-
> diction the equal protection of the laws; but
> this provision does not, any more than the
> one which precedes it, and which we have
> just considered, add any thing to the rights
> which one citizen has under the Constitution

---

*Section six of the Act of May 31, 1870 became, with immaterial changes, section 5508 of the revised statutes of 1874–1878. This section was repeated without change as section nineteen of the Criminal Code of 1909 (35 Stat. 1092). Section 241, United States Code, 1950 ed., repeated the terms of conspiracy, the fine and the imprisonment, but dropped the ineligibility clause.

against another. The equality of the rights of
citizens is a principle of republicanism. Every
republican government is in duty bound to
protect all its citizens in the enjoyment of this
principle, if within its power. That duty was
originally assumed by the States; and it still
remains there. The only obligation resting
upon the United States is to see that the
States do not deny the right. This the amendment guarantees, but no more. The power of
the national government is limited to the
enforcement of this guaranty.

But this unequivocal statement of the responsibility resting upon the federal government did not define the equality of the rights of citizens. When the
Court did rule on that question twenty years later, in Plessy *v.* Ferguson, it
declared that equality of right did not prevent segregation.

The Court, meanwhile, invoked the equal protection clause to limit the
exclusion of Negroes from jury service, the only cases during this period in
which the Court interpreted the Fourteenth Amendment in favor of Negroes.
The case of Strauder *v.* West Virginia established the precedent. West Virginia
statutes of 1872–1873 excluded Negroes from grand and petit juries. The
Court, in 1880, held that these laws flagrantly violated the equal protection
clause and were therefore unconstitutional. In the same decision, the Court
held valid that section of the Civil Rights Enforcement Act which authorized
the removal of a case into the United States courts when the equal rights of a
citizen were denied in a state court. During the same term, the Court ruled, in
Ex parte Virginia, that acts by officers and agents of a state constituted state
action under the Fourteenth Amendment. A county judge who had excluded
Negroes from jury service had therefore violated that amendment.

In both these cases, Justice William Strong, a Pennsylvania Republican,
made interesting observations that might be used today by organizations and
individuals seeking congressional legislation in behalf of Negroes. In the first
case, he expressed his conviction that the true spirit and meaning of the Reconstruction Amendments could not be understood without keeping in view "the
history of the times when they were adopted and the objects they plainly
sought to accomplish." He repeated this conviction in the second case, and
added that the amendments were intended to be and were "limitations of the
power of the States and enlargements of the power of Congress." It made no
difference that such legislation by Congress was restrictive of what a state
might have done before the amendments were adopted. He affirmed:

The prohibitions of the Fourteenth Amendment are directed to the States, and they are to
a degree restrictions of State power. . . . No such
enforcement is an invasion of State sovereignty.

No law can be, which the people of the United
States have, by the Constitution of the United
States, empowered Congress to enact.

Justice Harlan was to take an even stronger tone in his dissenting opinion in
the Civil Rights Cases, three years later.

The Supreme Court further strengthened the right of Negroes to serve on
juries, in Neal *v.* Delaware, 1880. The Court held that the Fifteenth Amendment *ipso facto* rendered inoperative the constitution and laws of Delaware
which, at the time the amendment was adopted, restricted jury service to
white persons who were qualified to vote. Since, moreover, the state had not
subsequently passed any law in violation of the Fifteenth Amendment,
Delaware recognized its binding force. Consequently, there was no denial of
equality on that score by the state. Since, however, the facts presented showed
that no Negroes had been called to jury service, the discrimination constituted
a "prima facie denial . . . of that equal protection which has been secured by
the Constitution and laws of the United States."

Two years later, the Court declared void the indictment of a Negro who had
been indicted and arraigned for trial under Kentucky laws which excluded
Negroes from all jury service. But, in Virginia *v.* Rives, 1880, the Court had
declared that the Fourteenth Amendment was not violated if, when the jury
was all white, it could not be shown that Negroes were excluded solely on the
ground of race or color.

To the traditional "man from Mars," it would be difficult to justify the ruling,
in 1882, that an Alabama statute which provided a more severe punishment in
cases of fornication and adultery between Negroes and whites than between
members of the same race did not violate the equal protection clause. As will be
seen later in this chapter, five other cases involving alleged exclusion of
Negroes from juries resulted in decisions against federal intervention and only
one in favor of it.

Meanwhile, the Supreme Court had handed down its first decision sanctioning
segregation in interstate traffic. This decision, Hall *v.* De Cuir, 1878—the year after
the withdrawal of federal troops from Louisiana and South Carolina—has not
been accorded the importance that it deserves. The decision is all the more fascinating against the background of the complex struggle over the federal regulation
of interstate commerce.

In the Granger Cases, 1877, the Court had upheld the right of states to regulate
railroads. Since most of the traffic was interstate, such regulation was clearly a
direct burden on interstate commerce. But, in Hall *v.* De Cuir, the Court held
unconstitutional a Louisiana statute forbidding discrimination on account of race,
because the law placed a direct burden on interstate commerce. In order to make
clear that this was true, the Court pointed out: "A passenger in the cabin class set
apart for the use of whites without the State must, when the boat comes within,
share the accommodations of that cabin with such colored passengers as may
come on board afterwards, if the law is enforced." The decision, written by Chief

Justice Waite, observed that "it was to meet just such a case that the commercial clause in the Constitution was adopted." While this may be doubted, it is none the less true that, as the Court stated, it would be difficult to conduct business if, in one state white and colored passengers were separated by law, and in another were required by law to be put in cabins together. The racial aspects of this burden on interstate commerce were further pointed up when the Court observed:

> If this statute can be enforced against those engaged in interstate commerce, it may be as well against those engaged in foreign; and the master of a ship clearing from New Orleans to Liverpool, having passengers on board, would be compelled to carry all, white and colored, in the same cabin during his passage down the river, or be subject to an action for damages, "exemplary as well as actual," by any one who felt himself aggrieved because he had been excluded on account of his color.

If these two cases had stood alone, a logician would have been justified in concluding that state regulation of interstate commerce was less a violation of the Constitution if it dealt with commerce *per se* than if it involved the mingling of the races. But in 1886 the Court ruled, in the Wabash Case, that rates fixed by state law could not be applied to transportation beginning or ending outside the state. Even after this decision the Court found it difficult to fix the exact line of demarcation between a direct and an indirect burden on interstate commerce. One of the most interesting decisions was the Lake Shore Case in 1889, since it required consideration of the De Cuir Case. An Ohio law required some interstate passenger trains to stop at certain points in Ohio in order to let off and receive passengers. Rejecting the appositeness of the De Cuir decision, the Court declared that the Ohio law did not at all interfere with the "management" of trains outside the state and that it applied only to some trains. The Ohio law so manifestly subserved the public convenience, and was "in itself so just and reasonable, as wholly to preclude the idea that it was, as the Louisiana statute was declared to be, a direct burden upon interstate commerce, or a direct interference with its freedom."

It was easier for the Supreme Court to find that laws requiring segregation in intrastate commerce did not violate the interstate commerce clause. In 1890, the Court held that a Mississippi statute requiring separate but equal accommodations did not violate the interstate commerce clause, since the Mississippi Supreme Court had construed the law as applying only to intrastate commerce. At the turn of the century, the Court ruled that a separate coach law applicable only to passengers within the state of Kentucky was valid.

While the Supreme Court was seeking to define the precise line of demarcation between state laws that placed a direct, and those that placed an indirect, burden on interstate commerce, the Court had little trouble in fixing the limits between state action and individual action. The principle that the first section of the Fourteenth Amendment was prohibitory upon states only, and not upon individuals, was first upheld in United States *v.* Harris, 1882. Those sections of the so-called Ku-Klux Act of April 20, 1871, which had laid severe penalties upon anyone conspiring to impede the effects of the Fourteenth and Fifteenth Amendments, were therefore declared unconstitutional. In accordance with this same principle, the Court in 1883 held the Civil Rights Act of 1875 unconstitutional.

The preamble of this law stated that Congress deemed it essential to just government that "we recognize the equality of all men before the law, and hold it is the duty of government in all its dealings with the people to mete out equal and exact justice to all, of whatever nativity, race, color, or persuasion, religious or political," and that it is "the appropriate object of legislation to enact great fundamental principles into law." The Act provided that all persons within the jurisdiction of the United States should be entitled to "the full and equal enjoyment of the accommodations, facilities, and privileges of inns, public conveyances on land or water, theaters, and other places of public amusement; subject only to the conditions and limitations established by law, and applicable alike to citizens of every race and color, regardless of any previous condition of servitude." The person aggrieved by a violation could recover $500; the offender was guilty of a misdemeanor, and federal courts were given exclusive jurisdiction. This law was the culmination of the various federal laws that were passed to counteract the post-Civil War Black Codes in the Southern states. More than any of the other laws it rankled Southern views on the proper place of the free Negro.

The aversion of white men to personal contacts with Negroes after the Civil War stemmed largely from the new status of Negroes as free men. Masters and mistresses had had personal contacts with their house slaves. Indeed, the not infrequent practice of cohabitation had caused Mrs. Mary Boykin Chesnut, the wife of a rich planter, to pour out in poignant passages her bitterness against the slave system which permitted Southern gentlemen to live "like the patriarchs of old, . . . all in one house with their wives and concubines; and the mulattoes one sees in every family partly resemble the white children." After emancipation personal contacts became social relations. The etiquette of slavery permitted, for example, a slave girl to travel as maid for her mistress on a train. The etiquette of freedom found it intolerable that a colored woman paying her own fare should travel in the same coach with a white woman. The extramarital activities of white men with a free colored woman were considered even more reprehensible than similar infidelities with a slave woman. The myth of the faithful slave was replaced by the legend of the Negro as a rapist. Attempts to give the freedmen political and economic equality threatened the old way of life. Social equality—the mingling of the races in schools, inns, theaters and on public carriers—would encourage black men, it was asserted, to dream of cohabitation with white women. While these fears were most deeply rooted in recollections of the slave system in the South, they prevailed also to some degree in the North where free men had suffered economic, political and social inequality.

The case of the United States *v.* Stanley, and other cases, or the Civil Rights Cases as the decision is better known, involved seven different incidents. These included the denial of hotel accommodations to Negroes in Kansas and Missouri; the denial to a Negro of a seat in the dress circle of a theater in San Francisco; the denial to a person (presumably a Negro) of the full enjoyment of the accommodations of the Grand Opera in New York; the refusal by a conductor on a passenger train to allow a colored woman to travel in the ladies' car of the Memphis and Charleston Railroad Company. Only two of the five cases originated in the South. This fact should not lead to the conclusion that the aversion was greater in the North than in the South, but rather that Negroes in the North had more frequent personal contacts with whites in public places.

The decision was written by Justice Bradley, the "Fifth Judge" of the Electoral Commission which had decided every controversial issue of the Hayes-Tilden election in favor of Hayes. Woodward finds it appropriate that Bradley should have written the decision since it "constituted a sort of validation of the Compromise of 1877." The essential points in the decision are two: the first section of the Fourteenth Amendment is prohibitory upon states only; Congress is authorized by the amendment to adopt only corrective, not general legislation. In brief, the person wronged must look for vindication or redress to the laws of the state. Since the cases considered arose within states, the constitutionality of the act with respect to territories and to the District of Columbia was not presented. As in the Cruikshank Case, the Court held that if state laws were to make any unjust discrimination, Congress would have the power under the Fourteenth Amendment to afford remedy.

Harlan, the Kentucky Unionist, opened his classic dissent by stating that the majority opinion proceeded upon grounds

> entirely too narrow and artificial. I cannot resist the conclusion that the substance and spirit of the recent amendments of the Constitution have been sacrificed by a subtle and ingenious verbal criticism. Constitutional provisions, adopted in the interest of liberty, and for the purpose of securing, through national legislation, if need be, rights inhering in a state of freedom, and belonging to American citizenship, have been so construed as to defeat the ends the people desired to accomplish by changes in the fundamental law.

This far-reaching decision thus legalized race distinctions by individuals with respect to enjoyment of facilities in carriers and places of public accommodation and amusement. In addition, it virtually assured the subsequent development of Jim Crow laws, and other forms of race discrimination, and the passivity of the Federal government in the face of this discrimination. The sequel proved that Harlan was correct when he declared in his dissenting opinion: "We shall enter upon an era of constitutional law, when the rights of freedom and American citizenship cannot receive from the nation that efficient protection which heretofore was unhesitatingly accorded to slavery and the rights of the master."

But the nation, as a whole, rejoiced over the decision. It is still the law of the land. Charles Warren, whose book *The Supreme Court in United States History* is considered one of the most authoritative treatises on the subject, commented with respect to the Civil Rights Cases, the Harris Case and others of a similar character:

> Viewed in historical perspective now [1922], however, there can be no question that the decisions in these cases were most fortunate. They largely eliminated from national politics the Negro question which had so long embittered Congressional debates; they relegated the burden and the duty of protecting the Negro to the states, to whom they properly belonged; and they served to restore confidence in the national court in the Southern states.

The decision, of course, had the reverse effect on many Negroes. Despite the admonition of the Court that Negroes were not justified in interpreting denials of equal accommodations as a badge of inferiority, they could hardly construe such discrimination otherwise. They found some solace in the fact that fifteen Northern states soon thereafter passed civil rights laws, and three others strengthened existing laws. But the lower courts frequently found loopholes which largely nullified these state laws. Moreover, the vast majority of Negroes still lived in the South where they were increasingly subjected to segregation and discrimination by law and custom.

While the Court upheld the right of individuals to discriminate in public places against Negroes on account of their race, in the following year, it construed the Civil Rights Act of 1870 as a valid exercise of the power granted under the Fifteenth Amendment. In the Cruikshank Case, the Court had dismissed the charge that Negroes had been denied the right to vote, because the allegations did not show that the denial had been based on race or color. But, in *Ex parte* Yarbrough, 1884, the Court ruled that the Fifteenth Amendment "does, *proprio vigore*, substantially confer on the negro the right to vote, and Congress has the power to enforce that right." The ineffectiveness of this 1870 law was so evident that Congress, in 1890, attempted to enact legislation that would give practical effect to the Fifteenth Amendment. That attempt not only failed but led to constitutional amendments by Southern states to "legalize" the disfranchisement of most Negroes.

No case involving the right of Negroes to engage in business came before the Supreme Court. But, in a case involving Chinese laundrymen in California, the

Court construed the equal protection clause of the Fourteenth Amendment to the advantage of the Chinese. Chinese who conducted their business in wooden buildings were denied licenses while white persons conducting laundries under similar conditions were left unmolested. The Court vigorously ruled:

> Though the law itself be fair on its face and impartial in appearance, yet, if it is applied and administered by public authority with an evil eye and an unequal hand, so as practically to make unjust and illegal discriminations between persons in similar circumstances, material to their rights, the denial of equal justice is still within the prohibition of the Constitution.

The Court pointed out that it had sanctioned this principle in a number of cases, including *Ex parte* Virginia, and Neal *v.* Delaware. In neither of these cases, however, did the Court use such strong language as it did in Yick Wo *v.* Hopkins. Moreover, the decision in this case was unanimous, whereas in the cases involving the right of Negroes to sit on juries, Justice Field of California had dissented in both, Justice Clifford in one and Chief Justice Waite in the other.

Thirteen years after the Supreme Court had sanctioned discrimination by individuals in public places and on public carriers, the Court approved separation of the races by state action. In Plessy *v.* Ferguson, 1896, the Court for the first time invoked the doctrine of police powers to deny in effect the equal protection which the framers of the Fourteenth Amendment thought they had established. It was this decision by which the Supreme Court accepted the doctrine of "separate but equal accommodations." Between 1882 and 1888, lower federal courts had upheld the principle in four cases. In three cases involving segregation on public carriers, the courts had held that separate cars were a proper exercise of the state's police powers. In the fourth case, dealing with an Ohio statute which authorized school boards to organize separate schools for colored children, the lower federal court ruled: "Equality of right does not mean identity of right and . . . so long as educational opportunities for Negroes were substantially equal to those for whites no denial of protection resulted.". . . 1888, and 1889 had approved this doctrine of separate but equal accommodations.

It was not until 1896, however, that the United States Supreme Court upheld this doctrine. A Louisiana law required separate but equal accommodations on public carriers and provided a penalty for passengers who sat in a car or compartment assigned to the other race. The petitioner, an octoroon in whom "Negro blood was not discernible," sat in a white car and was arrested. The Court held that the law was a reasonable exercise of the state police power and was therefore constitutional. Justice Henry B. Brown, a Republican from Michigan, speaking for the Court, made this revealing observation:

The object of the [Fourteenth] Amendment was undoubtedly to enforce the absolute equality of the two races before the law, but in the nature of things it could not have been intended to abolish distinctions based on color, or to enforce social, as distinguished from political equality, or a commingling of the two races upon terms unsatisfactory to either.

The Court added, as it had done in the Civil Rights Case, that laws requiring segregation did not necessarily imply "the inferiority of either race to the other." Moreover, the Court pointed out that separate schools had been held valid in several Northern states by the state courts. Expanding even further the social philosophy which controlled the thinking of the judges, the Court continued:

If the two races are to meet upon terms of social equality, it must be the result of natural affinities, a mutual appreciation of each other's merits and a voluntary consent of individuals. . . . If one race be inferior to the other socially, the Constitution of the United States cannot put them upon the same plane. The distinction between the two races, which was founded in the color of the two races, must always exist so long as white men are distinct from the other color.

Harlan, who had dissented in the Civil Rights Cases, again wrote a scorching dissent. Laws requiring segregation on public carriers, he declared, were unconstitutional, since they interfered with the personal freedom of citizens "under the guise of giving equal accommodations to whites and blacks." They fostered ideas of caste and inferiority and the majority decision would stimulate further aggressions upon the rights of Negroes. Giving his own social interpretation of the Constitution and laws, he insisted: "Our Constitution is blind, and neither knows nor tolerates classes among citizens. . . . The law regards man as man, and takes no regard of his surroundings or his color when his civil rights as guaranteed by the supreme law of the land are invoked."

It is easy enough, then, to understand why one student of the subject has written that "the invocation and application of the police power is nothing more than an appeal to the sociological method of interpreting our Constitution and laws." Justice Harlan prophesied that the decision—which is not mentioned in Warren's authoritative history of the Supreme Court—would prove as pernicious as the Dred Scott decision. The Washington *Post,* in 1949, editorially called Plessy *v.* Ferguson the "worst" decision in the history of the Supreme Court except the Dred Scott decision. But this decision is still the law of the land. In recent years the Supreme Court has sought to enforce "substantial equality" in the separate accommodations, but it has not yet ruled on the constitutionality of segregation itself under the equal protection clause.*

The principle of separate but equal accommodations was not again clearly presented to the Supreme Court during the period under study. The Court found an opportunity to avoid a direct ruling in a case originating in Richmond County, Georgia. Cummings, a Negro taxpayer, complained that the high school for Negroes in that county had been suspended "for economic reasons" while the high school for whites remained open. The constitutionality of all laws providing separate accommodations for whites and Negroes was attacked in the argument of the plaintiff's counsel, but the question was not presented in the record. Harlan, speaking for the Court, declared that the relief asked for was an injunction which would close the school for the whites without furnishing any additional opportunities for Negroes. The trial did not show any abuse of the discretion allowed by law to the County Board of Education. The Court further held that the education of people in schools maintained by state taxation was a matter belonging to the respective states, and interference could not be justified except in a case of "clear and unmistakable disregard of the rights secured by the supreme law of the land."

During the last six years of the century, Negroes found it increasingly difficult to establish that exclusion from juries violated the equal protection clause. In one case, the Court declared that the petitioner had used the wrong method of procedure, since the regular trial of a state court can not be reviewed by *habeas corpus* proceedings. The second case, Gibson *v.* Mississippi, 1895, is more significant, since it revealed a growing insistence by the Court that indisputable evidence be presented of the exclusion from juries because of race or color. The petitioner in this case sought removal of his case from a Mississippi state court on the ground that Negroes were excluded from the grand and petit juries in Mississippi. Counsel for the petitioner—this seems to have been the first case in which Negro lawyers appeared before the United States Supreme Court—contended that at the time of selecting jurors in Washington County there were 7,000 colored citizens competent to serve as jurors and only 1,500 whites. Nevertheless, no colored juror had been summoned for a number of years. The Court rejected the petition because no proof had been offered that Negroes were excluded solely because of race or color. In any event, as Justice Harlan pointed out: "It is clear in view of what has been said that these facts, even if they had been proved and accepted, do not show that the rights

---

*Title II of the Civil Rights Act of 1964 was based upon both the equal protection clause of the Fourteenth Amendment and the interstate commerce clause.

of the accused were denied by the Constitution and laws of the State." But the Court also declared that evidence of the failure to call Negroes to jury service would be for the consideration of the trial court upon motion by the accused to quash the indictment. The Court thus required the accused to establish proof in the court of a state which had rendered Negroes politically impotent. But in 1899, the Court reversed the decision of a Texas court and remanded the case on the ground that the state court had erred in refusing to receive proof that Negroes were excluded from the grand jury solely because of their race or color. In two other cases, the Court based its rulings on failure to prove that the exclusion was due to discrimination.*

Perhaps the least defensible decision of the United States Supreme Court on the right of Negroes to serve on juries was handed down in the too little known case of Williams *v.* Mississippi. Cornelius J. Jones, one of the colored lawyers who had appeared in Gibson *v.* Mississippi was determined that he would this time give the Court no loopholes. The accused had been indicted for murder by a grand jury of white men. Jones had made a motion to quash the indictment, on the ground that the state constitution required the ability to read and write and understand any section of that constitution for service on a jury. The motion had been denied, and the defendant had then moved to remove the case to the United States Circuit Court on substantially the same ground. This motion had likewise been denied. The defendant had thereupon been tried by a jury of white men and convicted. When his motion for a new trial had been denied, he had appealed to the United States Supreme Court.

The ruling of the Court was based upon the doctrine that possibility of evil administration of a law was not necessarily proof of the fact that the law itself was evil. This case does not, therefore, offer an exact parallel with Yick Wo *v.* Hopkins, in which it was clearly demonstrated that Chinese laundrymen had been deprived of their right to conduct a business solely because of their race. But, the Court in this Mississippi case had to fall back upon a decision of the Mississippi Supreme Court for proof that Negroes were not excluded from the jury lists because of their color. The Court observed:

> We gather from the statements of the motion that certain officers are invested with discretion in making up lists of electors, and that this discretion has been exercised against the colored race and that from these lists the jurors are selected. The Supreme Court of Mississippi, however, decided in a case presenting the same question as that at bar that jurors are not selected from or with reference to any lists furnished by such election officers.

*The Supreme Court ruled in Norris *v.* Alabama, 1935, that the systematic exclusion of Negroes from juries was *prima-facie* evidence of the denial of equal protection of the laws guaranteed by the Fourteenth Amendment.

By the beginning of the twentieth century, the first section of the Fourteenth Amendment—except the definition of citizenship—had been virtually nullified by decisions of the United States Supreme Court. The Court had ruled that most privileges and immunities of citizens inhered in state, rather than in United States, citizenship. The Fourteenth Amendment placed prohibitions upon states and not individuals. Under the doctrine of police powers the states could, however, do some of the very things which the framers of the Fourteenth Amendment thought they had prevented. Separation of the races, for example, was not a denial of equal protection of the laws, provided that the separate accommodations were substantially equal. Due process of law did not add to the rights of any citizens, but merely strengthened the procedure by which their rights were safeguarded. The only right of Negroes under the Fourteenth Amendment which the Court upheld was the right of Negroes to serve on juries when state laws and state officers clearly violated that right, and proof was presented at the trial that Negroes had been barred because of their race or color. The Supreme Court had further held that state law requiring separation of races was not a direct burden on interstate commerce and was, therefore, constitutional. The Interstate Commerce Commission had also upheld segregation in interstate travel, provided the accommodations were equal. The protection of the Negro was left to the states, which increasingly were relegating Negroes to what is today called second-class citizenship. The decision of the Supreme Court, that the Fifteenth Amendment did substantially confer on the Negro the right to vote, was being increasingly nullified by the revision of state constitutions that disfranchised most Negroes. No cases involving these new constitutions were presented to the Court during this period.

It is not clear whether Douglass meant abstract justice or the interpretation of the Constitution and laws when he listed "American justice" as the first principle which should apply alike to all Americans. Whichever he meant, the Supreme Court had been compelled to rule that, in substance, "Equal Justice under Law" did not guarantee to Negro Americans the same rights that other Americans enjoyed.

White English in Blackface, or Who Do I Be?
Geneva Smitherman

Black verbal style exists on a sacred-secular continuum, as represented by the accompanying scheme [see table below]. The model allows us to account for the many individual variations in black speech, which can all be located at some point along the continuum.

The sacred style is rural and Southern. It is the style of the black preacher and that associated with the black church tradition. It tends to be more emotive and highly charged than the secular style. It is also older in time. However, though I've called it "sacred," it abounds in secularisms. Black church service tends to be highly informal, and it ain't nothin for a preacher to get up in the pulpit and, say, show off what he's wearing: "Y'all didn't notice the new suit I got on today, did y'all? Ain the Lord good to us. . . ."

The secular style is urban and Northern, but since it probably had its beginnings in black folk tales and proverbs, its *roots* are Southern and rural. This is the street culture; the style found in barbershops and on street corners in the black ghettos of American cities. It tends to be more cool, more emotionally restrained than sacred style. It is newer and younger in time and only fully evolved as a distinct style with the massive wave of black migration to the cities.

Both sacred and secular styles share the following characteristics:

1. *Call and Response.* This is basic black oral tradition. The speaker's solo voice alternates or is intermingled with the audience's response. In the sacred style, the minister is urged by the congregation's Amen's, That's right, Reverend's, or Preach Reverend's. One also hears occasional Take your time's when the preacher is initiating his sermon, the congregation desiring to savor every little bit of this good message they bout to hear. (In both sacred and secular political rap styles, the "Preach Reverend" is transposed to "Teach Brother.") In the secular style, the response can take the form of a back-and-forth banter between the speaker and various members of the audience. Or the audience might manifest its response in giving skin (fives) when a really down

SACRED	SECULAR
Political Rap Style	*Political Rap Style*
Examples: Jesse Jackson	*Examples:* Malcolm X
Martin Luther King	Rap Brown
Political Literary Style	*Political Literary Style*
Examples: Barbara Ann Teer's	*Examples:* Don Lee
National Black Theater	Last Poets
Nikki Giovanni's "Truth Is	
on Its Way"	

Sacred and Secular Black Verbal Styles

verbal point is scored. Other approval responses include laughter and phrases like "Oh, you mean, nigger," "Get back, nigger," "Git down, baby," etc.

2. *Rhythmic Pattern.*   I refer to cadence, tone, and musical quality. This is a pattern that is lyrical, sonorous, and generally emphasizing sound apart from sense. It is often established through repetition, either of certain sounds or words. The preacher will get a rhythm going, conveying his message through sound rather than depending on sheer semantic import. "I-I-I-I-I-Oh-I-I-Oh, yeah, Lord-I-I-heard the voice of Jesus saying. . . ." Even though the secular style is characterized by rapidity, as in the toasts (narrative tales of bad niggers and they exploits like Stag-O-Lee, or bad animals and they trickeration, like the Signifying Monkey), the speaker's voice tone still has that rhythmic, musical quality, just with a faster tempo.

3. *Spontaneity.*   Generally, the speaker's performance is improvisational, with the rich interaction between speaker and audience dictating and/or directing the course and outcome of the speech event. Since the speaker does not prepare a formal document, his delivery is casual, nondeliberate, and uncontrived. He speaks in a lively, conversational tone, and with an ever-present quality of immediacy. All emphasis is on process, movement, and creativity of the moment. The preacher says "Y'all dont wont to hear dat, so I'm gon leave it lone," and his audience shouts, "Naw, tell it Reverend, tell it!," and he does. Or, like, once Malcolm [X] mentioned the fact of his being in prison, and sensing the surprise of his audience, he took advantage of the opportunity to note that all black people were in prison: "That's what American means: prison."

4. *Concreteness:*   The speaker's imagery and ideas center around the empirical world, the world of reality, and the contemporary Here and Now. Rarely does he drift off into esoteric abstractions; his metaphors and illustrations are commonplace and grounded in everyday experience. Perhaps because of his concreteness, there is a sense of identification with the event being described or narrated, as in the secular style where the toast-teller's identity merges with that of the protagonist of his tale, and he becomes Stag-O-Lee or Shine; or when the preacher assumes the voice of God or the person-

ality of a Biblical character. Even the experience of being saved takes on a pre-sentness and rootedness in everyday life: "I first met God in 1925. . . ."

5. *Signifying.* This is a technique of talking about the entire audience or some member of the audience either to initiate verbal "war" or to make a point hit home. The interesting thang bout this rhetorical device is that the audience is not offended and realizes—naw, expects—the speaker to launch this offensive to achieve this desired effect. "Pimp, punk, prostitute, Ph.D.—all the P's—you still in slavery!" announces the Reverend Jesse Jackson. Malcolm puts down the nonviolent movement with: "In a revolution, you swinging, not singing." (Notice the characteristic rhythmic pattern in the above examples—the alliterative poetic effect of Jackson's statement and the rhyming device in Malcolm's.)

An analysis of black expressive style, such as presented here, should facilitate the construction of a performance instrument to measure the degree of command of the style of any given BI speaker. Linguists and educators sincerely interested in black education might be about the difficult, complex business of devising such a "test," rather than establishing linguistic remediation programs to correct a nonexistent remediation. Like in any other area of human activity, some BI rappers are better than others, and today's most effective black preachers, leaders, politicians, writers are those who rap in the black expressive style, appropriating the ritual framework of the Oral Tradition as vehicle for the conveyance of they political ideologies. Which brings me back to what I said from Jump Street. The real heart of this language controversy relates to/is the underlying political nature of the American educational system. Brother Frantz Fanon is highly instructive at this point. From his "Negro and Language," in *Black Skin, White Masks*:

> I ascribe a basic importance to the phenome-non of language. . . . To speak means . . . above all to assume a culture, to support the weight of a civilization. . . . Every dialect is a way of thinking. . . . And the fact that the newly returned [i.e., from white schools] Negro adopts a language different from that of the group into which he was born is evidence of a dislocation, a separation. . . .

In showing why the "Negro adopts such a position . . . with respect to European languages," Fanon continues:

> It is because he wants to emphasize the rup-ture that has now occurred. He is incarnating a new type of man that he imposes on his associates and his family. And so his old mother can no longer understand him when

he talks to her about his *duds*, the family's *crummy joint*, the *dump*. . . all of it, of course, tricked out with the appropriate accent.

In every country of the world, there are climbers, 'the ones who forget who they are,' and in contrast to them, 'the ones who remember where they came from.' The Antilles Negro who goes home from France expresses himself in the dialect if he wants to make it plain that nothing has changed.

As black people go moving up toward separation and cultural nationalism, the question of the moment is not which dialect, but which culture, not whose vocabulary but whose values, not *I am* vs. *I be*, but WHO DO I BE?

Return Movements to West and East Africa: A Comparative Approach

Joseph E. Harris

The significant crosscurrents of mutual influence between blacks in the United States and the Caribbean, and among those two areas and Africa, as well as between India and Africa, have very deep historical roots that, from the perspective of the African heritage, form a useful Pan-African approach to the study of blacks throughout the world. The key problems of that approach are, first, to trace the changes that occurred among Africans as they adjusted to varied conditions abroad during the period of slavery, abolition, and after; second, to determine the extent to which African customs and memories survived abroad and in what form; third, to analyze the ways in which the idea of Africa arose and manifested itself in the diaspora and related itself to Africa and Africans; fourth, to assess the nature, extent, and significance of contacts between and within Africa and the areas of the diaspora.

The 1770s and 1780s were critical decades in African diaspora history. The key year was 1787. Its significance was twofold: first, because of European decisions about Africans in Europe and America; second, because of the decisions and actions Africans in the Americas were taking. In 1787 Americans wrote into their constitution a provision that permitted the termination of the slave trade in 1807. The consequences of this act resulted in a more limited source of slaves, a federal subsidy for disposal of slaves liberated on the high seas, and cooperation with the American Colonization Society, which founded Liberia in 1821. In Europe in 1787, a group of English abolitionists completed plans for the resettlement in Africa of Africans residing in England. In the wake of the 1772 decision against slavery in England, some abolitionists believed they could found a society of free labor, develop trade in goods, spread Christianity, and contribute to the abolition of slavery and the slave trade in Africa by settling Africa with unwanted, Christianized Africans. Thus, in 1787 some four hundred Africans left to begin that experiment in Sierra Leone; shortly thereafter they were joined by a group from the United States who came by way of Nova Scotia, Canada. A third group from Jamaica, West Indies, followed a few years later.

It was also in 1787 that Africans in the United States were formally organizing their separate institutions: the church, which became the largest black organization in the country; the African lodges; the African Free Schools; and so on. Not only did all these institutions bear the African label, they also expressed interest in the welfare of Africans. Some of them, notably the churches and schools, became seriously involved in the development of a deepening consciousness of and cooperation with Africans in the Caribbean and Africa.

Between 1820 and 1860 there occurred what is sometimes called the first black renaissance in the United States, a period when blacks expressed themselves and their heritage in literature, art, music, and dance. It was also the era when black schools and churches, in particular, sent representatives to Africa and the Caribbean as teachers and preachers. In 1841 Edward Jones, the first black college graduate in the United States, became president of the recently established Fourah Bay College in Sierra Leone. This and other examples confirmed that a situation had developed in the United States that provided a pool of educated and concerned Africans for work in the diaspora and in Africa at a time when such opportunities were rarely available elsewhere.

Because Sierra Leone's repatriates were from England and the Americas, they valued Western culture and education. They enrolled their children in the several mission schools and sent their sons and daughters to English universities. In fact, the liberated African's desire for Western education, and the missionary's commitment to education to "civilize" Africans, had led to the founding of Fourah Bay College by the Church Missionary Society (CMS) in 1826. In 1876 a connection was established between Fourah Bay and Durham University, thereby bringing university education to Sierra Leone, where it became available to students across West Africa, especially British West Africa. In a very real sense, therefore, Western education, in general, and Fourah Bay College, in particular, distinguished Sierra Leone in Africa and the diaspora.[1]

The very nature of these developments, and the fact that the repatriated Africans had not come from that area originally, provided Sierra Leone with the unique opportunity of spearheading a Pan-African tradition. As the repatriates began migrating throughout West Africa in search of their families, a way back home, opportunities to expand their business interests, or, in the case of some, to spread the faith, they took with them aspects of Western education and culture. Those trained at Fourah Bay College were selected by British missionaries, merchants, and colonial officials to entrench British influence. At the same time, however, there were men like Samuel Crowther, who wrote books in the Nupe and Ibo languages and compiled a Yoruba dictionary; Samuel Johnson, who wrote the valuable *History of the Yorubas*; and Thomas Macaulay, father of Herbert and sometimes known as the father of Nigerian nationalism. These were all either repatriates or their descendants and were graduates of Fourah Bay College. Many other examples could be given to show that although they were sometimes exploited for European purposes, the repatriated Africans still forged links in West Africa that broadened the horizons and expanded the channels of communication of several local societies, and thus facilitated Sierra Leone's role in this early Pan-Africanist tradition before a strong, independent base had emerged.

Sierra Leone's experiment had a significant impact on groups in the United States, although repatriation took a somewhat different course. Africans had on their own, early in the eighteenth century, petitioned for freedom and a return to Africa. But the real black repatriationist was Paul Cuffe, that black shipper who organized groups in the United States and Sierra Leone to assist in his efforts to settle Africans from the United States in that colony. He himself financed the settlement of thirty-eight persons in 1815. Cuffe's efforts and the success of Sierra Leone demonstrated the feasibility of black settlement in Africa. Within a few years, colonization schemes to rid America of free Africans became a serious concern of white Americans.

In the United States slave society, Africans were forbidden to speak their language or practice their religion; free blacks were denied many of the rights of freedom. In addition, with the independence of Haiti in 1804, many slave owners in the United States and the Caribbean referred to that black state as the "Black Menace," which could cause blacks elsewhere to revolt for freedom. For these and other reasons, many ordinary and prominent white Americans joined efforts that resulted in the organization of a society to settle "free" blacks in Africa. This endeavor led to the founding of Liberia.

Liberia's development was similar in several aspects to that of Sierra Leone, but there are some differences. First, although the overall number of Liberian settlers was much smaller than Sierra Leone's, the great majority in Liberia had previously resided in the United States. Second, although most of the Liberian settlers were poor, a significant number of them had been born free, were educated, and had owned property in the United States. Their connections with America were, thus, very real and strong. It is not surprising, therefore, that many of Liberia's institutions were patterned after American ones. In addition to the churches, the University of Liberia helped to prepare Liberians as agents of social change, Western-style, as Fourah Bay College was doing in Sierra Leone. But more than in Sierra Leone, Liberian settlers took greater responsibility for their own physical and social survival, which led to their independence in 1847.

With independence, Liberia became unique in Africa and in the diaspora. Not only was Liberia the result of repatriation of Africans from abroad, it also became the only internationally recognized independent black state in Africa until well into the twentieth century. And precisely because of its unique status and history, Liberia became a symbol of hope for many at home and abroad. The pioneer Liberians viewed their venture as an opportunity to exercise their freedom, and within a few years their leaders envisioned the country as destined to become a "province of freedom" for the uplift of all persons of African ancestry. The Liberian constitution noted that the object of forming the state was "to provide a home for the dispersed and oppressed children of Africa." Even more than the case of Sierra Leone, the Liberian situation facilitated continued close relations with Africans overseas, especially in America. The story here is well known: Joseph Roberts from the United States became the first president; John Russwurm, who cofounded with Samuel Cornish the first Afro-American newspaper in the United States, also founded the first newspaper in Liberia, the *Liberian Herald*; John Day left the United States to become the country's chief justice; and Edward Blyden, from the West Indies, became Liberia's most distinguished citizen, as publisher, diplomat, minister of state, and intellectual.[2]

Although Blyden is well known, he deserves special attention. His efforts on behalf of unity and freedom for Africa ranged across West Africa, as he held posts in Liberia, Sierra Leone, and Nigeria. His popular appeal to persons of African descent was extended to the diaspora and to the indigenous peoples on the continent. Blyden wanted to make Liberia College (the second Western-style college in Africa) one in which African religion, political systems, and other customs could be studied; and in this sense, he became the major proponent of black studies at the national and international levels. Later, he pioneered a synthesis of African and Western culture, a task that he realized would require the dedication and labor of large numbers of educated and skilled Africans from the diaspora. We will never know whether his objectives and the Liberian goals might have been achieved because the thrust of the nineteenth-century colonial rule diverted and delayed those efforts from establishing tangible and lasting ties between Africa and the American diaspora. Marcus Garvey through his Universal Negro Improvement Association, W. E. B. Du Bois and others through the several Pan-African congresses, the Harlem Renaissance, and Negritude movements, and the Nation of Islam (Black Muslims) continued that trend in the twentieth century and had a significant impact on nationalism in West Africa.[3]

The Brazilian returnees to West Africa are discussed in a later essay by Dr. Boadi-Siaw. However, it is important to note here that those returnees came voluntarily from communities in Brazil that had retained Yoruba language and culture. Indeed, other African cultural influences persisted in Brazil. Thus, the Brazilian returnees not only retained much of their Africanity, they could identify with the area to which they returned, unlike the returnees to Sierra Leone and Liberia. To be sure, they had adopted aspects of Portuguese culture and had not escaped the idea of redemption that motivated so many returnees. They regarded themselves as special agents of cultural change and were regarded by some as "half-baked Europeans," but, as Boadi-Siaw notes, they nonetheless combined their European and African ideas and skills and made notable contributions to Ghana, Togo, Benin, and Nigeria.[4]

Let us now examine developments on the other side of the continent, where the Indian Ocean slave trade was many centuries older than that of the Atlantic, and where Africans had been planted at various points in Asia from the Middle East probably as far as China since the first or second century A.D., if not earlier. These are episodes that require more extensive examination by researchers, for by the time of my own research—which focused on the nineteenth century primarily—African communities were already centuries old in India, Turkey, Arabia, Iraq, Iran, Yemen, Pakistan, China, and possibly elsewhere.[5]

In India, for example, frequent references to Africans may be found in records from the thirteenth century. Groups of Africans (referred to in Asia as *Habshis* and *Siddis*) revolted in Bengal, India, during the latter part of the fifteenth century and established control there for a few years before finally suffering defeat. During the sixteenth and seventeenth centuries, Africans in western India, Gujarat in particular, emerged in positions of prominence in military and administrative affairs. One such person was Malik Ambar, sold as a slave in Ethiopia, in Mocha, in Baghdad and finally in India in 1575. Malik Ambar had been taught clerical skills in Arabia and later was placed in important clerical positions in the Deccan. Because of his loyalty and military skills, he eventually became a commander of the slave guard in Ahmadnagar. Malik Ambar commanded a unit of a thousand African soldiers and built auxiliary units of Asians; with these two groups he seized power and emerged as the undisputed leader of the Ahmadnagar area between 1602 and 1626. In this role he prevented the Great Mughuls of Delhi from conquering the Deccan for more than a quarter of a century.[6]

Other groups of Africans became prominent on Janjira Island, some forty miles south of Bombay. They claim descent from Ethiopians and have several legends to support their claim. In any case, it appears that most of these people arrived by way of the Indian Ocean slave trade. By the seventeenth century the community had become large enough and had built a fleet strong enough to command control over the area between Bombay and Goa; they were therefore sought as allies not only by local Indian groups, Mughuls and Marathas, but also by European merchants—Dutch, Portuguese, and British. At various times during the seventeenth and eighteenth centuries the Janjira Africans played one group against the other and received subsidies to keep open the sea lanes around Bombay. However, when the economic and political stakes became higher during the eighteenth century, Britain invaded the island, destroyed the fleet, and declared it a colony in 1834.[7]

A different kind of African community in Asia sprang from the abolitionist campaign of the nineteenth century. Between 1820 and 1873, after the legal abolition of the West African slave trade in 1807, Britain negotiated a series of abolitionist treaties with Asian and African sovereigns. In addition to suppressing the slave trade, the British also pressed for the liberation of slaves on the Asian continent itself—and had a measure of success. Thus, Africans liberated from ships on the seas and those freed on the Asian main-land were channeled to three depots for settlement: Aden in Arabia, Bombay in India, and the Seychelles in the Indian Ocean. These places had long been frequented by Africans, and they attracted others seeking the economic and social security these depots provided during the nineteenth century.[8]

Africans resided in Bombay at least as early as the eighteenth century, when British merchants also engaged in the slave trade to India. Several documents refer to British cruiser commanders complaining about the difficulty of con-trolling the "Madagascar slaves." The British East India Company purchased, trained, and advertised Africans as contract slaves in the eighteenth century. And in the latter part of the century, an official British abstract listing persons who could be called on to defend Bombay included nearly a thousand Africans.

As a depot for liberated Africans, Bombay received its first allotment in 1835. That year a group of 200 African children came from Karachi and was sent to Bombay's police commissioner to place them among families, in employment, or in charitable institutions. From that time until the 1870s at least, European and Indian families in Bombay requested and received liber-ated Africans as domestics. In addition, the British navy in India enlisted so many liberated Africans that by the 1850s the government observed that the majority of its seamen were Africans.

Mission stations also accepted liberated Africans in India. The principal sta-tions were the Roman Catholic orphanage at Bandora, the American mission at Poona, and the Church Missionary Society (CMS) African Asylum at Nasik. In these cases the government contributed a monthly allowance for the chil-dren's upkeep. Thus, by the time of the Treaty of 1873, the East African slave trade was legally ended. When Bartle Frere recommended the establishment of settlements of liberated Africans on the East African coast, liberated Africans in India were prepared to return and make a meaningful contribution to East Africa.

The CMS mission at Nasik, in particular, was called on to provide the initial group. Nasik had been established in 1854 by the Reverend William Price with initial funds from fines imposed on convicted slave dealers in India. In 1857, the government of India began making annual awards from the public rev-enues. As a center for liberated African children, its responsibilities included the conduct of a school that taught history, geography, English, arithmetic, and Bible studies; in addition, the girls were trained in sewing and cooking, while the boys were trained as blacksmiths, carpenters, masons, and printers. At that time it was thought that the Africans should be prepared to seek jobs in addi-tion to their missionary work. David Livingstone was one of the staunch sup-porters of the school. In 1865 he visited the school and returned to Africa with nine of the boys, one of whom was with him when he died.[9]

Now, let us turn to the Kenya connection. In 1874, the CMS sent William Price, who had established the program at Nasik, to organize the station in Mombasa. Prior arrangements had already been undertaken as early as 1864 when William Henry Jones, who had been rescued as a slave and landed at Nasik in 1854, was sent to Mombasa to join Johann Rebmann, the CMS missionary. While on the coast, Jones visited several areas, including Zanzibar, to explore the possibilities of establishing mission stations for the resettlement of liberated Africans. He returned to Bombay in 1871 and appealed to Africans to return to the coast and to Zanzibar under the auspices of the CMS. Clearly, therefore, the movement to return was already in motion when Frere recommended that liberated and captured Africans be repatriated at Mombasa.[10]

The history of Nasik led to the selection of William Price, the former superintendent, to supervise the establishment of the community at Mombasa, which came to be known as Freretown and was patterned after Nasik. The aims of the CMS project were to form an industrial Christian settlement of liberated Africans at Freretown and Rabai, and to expand toward Kilimanjaro. To accomplish these objectives, a church and a school were built, and William Jones, Ismael Semler, David George, and their wives, all Africans formerly at the Nasik school became Price's principal assistants. They were joined later by others from the Bombay area, who, thus, have become known in some quarters as Bombay Africans, Bombay boys, and Nasik boys.[11]

The early settler Africans became pioneers in the Freretown settlement. They helped to set the cultural tone and substance of the community through their leadership roles in the churches, schools, media, trade unions, crafts, and civil service; and neighboring Africans, Europeans, Arabs, and Indians in Kenya viewed the Christian community of Freretown as an influential outpost of Western society.[12]

Freretown poses some contrasts to Sierra Leone and Liberia. First, unlike the two West African examples, Freretown was founded by repatriated Africans who, for the most part, were born in Africa, and who had been away only for up to twenty years before returning. They, therefore, retained much more of their culture, especially language (they spoke Swahili and some of the vernaculars); they also had not been abroad long enough to sever ties with families and friends (indeed, some among them were reunited with members of their families and friends at Freretown, and Rabai). In addition, because those who returned came from a mission station apart from Indian society, they had not been exposed to any great extent to the wider Indian community and, therefore, had little reason to identify with it, though several of them had been taught the Hindostani and Gujarati languages.

However, like their West African counterparts in Liberia and Sierra Leone, the Bombay group had had significant exposure to Western cultural values for up to a maximum of twenty years. They were Christians, spoke English, adopted European dress, and acquired skills as blacksmiths, carpenters, masons, and tailors. Some of them gained experience as railroad and dock workers. All of these activities made them attractive potential for European missionaries propagating the faith, for merchants expanding their businesses, for explorers venturing into the interior, and for colonial officials entrenching colonial rule. Thus, some of the repatriated Africans became missionaries who settled widely along the coast, establishing mission stations. The Imperial British East Africa Company (IBEA) and other businesses made use of repatriated Africans as clerks and interpreters, while explorers employed them to accompany caravans into the interior and relied heavily on their accounts of inland societies. William Jones, for example, accompanied Bishop Hannington to Uganda. In addition to returning with news of Hannington's death, Jones also provided valuable information on the state of affairs between the coast and Uganda.

With the establishment of colonial rule, people of Freretown were employed as clerks, interpreters, and advisers in the courts, post office, and other agencies. Indeed, one of the few highly qualified printers, African or otherwise, on the coast in the 1920s was James "Jimmy" Jones, son of William Jones.

No one at Freretown really compares with Blyden of Liberia, but there are some similarities with William Jones. He was an ex-slave who was reared in the Indian mission, where he received a good Western education. Like Blyden, he made several trips from Africa to India to encourage Africans to return to the continent. There seems to be no record of the number who responded to his appeals, but he must be given credit for having been responsible for encouraging some of the several hundred who ultimately joined the community directly from India. In Freretown and Rabai, Jones stimulated pride in Africans and provided a rationale for the responsible involvement of the liberated community on behalf of Africans, especially on the matter of slavery and human dignity. For this stance, Jones was denounced by his fellow European missionaries, but he became a hero to Africans.

Because of their background in a Western setting, the pioneer settlers in Freretown, Sierra Leone, and Liberia identified themselves with European culture and ideas. However, because of the great numbers of other Africans who also accepted Christianity and European ways, intermarriages occurred and—as in Sierra Leone—there emerged the Creole society, which represented a blend of African and European beliefs, languages, cuisine, and so on. This group, thus, became exclusive and achieved the greatest mobility in trade and Western-style professions, where Africans could earn the most money. This also happened in Liberia, where the repatriates believed that theirs was the task of redeeming Africa, which meant a special position for them in the country's affairs. In Liberia the strong impact of American racial denigration of blacks as well as the development of the "providential design" concept caused the "Americo-Liberians" to have a greater commitment to the gradual uplift of the masses than the other areas, especially after independence, which—at least theoretically—provided for greater authority in policy formulation for Liberians. A compulsory educational system to facilitate national integration did emerge in principle in the nineteenth century and slowly proceeded to incorporate other ethnic groups in Western-style activities.

Unlike Liberia, Sierra Leone remained a colony on which Britain placed some priority in Africa. Thus, Creoles received appointments to civil service posts and seats in the executive and legislative councils not only in Sierra Leone but also in other British West African colonies.[13] However, from 1896 when the British declared a colony over the hinterland, Creole fortunes diminished because interior peoples, the Mende and Temne in particular, regarded the Creoles as "black Englishmen."[14] The British then proceeded to limit Creole influence in the colony by restricting the expansion of Christianity in the hinterland and by appointing Englishmen to posts formerly held by the Creoles on the coast. This policy assured greater ethnic particularity.

At the same time, Creole merchants had to compete with European merchants whose presence in Africa increased perceptibly during the last quarter of the nineteenth century. And while the Creole community's influence in Sierra Leone declined during this period, and distrust between them and indigenous Africans increased, one should also note that Creole influence on business, education, journalism, the civil service, and other areas was deeply imprinted in neighboring countries of West Africa. The same imprint was made by Freretownians in Kenya and to lesser degrees in Uganda, Tanganyika and Zanzibar (Tanzania).

In Freretown there developed a generally steadier trend of identification with neighboring peoples than in either Sierra Leone or Liberia at the early stage of growth. This was probably because Freretownians had not been as completely alienated from the area as their West African counterparts had been and thus could more easily understand the indigenous groups. Certainly this was evident in their language. In addition, better preparations had been made for the return to Africa, which may have resulted in part from prior knowledge of the West African experiences. Jones had surveyed the area, and Frere discussed plans and negotiated an agreement with Arabs on the coast, and they readily accepted the idea and eventually benefited from the community's presence in such things as trade, medicine, and education. The Arab School in Mombasa drew on the Freretown community for some of its teachers in the 1920s, 1930s, and later. Freretownians thus served as a social and economic bridge between Africans and Arabs on the coast.[15]

Further, several of the local missionaries tolerated (and some, especially the Africans, welcomed) the presence of their brothers fleeing slavery. In addition, neighboring Africans were attracted to Freretown for education and economic survival, especially during the several famines of the 1880s and 1890s, and for security (particularly those running away from slavery). The close identification of the area with Swahili culture also facilitated the eventual development of closer cohesion among the repatriates, refugees, and indigenous Africans. Very early, therefore, Freretown became a mixture of several ethnic groups, and although the first settlers were viewed as, and considered themselves, a kind of elite, the fact is that they soon recognized that the Europeans, Arabs, and Asians did not accord them equality but regarded them as inferior, though a step above indigenous Africans. These factors had the effect of facilitating a fusion into the larger African community, a process that continues today.

The Freretown settlers never constituted a large group and were always dependent not only on the European missionaries but also on good relations with their neighbors, among whom they missionized and taught. Indeed, by the turn of the century, the "Bombay group" as a class had greatly diminished, as they moved to coastal towns and into the interior, fusing with other groups. Some of them migrated because of grievances against the white missionaries; others sought economic opportunities in the towns; still others joined different million stations. Today, therefore, the descendants of the first settlers are widely scattered on the coast, with only a few remaining in Freretown proper.

Many of the migrating Freretownians became teachers in various parts of the country. It is probably no exaggeration to say that most Africans educated in Kenya prior to World War II were taught by Freretownians or Freretown-trained teachers, and most Christian Africans in Kenya probably had close contact with Freretown. The Freretown Divinity School was the main source of primary and secondary education in the country until 1931, when it was relocated near Nairobi at Limuru. This educational and missionary influence was also spread in neighboring Tanganyika and Zanzibar (Tanzania), and Uganda; and Freretownians were also among the first pioneering Kenyan journalists, radio announcers, and trade unionists, especially among the Africans of Mombasa.

The first national political party among Kenya Africans, KASU/KAU (Kenya African Study Union/Kenya African Union), was founded by several repatriates, including Francis Khamisi, the first general secretary; Thomas Mbotela, assistant general secretary and later vice president under Jomo Kenyatra; and "Jimmy" Jeremiah; all from the Freretown tradition. Other leaders then and later received their education and had close contacts with Freretown. Indeed, the influence of ideas such as multiracialism, nonviolence, and a constitutional approach to independence became major objectives of KAU until late 1951, in large measure because of the impact of these men. It is noteworthy that when Jomo Kenyatta returned to Kenya in 1947 after many years abroad, his leadership depended on assistants who knew the country—the Europeans, Africans, and Asians—who could communicate easily in English and local languages and who had a "national image" to underscore the national character of the party. The Freretownians met those criteria better than anyone else and emerged as key party leaders until Mau Mau ushered in a more radical approach to replace the moderate, constitutional approach pursued by the repatriates and others.

In conclusion, Sierra Leone, Liberia, and Freretown are examples of an important physical return of African people from the diaspora to Africa, thereby greatly influencing not only their immediate settlements but surrounding societies as well. Whether the repatriates served as teachers or civil servants, doctors or trade unionists, journalists or politicians, they were conveyors of ideas and skills necessary to modernize Africa. Their contribution to the development of managerial skills and conceptual approaches necessary to understand international problems and interrelationships greatly accelerated modern freedom movements and the emergence of a national consciousness in several African states. This is not an argument that these developments would not have occurred without the returnees; it is an argument that they did occur with critical assistance from the diaspora.

The black returnees could not escape the influence of their physical and social environment abroad. That influence not only accounted for the contributions they made as returnees in Africa but also facilitated their continued links with the diaspora. Although their language and life-styles changed and their values and goals were modified, traces of several African languages persist in the Guianas and the islands of the southeastern United States; Yoruba became widely spoken in parts of Brazil; Swahili was planted in India; and Creole emerged in Africa and several diaspora communities. Indeed, evidence of cultural continuity continues to be uncovered, and it is likely that the continuity in substance rather than form is even greater. Without a doubt, therefore, cultural as well as biological links were forged between Africa and the diaspora communities, and those links facilitated a meaningful return to Africa.

Whether in music or literature, social or economic relations, military or political achievements, Africans in the diaspora have been major contributors to their adopted societies, in spite of inhibiting racial prejudices on the part of Euro-Americans. Perhaps the greatest contribution of Africans abroad was labor, which facilitated the accumulation of capital, the advance of technology, the internationalization of banking and insurance, and the general administrative organization, especially in the West, but also in the Persian Gulf region and southern Asia, where much additional research is needed.

In conclusion, Sierra Leone, Liberia, Freretown, and the scattered areas in Ghana, Togo, Benin, and Nigeria are examples of an important physical return. This comparative approach clearly has potential for the reconstruction of the history of Africa and its influence abroad; it also promises to provide a more realistic perspective on the history of Africa as well as the areas in which the African presence was established—Europe, the Americas, and Asia.

Notes

1. Many sources consider this subject: Christopher Fyfe, *A History of Sierra Leone* (London: Oxford University Press, 1962); John Peterson, *Province of Freedom: A History of Sierra Leone* (Evanston: University of Illinois Press, 1969); Johnson U. J. Asiegbu, *Slavery and the Politics of Liberation, 1787–1861* (New York: Longmans, 1969); Arthur Porter, *Creoledom* (New York, 1963); Leo Spitzer, *The Creoles of Sierra Leone: Responses to Colonialism, 1870–1945* (Madison: University of Wisconsin Press, 1974); Jean H. Kopytoff, *A Preface to Modern Nigeria: The Sierra Leoneans in Yoruba, 1880–1890* (Madison: University of Wisconsin Press, 1965); Kenneth L. Little, "The Significance of the West African Creole for Africanist and Afro-American Studies," *African Affairs* 49, 197 (1950); John D. Hargreaves, "African Colonization in the 19th Century: Liberia and Sierra Leone," *Sierra Leone Studies* 4.

2. The following are sources on Liberia: Raymond Buell, *Liberia: A Century of Survival, 1847–1947* (Philadelphia, 1947); Merran Fraenkel, *Tribe and Class in Monrovia* (New York: Oxford, 1964); Hollis Lynch, *Edward Wilmot Blyden: Pan Negro Patriot* (London: Oxford University Press, 1967); C. L. Simpson, *The Symbol of Liberia* (London: Oxford University Press, 1961); and several issues of *The Liberian Historical Review*.

3. These developments have received much scholarly and popular attention and do not need extended discussion here, especially since some of the contributors to this volume consider the topic.

4. See S. Y. Boadi-Siaw.

5. This is a largely unexplored dimension of the African diaspora. Consequently, most of the published sources are those of the author: Joseph E. Harris, *The African Presence in Asia: Consquences of the East African Slave Trade* (Evanston, Ill.: Northwestern University Press, 1971); *Abolition and Repatriation in Kenya* (Historical Association of Kenya, East African Publishing House, Nairobi, Kenya, 1977); "The Black Peoples of Asia," *World Encyclopedia of Black Peoples* (Scholarly Press, 1975); *Recollections of James Juma Mbotela* (East African Publishing House, Nairobi, Kenya, 1977).

6. Harris, *The African Presence in Asia* 87–98; Sheikh Chand, *Malik Ambar* (Hyderabad, 1931) in Urdu; D. R. Seth, "The Life and Times of Malik Ambar," *Islamic Culture: An English Quarterly* 31 (Hyderabad, January 1957); Bena Rasi Prasad Saksena, "Malik Ambar," *Hindustani Academy* 4 (October 1933), in Hindi; M. S. Commissariat, *A History of Gujarat* (Calcutta, 1957); E. Denison Ross, *An Arabic History of Gujarat* (London, 1921).

7. D. R. Banaji, *Bombay and the Siddis* (Bombay, 1933); R. V. Ramdas, "Relations between the Marathas and the Siddis of Janjira" (Ph.D. diss., University of Bombay, n.d.); Harris, *The African Presence in Asia*, 80–87.

8. India, Political Department, "Report on the Emigration of Siddhies of Hyderabad" (December 1882) 1; 110–13; Harris, *The African Presence in Asia*, 99–114.

9. Harris, *Abolition and Repatriation*, 19.

10. Ibid., 20.

11. Ibid., 21.

12. James Juma Mbotela, *The Freeing of the Slaves in East Africa* (London: Oxford, 1956) and in Swahili, *Uhuru wa Watumwa* (London: Oxford, 1934).

13. Kopytoff, *Preface to Modern Nigeria*; I. K. Sundiata, "Creolization on Fernando Po: The Nature of Society," *The African Diaspora: Interpretive Essays* (Cambridge: Harvard University Press, 1976).

14. Akintola Wyse modifies this characterization. See page 357 of this volume.

15. For a fuller discussion of this and the remainder of this section before the conclusion, see Joseph E. Harris, *Repatriates and Refugees in a Colonial Society: The Case of Kenya* (Washington, D. C.: Howard University Press, 1982).

African Roots of the African American Family
Joseph White

The Deficit-Deficiency Model

The view of the core structure of the Black family as an extended family group-ing is not shared by all observers. The traditional view of the Black family, which has evolved from the works of Frazier (1939), Elkins (1968), Moynihan (1965), and Rainwater (1970), is one of a disorganized, single-parent, subnu-clear, female-dominated social system. This is essentially the deficit-deficiency model of Black family life. The deficit-deficiency model begins with the his-torical assumption that there was no carry-over from Africa to America of any sophisticated African-based form of family life and communal living. Viable patterns of family life either did not exist because Africans were incapable of creating them, or they were destroyed beginning with slavery and the separa-tion of biological parents and children, forced breeding, the master's sexual exploitation of Black women, and the accumulative effects of three hundred years of economic and social discrimination. As a result of this background of servitude, deprivation, second-class citizenship, and chronic unemployment, Black adults have not been able to develop marketable skills, self-sufficiency, future orientation, and planning and decision-making competencies, instru-mental behaviors thought to be necessary for sustaining a successful two-parent nuclear family while guiding the children through the socialization process.

In a society that placed a premium on decisive male leadership in the fam-ily, the Black male was portrayed as lacking the masculine sex role behaviors characterized by logical thinking, willingness to take responsibility for oth-ers, assertiveness, managerial skills, achievement orientation, and occupa-tional mastery. The Black male in essence had been psychologically castrated and rendered ineffective by forces beyond his control. He is absent within the family circle and unable to provide leadership and command respect when he is present. After generations of being unable to achieve the ideal male role in the family and in American society, the Black male is likely to be inclined to compensate for his failure by pursuing roles such as the pimp, player, hustler, and sweet daddy, which are in conflict with the norms of the larger society. The appearance of these roles in male behavior in the Black community, rather than being interpreted as a form of social protest, reinforces the majority culture stereotypes of Black males as irresponsible, lazy, shiftless, and sociopathic.

The Black woman does not fare much better in terms of how she is portrayed in the deficit-deficiency model of Black family life. She is regarded as the head of the household, a matriarch who initially received her power because the society was unwilling to permit the Black male to assume the legal, economic, and social positions necessary to become a dominant force within the family and community life. Having achieved this power by default, the Black female is unwilling to share it. Her unwillingness to share her power persists even when the Black male is present and willing to assume responsibility in the family circle, since she is not confident of the male's ability to follow through on his commitments. Confrontation over decision making and family direction is usually not necessary because the Black male is either not present in the household on any ongoing basis or is regarded as ineffective by the female when he is present.

The proponents of the pathology-oriented, matriarchal family model did not consider the possibility that a single-parent Black mother could serve as an adequate role model for the children of both sexes. The notion that the mother could reflect a balance of the traditional male and female roles, with respect to mental toughness and emotional tenderness, was largely ignored because of the rigid classification of psychosexual roles in American society. In the Black community, however, the categorization of social role behaviors based on gender is not as inflexible. It is conceivable that a Black mother could project a combination of assertive and nurturant behaviors in the process of rearing children of both sexes as nonsexist adults.

With the reality of accelerating divorce rates, in recent years the single-parent family headed by a woman has become a social reality in Euro-America. This reality has been accompanied by an attempt on the part of social scientists to legitimate family structures that represent alternatives to the nuclear family while reconceptualizing the social roles of males and females with less emphasis on exclusive behaviors. The concept of androgyny has been introduced to cover the vast pool of human personality traits that can be developed by either sex (Rogers, 1978). A well-balanced person reflects a combination of both instrumental and expressive traits. The latter include feeling-oriented behaviors formerly considered feminine, such as tenderness, caring, and affection. Thus, it is conceptually possible for a white, single, and androgynous female parent to rear psychologically healthy, emotionally integrated children. It is interesting how the sociology of the times makes available to white Americans psychological concepts designed to legitimize changes in the family, in child-rearing patterns, and in relationships between the sexes. Yet, these same behaviors when first expressed by Afro-Americans were considered as pathological.

The Extended Family Model

The extended family, in contrast to the single-parent subnuclear family, consists of a related and quasi-related group of adults, including aunts, uncles, parents, cousins, grandparents, boyfriends, and girlfriends linked together in a kinship or kinlike network. They form a cooperative interface with each other in confronting the concerns of living and rearing the children. This model of family life, which seems able to capture not only the strength, vitality, resilience, and continuity of the Black family, but also the essence of Black values, folkways, and life styles, begins with a different set of assumptions about the development and evolution of Black family life in America.

The Black extended family is seen as an outgrowth of African patterns of family and community life that survived in America. The Africans carried with them through the Mid-Atlantic passage and sale to the initial slave owners a well-developed pattern of kinship, exogamous mating, and communal values, emphasizing collective survival, mutual aid, cooperation, mutual solidarity, interdependence, and responsibility for others (Nobles, 1974; Blassingame, 1972). These values became the basis for the Black extended family in America. They were retained because they were familiar and they allowed the slaves to have some power over destiny by enabling them to develop their own styles for family interaction. A consciousness of closeness to others, belongingness, and togetherness protected the slave from being psychologically destroyed by feelings of despair and alienation and the extended family provided a vehicle to pass the heritage on to the children (Fredrickson, 1976; Gutman, 1976). Slaves in essence created their own communal family space, regardless of whether the master was paternalistic or conducted a Nazi-like concentration camp.

To understand the cultural continuity, it is necessary to depart from the traditional hypothesis that slave masters and their descendants exercised total psychological and social control over the development of Black family life and community institutions. The slaves were much more than empty psychological tablets on which the master imprinted an identity. These early Blacks were able to find ways of creating psychological space and implementing African cultural forms that whites were unaware of and did not understand. Once in the New World the African recreated a sense of tribal community within the plantation milieu through a series of extended kin and kinlike family networks that carried on the cultural values of responsibility for others, mutual aid, and collective survival. First- and second-generation American slaves who were separated from biological kin by continued activity at the auction block and newly arriving slaves who were sold to different plantations were incorporated into the extended family structures of existing plantations. It was not essential for the survival of African conceptions of family life that biological or legal kinship ties be maintained. When a people share a philosophy of interdependence and collective survival, persons who are not biologically or legally related can become interwoven into newly created and existing kin-like networks. Cultural patterns once established seem to endure, especially if they work. The extended family survived because it provided Afro-Americans a support system within the context of a shared frame of reference. Along with other African customs and beliefs, an African family identity was passed along to the children as the link between generations through the oral tradition.

Once the philosophy of collective survival and interdependence was set into place as the foundation for community living, the extended family evolved through a series of cycles of formation, breakup, and reformation as the slaves who were without the recourse to legal rights to protect kinship structures and conjugal unions were transferred from place to place. Much later, with the beginnings of the Industrial Revolution after the Civil War, the pattern of Black family life based on combinations of kinship and kinlike networks continued, despite the emergence of the nuclear family among Euro-Americans. The growth of the individual nuclear family in Euro-America seemed to correspond with the competitive and individualistic values of the market place. The cycles of formation, breakup, and reformation of the extended family continued as Blacks migrated farther north and west towards the cities at the turn of the century during the pre and post periods of the two world wars and into the modern age.

The Black extended family, with its grandparents, biological parents, conjugal partners, aunts, uncles, cousins, older siblings, boyfriends, girlfriends, and quasi-kin, is an intergenerational group. The members of this three-generation family do not necessarily reside in the same household. Individual households are part of a sociofamilial network that functions like a minicommunity. The members band together to share information, resources, and communal concern (Stack, 1974). There is no central authority, matriarchal or patriarchal. Decisions are made on an equalitarian model with input and outcomes determined by who is available at a given time, who has expertise with reference to a given problem, and one's prior experience and track record in decision making. This is likely to give some edge to the tribal elders. They are looked up to within the extended family network as resource people and advisors because they have the life experience that is highly valued in the Black community. As in the past, the family is held together over time and across geographical space by a shared experience frame and a common set of values involving interdependence, mutual aid, resilience, communalism, and collective responsibility (Nobles, 1978). These values transcend sex roles and allow both men and women to participate in and contribute to the management of economic resources, child rearing, community activism, and other issues of family life without being categorically restricted on the basis of gender. The fluid distinction between social sex roles offers both men and women in the Black family network the opportunity to emerge as decision makers, influence molders, and household managers.

It could be argued that the Black extended family exists and persists primarily because Black people face the common fate of oppressive economic and social conditions, that it exists out of necessity as a way of surviving in an oppressive class system. Politically and economically oppressed people have historically banded together for survival, whether it be in internment camps, labor unions, or women's movements. It would follow from this argument that the Black extended family would disappear as Black people moved up the socioeconomic ladder. Yet the extended family does not appear to be disappearing with rising economic fortunes. McAdoo's (1979) work with upwardly mobile middle and upper-middle class Black families suggests that not only does the extended family model persist when Blacks move up the socioeconomic ladder but the Afro-American values of mutual aid, interdependence, and interconnectedness also remain as the guiding ethos of family existence.

Being part of a close-knit extended family group is a vital part of Afro-American life. Wherever Blacks appear in numbers of two or more, whether it be on predominantly white college campuses, professional baseball teams, fraternal groups, street corners, storefront churches, automobile factories, or professional conferences, they soon seem to form a quasi-family network, share information and resources, get together, git down, rap, and party. White folks don't know what to make of this. The idea of sharing closeness, and interdependence expressed in sociofamilial groups is so deeply ingrained in the fabric of the Afro-American ethos that it is not likely to give way to the nuclear family with its stress on isolation, competition, and independence. If anything, the traditional nuclear family may be moving toward becoming more like the Afro-American extended family.

Works Cited

Blassingame, John. *The Slave Community.* New York: Oxford University Press, 1972.

Elkins, Stanley. *Slavery: A Problem in American Institutions and Intellectual Life.* Chicago: University of Chicago Press, 1968.

Frazier, E. Franklin. *The Negro Family in the United States.* Chicago: University of Chicago Press, 1939.

Fredrickson, George. "The Gutman Report," *The New York Review*, September 30, 1976, pp. 18–22, 27.

Gutman, Herbert. *The Black Family in Slavery and Freedom, 1750–1925.* New York: Vintage Books, 1976.

McAdoo, Harriet. "Black Kinship," *Psychology Today,* May 1979, pp. 67–69, 79, 110.

Moynihan, Daniel Patrick. *The Negro Family: The Case for National Action,* Washington, D.C.: U.S. Government Printing Office, 1965.

Nobles, Wade. "Africanity: Its Role in Black Families," *The Black Scholar,* June 1974, pp. 10–17.

———. "Toward an Empirical and Theoretical Framework for Defining Black Families," *Journal of Marriage and Family,* November 1978, pp. 679–688.

Rainwater, Lee. *Behind Ghetto Walls: Black Family Life in a Federal Slum.* Chicago: Aldine, 1970.

Rogers, Dorothy. *Adolescence: A Psychological Perspective,* 2nd Edition. Monterey, Calif.: Brooks/Cole, 1978.

Stack, Carol. *All Our Kin: Strategies for Survival in a Black Community.* New York: Harper & Row, 1974.

The Transformation of Silence into Language and Action*
Audre Lorde

I have come to believe over and over again that what is most important to me must be spoken, made verbal and shared, even at the risk of having it bruised or misunderstood. That the speaking profits me, beyond any other effect. I am standing here as a Black lesbian poet, and the meaning of all that waits upon the fact that I am still alive, and might not have been. Less than two months ago I was told by two doctors, one female and one male, that I would have to have breast surgery, and that there was a 60 to 80 percent chance that the tumor was malignant. Between that telling and the actual surgery, there was a three-week period of the agony of an involuntary reorganization of my entire life. The surgery was completed, and the growth was benign.

But within those three weeks, I was forced to look upon myself and my living with a harsh and urgent clarity that has left me still shaken but much stronger. This is a situation faced by many women, by some of you here today. Some of what I experienced during that time has helped elucidate for me much of what I feel concerning the transformation of silence into language and action.

In becoming forcibly and essentially aware of my mortality, and of what I wished and wanted for my life, however short it might be, priorities and omissions became strongly etched in a merciless light, and what I most regretted were my silences. Of what had I *ever* been afraid? To question or to speak as I believed could have meant pain, or death. But we all hurt in so many different ways, all the time, and pain will either change or end. Death, on the other hand, is the final silence. And that might be coming quickly, now, without

---

* Paper delivered at the Modern Language Association's "Lesbian and Literature Panel," Chicago, Illinois, December 28, 1977. First published in *Sinister Wisdom 6* (1978) and *The Cancer Journals* (Spinsters, Ink, San Francisco, 1980).

regard for whether I had ever spoken what needed to be said, or had only betrayed myself into small silences, while I planned someday to speak, or waited for someone else's words. And I began to recognize a source of power within myself that comes from the knowledge that while it is most desirable not to be afraid, learning to put fear into a perspective gave me great strength.

I was going to die, if not sooner then later, whether or not I had ever spoken myself. My silences had not protected me. Your silence will not protect you. But for every real word spoken, for every attempt I had ever made to speak those truths for which I am still seeking, I had made contact with other women while we examined the words to fit a world in which we all believed, bridging our differences. And it was the concern and caring of all those women which gave me strength and enabled me to scrutinize the essentials of my living.

The women who sustained me through that period were Black and white, old and young, lesbian, bisexual, and heterosexual, and we all shared a war against the tyrannies of silence. They all gave me a strength and concern without which I could not have survived intact. Within those weeks of acute fear came the knowledge—within the war we are all waging with the forces of death, subtle and otherwise, conscious or not—I am not only a casualty, I am also a warrior.

What are the words you do not yet have? What do you need to say? What are the tyrannies you swallow day by day and attempt to make your own, until you will sicken and die of them, still in silence? Perhaps for some of you here today, I am the face of one of your fears. Because I am woman, because I am Black, because I am lesbian, because I am myself—a Black woman warrior poet doing my work—come to ask you, are you doing yours?

And of course I am afraid, because the transformation of silence into language and action is an act of self-revelation, and that always seems fraught with danger. But my daughter, when I told her of our topic and my difficulty with it, said, "Tell them about how you're never really a whole person if you remain silent, because there's always that one little piece inside you that wants to be spoken out, and if you keep ignoring it, it gets madder and madder and hotter and hotter, and if you don't speak it out one day it will just up and punch you in the mouth from the inside."

In the cause of silence, each of us draws the face of her own fear—fear of contempt, of censure, or some judgment, or recognition, of challenge, of annihilation. But most of all, I think, we fear the visibility without which we cannot truly live. Within this country where racial difference creates a constant, if unspoken, distortion of vision, Black women have on one hand always been highly visible, and so, on the other hand, have been rendered invisible through the depersonalization of racism. Even within the women's movement, we have had to fight, and still do, for that very visibility which also renders us most vulnerable, our Blackness. For to survive in the mouth of this dragon we call america, we have had to learn this first and most vital lesson—that we were never meant to survive. Not as human beings. And neither were most of you here today, Black or not. And that visibility which makes us most vulnerable is that which also is the source of our greatest strength. Because the machine will try to grind you into dust anyway, whether or not we speak. We can sit in our corners mute forever while our sisters and our selves are wasted, while our children are distorted and destroyed, while our earth is poisoned; we can sit in our safe corners mute as bottles, and we will still be no less afraid.

In my house this year we are celebrating the feast of Kwanza, the African-american festival of harvest which begins the day after Christmas and lasts for seven days. There are seven principles of Kwanza, one for each day. The first principle is Umoja, which means unity, the decision to strive for and maintain unity in self and community. The principle for yesterday, the second day, was Kujichagulia—self-determination—the decision to define ourselves, name ourselves, and speak for ourselves, instead of being defined and spoken for by others. Today is the third day of Kwanza, and the principle for today is Ujima—collective work and responsibility—the decision to build and maintain ourselves and our communities together and to recognize and solve our problems together.

Each of us is here now because in one way or another we share a commitment to language and to the power of language, and to the reclaiming of that language which has been made to work against us. In the transformation of silence into language and action, it is vitally necessary for each one of us to establish or examine her function in that transformation and to recognize her role as vital within that transformation.

For those of us who write, it is necessary to scrutinize not only the truth of what we speak, but the truth of that language by which we speak it. For others, it is to share and spread also those words that are meaningful to us. But primarily for us all, it is necessary to teach by living and speaking those truths which we believe and know beyond understanding. Because in this way alone we can survive, by taking part in a process of life that is creative and continuing, that is growth.

And it is never without fear—of visibility, of the harsh light of scrutiny and perhaps judgment, of pain, of death. But we have lived through all of those already, in silence, except death. And I remind myself all the time now that if I were to have been born mute, or had maintained an oath of silence my whole life long for safety, I would still have suffered, and I would still die. It is very good for establishing perspective.

And where the words of women are crying to be heard, we must each of us recognize our responsibility to seek those words out, to read them and share them and examine them in their pertinence to our lives. That we not hide behind the mockeries of separations that have been imposed upon us and which so often we accept as our own. For instance, "I can't possibly teach Black women's writing—their experience is so different from mine." Yet how many years have you spent teaching Plato and Shakespeare and Proust? Or another, "She's a white woman and what could she possibly have to say to me?" Or, "She's a lesbian, what would my husband say, or my chairman?" Or again, "This woman writes of her sons and I have no children." And all the other endless ways in which we rob ourselves of ourselves and each other.

We can learn to work and speak when we are afraid in the same way we have learned to work and speak when we are tired. For we have been socialized to respect fear more than our own needs for language and definition, and while we wait in silence for that final luxury of fearlessness, the weight of that silence will choke us.

The fact that we are here and that I speak these words is an attempt to break that silence and bridge some of those differences between us, for it is not difference which immobilizes us, but silence. And there are so many silences to be broken.

Hard Words and Clear Songs: The Writing of Black Poetry
Haki Madhubuti

Prologue

Writers write. What they write about tells the reader to what extent they are involved with the real world.

Writing for me is a difficult process. I write best under pressure, under a deadline set for me by someone or one that I set for myself. I am not a professional or leisure writer. I do not earn my livelihood from writing, nor do I allot special time in the day just to write. Much of my writing is notetaking. I take an abundance of notes and these notes, at a later time, are developed into poems, essays and occasional fiction. Writing for me is also a form of life-therapy, but it is not my life. My life is too complex to be limited to one stimulus.

Writers are questioners of the world and doers within the world. They question everything and are not satisfied with quick surface answers. Richard Wright was a questioner. We can see it in his works—the fiction and nonfiction. W.E.B. Du Bois was a questioner—his output was triple that of the "average" writer, but he always maintained a high level of quality and content. Both men were of the world, but in their own way refused to be subordinated to the world. They were fighters, always aware of the war, and writing was a war weapon. And writing at its best for them was a tool, a vocation, a hammer to be used for the survival and development of the Race.

Aims

The writer is also the lively but lonely investigator, the seeker of unknowns, the wanderer along back alleys, through power corridors, and into the far reaches of her or his own mind and that of his or her people. Essentially, the loneliness comes from the demands of the writing form; although there are exceptions, one usually does not write in a group. Writing is a personal occupation, one man or woman, one pen or typewriter. Once the writer leaves the research, the study, she or he does battle with the blank sheet of paper. The writer is alone. It is a lonely vocation that is bound to affect the writer and those closest to him or her. When the writer begins to work, the most important concern is the relationship between the writer and the subject. The central question becomes: How to bring life to the subject?

This process, above all, requires discipline. The creative process is a disciplined process which most writers have had to teach themselves. In most cases, as soon as the writing begins, the interruptions seem to multiply—these interruptions are both real and unreal. Each phone call is attacked or ignored because the writer is more, or less, sensitive to the uses of his or her time. Family relationships are altered during this period. Also, the book that could have been read easily two months ago becomes a *priority* now—not because the book is essential to the writer's subject, but because it becomes a part of the writer's internal interruptions. These types of interference are often rationalized as direct contributions to the writing. Nonsense. Writers waste time, as do most people; this is why discipline is so important.

In many ways all writers are re-creators. They take in the world and retell it, reinterpret it for others in a form and style that should be unique for them, the readers, and the times. These times are space age times, and words come and go like Chicago's weather. The way the writer uses the words tells as much about him or her as a word-user as anything else can. The major distinction that can be made between writers (other than forms they work in) is their ability to say the same thing differently, originally using and "misusing" the language at will. The language is the tool, the weapon, and writers must train themselves to use it as a carpenter trains to use wood and nails, or as a farmer trains to use the earth.

Writer and Teacher

Just as I am a writer, I am also a teacher, and one of the most important tasks that I have as a teacher is to demystify the act of writing, particularly as it applies to the writing of poetry. I have discovered through years of experience that one of the best ways to teach young people how to develop their interests in poetry is to use music and recorded poems as they engage in the writing act. Both of these approaches I find personally rewarding, and as a result, I am able to heighten the students' interests not only in content but in the poet's craft as well. By increasing their awareness of the form and structure of poetry, through a rigorous examination and discussion of poems, students are better able to understand that the poet—like other writers—does more than record first impressions. The students also come to recognize that the writing of poetry is a complicated process requiring all the skills needed by writers of other forms, plus additional ones as well. Most important, these students begin to perceive that the poet, just as other writers, must develop—or rather possess—a keen eye, catching and questioning everything, the largest and the smallest detail, and reproducing it in a condensed form that challenges the readers' minds and emotions.

I have found that many poems written by Afro-American poets can be used to serve this purpose. I find that as a teacher, I can take the best of these writers and use their works as examples of how young people can begin to fashion language into a memorable experience, a form that challenges the reader on several levels. After all, that is what poetry does.

The writers who provide the best examples are not necessarily the best. Yet most do have something to say and say it in a way that people can understand and relate to. Langston Hughes's work is an excellent example of style and content that black people can relate to. His jazz poetry and "simple" folk tales not only established him as a "professional" writer of the very best order, but earned him the title "Dean" of black writers from his own people. Sterling Brown also comes to mind in terms of original style and content; his poetry and essays exemplify the highest tradition of black oral communication combined with scholarly research. For me, the content is as important as the style. Beautiful writing that does not say anything is only that—beautiful writing. Yet, bad writing containing the most revolutionary ideas is equally—first and last—bad writing. A standard must be met if the writer is to communicate effectively. The ability to develop a style that is clear, original, and communicative is what separates writers from nonwriters.

There are many ways to make a poem "a memorable experience," Gwendolyn Brooks says. One can use images, that is pictures, visible pictures, which carry the characteristics of the subject or which suggest the meaning and mood the writer is trying to create. One of the strengths of using images and metaphors is that often they carry the weight of symbols; that is they suggest multiple levels of meaning to the reader as well as allow the reading of his or her own experience into the image or metaphor. Another important technique for making the poem a "memorable experience" is to create characters, real people with whom the reader can feel and empathize. In poetry, however, when creating characters, the poet should search for only those crucial characteristics which symbolize what the character is most essentially about. Images, metaphors, characters take on visibility and become memorable by the use of concrete details. The following are examples of what I mean.

> . . . Prophet Williams, young beyond St. Julia,
> and rich with Bible; pimples, pout; who reeks
> with lust for his disciple, is an engine
> or candid steel hugging combustibles.

Gwendolyn Brooks created this character in the poem *In the Mecca*. She is able to establish through suggestion the real character of Prophet Williams. She does this in part through concrete choice of metaphor. When she compares the prophet's passion (for his disciples) to an "engine of candid steel hugging combustibles," she is able to suggest, on the one hand, the great power, probably physical power, of the prophet, and on the other, the coldness and real dispassion or lack of passion of the prophet. In this case, then, the metaphor allows her to make several statements at the same time, using very few words (simple words).

In the long poem *In the Mecca*, Ms. Brooks chooses those select, concrete details which are crucial to an intimate understanding of that character. She says of Briggs, a young brother intimate with the neighborhood gang, "Briggs is adult as a stone." The stone as an image or metaphor for Briggs's development is most appropriate as it allows her to make several profound statements with only six simple words. A stone is hard as Briggs is hard. A stone does not grow as organic matter as human beings grow, thus suggesting Briggs has reached a point beyond which he cannot go. It also suggests a certain one-dimensional aspect of Briggs's character.

The Use of Words

The raw materials of the poet are the words and sounds. The right, most appropriate, most exact choice of words is part of what makes the experience of the poem memorable. The following examples from Ms. Brooks illustrate how the right word is specific and concrete in nature, yet often carries the massive power of the symbol (allowing each reader to be consciously directed into a myriad of experiences, emotions, and meanings). We see also from Sister Brooks (again, *In the Mecca*) that this appropriate choice of the exact word need not be a long, multisyllabic, "difficult" word.

> Conduct your blooming in the noise and
> whip of whirlwind

Blooming and *whirlwind* are concrete, visible, physical realities, and because of their concreteness, we immediately recognize that each belongs to opposite categories of reality; in fact, the nature and purpose of the whirlwind is to destroy all blooming. Thus Sister Brooks is able to make a very strong political comment without resorting to trite political clichés. The use of words which have physical, visible existence is often more powerful, more clear than abstractions like "the universe" and "the cosmos."

St. Julia, a character described by Sister Brooks in the poem *In the Mecca*, is a "good" church-going sister who dearly loves Jesus. Ms. Brooks has St. Julia cry out:

> He's the comfort and wine
> and piccalilli for my soul

Piccalilli here is another extremely concrete word, a simple word that reveals Sister Brooks's intimate knowledge of the black community's eating habits (piccalilli being just the right topping for black-eyed peas and rice, she didn't say "relish"). Through this word, we can make some very concrete deductions about where and how St. Julia grew up as well as how she feels about Jesus.

Sometimes the beginning poet will use complete grammatical sentences (using connectives like "and," etc.) when often just an elliptical phrase will do. It is just as important for the poet to know what to take out as to know what to put in. The following example from Johari Amini ("Let's Go Somewhere") shows how effective the use of only those words (carefully chosen) necessary to create the intense moment of message and mood can be.

> I am too past youth
> too strong
> too black
> to cry
>   still. . . .
> need
> comes: a steadied,
> profuseness; insensitive
> spreading
> spreading

The problem of triteness—that of using words and phrases which have been used over and over again and are no longer fresh and vivid—usually falls into the category of street rap or in the form of imitating nineteenth-century European phrases (personifying the sun and moon, "thou," etc.). The problem with the rap is that it is a potentially very powerful form. To exert its power, the writer who uses it must do more than copy or imitate the vocabulary of the rap. He or she must create an originality and a tension on the printed page; using the words of the rap alone on a piece of paper cannot of itself carry the nuance and rhythm of a brother on the corner rapping out his mouth. In the same way, for example, Langston Hughes in his blues poems—because he only "copied" the superficial form of the blues lyric—could not really reach the power of a Blind Lemon or a Muddy Waters. The printed page imposes limitations that sound does not.

A Sense of Direction

Actually, a sense of direction comes from the world that students are involved in every day. If a student's work is putting comic books together or is being a professional student, he or she will see the world differently than a person working on the line at Ford Motor Company. If students question what they see, a whole new world opens up.

If what young people write about is to be meaningful, it must have some relationship to reality. And reality is not the same to the doer as it is to the sayer. There are four areas in which students should concentrate much of their efforts if they are to develop as a person and a writer:

1. Study and Research: This is of the utmost importance for writers of nonfiction and certain kinds of fiction such as historical fiction. Margaret Walker's research for her novel, *Jubilee*, took almost a lifetime, and Chancellor William's research for his monumental study, *The Destruction of Black Civilization*, took eighteen years. The two books mentioned will live because they are packed with life-giving and stimulating information written in a readable style.

2. Writing: The major endeavor for the beginning writer must be writing. The writer should at first put him or herself on a schedule in order to acquire discipline. Discipline in doing anything that is important is a must for the writer. The writer is his or her own whip. Self-discipline is the hardest to achieve but if achieved is the writer's most important asset. He or she should keep a small notebook in which to jot down all ideas. Writers should never rely solely on memory. They should not throw any of the notes away but keep the unused ones for later. Though students may want to concentrate in one area of writing, they should gain knowledge of all kinds of writing—fiction, nonfiction, children's, radio and television, magazine-journalism, poetry, and drama.

3. Revision: Writers never accept a first draft of their work. The art of writing is frequent revising. Writers must be their own worst critics. Writers must be their own editors.

4. Workshop: For the beginning and the inexperienced writer, workshops are good mostly for the associations that are formed with other writers. Also, workshops are probably one of the few places a young writer can get competent and truthful direct criticism. Many good writers have been involved in workshop experiences.

Final Words

Writing is a form of self-definition and communication through which writers basically define themselves and their relationship to the world. The writer is essentially always searching for the core of the definition, looking for the gut—the truth. There are few good writers who lie; there are a lot of liars who try to write, and unfortunately, they are in the majority. But they come and go, passing through like a European wind penetrating the African heat only to be eliminated by the warmth of reality.

A writer is a questioner, always asking, always seeking the bottom line, always looking for the essences within the essence—always looking for the enemies of the world. When writers stop questioning, they stop having anything to say. When writers question, they are doing more than admitting that they don't know everything, they're assuming a posture, a relationship with the world that is conducive to creativity. Writers who humble themselves before knowledge of any kind generally end up wiser and as voices with something meaningful to say.

The Politics of Language
Ngugi wa Thiong'o

Language, any language, has a dual character: it is both a means of communication and a carrier of culture. Take English. It is spoken in Britain and in Sweden and Denmark. But for Swedish and Danish people English is only a means of communication with non-Scandinavians. It is not a carrier of their culture. For the British, and particularly the English, it is additionally, and inseparably from its use as a tool of communication, a carrier of their culture and history. Or take Swahili in East and Central Africa. It is widely used as a means of communication across many nationalities. But it is not the carrier of a culture and history of many of those nationalities. However, in parts of Kenya and Tanzania, and particularly in Zanzibar, Swahili is inseparably both a means of communication and a carrier of the culture of those people to whom it is a mother-tongue.

Language as communication has three aspects or elements. There is first what Karl Marx once called the language of real life, the element basic to the whole notion of language, its origins and development: that is, the relations people enter into with one another in the labour process, the links they necessarily establish among themselves in the act of a people, a community of human beings, producing wealth or means of life like food, clothing, houses. A human community really starts its historical being as a community of co-operation in production through the division of labour; the simplest is between man, woman and child within a household; the more complex divisions are between branches of production such as those who are sole hunters, sole gatherers of fruits or sole workers in metal. Then there are the most complex divisions such as those in modern factories where a single product, say a shirt or a shoe, is the result of many hands and minds. Production is co-operation, is communication, is language, is expression of a relaxation between human beings and it is specifically human.

The second aspect of language as communication is speech and it imitates the language of real life, that is communication in production. The verbal signposts both reflect and aid communication or the relations established between human beings in the production of their means of life. Language as a system of verbal signposts makes that production possible. The spoken word is to relations between human beings what the hand is to the relations between human beings and nature. The hand through tools mediates between human beings and nature and forms the language of real life: spoken words mediate between human beings and form the language of speech.

The third aspect is the written signs. The written word imitates the spoken. Where the first two aspects of language as communication through the hand and the spoken word historically evolved more or less simultaneously, the written aspect is a much later historical development. Writing is representation of sounds with visual symbols, from the simplest knot among shepherds to tell the number in a herd or the hieroglyphics among the Agīkūyū gicaandi singers and poets of Kenya, to the most complicated and different letter and picture writing systems of the world today.

In most societies the written and the spoken languages are the same, in that they represent each other: what is on paper can be read to another person and be received as that language which the recipient has grown up speaking. In such a society there is broad harmony for a child between the three aspects of language as communication. His interaction with nature and with other men is expressed in written and spoken symbols or signs which are both a result of that double interaction and a reflection of it. The association of the child's sensibility is with the language of his experience of life.

But there is more to it: communication between human beings is also the basis and process of evolving culture. In doing similar kinds of things and actions over and over again under similar circumstances, similar even in their mutability, certain patterns, moves, rhythms, habits, attitudes, experiences and knowledge emerge. Those experiences are handed over to the next generation and become the inherited basis for their further actions on nature and on themselves. There is a gradual accumulation of values which in time become almost self-evident truths governing their conception of what is right and wrong, good and bad, beautiful and ugly, courageous and cowardly, generous and mean in their internal and external relations. Over a time this becomes a way of life distinguishable from other ways of life. They develop a distinctive culture and history. Culture embodies those moral, ethical and aesthetic values, the set of spiritual eyeglasses, through which they come to view themselves and their place in the universe. Values are the basis of a people's identity, their sense of particularity as members of the human race. All this is carried by language. Language as culture is the collective memory bank of a people's experience in history. Culture is almost indistinguishable from the language that makes possible its genesis, growth, banking, articulation and indeed its transmission from one generation to the next.

Language as culture also has three important aspects. Culture is a product of the history which it in turn reflects. Culture in other words is a product and a reflection of human beings communicating with one another in the very struggle to create wealth and to control it. But culture does not merely reflect that history, or rather it does so by actually forming images or pictures of the world of nature and nurture. Thus the second aspect of language as culture is as an image-forming agent in the mind of a child. Our whole conception of ourselves as a people, individually and collectively, is based on those pictures and images which may or may not correctly correspond to the actual reality of the struggles with nature and nurture which produced them in the first place. But our capacity to confront the world creatively is dependent on how those images correspond or not to that reality, how they distort or clarify the reality of our struggles. Language as culture is thus mediating between me and my own self; between my own self and other selves; between me and nature. Language is mediating in my very being. And this brings us to the third aspect of language as culture. Culture transmits or imparts those images of the world and reality through the spoken and the written language, that is through a specific language. In other words, the capacity to speak, the capacity to order sounds in a manner that makes for mutual comprehension between human beings is universal. This is the universality of language, a quality specific to human beings. It corresponds to the universality of the struggle against nature and that between human beings. But the particularity of the sounds, the words, the word order into phrases and sentences, and the specific manner, or laws, of their ordering is what distinguishes one language from another. Thus a specific culture is not transmitted through language in its universality but in its particularity as the language of a specific community with a specific history. Written literature and orature are the main means by which a particular language transmits the images of the world contained in the culture it carries.

Language as communication and as culture are then products of each other. Communication creates culture: culture is a means of communication. Language carries culture, and culture carries, particularly through orature and literature, the entire body of values by which we come to perceive ourselves and our place in the world. How people perceive themselves affects how they look at their culture, at their politics and at the social production of wealth, at their entire relationship to nature and to other beings. Language is thus inseparable from ourselves as a community of human beings with a specific form and character, a specific history, a specific relationship to the world.

So what was the colonialist imposition of a foreign language doing to us children?

The real aim of colonialism was to control the people's wealth: what they produced, how they produced it, and how it was distributed; to control, in other words, the entire realm of the language of real life. Colonialism imposed its control of the social production of wealth through military conquest and subsequent political dictatorship. But its most important area of domination was the mental universe of the colonised, the control, through culture, of how people perceived themselves and their relationship to the world. Economic and political control can never be complete or effective without mental control. To control a people's culture is to control their tools of self-definition in relationship to others.

For colonialism this involved two aspects of the same process: the destruction or the deliberate undervaluing of a people's culture, their art, dances, religions, history, geography, education, orature and literature, and the conscious elevation of the language of the coloniser. The domination of a people's language by the languages of the colonising nations was crucial to the domination of the mental universe of the colonised.

Take language as communication. Imposing a foreign language, and suppressing the native languages as spoken and written, were already breaking the harmony previously existing between the African child and the three aspects of language. Since the new language as a means of communication was a product of and was reflecting the "real language of life" elsewhere, it could never as spoken or written properly reflect or imitate the real life of that community. This may in part explain why technology always appears to us as slightly external, *their* product and not *ours*. The word "missile" used to hold an alien faraway sound until I recently learnt its equivalent in Gĩkũyũ, *ngurukuhi*, and it made me apprehend it differently. Learning, for a colonial child, became a cerebral activity and not an emotionally felt experience.

But since the new, imposed languages could never completely break the native languages as spoken, their most effective area of domination was the third aspect of language as communication, the written. The language of an African child's formal education was foreign. The language of the books he read was foreign. The language of his conceptualisation was foreign. Thought, in him, took the visible form of a foreign language. So the written language of a child's upbringing in the school (even his spoken language within the school compound) became divorced from his spoken language at home. There was often not the slightest relationship between the child's written world, which was also the language of his schooling, and the world of his immediate environment in the family and the community. For a colonial child, the harmony existing between the three aspects of language as communication was irrevocably broken. This resulted in the disassociation of the sensibility of that child from his natural and social environment, what we might call colonial alienation. The alienation became reinforced in the teaching of history, geography, music, where bourgeois Europe was always the centre of the universe.

This disassociation, divorce, or alienation from the immediate environment becomes clearer when you look at colonial language as a carrier of culture.

Since culture is a product of the history of a people which it in turn reflects, the child was now being exposed exclusively to a culture that was a product of a world external to himself. He was being made to stand outside himself to look at himself.

Since culture does not just reflect the world in images but actually, through those very images, conditions a child to see that world in a certain way, the colonial child was made to see the world and where he stands in it as seen and defined by or reflected in the culture of the language of imposition.

And since those images are mostly passed on through orature and literature it meant the child would now only see the world as seen in the literature of his language of adoption. From the point of view of alienation, that is of seeing oneself from outside oneself as if one was another self, it does not matter that the imported literature carried the great humanist tradition of the best in Shakespeare, Goethe, Balzac, Tolstoy, Gorky, Brecht, Sholokhov, Dickens. The location of this great mirror of imagination was necessarily Europe and its history and culture and the rest of the universe was seen from that centre.

But obviously it was worse when the colonial child was exposed to images of his world as mirrored in the written languages of his coloniser. Where his own native languages were associated in his impressionable mind with low status, humiliation, corporal punishment, slow-footed intelligence and ability or downright stupidity, non-intelligibility and barbarism, this was reinforced by the world he met in the works of such geniuses of racism as a Rider Haggard or a Nicholas Monsarrat; not to mention the pronouncement of some of the giants of western intellectual and political establishment, such as Hume ("... the negro is naturally inferior to the whites ..."), Thomas Jefferson ("... the blacks ... are inferior to the whites on the endowments of both body and mind ..."), or Hegel with his Africa comparable to a land of childhood still enveloped in the dark mantle of the night as far as the development of self-conscious history was concerned. Hegel's statement that there was nothing harmonious with humanity to be found in the African character is representative of the racist images of Africans and Africa such a colonial child was bound to encounter in the literature of the colonial languages. The results could be disastrous.

Black Men and Public Space
Brent Staples

My first victim was a woman—white, well dressed, probably in her late twenties. I came upon her late one evening on a deserted street in Hyde Park, a relatively affluent neighborhood in an otherwise mean, impoverished section of Chicago. As I swung onto the avenue behind her, there seemed to be a discreet, uninflammatory distance between us. Not so. She cast back a worried glance. To her, the youngish black man—a broad six feet two inches with a beard and billowing hair, both hands shoved into the pockets of a bulky military jacket—seemed menacingly close. After a few more quick glimpses, she picked up her pace and was soon running in earnest. Within seconds she disappeared into a cross street.

That was more than a decade ago. I was twenty-two years old, a graduate student newly arrived at the University of Chicago. It was in the echo of that terrified woman's footfalls that I first began to know the unwieldy inheritance I'd come into—the ability to alter public space in ugly ways. It was clear that she thought herself the quarry of a mugger, a rapist, or worse. Suffering a bout of insomnia, however, I was stalking sleep, not defenseless wayfarers. As a softy who is scarcely able to take a knife to a raw chicken—let alone hold one to a person's throat—I was surprised, embarrassed, and dismayed all at once. Her flight made me feel like an accomplice in tyranny. It also made it clear that I was indistinguishable from the muggers who occasionally seeped into the area from the surrounding ghetto. That first encounter, and those that followed, signified that a vast, unnerving gulf lay between nighttime pedestrians—particularly women—and me. And I soon gathered that being perceived as dangerous is a hazard in itself. I only needed to turn a corner into a dicey situation, or crowd some frightened, armed person in a foyer somewhere, or make an errant move after being pulled over by a policeman. Where fear and weapons meet—and they often do in urban America—there is always the possibility of death.

In that first year, my first away from my hometown, I was to become thoroughly familiar with the language of fear. At dark, shadowy intersections, I could cross in front of a car stopped at a traffic light and elicit the *thunk*,

thunk, thunk, thunk of the driver—black, white, male, or female—hammering down the door locks. On less traveled streets after dark, I grew accustomed to but never comfortable with people crossing to the other side of the street rather than pass me. Then there were the standard unpleasantries with police-men, doormen, bouncers, cabdrivers, and others whose business it is to screen out troublesome individuals *before* there is any nastiness.

I moved to New York nearly two years ago and I have remained an avid night walker. In central Manhattan, the near-constant crowd cover minimizes tense one-on-one street encounters. Elsewhere—in SoHo, for example, where sidewalks are narrow and tightly spaced buildings shut out the sky—things can get very taut indeed.

After dark, on the warrenlike streets of Brooklyn where I live, I often see women who fear the worst from me. They seem to have set their faces on neu-tral, and with their purse straps strung across their chests bandolier-style, they forge ahead as though bracing themselves against being tackled. I understand, of course, that the danger they perceive is not a hallucination. Women are par-ticularly vulnerable to street violence, and young black males are drastically overrepresented among the perpetrators of that violence. Yet these truths are no solace against the kind of alienation that comes of being ever the suspect, a fearsome entity with whom pedestrians avoid making eye contact.

Over the years, I learned to smother the rage I felt at so often being taken for a criminal. Not to do so would surely have led to madness. I now take precau-tions to make myself less threatening. I move about with care, particularly late in the evening. I give a wide berth to nervous people on subway platforms during the wee hours, particularly when I have exchanged business clothes for jeans. If I happen to be entering a building behind some people who appear skittish, I may walk by, letting them clear the lobby before I return, so as not to seem to be following them. I have been calm and extremely congenial on those rare occasions when I've been pulled over by the police.

And on late-evening constitutionals I employ what has proved to be an excellent tension-reducing measure: I whistle melodies from Beethoven and Vivaldi and the more popular classical composers. Even steely New Yorkers hunching toward nighttime destinations seem to relax, and occasionally they even join in the tune. Virtually everybody seems to sense that a mugger wouldn't be warbling bright, sunny selections from Vivaldi's *Four Seasons*. It is my equivalent of the cowbell that hikers wear when they know they are in bear country.

Revolutionary Struggle
Assata Shakur

I was surprised to find that the Black Liberation Army was not a central-ized, organized group with a common leadership and chain of command. Instead, there were various organizations and collectives working out of dif-ferent cities, and in some of the larger cities there were often several groups working independently of each other. Many members of the various groups had been forced into hiding as a result of the extreme police repression that took place during the late sixties and early seventies. Some had serious cases, some had minor ones, and others, like me, were just wanted for "questioning."

Sisters and brothers joined these groups because they were committed to revolutionary struggle in general and armed struggle in particular and wanted to help build the armed movement in amerika. It was the strangest feeling. People i used to run into at rallies were now in hiding, sending mes-sages that they wanted to hook up. Sisters and brothers from just about every revolutionary or militant group in the country were either rotting away in prison or had been forced underground. Everyone i talked to was interested in taking the struggle to a higher level. But the question was how. How to bring together all those people scattered around the country into an organized body that would be effective in struggling for Black liberation.

It became evident, almost from the beginning, that consolidation was not a good idea. There were too many security problems, and different groups had different ideologies, different levels of political consciousness and different ideas about how armed struggle in amerika should be waged. On the whole, we were weak, inexperienced, disorganized, and seriously lacking in training. But the biggest problem was one of political development. There were sisters and brothers who had been so victimized by amerika that they were willing to fight to the death against their oppressors. They were intelligent, courageous and dedicated, willing to make any sacrifice. But we were to find out quickly that courage and dedication were not enough. To win any struggle for libera-tion, you have to have the way as well as the will, an overall ideology and strategy that stem from a scientific analysis of history and present conditions.

Some of the groups thought they could just pick up arms and struggle and that, somehow, people would see what they were doing and begin to struggle themselves. They wanted to engage in a do-or-die battle with the pig power structure in amerika, even though they were weak and ill prepared for such a fight. But the most important factor is that armed struggle, by itself, can never bring about a revolution. Revolutionary war is a people's war. And no people's war can be won without the support of the masses of people. Armed struggle can never be successful by itself; it must be part of an overall strategy for winning, and the strategy must be political as well as military.

Since we did not own the TV stations or newspapers, it was easy for the news media to portray us as monsters and terrorists. The police could terrorize the Black community daily, yet if one Black person successfully defended himself or herself against a police attack, they were called terrorists. It soon became clear to me that our most important battle was to help politically mobilize, educate, and organize the masses of Black people and to win their minds and hearts. It was inconceivable that we could survive, much less win anything, without their support.

Every group fighting for freedom is bound to make mistakes, but unless you study the common, fundamental laws of armed revolutionary struggle you are bound to make unnecessary mistakes. Revolutionary war is protracted warfare. It is impossible for us to win quickly. To win we have got to wear down our oppressors, little by little, and, at the same time, strengthen our forces, slowly but surely. I understood some of my more impatient sisters and brothers. I knew that it was tempting to substitute military for political struggle, especially since all of our aboveground organizations were under vicious attack by the FBI, the CIA, and the local police agencies. All of us who saw our leaders murdered, our people shot down in cold blood, felt a need, a desire to fight back. One of the hardest lessons we had to learn is that revolutionary struggle is scientific rather than emotional. I'm not saying that we shouldn't feel anything, but decisions can't be based on love or on anger. They have to be based on the objective conditions and on what is the rational, unemotional thing to do.

In 1857 the u.s. supreme kourt ruled that Blacks were only three-fifths of a man and had no rights that whites were bound to respect. Today, more than a hundred and twenty-five years later, we still earn less than three-fifths of what white people earn. It was plain to me that we couldn't look to the kourts for freedom and justice anymore than we could expect to gain our liberation by participating in the u.s. political system, and it was pure fantasy to think we could gain them by begging. The only alternative left was to fight for them, and we are going to have to fight like any other people who have fought for liberation.

Brown v. Board of Education of Topeka, Kansas:
Our Twentieth Century Legacy
Constance Baker Motley

Justice Harlan's dissent in *Plessy* formed the basis of our legal arguments to end segregation in education. We abandoned his Thirteenth Amendment argument, however, since we had successfully invoked the equal protection clause of the Fourteenth Amendment in other cases involving state action. We consistently argued that the state was powerless, under the Fourteenth Amendment, to make racial distinctions with respect to civil or political rights. But we needed a persuasive argument as to why, even when the facilities provided black children were equal, segregation violated this amendment. After all, Harlan's Fourteenth Amendment argument was rejected by the overwhelming majority of the Court in *Plessy*, a powerful precedent against us. We had to convince the Court that *Plessy* either was wrongly decided or should not be extended to public education. We were fully aware that getting the Supreme Court to reverse long-standing precedent would be virtually impossible without new evidence of the harmful effects of segregation on a state's black citizens.

We needed to prove that segregation, even where facilities are equal, has a harmful psychological effect on the ability of black children to learn. This new evidence was developed at the trial of the *Brown* case. All the lawyers involved in preparing the brief were convinced that it was necessary to allege and prove some injury to black children from the state's segregation policies. But the majority in *Plessy* had found Plessy's argument about the effect of state-decreed segregation on nonwhites fanciful.

Kansas permitted (but did not require) segregation in elementary schools in first-class (large) cities as defined by statute, which applied only to these schools, apparently because few blacks went to high school. There was only one city that met the definition, Topeka. All other public school systems in Kansas were integrated. A large black population had moved to Topeka in connection with railroad construction in the last century, so most blacks in the state lived there.

I sent a draft complaint to our lawyers in the Kansas case as early as 1950, right after the Supreme Court's decision in *Sweatt*, in accordance with our plan to tackle the public schools. Similar model complaints were sent to other local NAACP lawyers who requested LDF assistance.

Robert Carter was lead counsel in the trial court in Kansas and argued the case on direct appeal to the Supreme Court. Jack Greenberg participated in the trial. Psychologist Kenneth Clark's work (along with others) on the psychological effects of segregation on black children, their self-image, and their ability to learn had been introduced at the Kansas trial and was, indeed, new. The trial was held in a three-judge federal district court, because a state statute was under attack on federal constitutional grounds. It found that segregation in public education had a detrimental effect on Negro (as we were called then) children but denied injunctive relief enjoining the Kansas statute, on the ground that the Negro and white schools in Topeka were substantially equal. The federal statute allowed for a direct appeal of the three-judge-court ruling to the Supreme Court. The appeal was taken and consolidated by the Supreme Court with school segregation cases in four other jurisdictions: South Carolina, Virginia, Delaware, and the District of Columbia.

In the cases involving two predominantly black rural counties, Clarendon, in South Carolina, and Prince Edward, in Virginia, the three-judge federal district court panels upheld the constitutionality of the state's laws on compulsory segregation in public education, even though the facilities for Negro children were found unequal to those for white children. In both instances, the local school board was ordered to equalize the facilities for Negro children, and when Thurgood and Spottswood Robinson III proceeded with the oral argument in Supreme Court, the plaintiffs conceded that the facilities had been equalized.

In the Delaware case, involving New Castle County, both elementary and high school students were plaintiffs. Their action was brought in the state court, the Delaware Court of Chancery, to enjoin state statutory and constitutional provisions that required racial segregation in education. The chancellor, Collin Seitz, ruled in favor of the Negro children and ordered their immediate admission to white schools on the ground that the schools provided for them were inferior with respect to teacher training, pupil-teacher ratio, extracurricular activities, physical plant, and time and distance involved in travel. The chancellor also found that segregation itself resulted in an inferior education for Negro children but did not rest his decision on that ground. The Supreme Court of Delaware, affirming the chancellor's decree, suggested that a modification of the decree might be in order if the schools were equalized later but found the Negro schools unequal under *Plessy v. Ferguson*. The school authorities appealed to the U.S. Supreme Court. The argument there was made by Louis Redding of Wilmington, Delaware, assisted by Jack Greenberg (both had been trial counsel). The Supreme Court also agreed to review a case filed in U.S. District Court for the District of Columbia seeking admission of Negro children to schools attended by white children. The district court dismissed the complaint, and an appeal was taken to the U.S. Court of Appeals for the District of Columbia Circuit. The Supreme Court, in an unprecedented move, issued a writ of certiorari to the court of appeals before judgment, because of the importance of the constitutional question presented as to federal authority, so that it could hear the case along with the four state cases. The case was argued in Supreme Court by trial counsel George E. C. Hayes and Frank Reeves, both of Washington, D.C., and members of Marshall's inner circle.

In its opinion relating to the four state cases, the Court first dealt with the history and intent of the framers of the Fourteenth Amendment and the states in ratifying it and found the issues inconclusive. It then reviewed the status of public education at the time the amendment was proposed and ratified and found it far from comparable to the status of public education in 1954. The Court next reviewed how earlier Courts had construed the amendment from shortly after its adoption until the 1950 decision in *Sweatt*, where it had expressly reserved judgment on whether *Plessy v. Ferguson* should be held inapplicable to public education. The Court then noted that this question was directly presented by the *Brown* cases. It said: "Here, unlike *Sweatt v. Painter*, there are findings below that the Negro and white schools involved have been equalized, or are being equalized, with respect to buildings, curricula, qualifications and salaries of teachers, and other tangible factors. Our decision, therefore, cannot turn on merely a comparison of these tangible factors in the Negro and white schools involved in each of the cases. We must look instead to the effect of segregation itself on public education." The Court first concluded that education today is perhaps the most important function of state government.

It then said: "We come then to the question presented: Does segregation of children in public schools solely on the basis of race, even though the physical facilities and other tangible factors may be equal, deprive the children of the minority group of equal education opportunities? We believe that it does." Its basic holding was: "To separate them from others of similar age and qualifications solely because of their race generates a feeling of inferiority as to their status in the community that may affect their hearts and minds in a way unlikely ever to be undone." In reaching its conclusion, the Supreme Court adopted the findings of the Kansas court: "The effect of this separation on their educational opportunities was well stated by a finding in the Kansas case by a court which nevertheless felt compelled to rule against the Negro plaintiffs: 'Segregation of white and colored children in public schools has a detrimental effect upon the colored children. The impact is greater when it has the sanction of the law; for the policy of separating the races is usually interpreted as denoting the inferiority of the Negro group. A sense of inferiority affects the motivation of a child to learn. Segregation with the sanction of the law, therefore, has a tendency to [retard] the educational and mental development of Negro children and to deprive them of some of the benefits they would receive in a racial[ly] integrated school system.'

"Whatever may have been the extent of psychological knowledge at the time of *Plessy v. Ferguson*, this finding is amply supported by modern authority. Any language in *Plessy v. Ferguson* contrary to this finding is rejected."

In the District of Columbia case, the Court said: "We have this day held that the Equal Protection Clause of the Fourteenth Amendment prohibits the states from maintaining racially segregated public schools. The legal problem in the District of Columbia is somewhat different, however. The Fifth Amendment, which is applicable in the District of Columbia, does not contain an equal protection clause as does the Fourteenth Amendment which applies only to the states. But the concepts of equal protection and due process, both stemming from our American ideal of fairness, are not mutually exclusive. The equal protection of the laws is a more explicit safeguard to prohibited unfairness than due process of law, and, therefore, we do not imply that the two are always interchangeable phrases. But, as this Court has recognized, discrimination may be so unjustifiable as to be violative of due process."

The Supreme Court then set the cases down for re-argument on the two questions addressed in the briefs relating to the relief to be granted in these cases in the event that the plaintiffs should prevail. That is, if segregation was deemed unconstitutional, should Negro students be admitted forthwith or after a reasonable time for adjustment, and how should the courts proceed in determining a reasonable time?

No one associated with us in preparing the briefs or oral arguments called to see if there was going to be a victory party. Those who knew Thurgood knew that "party" was his middle name. Everyone converged on LDF's offices, which were then on West Forty-third Street next to Town Hall and not far from the NAACP national headquarters on Fortieth Street. It was bedlam; the party went on most of the night. I remember being there when the clock struck 3:30 A.M.

Becoming a part of history is a special experience, reserved for only a few. It's like earning a law degree or a Ph.D.; nobody can take it away from you. You may be forgotten, but it's like immortality: You will always be there.

As the night went on, Marshall began to worry about the dawn. It might even be fair to say that, as people left, he sensed the new reality in personal terms—a task ahead even greater than the one he had just accomplished. He kept saying to those assembled, "There is nothing to party about—your task has just begun." Work on the two procedural questions started immediately— day and night discussions mainly with the same lawyers who had helped with the case before.

In early July, LDF lawyers, as customary, attended the NAACP's annual convention in Dallas, Texas. The local convention organizers succeeded in getting a new motel, which had not yet opened, to house some of the NAACP delegates. During past conventions in the South, delegates had stayed in private homes or in black-college dormitories, but in light of the Supreme Court's May 17, 1954, decision, a larger crowd than usual was expected that July. LDF staff lawyers, led by Thurgood, lawyers on the national board of the NAACP, and those working with major NAACP branches around the country met at that euphoric convention to savor victory. The Supreme Court's 1955 decision in the *Brown* case applying "all deliberate speed" to implement its 1954 decision had not yet been announced, but the pivotal battle, it was felt by all, had been won. Black America faced a new day, for the Supreme Court's ruling in *Brown I* foreshadowed the end of all public segregation. Although it did not expressly overrule *Plessy*, its overruling was implicit.

In discussing our overall strategy for implementing the *Brown* decision, the lawyers at the Dallas convention unanimously agreed that we would start bringing public school desegregation cases in border states (Missouri, Maryland, Tennessee, and Kentucky) before confronting Deep South states (Mississippi, Alabama, Louisiana, Texas, Georgia, South Carolina, and Florida), all of which (except South Carolina) were within the jurisdiction of the U.S. Court of Appeals for the Fifth Circuit, a circuit hostile to civil rights claims.

Oliver Hill of Richmond, Virginia, was at the convention. A classmate of Thurgood's at Howard Law School, he had been one of the local counsel in the Prince Edward County, Virginia, case, one of the five school desegregation cases still pending before the Supreme Court. At the lawyers' meeting, Oliver suggested that, since we had achieved our goal of ending segregation in public education, we turn our attention to public transportation. He believed black people in Richmond, for example, were not as concerned about segregated education as they were about segregated public transportation, which every black, child or adult, confronted each day and found more degrading than public school segregation. Oliver was hooted down—especially by Thurgood, as I recall. The focus of the meeting was on implementing *Brown I*, not on taking on new major challenges. Thurgood had the feeling—as we all did—that our work was cut out for us and that implementing *Brown I* would fully occupy LDF lawyers for at least five years. Physically and mentally exhausted from working on *Brown I*, he found the idea of a brand-new challenge on a different front out of the question. (The Montgomery bus boycott of 1955–56 proved Oliver right, however.)

The Supreme Court's decision in *Brown II*, on the relief to be afforded in school desegregation cases, came on May 31, 1955. The Court invited the U.S. attorney general and the attorneys general of all states requiring or permitting racial discrimination in public education to present their views on the issue. The parties in the five cases, the United States, and the states of Florida, North Carolina, Arkansas, Oklahoma, Maryland, and Texas filed briefs and participated in the oral arguments on remedy.

As the Court pointed out, the briefs demonstrated that substantial steps to eliminate racial discrimination in public schools had already been taken not only in some of the communities in which the cases arose but in some of the states appearing as amici curiae and other states as well. It noted that progress had been made in the District of Columbia, Kansas, and Delaware. However, the defendants in the cases from South Carolina and Virginia were awaiting the Court's decision. Where were Georgia, Alabama, Louisiana, Mississippi, and Arkansas? No one needed to ask, but we suspected that their absence meant storm clouds were gathering.

The Court's directions to the trial courts were straightforward and explicit: "[T]he courts will require that the defendants make a prompt and reasonable start toward full compliance with our May 17, 1954, ruling. Once such a start has been made, the courts may find that additional time is necessary to carry out the ruling in an effective manner. The burden rests upon the defendants to establish that such time is necessary in the public interest and is consistent with good faith compliance at the earliest practicable date. To that end, the courts many consider problems related to administration, arising from the physical condition of the school plant, the school transportation systems, personnel, revision of school district and attendance areas into compact units to achieve a system of determining admission to the public schools on a nonracial basis, and revision of local laws and regulations which may be necessary in solving the foregoing problems. They will also consider the adequacy of any plans the defendants may propose to meet these problems and to effectuate a transition to a racially nondiscriminatory school system. During this period of transition, the courts will retain jurisdiction of these cases."

Why the Supreme Court did not expressly overrule *Plessy v. Ferguson* has always been a mystery to me. Some lawyers have suggested that the most obvious reason was that *Plessy* dealt with a different era in American history, while *Brown* dealt with America's then fully developed public school system in the second half of the twentieth century. Moreover, the Court, some argue, and I agree, did not want to render a decision that would remove the legal props for racial segregation in all areas of public life at once. School desegregation was, in and of itself, such a wrenching societal change for the Deep South states that the Court, perhaps, did not want to bring on a major social crisis by casting *Brown*'s net too far. However, the Court ruled immediately after *Brown I* on a case involving state-enforced racial segregation in other areas, most notably recreation, and as time has demonstrated, *Brown* itself quickly ushered in our greatest period of social upheaval since the Civil War.

The Court's decision in *Brown I*—sweeping, unusually straightforward, simply written, and unanimous—gained the status of a Magna Carta in the black community. Laymen read it as a mandate to end all state-sanctioned segregation. The Montgomery bus boycott was the best evidence of this new vision of the Constitution among grassroots blacks. When the three-judge federal district court in Montgomery, Alabama, issued its injunction (two to one) enjoining intrastate segregation in transportation facilities in Montgomery under both state and local law, it ruled that the Supreme Court had implicitly overruled *Plessy* and had not intended to limit *Brown I* to schools, as evidenced by the fact that, on the same day it ruled in *Brown*, it sent a case back for reconsideration in light of *Brown*, a decision upholding segregation in the park system of Louisville, Kentucky, *Muir v. Louisville Park Theatrical Association.* Judge Seybourn H. Lynne of Birmingham dissented. One would have to read his dissent to see just how hard segregationists sitting on the federal bench died. There were many more such deaths on that bench to come. The majority opinion was written by Judge Richard Rives of the Fifth Circuit, who was joined by Judge Frank Johnson, both of Montgomery. Rives's decision was rendered on June 5, 1956, two years after *Brown I*. The Montgomery city fathers took a direct appeal to the Supreme Court, which refused to hear oral argument, as it often did in such cases after *Brown I* when the outcome was obvious. It merely affirmed the injunction, citing *Brown I* and cases from Baltimore and Atlanta that enjoined segregation in municipal recreational facilities. Thus, although the Supreme Court initially tried to limit *Brown I* to schools by letting *Plessy* stand unreversed, within a decade the Court (citing *Brown I*) had declared unconstitutional all state-enforced or state-supported segregation in public facilities.

One of the last segregated public institutions to fall were courthouses in Virginia. In its 1963 per curiam decision in *Johnson v. Virginia*, rendered without argument, the Supreme Court said: "State-compelled segregation in a court of justice is a manifest violation of the State's duty to deny no one the equal protection of its laws." Citing *Brown I*, the Court also said: "[I]t is no longer open to question that a state may not constitutionally require segregation of public facilities."

In my view, the Supreme Court interpreted Truman's politically courageous action of integrating the armed forces in 1948 as a sign of executive-branch support for its decision in *Brown I*, which required a major reversal in national policy. When the Supreme Court rendered its 1954 decision, the NAACP and its legal arm achieved its primary goal, the end of legal segregation in American society. The doubting Thomases in the black community disappeared. Even the most unsophisticated American grasped *Brown*'s historic impact. A new day had dawned. It was the kind of sweeping sea change in a nation's social policy that occurs once in a century. It was particularly significant for American society, which had been segregated for centuries.

Thurgood justifiably received the major credit for this monumental legal achievement. He had convened the lawyers, historians, psychologists, and sociologists who worked on the two main briefs. He had worked out the delicate negotiations regarding who would argue which case in the Supreme Court. He had raised most of the meager funds from speaking to NAACP branches and large individual contributors. He had organized the moot courts at Howard Law School that preceded each Supreme Court argument. He had persuaded lawyers to put other school desegregation cases on the back burner until the Supreme Court ruled in *Brown I*. He was the spokesman for the lawyers involved and, in 1954, the undisputed spokesman for black America. His picture appeared on the cover of *Time* magazine as Man of the Year. He was simultaneously exhilarated and awestruck by his leadership position in black people's struggle for equality. At times, he seemed immobilized by the inherent responsibility to move forward with implementation; at other times, he was literally overwhelmed by the onrush of events that the decision set in motion. It was like trying to navigate a ship in a hurricane, a fate that none of us had thought about very much.

My feeling after *Brown I* was often one of depression. Awaiting the Court's 1954 decision had been about all the stress we could bear. I kept thinking: How will we manage? The staff was small, our funds meager, our plans sketchy; thousands of school districts were involved.

The President, Dwight Eisenhower, was not enthusiastic about enforcing the Supreme Court's decision. This was a national development that had not been anticipated. He made no strong statement endorsing *Brown I*, so, in practical terms, there was no support from the executive branch for desegregating Southern schools. Eisenhower should never be forgiven for his failure to lead the nation into its new era at that critical time. Segregationists noted this lack of support for the most important Supreme Court decision to affect their societal organization in this century.

Although we had anticipated resistance in the Deep South, there was no plan in place to meet the Southern states' wholesale defiance. Such a plan would have required executive-branch involvement. There was not yet enough money in the coffers of the NAACP or LDF to support even a moderately scaled program of desegregation at the elementary and high school levels in all the Southern states in 1955. Most difficult of all, we had no crystal ball or other way of predicting the reactions of the rank and file to the Supreme Court's historic move. Montgomery took us completely by surprise.

When the Supreme Court's second *Brown* decision came down in May 1955, we saw it as a major block in the enforcement process. This time there was no party, and nobody called with congratulations. We all were depressed and befuddled. Of course, we had anticipated resistance in the Deep South, but we felt that *Brown II* would encourage delay and evasion. However, it should be noted that, when Thurgood argued *Brown I* in 1954, he emphasized in closing that the Court's ruling in our favor simply would allow us to begin the long journey toward desegregating public education. He repeated this stance in *Brown II*. Arguing that desegregation in education should take place at once was not our legal position, yet the Supreme Court in *Brown II* refused to order the immediate admission of the named plaintiffs, in line with its 1950 ruling in *Sweatt* to the effect that constitutional rights are "personal and present." As noted above, the Supreme Court had ordered Sweatt admitted to the University of Texas Law School, notwithstanding that Texas was in the process of building a separate law school for its black citizens. Group rights, thus, became substantively as well as procedurally a distinct, new area in constitutional adjudication.

The Supreme Court's decision in *Brown II* dealt with how *Brown I* was to be implemented for the class of plaintiffs as a whole. All five cases were brought as class actions. *Brown II* specifically contemplated a merger of the black and white public school systems. A few communities in the border states had already begun the process of desegregation on their own in 1955 in response to the 1954 decision. Schools in the District of Columbia soon began consolidation, as the Court noted. West Virginia's college for blacks, West Virginia State, promptly opened to local whites and became a fully integrated, predominantly white college. The black former president of that college, John W. Davis, was then employed by LDF to work with black teachers who feared loss of employment. The Court's *Brown II* decision simply noted that a particular school district's desegregation plan might entail personnel problems. *Brown I* dealt solely with the effects of segregation on black children. The fate of black teachers and administrators was not viewed as a major problem by either the Court or the plaintiffs' lawyers. Only after the 1955 decision did we realize that black personnel might prove a major foe of school desegregation.

America:
The Multicultural Society
Ishmael Reed

> At the annual Lower East Side Jewish Festi-
> val yesterday, a Chinese woman ate a pizza
> slice in front of Ty Thuan Duc's Vietnamese
> grocery store. Beside her a Spanish-speaking
> family patronized a cart with two signs: "Ital-
> ian Ices" and "Kosher by Rabbi Alper." And
> after the pastrami ran out, everybody ate
> knishes.
>
> *New York Times*, June 23, 1983

On the day before Memorial Day, 1983, a poet called me to describe a city he had just visited. He said that one section included mosques, built by the Islamic people who dwelled there. Attending his reading, he said, were large numbers of Hispanic people, forty thousand of whom lived in the same city. He was not talking about a fabled city located in some mysterious region of the world. The city he'd visited was Detroit.

A few months before, as I was leaving Houston, Texas, I heard it announced on the radio that Texas's largest minority was Mexican-American, and though a foundation recently issued a report critical of bilingual education, the taped voice used to guide the passengers on the air trams connecting terminals in Dallas Airport is in both Spanish and English. If the trend continues, a day will come when it will be difficult to travel through some sections of the country without hearing commands in both English and Spanish; after all, for some western states, Spanish was the first written language and the Spanish style lives on in the western way of life.

Shortly after my Texas trip, I sat in an auditorium located on the campus of the University of Wisconsin at Milwaukee as a Yale professor—whose original work on the influence of African cultures upon those of the Americas has led to his ostracism from some monocultural intellectual circles—walked up and down the aisle, like an old-time southern evangelist, dancing and drumming the top of the lectern, illustrating his points before some serious Afro-American intellectuals and artists who cheered and applauded his performance and his mastery of information. The professor was "white." After his lecture, he joined a group of Milwaukeeans in a conversation. All of the participants spoke Yoruba, though only the professor had ever traveled to Africa.

One of the artists told me that his paintings, which included African and Afro-American mythological symbols and imagery, were hanging in the local McDonald's restaurant. The next day I went to McDonald's and snapped pictures of smiling youngsters eating hamburgers below paintings that could grace the walls of any of the country's leading museums. The manager of the local McDonald's said, "I don't know what you boys are doing, but I like it," as he commissioned the local painters to exhibit in his restaurant.

Such blurring of cultural styles occurs in everyday life in the United States to a greater extent than anyone can imagine, and is probably more prevalent than the sensational conflict between people of different backgrounds that is played up and often encouraged by the media. The result is what the Yale Professor, Robert Thompson, referred to as a cultural bouillabaisse, yet members of the nation's present educational and cultural Elect still cling to the notion that the United States belongs to some vaguely defined entity they refer to as "Western civilization," by which they mean, presumably, a civilization created by the people of Europe, as if Europe can be viewed in monolithic terms. Is Beethoven's Ninth Symphony, which includes Turkish marches, a part of Western civilization, or the late nineteenth- and twentieth-century French paintings, whose creators were influenced by Japanese art? And what of the cubists, through whom the influence of African art changed modern painting, or the surrealists, who were so impressed with the art of the Pacific Northwest Indians that, in their map of North America, Alaska dwarfs the lower forty-eight in size?

Are the Russians, who are often criticized for their adoption of "Western" ways by Tsarist dissidents in exile, members of Western civilization? And what of the millions of Europeans who have black African and Asian ancestry, black Africans having occupied several countries for hundreds of years? Are these "Europeans" members of Western civilization, or the Hungarians, who originated across the Urals in a place called Greater Hungary, or the Irish, who came from the Iberian Peninsula?

Even the notion that North America is part of Western civilization because our "system of government" is derived from Europe is being challenged by Native American historians who say that the founding fathers, Benjamin Franklin especially, were actually influenced by the system of government that had been adopted by the Iroquois hundreds of years prior to the arrival of large numbers of Europeans.

Western civilization, then, becomes another confusing category like Third World, or Judeo-Christian culture, as man attempts to impose his small-screen view of political and cultural reality upon a complex world. Our most publicized novelist recently said that Western civilization was the greatest achievement of mankind, an attitude that flourishes on the street level as scribbles in public restrooms: "White Power," "Niggers and Spics Suck," or "Hitler was a prophet," the latter being the most telling, for wasn't Adolph Hitler the archetypal monoculturalist who, in his pigheaded arrogance, believed that one way and one blood was so pure that it had to be protected from alien strains at all costs? Where did such an attitude, which has caused so much misery and depression in our national life, which has tainted even our noblest achievements, begin? An attitude that caused the incarceration of Japanese-American citizens during World War II, the persecution of Chicanos and Chinese-Americans, the near-extermination of the Indians, and the murder and lynchings of thousands of Afro-Americans.

Virtuous, hardworking, pious, even though they occasionally would wander off after some fancy clothes, or rendezvous in the woods with the town prostitute, the Puritans are idealized in our schoolbooks as "a hardy band" of no-nonsense patriarchs whose discipline razed the forest and brought order to the New World (a term that annoys Native American historians). Industrious, responsible, it was their "Yankee ingenuity" and practicality that created the work ethic. They were simple folk who produced a number of good poets, and they set the tone for the American writing style, of lean and spare lines, long before Hemingway. They worshiped in churches whose colors blended in with the New England snow, churches with simple structures and ornate lecterns.

The Puritans were a daring lot, but they had a mean streak. They hated the theater and banned Christmas. They punished people in a cruel and inhuman manner. They killed children who disobeyed their parents. When they came in contact with those whom they considered heathens or aliens, they behaved in such a bizarre and irrational manner that this chapter in the American history comes down to us as a late-movie horror film. They exterminated the Indians, who taught them how to survive in a world unknown to them, and their encounter with the calypso culture of Barbados resulted in what the tourist guide in Salem's Witches' House refers to as the Witchcraft Hysteria.

The Puritan legacy of hard work and meticulous accounting led to the establishment of a great industrial society; it is no wonder that the American industrial revolution began in Lowell, Massachusetts, but there was the other side, the strange and paranoid attitudes toward those different from the Elect.

The cultural attitudes of that early Elect continue to be voiced in everyday life in the United States: the president of a distinguished university, writing a letter to the *Times*, belittling the study of African civilizations; the television network that promoted its show on the Vatican art with the boast that this art represented "the finest achievements of the human spirit." A modern up-tempo state of complex rhythms that depends upon contacts with an international community can no longer behave as if it dwelled in a "Zion Wilderness" surrounded by beasts and pagans.

When I heard a schoolteacher warn the other night about the invasion of the American educational system by foreign curriculums, I wanted to yell at the television set, "Lady, they're already here." It has already begun because the world is here. The world has been arriving at these shores for at least ten thousand years from Europe, Africa, and Asia. In the late nineteenth and early twentieth centuries, large numbers of Europeans arrived, adding their cultures to those of the European, African, and Asian settlers who were already here, and recently millions have been entering the country from South America and the Caribbean, making Yale professor Bob Thompson's bouillabaisse richer and thicker.

One of our most visionary politicians said that he envisioned a time when the United States could become the brain of the world, by which he meant the repository of all of the latest advanced information systems. I thought of that remark when an enterprising poet friend of mine called to say that he had just sold a poem to a computer magazine and that the editors were delighted to get it because they didn't carry fiction or poetry. Is that the kind of world we desire? A humdrum homogeneous world of all brains and no heart, no fiction, no poetry; a world of robots with human attendants bereft of imagination, of culture? Or does North America deserve a more exciting destiny? To become a place where the cultures of the world crisscross. This is possible because the United States is unique in the world: The world is here.

Black vs. Blue:
Time for a Cease-Fire?
Meta Carstarphen

When the red and blue flashing lights reflected off my rearview mirror, I froze. Still moving, the tires still turning, my car was momentarily driverless. Instinctively, I slowed to an uneasy halt by the side of a small street, in the dark, waiting. With a sideways and cautious glance, I watched the uniformed stranger walk—no, swagger—toward me. I hadn't been speeding. I hadn't run through any red lights. I hadn't violated any traffic law as far as I knew. That sure knowledge, however, did not give me confidence. Instead, I braced myself cautiously and prepared to say or do nothing that might upset him. For anything could happen, anything, when white police and black civilians cross paths.

Strife, even violence, between white policemen and African Americans seems to be an ever-present reality, unlimited by time or locality. In Dallas, Texas, a young white officer died after being shot by a black vagrant, and this incident sparked tensions which threatened to tear the city asunder. Reports surfaced that the mainly black inner city onlookers cheered the mentally unstable assailant on to assault Officer Glen Chase. With this discovery, police administrators decried the entire incident as evidence that police were not supported by the very communities which needed them most. Black officials, meanwhile, used the same occurrence as proof that a history of racist actions by Dallas police had so hardened the residents that unequivocal support of the "blue" was impossible.

In Miami, Florida, a white Hispanic officer shot an unarmed black motor-cyclist whose death provoked riots, fires, and protests in the black neighbor-hood where it occurred. While community leaders fought to appease the residents' anger and prod the Chief of Police into retributive action against Officer Lozano, they noted the irony. In the face of high unemployment and fiscal restraints, the city of Miami had just spearheaded a massive resettlement project for Central American refugees that appeared to give them so easily the economic assistance that was utterly lacking for its poorest citizens. Officer Lozano's assault of an unarmed black, they said, was just one more proof of the system's assault against its black residents.

More and more, contentious relations between police departments and black residents are surfacing. What is more alarming than the frequency of these events are the similarities. Change the players and the results still remain the same: police actions involving African Americans in a dispute, regardless of the issue, are tinged by racial tensions. The humanity of both the police officer and black citizen evaporates, leaving only mutual targets in their places.

When did police officers become symbols of evil instead of representatives of good in the black community? Frankly, if there has ever been a time of harmony between the two, most blacks are unaware of it. In 1966, as a result of earlier surveys conducted for *Newsweek* by political pollster Louis Harris, two of the magazine's staffers wrote *Black and White: A Study of U.S. Racial Attitudes Today*. Taken by 1000 African Americans and 1200 whites, the surveys posed similar questions to both groups to gauge their perceptions about the society and its major institutions. One striking element showed the disparity of opinion between blacks and whites over how helpful, or harmful, local authorities were to blacks.

According to the survey, 58 percent of the whites polled felt local authorities were "more helpful" to blacks than not; only 35 percent of the black respondents felt that way. When pointedly questioned about local police, only 26 percent of the blacks felt that law enforcement officials were "more helpful" to them, whereas 74 percent were either not sure or decidedly convinced that the police were "more harmful" to blacks.

Such a high level of mistrust among blacks had its roots in widespread patterns of frustrating experiences with police. So similar were these interactions across a variety of black communities throughout the country that, in 1968, a special task force created by President Lyndon B. Johnson brought special attention to this problem. Dubbed *The Kerner Report*, this groundbreaking study, issued by the National Advisory Commission on Civil Disorders, noted that strained police-community relations contributed much during the mid-sixties to the series of racial riots which had just rocked the nation:

> All major outbursts of recent years . . . were precipitated by arrests of Negroes by white police for minor offenses. . . . Thus, to many Negroes, police have come to symbolize white power, white racism and white repression. And the fact is that many police do reflect and express these white attitudes. (200)

Until the civil rights movements of the fifties and the sixties culminated in instigating significant legislation—most notably the Civil Rights Act of 1964—segregation blocked most blacks from the mainstream of virtually every aspect of American society. What the new age of integration inherited, despite its promise of better days ahead, was an ominous legacy of exclusion and mistrust.

No two areas reflected this estrangement more than housing and jobs. For blacks, this usually meant that no matter how much money they may have had, they were prevented from buying houses outside predominantly black neighborhoods. And their sons living in those neighborhoods who grew up playing "cops and robbers" may have rudely discovered in manhood that real careers in law enforcement were closed to them because of their color.

A context eventually developed that seemed unchanging. Crimes committed in black neighborhoods by black criminals were to be stopped by white police in blue uniforms, who usually only saw black people in times of crisis, or in handcuffs. On the other hand, blacks were quite used to interacting with whites in positions of authority, whites who represented a system that seemed determined to separate them into their respective places. The white police officer, especially if his actions and words were aggressive or brutal, was just another reminder of the same. However, because he could enter their neighborhoods more freely than blacks could enter his, he became an even more menacing personal threat.

In the sixties, one of the most strident voices expressing this enmity was that of the Black Panther Party, which argued that passive, though organized resistance by blacks to social and political inequities was not enough. Instead, the Black Panthers advocated aggressive, even armed, defense of black life and property against white authorities. And, the Panthers charged, no one seemed to be more identified with all that was wrong and perverse in America than her police officers.

By 1969, the Black Panther's Minister of Information, Eldridge Cleaver, was a key party member who had become famous for explaining the party philosophy through published articles and books. In one of them, *Post-Prison Writings & Speeches,* Cleaver described his perception of police/community relations in Oakland, California:

> The notorious, oppressive, racist and brutal Oakland Police Department is at the heart of the matter. This Gestapo force openly and flagrantly terrorizes the black people of Oakland. . . . The OPD has increased its patrols of the black community to the saturation point and become like a sword buried in the heart of the people. The Black Panther Party intended to remove that sword. (101–2)

This was not a sentiment felt only by an eccentric group of hotheads, ex-cons, and radicals as the Black Panther members were often portrayed. Repeated experiences of brutality and corruption by police convinced most blacks that law enforcement meant separate and unequal treatment.

Over the years since the turbulent times of the Black Panthers, urban riots, and "race" studies, little seems to have improved. Recently, just outside of Los Angeles in the decidedly upscale community of Long Beach, California, a "sting" operation was deliberately planned. Designed to capture some truths about white police behavior toward black civilians, the experiment yielded chilling results. A black motorist (and undercover police officer) did not have to drive long in the predominantly white neighborhoods before he was noticed and stopped by a white officer. The motorist, without provocation, was harassed and assaulted by the officer as a nearby hidden TV camera recorded it all, including the uniformed officer smashing the undercover officer's head through a plate glass window.

But there may be hope. Just 35 miles north of the sprawling metropolitan area of Dallas, another small community is attempting a change. In the university city of Denton, an integrated team of seven officers formed the core of a new, volunteer initiative: "C.O.P.," for Community-Oriented Policing. Contrary to traditional police practices, C.O.P. members try to allay black residents' latent suspicions about police with a different set of experiences. C.O.P. officers knock on doors in the city's predominantly black neighborhoods, meet the residents, learn their first names, listen to their concerns. As for the African American community members, they hope to prevent their neighborhoods from becoming another potential battleground between black and white, between the police and the citizens.

Perhaps change is possible. My own encounter with a white police officer ended surprisingly. After the obligatory check of license and insurance, the officer told me why I had been stopped. He had observed that both of my brake lights had been out and thought perhaps I had been unaware of that fact. He gave me no ticket, no citation. In the friendliest of voices, he advised me to repair the lights "for my own safety." And, if I ever see him again, the first thing I do may be to smile instead of panic. Perhaps, just perhaps, change is possible.

Works Cited

Cleaver, Eldridge. *Post-Prison Writings & Speeches.* New York: Putnam, 1981.

Doe, Jane, and John Doe. *Black and White: A Study of U.S. Racial Attitudes Today.* New York: Newsweek, 1966.

National Advisory Commission on Civil Disorders. *The Kerner Report.* Washington, DC: GPO, 1968.

Black and Latino
Roberto Santiago

"There is no way that you can be black and Puerto Rican at the same time." What? Despite the many times I've heard this over the years, that statement still perplexes me. I *am* both and always have been. My color is a blend of my mother's rich, dark skin tone and my father's white complexion. As they were both Puerto Rican, I spoke Spanish before English, but I am totally bilingual. My life has been shaped by my black and Latino heritages, and despite other people's confusion, I don't feel I have to choose one or the other. To do so would be to deny a part of myself.

There has not been a moment in my life when I did not know that I looked black—and I never thought that others did not see it, too. But growing up in East Harlem, I was also aware that I did not "act black," according to the African-American boys on the block.

My lighter-skinned Puerto Rican friends were less of a help in this department. "You're not black," they would whine, shaking their heads. "You're a *boriqua* [slang for Puerto Rican], you ain't no *moreno* [black]." If that was true, why did my mirror defy the rules of logic? And most of all, why did I feel that there was some serious unknown force trying to make me choose sides?

Acting black. Looking black. Being a real black. This debate among us is almost a parody. The fact is that I am black, so why do I need to prove it?

The island of Puerto Rico is only a stone's throw away from Haiti, and, no fooling, if you climb a palm tree, you can see Jamaica bobbing on the Atlantic. The slave trade ran through the Caribbean basin, and virtually all Puerto Rican citizens have some African blood in their veins. My grandparents on my mother's side were the classic *negro como carbón* (black as carbon) people, but despite the fact that they were as dark as can be, they are officially not considered black.

There is an explanation for this, but not one that makes much sense, or difference, to a working-class kid from Harlem. Puerto Ricans identify themselves as Hispanics—part of a worldwide race that originated from eons of white Spanish conquests—a mixture of white, African, and *Indio* blood, which, categorically, is apart from black. In other words, the culture is the predominant and determinant factor. But there are frustrations in being caught in a duo-culture, where your skin color does not necessarily dictate what you are. When I read Piri Thomas's searing autobiography, *Down These Mean Streets,* in my early teens, I saw that he couldn't figure out other people's attitudes toward his blackness, either.

My first encounter with this attitude about the race thing rode on horseback. I had just turned six years old and ran toward the bridle path in Central Park as I saw two horses about to trot past. "Yea! Horsie! Yea!" I yelled. Then I noticed one figure on horseback. She was white, and she shouted, "Shut up, you f—g nigger! Shut up!" She pulled back on the reins and twisted the horse in my direction. I can still feel the spray of gravel that the horse kicked at my chest. And suddenly she was gone. I looked back, and, in the distance, saw my parents playing Whiffle Ball with my sister. They seemed miles away.

They still don't know about this incident. But I told my Aunt Aurelia almost immediately. She explained what the words meant and why they were said. Ever since then I have been able to express my anger appropriately through words or action in similar situations. Self-preservation, ego, and pride forbid men from ever ignoring, much less forgetting, a slur.

Aunt Aurelia became, unintentionally, my source for answers I needed about color and race. I never sought her out. She just seemed to appear at my home during the points in my childhood when I most needed her for solace. "Puerto Ricans are different from American blacks," she told me once. "There is no racism between what you call white and black. Nobody even considers the marriages interracial." She then pointed out the difference in color between my father and mother. "You never noticed that," she said, "because you were not raised with that hang-up."

Aunt Aurelia passed away before I could follow up on her observation. But she had made an important point. It's why I never liked the attitude that says I should be exclusive to one race.

My behavior toward this race thing pegged me as an iconoclast of sorts. Children from mixed marriages, from my experience, also share this attitude. If I have to beat the label of iconoclast because the world wants people to be in set categories and I don't want to, then I will.

A month before Aunt Aurelia died, she saw I was a little down about the whole race thing, and she said, "Roberto, don't worry. Even if—no matter what you do—black people in this country don't, you can always depend on white people to treat you like a black."

Split Image
African Americans in the Mass Media

Edited by Jannette L. Dates
and William Barlow

Introduction: A War of Images
Jannette L. Dates and William Barlow

———————

Writing at the dawn of the twentieth century, W. E. B. Du Bois in *The Souls of Black Folk* prophesied more than once that "the problem of the color line" would dominate the planet's historical landscape for at least the next one hundred years. Having thus established race as the primary theoretical framework for his perceiving and being perceived by the world, Du Bois proceeded to delineate the cultural legacy of the "color line" with respect to African Americans, revealing that a deeply rooted "double consciousness" lay at the heart of his people's common racial memory. In his own words:

> After the Egyptian and the Indian, the Greek and Roman, the Teuton and Mongolian, the Negro is a sort of seventh son, born with a veil, and gifted with second sight in this American world, a world which yields him no true self-consciousness, but only lets him see himself through the revelation of the other world. It is a peculiar sensation this double consciousness, this sense of always looking at one's self through the eyes of others, of measuring one's soul by the tape of a

———————

Note: The terms Colored, Negro, black, Black American, Afro-American, and African American are all used to designate Americans of African ancestry more or less in correspondence with the trend of the period under discussion.

world that looks on in amused contempt and
pity. One ever feels his twoness, an American, a Negro; two souls, two thoughts, two
unreconciled strivings, two warring ideals in
one dark body, whose dogged strength alone
keeps it from being torn asunder.

The history of the American Negro is the
history of this strife, this longing to attain self-
conscious manhood, to merge his double self
into a better and truer self. In this merging he
wishes neither of the old selves to be lost. He
would not Africanize America, for America
has too much to teach the world and Africa.
He would not bleach his Negro soul in a flood
of white Americanism, for he knows that
Negro blood has a message for the world. He
simply wishes to make it possible for a man to
be both a Negro and an American, without
being cursed and spit upon by his fellows,
without having the doors of opportunity
closed roughly in his face.[1]

In many respects, the "double self" that Du Bois describes in the above passage is the inverse of the "split image" which, we shall argue, has characterized African American representations in the mass media throughout the
twentieth century. When juxtaposed, the exterior "image" and the interior
"self" constitute the complex and interdependent relationships between the
media and society, as well as between the individual and the mass, which this
book seeks to scrutinize through the cultural prism of race.

Sterling A. Brown was one of the first African American scholars to identify
and comment extensively on the bifurcation of black images in American culture along racial lines. In his pioneering study, *The Negro in American Fiction*,
he discussed the striking differences between fictional representations of
African Americans by white authors and those by black authors. In the
process, Brown identified recurring caricatures, particularly the "contented
slave," the "wretched freedman," the "tragic mulatto," the "brute Negro," and
the "comic Negro," as the most persistent African American stereotypes to
emerge from the nineteenth century and carry over into his era.[2] Likewise, his
Negro Poetry and Drama drew distinctions between "Negro poetry" and "white
poetry of Negro life" as well as between "Negro folk drama" and blackface
minstrelsy: "The minstrel show had a great deal to do with setting up the
American stereotype of the comic Negro, addicted to the use of big words, to
gaudy finery, to brawling with a razor, and to raiding chicken roosts." It was
"produced by whites for whites, and soon lost even its most rudimentary realism; the dialect became gibberish and the caricature a cartoon."[3]

It is interesting to note that Brown was also one of the first scholars of American culture to use Walter Lippmann's media-centered concept of the stereotype in his writings on literature, the arts, and the African American oral folk tradition. According to Lippmann's classic formulation, the stereotype "precedes reason" and "as a form of perception imposes a certain character on the data of our senses."[4] Hence, to be effective a stereotype must be anticipated by the conditioned perceptions of the beholder as well as existent in the imagination of the image maker. Ten years after Lippmann introduced the concept, Brown used it to characterize distinctive clusters of black representations in novels, poetry, and on the stage. Like the revelation implicit in Du Bois's "double consciousness" trope, Brown's unmasking of black stereotypes worked to deconstruct them, both metaphorically and mythically. His purpose was to expose the racial bias inherent in the most persistent caricatures of African Americans in the popular culture and then to replace them with less contrived and more authentic characterizations created, for the most part, by black image makers.

This collection of historical essays seeks to follow the intellectual lead of Du Bois and Brown by using the cultural prism of race to examine critically the images of African Americans that exist in the mass media. As our title suggests, the study focuses on the schizoid nature of these black representations. The dominant trend in African American portraiture has been created and nurtured by succeeding generations of white image makers, beginning as far back as the colonial era. Its opposite has been created and maintained by black image makers in response to the omissions and distortions of the former. This war of images casts light on the historical trajectory of the race issue in American society from both sides of the controversy. Thus, the definition and control of black images in the mass media have been contested from the outset along racial lines, with white cultural domination provoking African American cultural resistance. This theoretical framework is drawn from the Gramscian concept of ideological hegemony, of which it is an integral part. In brief, Antonio Gramsci argues that ruling-class alliances in modern societies maintain their power by cultivating a consensus among subordinate classes; coercion is used only as a last resort. Cultural domination is the best means of achieving ideological hegemony because it ensures the triumph of a single consensus, or "common sense," among all sectors of the social order. But hegemony is always in the making—or unmaking—for Gramsci also argues that cultural domination provokes its opposite, cultural resistance, in subordinate classes. Hence, even at its best, ideological hegemony is still an "unstable equilibrium." The dominant culture must constantly strive to expand its hegemony while fending off challenges and interventions from the very classes and groups it seeks to subjugate. Consequently, culture itself becomes an arena for historical contest.[5]

In the wake of Gramsci's formulations on class, culture, and ideological hegemony, Stuart Hall and his associates have more recently focused attention on popular culture and the mass media as sites of ideological struggle between the dominant culture and those subordinate classes and/or groups threatened by its cultural imperialism. In his studies of representation and ideology, Hall and others have noted the importance of the rituals of social behavior in which ideologies imprint or inscribe themselves. "These rituals . . . occur in social sites and are linked with social apparatuses. This is why we need to deconstruct language and behavior in order to decipher the patterns of ideological thinking which are inscribed in them."[6] The mass media function as the producers and transmitters of ideologies because the rituals and myths they reproduce for public consumption "explain, instruct and justify practices and institutions . . . linking symbols, formulas, plot and characters in a pattern that is conventional, appealing and gratifying . . . in tales of redemption that show how order is restored."[7] This is done routinely to encourage dutiful submission to authority.

In American society, by reproducing the ideological hegemony of the dominant white culture, the mass media help to legitimate the inequalities in class and race relations. In *Beyond Agenda-Setting*, Oscar Gandy argues that there is strong evidence that the media tilt toward the upper classes, that information systems "tend to distribute information, including the mass media, in a form most familiar to users with more education,"[8] thus widening the knowledge gap between the poor and poorly educated and the rich and well-educated as well as the disparity between the races.

In addition, racial images in the mass media are infused with color-coded positive and negative moralistic features. Once these symbols become familiar and accepted, they fuel misperceptions and perpetuate misunderstandings among the races. Hall, Jefferson, and other researchers point out that groups and classes are ranked in relation to each other in terms of productivity, wealth, and power, and that cultures may be similarly ranked in terms of "domination and subordination, along the scale of 'cultural power.' " Further, they support the position that the ruling class rules as thinkers and producers of ideas, as well as regulating their distribution. Its ideas, therefore, are the dominant ideas of any period.[9] When this framework is applied to race relations in American society, a similar pattern of unequal cultural power emerges. Racial representations help to mold public opinion, then hold it in place and set the agenda for public discourse on the race issue in the media and in the society at large. Black media stereotypes are not the natural, much less harmless, products of an idealized popular culture; rather, they are more commonly socially constructed images that are selective, partial, one-dimensional, and distorted in their portrayal of African Americans. Moreover, stereotyped black images most often are frozen, incapable of growth, change, innovation, or transformation. As T. W. Adorno has observed: "The more stereotypes become reified and rigid in the present setup of the culture industries, the less people are likely to change their preconceived ideas with the progress of experience. The more opaque and complicated modern life becomes, the more people are tempted to cling desperately to clichés which seem to bring some order into the otherwise un-understandable."[10]

Stereotypes are especially effective in conveying ideological messages because they are so laden with ritual and myth, particularly in the case of African Americans; but, invariably, these black representations are totally at odds with the reality of African Americans as individual people. The end result, a series of sharply conflicting black images in the mass media, has grave implications for American society as a whole. The conflict is indicative of a deep cultural schism, which precipitated the ideological struggle between white and black image makers in the first place. Hence the situation offers scholars a unique opportunity to explore the dynamics of cultural conflict as manifested in mass-media imagery. By tracking African American images, their audience, and their producers over time and across the various media strategically involved in the production and distribution of those images, we can pinpoint their common characteristics and sources, the ways in which they evolved, and the context in which they competed for the attention of both black and white Americans. Ultimately, this unmasking of black stereotypes deeply embedded in the popular culture brings the question of racial identity to the forefront, both at the individual and the national level. It was James Baldwin who expressed the quintessential paradox of America's race relations when he stated prophetically to a white television audience: "If I'm not who you say I am, then you're not who you think you are."[11]

Antebellum Popular Culture

The roots of the schism go back to slavery. Both the popular theater and the literature of the antebellum period created standardized images of slaves and their masters. These initial representations were used to rationalize the enslavement of African people and to justify the institution of slavery in the South. As early as 1781, in a play called *The Divorce*, and then again in 1795, in a romantic farce entitled *The Triumphs of Love*, a black character named Sambo appeared on the American stage. In both cases, he was cast in a familiar mold: always singing nonsense songs and dancing around the stage. His dress was gaudy, his manners pretentious, his speech riddled with malapropisms, and he was played by white actors in blackface. The subsequent popularity of the "comic Negro" stereotype had profound social implications. As historian Joseph Boskin noted:

> Sambo was an extraordinary type of social control, at once extremely subtle, devious, and encompassing. To exercise a high degree of control meant also to be able to manipulate the full range of humor; to create, ultimately, an insidious type of buffoon. To make the black male into an object of laughter, and conversely, to force him to devise laughter, was to strip him of masculinity, dignity, and self-respect. Sambo was, then, an illustration of

humor as a device of oppression, and one of
the most potent in American popular culture.
The ultimate objective for whites was to effect
mastery, to render the black male powerless
as a potential warrior, as a sexual competitor,
as an economic adversary.[12]

The first slave to appear in a major American novel was Caesar Thompson
Wharton, a house servant in James Fenimore Cooper's *The Spy.* Caesar was the
epitome of the early contented slave stereotype. He was loyal, devoted to his
master's welfare, and seemingly comfortable with his own servitude. He also
provided the story with comic relief due to his fear of ghosts and other superstitions. The novel was adapted to the stage soon after it was written and
became one of the most popular plays of the era. Theater and literature were
the major conduits for cultural images in America throughout the nineteenth
century. Popular songs were integral to both, being performed on stage and
published as sheet music or broadsides. Late in the 1820s, white actors began
doing imitations of African American song and dance in urban theaters in the
North and South. Their performances presented clownlike images of black
Americans, portraying them as comic buffoons. The actors continued the practice of blackening their faces with burnt cork to accent the caricatures. The
most renowned of the early blackface performers was Thomas D. Rice, who
popularized the song and dance, "Jump Jim Crow," a theatrical sensation in
the 1830s. Rice modeled his famous character on an elderly, crippled African
American stable hand and reputedly even borrowed his suit of ragged clothing for the first stage performance. His new stage act was an instant success,
catapulting him into a much heralded tour of the major entertainment halls in
the United States and England. In the process, the "Jim Crow" stereotype was
born. He was a comically deformed song-and-dance man, wearing ragged, ill-
fitting clothes—a burlesque of African American fashion, speech, and phys-
iognomy.[13] As historian William Van Deburg observed: "The early slave image
offered white audiences a comforting psychological reassurance. In the real
world of . . . Santo Domingo, or Stono, South Carolina, rebellious African
slaves might conspire and revolt, but on stage blackface bondsmen were loy-
ally imitative and greatly dependent on their masters. Such intellectually inferior clowns posed little threat to white hegemony."[14]

By the 1840s, blackface minstrelsy had evolved into a formalized entertainment genre, complete with a standardized stage extravaganza that required an
entire troupe of actors. But from its inception, antebellum minstrelsy's characterization of black Americans was a damaging one. African Americans living
in the cities were invariably portrayed as urban dandies and dummies who
futilely aped white manners. Plantation slaves were depicted as childlike,
comical, and contented with their lot. With the slavery issue increasingly pre-
occupying the nation, such representations tended to reinforce the ideology of

racism, especially in the minds of white working-class males, the major audience of the minstrel shows. As a result, they were not inclined to want the slaves emancipated, and most of them were openly hostile to the abolitionist movement.

Many of the popular white performers in antebellum minstrel shows had some knowledge of black folklore prior to putting on the burnt cork. The most prominent of these performers were Thomas Rice, George Dixon, Dan Emmett, E. P. Christy, and Stephen Foster. But their assumption of the slave population's inherent inferiority and their perceptions of African American "peculiarities" were in league with the condescending and inhumane views advanced by southern slave owners. Historian Robert Toll ably summarized the social dynamics of antebellum ministrelsy:

> Blackface performers were like puppets operated by a white puppet master. Their physical appearance proclaimed their non-humanity; yet they could be manipulated not only to mock themselves but also to act like human beings. They expressed human emotions such as joy and grief, love, fear, longing. The white audience then identified with the emotions, admired the skills of the puppeteer, even sympathized laughingly with the hopeless aspiration of the puppets to become human, and at the same time feasted on the assurance that they could not do so. Blackface minstrelsy's dominance of popular entertainment amounted to a half a century of inurement to the uses of white supremacy.[15]

By the 1850s, the slavery controversy had engulfed the nation in a war of political rhetoric and racial imagery. For the first time, key stereotypes in the arsenal of the proslavery forces, like the contented slave and the benevolent master, were being seriously challenged by antislavery activists at public forums and in the media. In particular, white abolitionists rallied around the publication of Harriet Beecher Stowe's *Uncle Tom's Cabin*, which they found to be an ideal vehicle for projecting their image of African American slaves and their antislavery sentiments. The book received a great deal of fanfare, inspiring a rash of imitative fiction and stage melodramas, and ultimately becoming the media event of the decade. Although Stowe stood the stereotype of the benevolent slave master on its head, portraying him as the novel's lecherous and malevolent villain, it was her reworking of the slave stereotype through the character of Uncle Tom that attracted the most attention. Uncle Tom was hardly a contented or comic slave, but neither was he an angry or rebellious one; instead, he was a gentle and long-suffering bondsman, imbued with childlike innocence and a "natural" Christian piety. Lurking behind these idealized character traits was an unusual collusion of middle-class white abolitionist and feminist beliefs, referred to by historian George Fredrickson as "romantic racialism."[16] Through the Uncle Tom stereotype, the major Christian virtues associated with the domestic realm of women were elevated and favored over secular patriarchial virtues. As one enthusiastic male supporter proclaimed: "It is sometimes said . . . that the Negro race is the feminine race of the world. This is not only because of [the Negro's] social and affectionate nature, but because he possesses that strange, moral, instinctive insight that belongs more to women than men."[17]

While Uncle Tom proved to be a prized new addition to the pantheon of popular American racial stereotypes, the other major black figures in Stowe's book were pretty much old hat, even back then. Like her white proslavery adversaries, Stowe resorted to longstanding popular cultural stereotypes in order to round out her cast of characters. The tragic mulattoes are represented by Cassy and George Harris, whose white blood gives them a genetic edge in intellect and temperament over their full-blooded African compatriots, but whose mixed blood dooms them to a life in limbo, stranded indefinitely between two cultures. The comic minstrel stereotypes are present in the slave duo of Sam and Andy, who could easily be considered the original Amos 'n' Andy prototypes. There is a black pickaninny child, Topsy, who is juxtaposed to her angelic blond opposite, Little Eva. Although there are no misguided rebel slaves in *Uncle Tom's Cabin*, Stowe made amends by devoting her next novel, appropriately named *Dred*, to just such a figure. Based in part on Nat Turner, the slave insurrectionist is depicted as a religious fanatic tormented by evil spirits and visions, while the idealized virtues of Uncle Tom are transferred to Dred's patient and docile wife, Milly.[18]

The nationwide publicity surrounding the publication of *Uncle Tom's Cabin* provoked a deluge of schemes to cash in on its popularity. These included everything from a cornucopia of Uncle Tom memorabilia to a plethora of amateurish "Uncle Tom Shows" that crisscrossed the country, staging the melodrama wherever they could solicit an audience. As one amused observer noted, " 'Uncle Tom' became, in his various forms, the most frequently sold slave in American history."[19] The longevity of Uncle Tom's lifespan as a well-known national stereotype, rivaled only by the ubiquitous Sambo, is testimony to his staying power—especially with white audiences. As recently as 1946, *The Negro Digest* reported that a large majority of the whites they polled thought that *Uncle Tom's Cabin* was not an "Anti-Negro" fable, while a clear majority of the African Americans polled viewed the same story and its hero as "Anti-Negro."[20]

The contested image of the slave in the antebellum era was at the eye of an ideological storm that shattered the hegemony of the dominant white culture, eventually dividing the country into two camps. For the white proslavery apologists, the black bondsmen were invariably a happy lot who had much to be thankful for while living on plantations. In contrast, white antislavery advocates depicted the black bondsmen as victims of an inhumane plantation system, waiting patiently to be set free by righteous white emancipators. It was left to ex-bondsmen such as Frederick Douglass, Soloman Northrup, William Wells Brown, and Henry Bibb to publicize accounts of defiant slaves who took their lives into their own hands. Each of them wrote a slave narrative detailing the inhumane conditions of their captivity and their eventual escape to freedom.

It is interesting to note that the mastery of reading, and especially writing, was also seen as an act of liberation for these former bondsmen. The slave narratives were the first instances of African American voices reaching the outside world, moving beyond the black oral tradition and the slave community. In essence, these written narratives are the beginnings of an African American literary tradition, one that responded to the pervasive white images of slavery by becoming "double voiced." Former slaves were recognized as speaking subjects in the dominant culture only to the extent that they could inscribe their voices in the written word. It was only by writing their thoughts down on paper that slaves could obtain a hearing in the outside world. Ironically, learning to read and write was strictly prohibited to slaves. Moreover, as Henry Louis Gates, Jr., has observed: "In slave narratives . . . making the white written text speak with a black voice is the initial mode of inscription of the double voiced."[21]

In addition to the slave narratives, the fiction written by former bondsmen during the antebellum era also championed bold and rebellious slave heroes who actively opposed their bondage. Frederick Douglass's *The Heroic Slave* is a classic example of this genre. It is based on a real mutiny carried out by bondsmen aboard the slaveship *Creole* in 1841. The novel's black hero is Madison Washington, who, after leading the successful slave revolt, returns to the South to rescue his kin, even though this action places his newly won freedom in great jeopardy. Another example of this genre is J. T. Trowbridge's *Cudjo's Cave*, the story of two escaped slaves in eastern Tennessee who live in a secret cave and wage guerrilla warfare against the Confederacy in the region. In both novels, the slave protagonists' active resistance to the bondage of their people stands in sharp contrast to Uncle Tom's passive resistance to slavery.[22]

Postbellum Popular Culture

After the Civil War, popular literature and the stage continued to be the chief media channels for cultural images of African Americans. Likewise, the debate over slavery continued, but now from a historical vantage point. Most white southern writers in the postbellum era routinely romanticized the Confederacy. Genteel slave masters and chivalrous military leaders were venerated as the cultural heroes of a mythical golden age of southern gallantry and glory—gone but not forgotten. Slaves continued to be characterized as contented and comical. But as a postbellum literature evolved, new black stereotypes emerged, updating those from the antebellum period. The place of the contented slave was taken over by the faithful servant: the female side of this stereotype became the domestic mammy caricature, while the male side matured into elderly Uncle Toms. Thomas Nelson Page invented Uncle Billy to sing the author's praises of slavery days in the slaves' own vernacular. Joel Chandler Harris created Uncle Remus as a sort of folksy apologist for the plantation social system and antebellum southern culture. His stories were expropriated from the African American oral tradition and related in black dialect. Next, the wretched freedman stereotype devolved into the bestial, brutish Negro, also a doomed figure—but in this case because of his ignorance, insolence, and lust for white women. Likewise, the mulatto became more degenerate as well as more tragic. Thomas Nelson Page helped to popularize the brute Negro stereotype in his novel *Red Rock* by inventing the character Moses, a mulatto villain who lusts after political power and white females. He is described by the author as a "reptile" and a "wild beast." Perhaps the most notorious of the depraved mulatto creatures, Silas Lynch, first appeared in Thomas Dixon's novel *The Clansmen* and then later in D. W. Griffith's film "Birth of a Nation." Dixon was an infamous southern Negrophobe who was also responsible for inventing the renegade Gus, a classic brute Negro stereotype equally prominent in Griffith's controversial film.[23]

In contrast and reaction to this new onslaught of black stereotypes from the southern white literary mainstream, African American writers created cultural heroes who were masters of their own destiny, and they also sought to repossess the black vernacular tradition for their own literature. The first order of business was the veneration of African American heroes. In William Still's *The Underground Railroad*, a fugitive slave who works as an underground railroad conductor is the novel's major character and role model.[24] Another favorite fictional African American hero during this period was the black soldier who fought for the Union during the Civil War. His courage and skill as a combatant was lauded in novels, histories, and personal reminiscences.

It was Charles Chesnutt, however, who first used black dialect and parody, cultural resources drawn from the wellspring of the black oral tradition, as a means of undermining the dominant white literary discourse on African Americans and their vernacular. In addition to the masking function of the dialect, what Gates refers to as "the self-conscious switch of linguistic codes from white to black, or more properly, from standard English to black vernacular," Chesnutt also made use of its subversive qualities.[25] His dialect-speaking folk hero in *The Conjure Woman*, Uncle Julius, is the antithesis of Uncle Remus; this wily raconteur is more interested in preserving his integrity and surviving in the postbellum era than in glorifying antebellum slavery and remaining loyal to his former masters. Moreover, Uncle Julius also uses witchcraft in his adversarial relationships with white people.[26] Chesnutt's use of black folklore and dialect in his writing set the stage for other African American authors—from Jean Toomer to Langston Hughes,

Zora Neal Hurston, and Sterling A. Brown—to mine the black oral tradition for materials to incorporate into their novels, short stories, and poetry. As Gates points out: "The poet has in this mutation—this dialect—an accessible linguistic system that turns the literate language upon itself, exploiting the metaphor against the master."[27] In the ongoing war of racial images during this period, "one didn't believe one's eyes, if one were black," according to Sterling Brown, "one believed one's ears."[28]

Within the context of the black vernacular, two key strategies were readily adopted by black writers: parody and signifying. Literary scholar Mikhail Bakhtin defines the former as follows. In parody, "the author employs the speech of another . . . he introduces into that other speech an intention which is directly opposed to the original one. The second voice, having lodged in the other speech, clashes antagonistically with the original, host voice and forces it to serve directly opposite aims. Speech becomes a battlefield for opposing intentions."[29] In light of this definition, parody has a very special significance for an African American literary tradition because of its tendency to invert social hierarchies: "By appropriating an existing discourse for its own ends, parody is especially well-suited to the needs of the powerless, precisely because it assumes the force, of the dominant discourse only to deploy that force, through a kind of artistic jujitsu, against domination."[30] Signifying, on the other hand, is a rhetorical strategy calculated to reverse dialogue by turning a statement back on itself in order to gain the upper hand in a verbal contest; it is yet another "double-voiced" or intertextual practice that seeks to subvert existing power relations. The act of signifying is, of course, associated with the "Signifying Monkey," a well-known fixture in African American folklore; but its roots go all the way back to trickster figures from traditional West African cultures like the Yoruban Esu-Elegbara and the Fon's Legba. One of the most famous examples of literary signifying was created by Sterling A. Brown: in response to Robert Penn Warren's line from his poem, "Piney Woods," "Nigger, your breed ain't metaphysical," Brown retorts, "Cracker, your breed ain't exegetical."[31]

Popular theater was also an important cultural arena in which racial images were contested during the postbellum period. In the aftermath of the Civil War, African American minstrel troupes began appearing before both white and black audiences. These entertainers adopted the blackface minstrelsy format, the plantation subject matter, and, to a certain extent, the blackface stereotypes of slave life; but they did so while infusing their minstrel routines with authentic folk materials drawn from the African American oral tradition. This contradiction set the stage for what would follow: a protracted tug-of-war within minstrelsy between the forces of the still dominant antebellum blackface tradition and those of a slowly emerging postbellum African American minstrelsy.

Although black entertainers eventually came to dominate post-bellum minstrelsy, white businessmen owned and controlled it. In addition to reaping the profits, these white entrepreneurs insisted that the material and structure of the shows remain faithful to the content and the format of the early blackface tradition. They demanded that the black performers they hired reproduce the outdated routines and caricatures of the antebellum minstrel show. In essence, they functioned as guardians of the old cultural order, and their collective influence resulted in the perpetuation of demeaning racial stereotypes in American show business, a trend that persisted well into the twentieth century. Talented black entertainers who worked for white-owned minstrel troupes often found themselves between the hammer and the anvil with respect to their artistic and racial integrity. The white owners decided who could work in the most prestigious troupes and offered a certain amount of fame and fortune in exchange for African American compliance with the blackface legacy. Although there was some latitude in negotiating these arrangements, even the most popular, and therefore potentially the most powerful, of the black performers in these shows sacrificed a good deal of their artistic independence in return for stardom and financial gain. The careers of James Bland, Billy Kersands, and Bert Williams offer clear, if somewhat disheartening, illustrations of the pitfalls inherent in postbellum minstrelsy. Each of them accommodated minstrel stereotypes on the road to success. Bland's song "Carry Me Back to Old Virginny" told the story of a former slave longing for his master and his life on the old plantation. It became the state anthem of Virginia. Bert Williams was the last significant African American entertainer to perform in blackface on the American stage.[32]

Toward the end of the nineteenth century, the infamous "coon song" became fashionable. The term "coon" was a shortened version of raccoon used by southern whites as a derisive reference to black males. Gradually it came to represent the image of a dandified urban black male. In 1896, the African American songwriter Ernest Hogan published "All Coons Look Alike to Me." The song became an overnight sensation, inspiring a flood of commercial coon songs over the next two decades. Hogan would later regret that he had helped to popularize the derogatory connotations of the term and its image. At their worst, the coon songs were degrading burlesques of African American physical and cultural traits. However, the songs written by black composers for their new vaudeville musical revues were also commonly referred to as coon songs during this period. They were usually optimistic, ragtime numbers tinged with a whimsical sort of irony. "Darktown Is Out Tonite" by Will Marion Cook is an example of this sort of coon song. It celebrated the good times and musical vitality found in black urban enclaves, while also playfully chiding whites for their inability to break through their own rigid formalities and move past racial stereotypes to have some fun themselves. African American tunesmiths were thus able to reclaim a portion of a song genre that was rightfully theirs, but only after it had been thoroughly exploited by Tin Pan Alley and Broadway. As late as 1925, black entertainment columnist S. T. Whitney, after complaining bitterly about the white business interests in control of black show business, acknowledged that "the real musical show and drama of race life will have to be promoted by our own men before the desired result is obtained."[33]

Enter the Mass Media

Like popular theater and literature, popular song was another battlefield in the war of images between black and white image makers. With the advent of phonograph recordings, motion pictures, and radio broadcasting, the end of an era in American culture was close at hand. Popular theater and literature were no longer the dominant image making media in the country. Minstrelsy and its offspring, vaudeville, were fast becoming relics of the past. Unfortunately, the legacy of derogatory racial caricatures and restricted employment opportunities reemerged in the new mass-media industries that dominated the production and distribution of African American images in the twentieth century. White-owned record, film, radio, advertising, news, and later television industries based most of the black images they produced on the prevailing nineteenth-century stereotypes. They also continued the discriminatory practice of limiting the roles African Americans could play in these media.

This study is first and foremost a historical and comparative analysis of African American portrayal and participation in the mass media in the United States. It develops the theme of "the war of images" to foster some understanding of how and why the mass media have evolved as they have with respect to African American imagery and participation. Every chapter addresses the racial duality of the individual media industries under scrutiny. Each one explores the ways in which, on the one hand, African American images have been distorted and talent exploited, while, on the other hand, African Americans have been systematically denied by those in power the opportunity to act as full participants in the industries. What evolved were mass media that favored black stereotypes created by whites over the more authentic and positive black characters created by black image makers. It is therefore understandable that, for the most part, African Americans have been disappointed in many of the mass-media products featuring their group as seen in mainstream America's popular culture, because so little of their own culture and values that differ from the mainstream has been given any exposure. Thus, whenever and wherever they could, African Americans tried to develop their own media products and their own means of distributing them. White domination of mainstream culture inevitably gave rise to African American cultural resistance, splitting the black image.

As could be expected, very few scholarly books or critical articles have focused substantively on the participation and portrayal of African Americans in media industries, contributing to the perception that black Americans have played no part in the creation and evolution of the various mass media. Almost all the scholarly material written on African Americans in the mass media has been published since 1970.

While disparate amounts of scholarship on African American participation and portrayal in each of the media industries discussed here do exist, there is no book that attempts to survey all of them in historical and comparative terms. This study conscientiously attempts to use the cultural prism of race in order to assess the development of the American mass media in the twentieth century and, within this historical context, specifically to trace the negative portrayals and restricted participation of African Americans in the mass media, on the one hand, and their responses to such stereotyping and discrimination, on the other. These responses have been varied, ranging from cautious accommodation, through angry protest, to endeavors to create alternatives both inside and outside the dominant white media.

In "Cashing In: 1900–1939," William Barlow analyzes the commercial music industry's relationship to African American music from the turn of the century to World War II. He shows in detail how the industry served as an important catalyst in the development of certain styles of popular black music, while in the process financially and artistically exploiting African American musicians. The financial exploitation usually involved the theft of royalty monies and/or song copyrights. The artistic exploitation involved the expropriation of new styles of African American music by the white-dominated music industry, which, in turn, diluted its rhythms and trivialized its content in order to make it more palatable to white music consumers.

In "Crossing Over: 1939–1989," Reebee Garofalo extends the line of analysis to the postwar development of rhythm and blues and its offspring, rock 'n' roll. He points out that most white artists who "covered" songs originally conceived by black artists were able to reap huge profits and achieve tremendous popularity while exerting little or no original creativity of their own. At the same time, many of the black artists who were responsible for the popular music of the era went unrecognized and unrewarded. Garofalo demonstrates how this pattern of expropriation repeated itself in the rock music of the 1960s and the disco music of the 1970s. But he also describes how black popular music continued to rejuvenate its traditions and styles as a means of resisting such expropriation—rap music being the latest innovation that demonstrates this effort. As a result of this continuous creative output on a collective level, black music makers are able to control their own images and musical products better vis-à-vis the music industry.

In "Film," Thomas Cripps analyzes the portrayal and the participation of African Americans in motion pictures, revealing how black cinema evolved from African American history. Noting how African Americans by their very presence altered the substance of American politics, Cripps explores the participation of blacks in films made by whites and by themselves. By the time the film industry developed sound and settled into Hollywood, motion picture roles for African Americans had already become narrowly proscribed. During the 1920s and 1930s the two roles open to them were either as entertainers or servants. After World War II, some progress was made toward broadening that image, as African American characters became more realistic and a token black hero, Sidney Poitier, made his film debut. Most African American actors and directors, however, still could not gain entrance into the Hollywood film industry, and the old stereotypes never faded away. The political and cultural ferment of the 1960s brought stronger black role models into Hollywood motion pictures, but then came the "Blaxploitation" films of the 1970s, which glamorized African American decadence, hedonism, and violence. Cripps concludes his chapter by arguing that even now, although some African Americans have moved into directing and producing Hollywood movies, the film industry continues to limit black participation in its work force and still controls, in the majority of cases, the black screen image. Thus, in spite of some important gains made by stars like Richard Pryor, Eddie Murphy, and Spike Lee, Hollywood's hegemony over African Americans in the film industry is still formidable.

In "Commercial and Noncommercial Radio," William Barlow critically assesses the radio industry's portrayal of African Americans since the 1920s, the limited nature of black participation in the industry, and the role African Americans have managed to play in fashioning radio's black audio images. Prior to the 1950s, when radio was the country's most popular form of mass media, African Americans were systematically excluded from working in the industry; most black characters were created and played by white writers and performers. With the advent of television, the radio networks lost their national audience. The radio market became more localized and thus demographically segmented, resulting in the rise of black formatted radio stations in the 1950s and 1960s. The tendency has continued up to the present; yet, even though these stations are programmed for black listeners, they remain for the most part white-owned. On the other hand, Barlow points out that this pattern of white control in African American radio operations is not found presently in the fifty-odd noncommercial black university and community radio stations established since the 1960s.

In "Commercial Television," Jannette L. Dates argues that commercial television failed to reflect African American culture adequately, and distorted the few aspects of the culture it did include. It systematically deterred whites from learning about blacks while it prevented blacks from fully participating in the industry. Despite these constraints, African Americans gained entrance into the medium in whatever ways they could. Their presence developed over the years, and by the mid-1980s African Americans were a potent force in network commercial television, particularly on camera.

In "Public Television," Dates argues that the nonprofit public sector sought access to noncommercial television in order to offer a viable alternative to commercial enterprises. It sought an avenue for meeting the needs of minorities not served by commercial broadcasting, including cultural, regional, and, eventually, racial minorities. She concludes that, for the most part, public television failed to address the needs or desires of African American audiences, despite the fact that the system was subsidized by the public purse. She goes on to demonstrate how, like its commercial counterpart, public television gradually began to include racial minority groups in program offerings, personnel, and ownership/licensing, but these changes occurred well after the time of the civil rights movement.

In "Print News," Dates describes the portraiture of African Americans found in the black press in comparison with the white print media. She argues that the black press has historically seen the black community from a vastly different perspective from that of the white press, thus providing the raison d'être for the existence and continuation of the black press. She argues that, despite black press enfeeblement resulting from the very integration for which it had so conscientiously fought, the black press, particularly magazines, continues to offer viable alternatives for expressing African American views and perspectives.

Lee Thornton, "Broadcast News," focuses on the strides African Americans made between 1955 and 1990 in radio and television newsrooms. In 1955, for example, there was not a single black person in radio or television newsrooms above the caretaker level, whereas in the 1980s Americans saw Ed Bradley, Carole Simpson, George Strait, Bernard Shaw, and other black people reporting regularly. Thornton documents and analyzes how and why these dramatic changes came about. She concludes that broadcast journalists in general, and African Americans in particular, have a responsibility to African Americans and other minorities to bring the media at all levels into greater congruence with the institutional, cultural, and intellectual diversity of American society.

In "Advertising," Dates develops the argument that African American consumers were seldom courted as an actively targeted advertising market until years after the civil rights movement had ground to a halt. She demonstrates how the African American consumer, practitioner, and activist all figured in the development of the advertising industry's increased interest in the black community as a market. She also discusses how advertising opportunities became more available to African Americans as the new electronic environment emerged.

The Conclusion identifies the major contradictions still evident in the portrayals and participation of African Americans in the media industries. Within the framework of the tension between the potential of African Americans in the mass media and the constraints encountered by black people in those same media, the writers suggest a strategy for the future. This would involve both working within the media industries to broaden black participation and upgrade black images and working outside the industries to develop alternatives that would make users and suppliers aware of the power that resides in the hands of those who shape the image of the African American. The strategy also involves a new and more accurate understanding of the role played by economics and distribution in media operations, from the perspective of the African American entrepreneur. Only through the implementation of this dual strategy, the authors argue, can the schism between black and white images of the African American be significantly narrowed. Only by struggling on at least two fronts, we believe, can the split in the black image be minimized.

Notes

1. W. E. B. Du Bois, *The Souls of Black Folk* (New York: Fawcett, 1961), 16–17.

2. Sterling A. Brown, *The Negro in American Fiction*, 2d ed. (New York: Atheneum, 1972).

3. Sterling A. Brown, *Negro Poetry and Drama*, 2d ed. (New York: Atheneum, 1972), 106.

4. Walter Lippmann, *Public Opinion* (New York: Macmillan, 1922), 88–89.

5. Antonio Gramsci, *Selections from the Prison Notebooks* (New York: International Publishers, 1971); Stuart Hall, "Gramsci's Relevance for the Study of Race and Ethnicity," *Journal of Communication Inquiry* 10 (Summer 1986): 5–27.

6. Stuart Hall, "Signification, Representation, Ideology: Althusser and the Post-structuralist Debates," *Critical Studies in Mass Communication* (June 1985):98–100.

7. Douglas Kellner, "Television, Ideology and Emancipatory Popular Culture," in *Television: The Critical View*, 4th ed., ed. Horace Newcomb (New York: Oxford University Press, 1987), 471–506.

8. Oscar H. Gandy, Jr., *Beyond Agenda Setting: Information Subsidies and Public Policy* (New Jersey: Ablex, 1982), 178–81; D. Roberts and C. Bachen "Mass Communication Effects," *Annual Review of Psychology* 32 (1981): 307–56; and Oscar H. Gandy, Jr. and M. ElWaylly, "The Knowledge Gap and Foreign Affairs: The Palestinian-Israeli Conflict," *Journalism Quarterly* 62 (1985): 777–83.

9. John Clarke, Stuart Hall, Tony Jefferson, and Brian Roberts, "Subcultures, Cultures and Class," in *Resistance Through Rituals: Youth Subcultures in Post-War Britain*, ed. Stuart Hall and Tony Jefferson (London: Hutchinson & Company, 1980), 11.

10. T. W. Adomo, "Television and Patterns of Mass Culture," in *Mass Culture: The Popular Arts in America*, ed. Bernard Rosenburg and David Manning White (New York: Free Press, 1957), 484.

11. James Baldwin, interviewed on CBS News, October 1967.

12. Joseph Boskin, *Sambo: The Rise and Demise of an American Jester* (New York: Oxford University Press, 1986), 13–14.

13. Brown, *Negro Poetry and Drama*, 105.

14. William L. Van Deburg, *Slavery and Race in American Popular Culture* (Madison: University of Wisconsin Press, 1984), 24.

15. Richard C. Toll, *Blacking Up: The Minstrel Show in Nineteenth-Century America* (New York: Oxford University Press, 1974), 274.

16. George M. Fredrickson, *The Black Image in the White Mind* (Middletown, Conn.: Wesleyan University Press, 1971), 101–2, 125–27.

17. Ibid., 114–15.

18. Harriet Beecher Stowe, *Dred: A Tale of the Great Dismal Swamp* (Boston: Phillips Sampson & Company, 1856).

19. Richard Yarborough, "Strategies of Black Characterization in 'Uncle Tom's Cabin' and the Early Afro-American Novel," in *New Essays on Uncle Tom's Cabin*, ed. Eric J. Sundquist (Cambridge: Cambridge University Press, 1986), 63.

20. Wallace Lee, "Is 'Uncle Tom's Cabin' Anti-Negro?", *Negro Digest*, January 1946, 68.

21. Henry Louis Gates, Jr., *The Signifying Monkey: A Theory of Afro-American Literary Criticism* (New York: Oxford University Press, 1988), 131.

22. See Frederick Douglass, *The Heroic Slave* 1853; J.T. Trowbridge, *Cudjo's Cave* (1863).

23. See Thomas Nelson Page, *Red Rock* (1900); Joel Chandler Harris, *Tales of Uncle Remus*; and Thomas Dixon, *The Clansmen* (1905).

24. William Still, *The Underground Railroad: A Record of Facts, Authentic Narratives, Letters, & C., Narrating the Hardships, Hair-breadth Escapes and Death Struggles of the Slaves in Their Efforts for Freedom* (Philadelphia, Pa.: Porter & Coates, 1872).

25. Henry Louis Gates, Jr., *Figures in Black: Words, Signs and the Racial Self* (New York: Oxford University Press, 1987), 171.

26. Charles Chesnutt, *The Conjure Woman* (Boston and New York: Houghton Mifflin, 1899).

27. Gates, *Figures in Black*, 172.

28. Ibid., 186.

29. Mikhail Bakhtin, "Discourse Typology in Prose," in *Readings in Russian Poetics: Formalist and Structuralist Views*, ed. Ladislav Matejka and Kaystyna Pomorska (Cambridge, Mass.: MIT University Press, 1971), 185–86.

30. Robert Stam, "Mikhail Bakhtin and Left Cultural Critique," in *Postmodernism and Its Discontent: Theories, Practices*, ed. E. Ann Caplan (London: Verso, 1988), 139.

31. Interview with Sterling Brown by William Barlow, 4 May 1984.

32. Lewis Bland, "James Allen Bland, Negro Composer: A Study of His Life and Work," MA. thesis, Howard University, 1958; Ann Charters, *Nobody: The Story of Bert Williams* (New York: Macmillan, 1970); and Toll, *Blacking Up*.

33. Daphne Duval Harrison, *Black Pearls: Blues Queens of the 1920s* (New Brunswick, N.J.: Rutgers University Press, 1988), 30.

Conclusion: Split Images and Double Binds
Jannette L. Dates and William Barlow

White domination of the mass media, with its pervasive control over the portrayal and participation of African Americans in those media, has disclosed major cultural contradictions. In all the media industries surveyed in this study, white owners and producers have appropriated aspects of African American culture to enrich the mass-media mainstream and enrich themselves. The black images mass-produced by them, however, have been filtered through the racial misconceptions and fantasies of the dominant white culture, which has tended to deny the existence of a rich and resilient black culture of equal worth. Throughout most of the twentieth century, whenever white image makers have developed media products (records, films, radio and television programs, news stories, and advertising campaigns) featuring African Americans, they invariably did so in terms of codes and criteria based on their own racial and class background. Historically, there has been very little African American involvement at decision-making levels in these industries.

Given this situation, it has been only natural that African Americans should devise their own ways of resisting white domination, just as they had in the past, and that one of their first priorities would be to reconstruct more accurate images of themselves. Both the social reconstruction and the control of black images in the mass media came to be additional points of contention along Du Bois's prophetic "color line."

In the preceding chapters, we have focused on this schizoid racial representation in the American mass media, noting how, more often than not, the images of African Americans favored by the mainstream media were based on long-standing black stereotypes. These one-dimensional caricatures not only gave white Americans a false impression of black life, art, and culture but they also helped to mold white public opinion patterns, and set the agenda for public discourse on the race issue, thus broadening the cultural gap between black and white Americans. On the other side of the racial divide, the stereotyped imagery provoked a defiant response from many black image makers, who consciously sought to undermine the prevailing black representations by parodying or negating those stereotypes.

This war between white and black image makers and media practitioners over the African American image is a classic example of group/class power relations, where social class divisions have been complicated by the added dimension of race. Incorporating insights and concepts gleaned from thinkers like Du Bois, Gramsci, Lippmann, Brown, Hall, Gandy, Bakhtin, and Gates, we have endeavored to show how the dominant cultural group has worked to define, control, and maintain its influence over the subordinate one, while the latter has struggled to recreate an authentic self-image, and hence to reclaim its historical identity.

In the mainstream media industries, the overwhelming constraints placed on African Americans have forced them to adopt (sometimes consciously and sometimes unconsciously) a dual strategy in the ongoing chess match to control the destiny of the black image. Within the corporate mass media there are African American "insiders," media professionals who are working to broaden and upgrade black images and input as best they can, even as they establish their own credentials at the various levels of those industries. A second strategy has involved cultural entrepreneurs and activists who have developed alternative media products, outlets, and services that target the interests and needs of African American audiences and consumers. Some of these black media practitioners outside the mainstream have increasingly gained a modicum of both control over their products and success in marketing them, but a far greater number have paid the price for going against the corporate current and are no longer in business. Another factor in the cultural resistance equation has been the organized political action of African Americans, most often led by progressive media professionals or civil rights groups. They have worked diligently to expose and discredit the lingering black stereotypes, as well as to agitate for greater black participation and ownership in the media industries. Yet while considerable progress has been made in all of these areas, especially during the past twenty years, new factors are emerging that can only complicate the racial situation in the mass media in the very near future.

As the twenty-first century looms on the horizon, African Americans have made some significant inroads as entrepreneurs and decision makers within the white-dominated media industries, which suggests that a promising trend may be in the making. Oprah Winfrey's Harpo Production Company marks only the third time in American history that a woman has owned her own production facility and produced her own media products. Obviously, it is the first instance for an African American woman. Spike Lee, the African American independent filmmaker, director, and actor, with his three films "She's Gotta Have It," "School Daze," and "Do the Right Thing," seems to promise a new wave of cinema that speaks with a black voice rather than the white one hitherto dominant in films about African Americans. However, there is also a growing disparity between the demographic projections of the general population, on the one hand, and both current ownership and employment patterns in the media industries, on the other. The white population in the United States is projected to lose its numerical majority to nonwhite populations in the country sometime toward the end of the next century.[1] In contrast, even the projected gains in ownership of media outlets by American minorities, including African Americans, lag far behind their current percentage in the total population.[2] Moreover, the gap is growing wider, not vice versa.

Another contradictory tendency, or double bind, that has emerged recently concerns the new revisionist black representations in the mass media, best exemplified by the popular acclaim and success of "The Cosby Show" on network television. Henry Louis Gates, Jr. has characterized Cosby's character of Cliff Huxtable as a new "Noble Negro" stereotype living in an upper-middle-class utopia. Furthermore, Gates attributes the popularity of the programs to the "black characters in them," who have "finally become, in most respects, just like white people":

> As long as all blacks were represented in demeaning or peripheral roles, it was possible to believe that American racism was, as it were, indiscriminate. The social vision of Cosby, however, reflecting the minuscule integration of blacks into the upper middle class (having "white money," my mother used to say, rather than "colored money"), reassuringly throws the blame for black poverty back onto the impoverished.[3]

The selective bifurcation of the black television image along class lines has been the focus of sociologist Herman Gray's recent research. Gray has found that, while idealized black middle-class families living the American Dream have come to the forefront of mainstream fictional television fare, in particular entertainment television, the black underclass, in contrast, has been a major focus of television newscasts and documentaries. These two seemingly disparate black representations are linked, because they tell opposite sides of the same mythical story of African American success and failure. As Gray points out:

> The assumptions that organize our understanding of black middle-class success and underclass failure are expressed and reinforced in the formal organization of television programming. . . . Where representations of the underclass are presented in the routine structure of network news programming, it is usually in relationship to such extraordinary offenses as drugs, homicide and crime. In contrast, middle-class blacks are very much integrated into the programming mainstream. . . . The failure of blacks in the urban underclass . . . is their own, since they live in an isolated world where contemporary racism is no longer a significant factor in their lives. The success of blacks in the television middle class suggests as much. In the

television world of the urban underclass, unemployment, industrial relocation, ineffective social policies, power inequalities and racism do not explain failure, just as affirmative action policies, political organization, collective social and cultural challenges to specific forms of racial domination, and the civil rights movement do not explain the growth of the black middle class.[4]

Similar reservations have been expressed by media critic Nelson George concerning crossover acts in black music and crossover formats in black commercial radio. George equates the crossover phenomenon with black yuppie assimilation into the dominant corporate structure of the media industries. He warns that such an exodus from the black community by the black bourgeoisie is tantamount to "cultural suicide" because it undermines the ability of the community to develop indigenous cultural institutions, while exacerbating the class divisions among African Americans.[5] Success and failure, middle class and underclass, the noble Negro and the brute Negro, crossover and stand pat, divide and conquer—these are just some of the double binds confronting African Americans in the mass media as they look toward the future.

This study has raised issues and offered explanations concerning the role of African Americans in the mass media. In the future, the authors believe that the task of making media systems more congruent with the increasing cultural diversity of American society does not rest solely on the shoulders of African Americans and other minority groups. Only a concerted, systematic effort within the media mainstream, academia, and industry can ensure that the future will be different from the past for African American and other minorities with respect to the development and control of their media images. Respect for the multicultural society that will characterize America in the twenty-first century must be engendered by all image makers who shape the worldviews of the American public, regardless of their race. America's future can be one of either relatively smooth transition or great upheaval. The task is great and the hour is late. We encourage all those of goodwill and stout heart to begin the transformation now.

Notes

1. Clint C. Wilson II and Felix Gutierrez, *Minorities and Media: Diversity and the End of Mass Communication* (Beverly Hills, Calif.: Sage Publications, 1985), 19–20.

2. John Downing, "Minority Radio in the United States," *Howard Journal of Communications* (Spring 1990): 31.

3. Louis Henry Gates, Jr., "TV's Black World Turns—But Stays Unreal," *New York Times*, 12 November 1989, sec. 2, 40.

4. Herman Gray, "Television, Black Americans, and the American Dream," *Critical Studies in Mass Communication 6* (December 1989): 384.

5. Nelson George, *The Death of Rhythm and Blues* (New York: Pantheon, 1988), 200.

Saving a Life
Ben Carson

Surgeons had recorded so few cases of full functional recovery that most doctors wouldn't consider a hemispherectomy as viable.

I was going to do my best. And I went into the surgery with two things clear. First, if I didn't operate, Maranda Francisco would worsen and die. Second, I had done everything to prepare myself for this surgery, and now I could leave the results in God's hands.

To assist me I asked Dr. Neville Knuckey, one of our chief residents, whom I had met during my year in Australia. Neville had come to Hopkins to do a fellowship, and I considered him extremely capable.

Right from the beginning of the surgery we had problems, so that instead of the expected five hours we stayed at the operating table exactly twice that long. We had to keep calling for more blood. Maranda's brain was very inflamed, and no matter where an instrument touched, she started to bleed. It was not only a lengthy operation but one of the most difficult I'd ever done.

The dramatic surgery began simply, with an incision drawn down the scalp. The assisting surgeon suctioned away blood with a hand-held tube while I cauterized small vessels. One by one, steel clips were placed on the edge of the incision to keep it open. The small operating room was cool and quiet.

Then I cut deeper through a second layer of scalp. Again small vessels were sealed shut, and a suction tube whisked away blood.

I drilled six holes, each the size of a shirt button, in Maranda's skull. The holes formed a semicircle, beginning in front of her left ear and curving up across her temple, above and down behind the ear. Each hole was filled with purified beeswax to cushion the saw. Then with an air-powered saw I connected the holes into an incision and lifted back the left side of Maranda's skull to expose the outer covering of her brain.

Her brain was swollen and abnormally hard, making the surgery more difficult. The anesthesiologist injected a drug into her IV line to reduce the swelling. Then Neville passed a thin catheter through her brain to the center of her head where it would drain off excess fluid.

Slowly, carefully, for eight tedious hours I inched away the inflamed left hemisphere of Maranda's brain. The small surgical instruments moved carefully, a millimeter at a time, coaxing tissue away from the vital blood vessels, trying not to touch or damage the other fragile parts of her brain. The large veins along the base of her brain bled profusely as I searched for the plane, the delicate line separating brain and vessels. It was not easy to manipulate the brain, to ease it away from the veins that circulated life through her small body.

Maranda lost nearly nine pints of blood during the surgery. We replaced almost twice her normal blood volume. Throughout the long hours, nurses kept Maranda's parents up-to-date on what was happening. I thought of their waiting and wondering. When my thoughts turned to God, I thanked Him for wisdom, for helping to guide my hands.

Finally we were finished. Maranda's skull was carefully sewed back in place with strong sutures. At last Neville and I stood back. The OR technician took the last instrument from my hand. I allowed myself the luxury of flexing my shoulders, rotating my head. Neville and I and the rest of our team knew we had successfully removed the left hemisphere of Maranda's brain. The "impossible" had been accomplished.

The Measure of Our Success:
A Letter to My Children and Yours
Marian Wright Edelman

It is not easy for anybody to grow up, to craft a purposeful role in the world, to develop a positive passion for life, and to discover God's will. If you are of mixed racial and religious heritage, as you are, some small and insecure people whose self-esteem seems to rest on looking down on others whom they perceive as "different" may make growing up and life more challenging. But I hope you will always recognize your rich dual heritage as the special gift and blessing that it is; know deep within yourself who you are; and draw strength and pride from the legacies you have inherited from two peoples—Blacks and Jews—who have survived the worst persecution the world can offer. That in recent history these two peoples were slaves and not enslavers, were segregated and discriminated against and were not segregators and discriminators, is an achievement to be proud rather than ashamed of if you take seriously, as I do, the first principle of every great religion: to treat others as you'd like to be

It is utterly exhausting being Black in America—physically, mentally, and emotionally. While many minority groups and women feel similar stress, there is no respite or escape from your badge of color. The daily stress of nonstop racial mindfulness and dealings with too many self-centered people who expect you to be cultural and racial translators and yet feel neither the need nor responsibility to reciprocate—to see or hear you as a human being rather than just as a Black or a woman or a Jew—is wearing. It can be exhausting to be a Black student on a "white" college campus or a Black employee in a "white" institution where some assume you are not as smart as comparable whites. The constant burden to "prove" that you are as smart, as honest, as interesting, as wide-gauging and motivated as any other individual tires you out—as does the need to decide repeatedly whether you'll prove to anybody what they have no right to assume or demand.

I understand the resentment of some young Blacks who have decided "who needs it?" and are opting for Black colleges where their "personness" is not

under constant assault and testing. They are freed (for a short while) from having to decide whether to ignore, think about, or challenge the constant daily
insensitivities of some whites who expect every Black to be a general expert on
everything Black at breakfast, lunch, and dinner when you'd rather discuss
art, gossip, or simply listen, or who assume you are less competent than they
are because of "affirmative action." Black colleges have done an extraordinary
job in preparing many of our young to swim in mainstream society. But there
really is no hiding place out there or escape from negative racial attitudes in
this era of racial backlash fueled by clever and cynical political and media
manipulation. So you have to be ready to meet those attitudes and change
them.

Affirmative action does not and should not mean that unqualified people
get an advantage. Everybody has to be able to do the work in school or on the
job to succeed. Nobody should use affirmative action as a favor, a crutch, or as
an excuse not to be prepared or not to do a first-rate job—or to stigmatize.

White Anglo-Saxon males never have felt inferior as a result of their centuries of "affirmative action" and quotas (which are *not* the same) in jobs from
which Jews, racial minorities, and women were excluded and too often still
are. So while you and your brothers must and can make it on the basis of your
individual ability, motivation, and disciplined hard work, do not feel defen-
sive about the judgments of some that affirmative action somehow taints a
whole race or you as individuals. Just work as hard as you can to perform up
to your ability. You are the person you must compare yourself to. Have your
own high standards for performance and conduct, not mine or your Dad's or
your employers' or your peers'.

There are no easy answers to the continuing dilemmas of race in America.
You must grapple with them like those who have gone before you: DuBois in
The Souls of Black Folk and James Weldon Johnson and Countee Cullen and
Paul Laurence Dunbar and Ralph Ellison and Maya Angelou and James Baldwin and Toni Morrison and Alice Walker and countless Black bards and writers who speak to this extra Black burden. The bottom line, however, is to
believe in yourself and not let anybody—of any color—limit or define you
solely by race or undermine your acceptance and love inside yourself for who
you are. Race and gender are givens of God, which neither you nor anyone
else chose or earned at birth. Your race is a fact. Being racist and sexist are a
state of mind and a choice.

Dr. King, James Baldwin, and Malcolm X all reminded us that "whiteness is
a state of mind" and that the struggle for racial justice is a struggle of conscience
and not of race. As such, it is not just a minority responsibility. (And who created
the problem?) Nor can minorities be justified in fueling racial divisions any
more than those who mistreated them, however understandable the temptation
may be. George Washington Carver once warned against letting any man drag
you so low as to make you hate him.

Gandhi advised: "Let our first act every morning be the following resolve: 'I shall not fear anyone on earth. I shall fear only god. I shall bear ill-will towards no one. I shall not submit to injustice from anyone.' " No one, Eleanor Roosevelt said, can make you feel inferior without your consent. *Never* give it. Respect other people only on the basis of their individual character and personal efforts, struggles, and achievements. Never defer to another on the basis of his or her race, religion, gender, class, fame, wealth, or position. Whites did not create Blacks. Men did not create women nor Christians Jews. What then gives any human being the presumption to judge, diminish, or exclude another or expect deference solely on such bases? It does not take character, intellect, or talent to inherit a million dollars or to be born white or male. Why should more admiration be given to those who started life with far more advantages and supports than those with none or few? No person has the right to rain on your dreams. No person has a right to define you on the basis of what you have or what you look like.

Affirm who you are inside regardless of the world's judgments: God's and my very precious children who are loved unconditionally, not for what you do, look like, or own, but simply because you are a gift of a loving God. As parents we often forget to convey this, and I have been as guilty as any, as you well know. Many young people feel, as you have, so much pressure to achieve, to get top grades, high test scores, and good jobs, and to perform well in nonacademic ventures—all of which are important for acquiring the self-discipline needed to improve your life choices. But it is important for us overly perfectionist parents to make clear that you are far more than your SATs, good grades, and trophies. However desirable these achievements are and however proud we are of them, they have no bearing on your intrinsic value or on our love for and acceptance of you as a person. No awards can ever rival the countless little and big joys you have given and continue to give us.

I seek your forgiveness for all the times I talked when I should have listened; got angry when I should have been patient; acted when I should have waited; feared when I should have delighted; scolded when I should have encouraged; criticized when I should have complimented; said no when I should have said yes and said yes when I should have said no. I did not know a whole lot about parenting or how to ask for help. I often tried too hard and wanted and demanded so much, and mistakenly sometimes tried to mold you into my image of what I wanted you to be rather than discovering and nourishing you as you emerged and grew.

Even though I am so proud of each of you in every way, and thank you for making your parents look terrific, I still feel twinges of guilt. As many baseball games as I did attend, I still think about the ones I was late for or missed, when you hit those mighty home runs or pitched a no hitter or caught that impossible ball or got hit by the baseball and had to be rushed to the emergency room. But I was so proud on the latter occasion when

Joshua responded to his younger brother Ezra's accident, transported him to the hospital, and calmly summoned us parents.

Most of all, I am sorry for all the times I did not affirm all the wonderful things you are and did that got lost in parental admonitions about things left undone or thought not well enough done. A mixed blessing inherited from my childhood that I still struggle with in my relationship with you, with Dad, with colleagues, and most of all, with myself, is the expectation that things be done well. I admit I still recoil against a society that has so slipped in caring that ordinary human sharing and thoughtfulness appears to warrant a "humanitarian award" and diligent effort seems too often the exception rather than the rule. I loved it when Mother Hale in Harlem, who takes in AIDS and crack babies, responded in an interview: "I'm not an American hero, I'm a person that loves children." But I regret that with you, my children, I have often tended to point out shortcomings rather than to affirm strengths and extraordinary accomplishments.

Finally, I worry about the effects of my sometimes difficult, even frantic, efforts to balance my responsibilities to you, my own children, and to other people's children with whom you must share schools and streets, the nation and world. Paradoxically, the more I worried about and wanted for you, the more I worried about the children of parents who have so much less. When one of you got a high fever, painful earache, asthma attack, or sports injury, how reassuring it was to be able to pick up the phone and call our pediatrician and take you right in. How enraged I am to think that other parents cannot ease their children's suffering and their own fears because they happened to be born on the wrong side of the tracks, the wrong color, or to lack a job with health insurance or the means to get health care.

Because I am my own boss, I could follow my own rule that you came first in any crunch, and that I would always stay home if you were sick if your Dad couldn't. There were nonetheless times of agonizing choices. But I am ever mindful that I had and have real choices. I could leave my office and skip a meeting to care for you or to meet with your teacher without fear of loss of job. Besides, I had two partners in raising you: your Dad and Miz Amie, our live-in "grandmother" for thirteen years, who treated you as her own. Still I felt uneasy leaving and not being home on a few occasions when you were ill, even with these equally good caregivers. These queasy feelings have goaded me to battle senseless and insensitive national and corporate policies and priorities that don't enable most parents to leave work to care for sick family members, unlike so many other industrialized nations. I cannot imagine leaving you home alone sick and being able to focus on my work.

While I have attended most school parent meetings, I've done so often tired or stressed. When you were in three different schools and I was trying to keep up with your activities and teachers and go off to PTA meetings at night and to attend important school meetings, assemblies, or teacher conferences during the day, I'd imagine what it's like for millions of poor or single parents in unsafe neighborhoods trying to stay actively involved in their children's school without a car or a babysitter. I've tried to cook my share of brownies and chocolate chip cookies, but I've also tried, like my parents, to face the reality that there are problems in the world that all of us must try to address in our own ways. As a parent I believe that protecting you—my own children—does not end in our kitchen or at our front door or with narrow attention just to your personal needs.

As you have grown toward adulthood, you have become increasingly aware that your educationally and financially privileged lives are not typical of other children in this world, nation, or even our own city. We live in one of the wealthiest neighborhoods of Washington, D.C., while thousands of children ten minutes away are living in a war zone that imprisons them in fear and near–Third World poverty. First World privilege and Third World deprivation and rage are struggling to coexist not only in our nation's capital but all over an America that has the capacity but not the moral commitment and political will to protect all its young.

You must walk the streets with other people's children and attend schools with other people's children. You breathe polluted air and eat polluted food like millions of other children and are threatened by pesticides and chemicals and toxic wastes and a depleted ozone layer like everybody's children. Drunken drivers and crack addicts on the streets are a menace to every American child. So are violent television shows and movies and incessant advertising and cultural signals that hawk profligate consumption and excessive violence and tell you slick is real. It is too easy and unrealistic to say these forces can be tuned out just by individual parental vigilance.

So as a parent I wanted to make sure you had all your physical needs met and a lot of love. But as a parent I could not ignore other people's children or pain that spills over to public space and threatens the safety and quality of life and pocketbook and future of every American. I also wanted to make sure I left you a community and future more safe and hopeful than the one I inherited, and an example of one person trying to make a difference.

Just as parents help shape children, children help shape parents, and you have helped me grow. Thank you for being so helpful and so forbearing.

I hope so much that the balance of your childhood memories will be positive and loving. I worry God a lot not to let my shortcomings as a mother limit your growth or weaken your self-esteem. Indeed, I pray that my weaknesses will strengthen you and that my never-ending and always failing struggle to live what I preach will be a goad rather than impediment to your healthy development.

Parents are sometimes frail and troubled, but also strong and resilient human beings—just like you—if we get the nurturing and support all humans need. Most of us try to keep growing just as you do, although we make lots of mistakes all the time. What we owe you, our children, is our best effort to be a person worth emulating and to send through our lives a message to the future we hope you will feel is worth transmitting to your children and grandchildren. I hope I can grow big enough one day to feel I have done that.

You may think I think that I have all the answers, but like so many of my elders whom I seek to follow, I am often filled with uncertainties. There are a whole lot of mornings when I can barely face the work I know I must do and feel discouraged and hopeless about whether America is ever going to finish the business of ensuring racial and economic and gender justice. And then I see cynical and racist politicians on the television screen and I wonder how we have come to this point *again* in America—after all the struggles and progress of the past thirty years. I cannot believe that you, my children, may have to fight all over again the battles I thought were over.

I won't stop fighting as long as those who would turn us back won't stop. I am terrified by the escalating violence in our country and the apathy and ignorance that feed it. But I ask myself if I believe in my vision of America any less than the hatemongers and those who support them do in theirs. And I remember everything I have been given and all the chances each of us in this country has been given to make a difference.

My life is one of the countless lives that attest to the vibrancy of the American Dream under circumstances much harder than today's. The segregated world of my childhood in the 1940s and early 1950s seemed impenetrable. Never could I have envisaged the positive changes I have seen since my youth. But my parents and elders dreamed of them and never lost hope. So neither will I lose hope that America's best self will overcome growing racial and class divisions. President Havel of Czechoslovakia, when he was in prison, described hope as a state of mind, not a state of the world: "Either we have hope within us or we don't: it is a dimension of the soul. . . . Hope in this deep and powerful sense is . . . an ability to work for something because it is good, not just because it stands a chance to succeed. . . . It is also this hope, above all, which gives us the strength to live and continually to try new things, even in conditions that seem as hopeless as ours do here and now."

I therefore hope you find a positive passion in your life that gives meaning. I hope you find a loving partner to share the way. I hope some of the twenty-five lessons, offered with great love and prayers, will help you around and over some of the rocks ahead that I know you will negotiate with confidence and grace.

Please take this letter and the lessons that follow it in the spirit in which they are given—as tokens of how much you mean to me and as the best road maps I can share with you today. You will obviously ignore, revise, or use all or any of them as you see fit. I have every confidence in your ability to make your own choices. I hope some of these bits of your heritage will be worthy of carrying along to your children and to their children's children—as lanterns of love to lighten and enlighten your and their paths. I am so proud of you in every way and love you more than I can ever say.

Nihilism in Black America
Cornel West

The proper starting point for the crucial debate about the prospects for black America is an examination of the nihilism that increasingly pervades black communities. *Nihilism is to be understood here not as a philosophic doctrine that there are no rational grounds for legitimate standards or authority; it is, far more, the lived experiences of coping with a life of horrifying meaninglessness, hopelessness, and (most important) lovelessness.* The frightening result is a numbing detachment from others and a self-destructive disposition toward the world. Life without meaning, hope, and love breeds a cold-hearted, mean-spirited outlook that destroys both the individual and others.

Nihilism is not new in black America. The first African encounter with the New World was an encounter with a distinctive form of the Absurd. The initial black struggle against degradation and devaluation in the enslaved circumstances of the New World was, in part, a struggle against nihilism. In fact, the major enemy of black survival in America has been and is neither oppression nor exploitation but rather the nihilistic threat—that is, loss of hope and absence of meaning. For as long as hope remains and meaning is preserved, the possibility of overcoming oppression stays alive. The self-fulfilling prophecy of the nihilistic threat is that without hope there can be no future, that without meaning there can be no struggle.

The genius of our black foremothers and forefathers was to create powerful buffers to ward off the nihilistic threat, to equip black folk with cultural armor to beat back the demons of hopelessness, meaningless, and lovelessness. These buffers consisted of cultural structures of meaning and feeling that created and sustained communities; this armor constituted ways of life and struggle that embodied values of service and sacrifice, love and care, discipline and excellence. In other words, traditions for black surviving and thriving under usually adverse New World conditions were major barriers against the nihilistic threat. These traditions consist primarily of black religious and civic institutions that sustained familiar and communal networks of support. If cultures are, in part, what human beings create (out of antecedent fragments of other cultures) in order to convince themselves not to commit suicide, then black foremothers and forefathers are to be applauded. In fact, until the early seventies black Americans had the lowest suicide rate in the United States. But now young black people lead the nation in the rate of increase in suicides.

What has changed? What went wrong? The bitter irony of integration? The cumulative effects of a genocidal conspiracy? The virtual collapse of rising expectations after the optimistic sixties? None of us fully understands why the cultural structures that once sustained black life in America are no longer able to fend off the nihilistic threat. I believe that two significant reasons why the threat is more powerful now than ever before are the saturation of market forces and market moralities in black life and the present crisis in black leadership. The recent market-driven shattering of black civil society—black families, neighborhoods, schools, churches, mosques—leaves more and more black people vulnerable to daily lives endured with little sense of self and fragile existential moorings.

Black people have always been in America's wilderness in search of a promised land. Yet many black folk now reside in a jungle ruled by a cutthroat market morality devoid of any faith in deliverance or hope for freedom. Contrary to the superficial claims of conservative behaviorists, these jungles are not primarily the result of pathological behavior. Rather, this behavior is the tragic response of a people bereft of resources in confronting the workings of U.S. capitalist society. Saying this is not the same as asserting that individual black people are not responsible for their actions—black murderers and rapists should go to jail. But it must be recognized that the nihilistic threat contributes to criminal behavior. It is a threat that feeds on poverty and shattered cultural institutions and grows more powerful as the armors to ward against it are weakened.

But why is this shattering of black civil society occurring? What has led to the weakening of black cultural institutions in asphalt jungles? Corporate market institutions have contributed greatly to their collapse. By corporate market institutions I mean that complex set of interlocking enterprises that have a disproportionate amount of capital, power, and exercise a disproportionate influence on how our society is run and how our culture is shaped. Needless to say, the primary motivation of these institutions is to make profits, and their basic strategy is to convince the public to consume. These institutions have helped create a seductive way of life, a culture of consumption that capitalizes on every opportunity to make money. Market calculations and cost-benefit analyses hold sway in almost every sphere of U.S. society.

The common denominator of these calculations and analyses is usually the provision, expansion, and intensification of *pleasure*. Pleasure is a multivalent term; it means different things to many people. In the American way of life pleasure involves comfort, convenience, and sexual stimulation. Pleasure, so defined, has little to do with the past and views the future as no more than a repetition of a hedonistically driven present. This market morality stigmatizes others as objects for personal pleasure or bodily stimulation. Conservative behaviorists have alleged that traditional morality has been undermined by radical feminists and the cultural radicals of the sixties. But it is clear that corporate market institutions have greatly contributed to undermining traditional morality in order to stay in business and make a profit. The reduction of individuals to objects of pleasure is especially evident in the culture industries—television, radio, video, music—in which gestures of sexual foreplay and orgiastic pleasure flood the marketplace.

Like all Americans, African-Americans are influenced greatly by the images of comfort, convenience, machismo, femininity, violence, and sexual stimulation that bombard consumers. These seductive images contribute to the predominance of the market-inspired way of life over all others and thereby edge out nonmarket values—love, care, service to others—handed down by preceding generations. The predominance of this way of life among those living in poverty-ridden conditions, with a limited capacity to ward off self-contempt and self-hatred, results in the possible triumph of the nihilistic threat in black America.

A major contemporary strategy for holding the nihilistic threat at bay is a direct attack on the sense of worthlessness and self-loathing in black America. This *angst* resembles a kind of collective clinical depression in significant pockets of black America. The eclipse of hope and collapse of meaning in much of black America is linked to the structural dynamics of corporate market institutions that affect all Americans. Under these circumstances black existential *angst* derives from the lived experience of ontological wounds and emotional scars inflicted by white supremacist beliefs and images permeating U.S. society and culture. These beliefs and images attack black intelligence, black ability, black beauty, and black character daily in subtle and not-so-subtle ways. Toni Morrison's novel, *The Bluest Eye,* for example, reveals the devastating effect of pervasive European ideals of beauty on the self-image of young black women. Morrison's exposure of the harmful extent to which these white ideals affect the black self-image is a first step toward rejecting these ideals and overcoming the nihilistic self-loathing they engender in blacks.

The accumulated effect of the black wounds and scars suffered in a white-dominated society is a deep-seated anger, a boiling sense of rage, and a passionate pessimism regarding America's will to justice. Under conditions of slavery and Jim Crow segregation, this anger, rage, and pessimism remained relatively muted because of a well-justified fear of brutal white retaliation. The major breakthroughs of the sixties—more physically than politically—swept this fear away. Sadly, the combination of the market way of life, poverty-ridden conditions, black existential *angst,* and the lessening of fear of white authorities has directed most of the anger, rage, and despair toward fellow black citizens, especially toward black women, who are the most vulnerable in our society and in black communities. Only recently has this nihilistic threat—and its ugly inhumane outlook and actions—surfaced in the larger American society. And its appearance surely reveals one of the many instances of cultural decay in a declining empire.

What is to be done about this nihilistic threat? Is there really any hope, given our shattered civil society, market-driven corporate enterprises, and white supremacism? If one begins with the threat of concrete nihilism, then one must talk about some kind of *politics of conversion.* New models of collective black leadership must promote a version of this politics. Like alcoholism and drug addiction, nihilism is a disease of the soul. It can never be completely cured, and there is always the possibility of relapse. But there is always a chance for conversion—a chance for people to believe that there is hope for the future and a meaning to struggle. This chance rests neither on an agreement about what justice consists of nor on an analysis of how racism, sexism, or class subordination operate. Such arguments and analyses are indispensable. But a politics of conversion requires more. Nihilism is not overcome by arguments or analyses; it is tamed by love and care. Any disease of the soul must be conquered by a turning of one's soul. This turning is done through one's own affirmation of one's worth—an affirmation fueled by the concern of others. A love ethic must be at the center of a politics of conversion.

A love ethic has nothing to do with sentimental feelings or tribal connections. Rather it is a last attempt at generating a sense of agency among a downtrodden people. The best exemplar of this love ethic is depicted on a number of levels in Toni Morrison's great novel *Beloved.* Self-love and love of others are both modes toward increasing self-valuation and encouraging political resistance in one's community. These modes of valuation and resistance are rooted in a subversive memory—the best of one's past without romantic nostalgia—and guided by a universal love ethic. For my purposes here, *Beloved* can be construed as bringing together the loving yet critical affirmation of black humanity found in the best of black nationalist movements, the perennial hope against hope for transracial coalition in progressive movements, and the painful struggle for self-affirming sanity in a history in which the nihilistic threat *seems* insurmountable.

The politics of conversion proceeds principally on the local level—in those institutions in civil society still vital enough to promote self-worth and self-affirmation. It surfaces on the state and national levels only when grass-roots democratic organizations put forward a collective leadership that has earned the love and respect of and, most important, has proved itself *accountable* to these organizations. This collective leadership must exemplify moral integrity, character, and democratic statesmanship within itself and within its organizations.

Like liberal structuralists, the advocates of a politics of conversion never lose sight of the structural conditions that shape the sufferings and lives of people. Yet, unlike liberal structuralism, the politics of conversion meets the nihilistic threat head-on. Like conservative behaviorism, the politics of conversion openly confronts the self-destructive and inhumane actions of black people. Unlike conservative behaviorists, the politics of conversion situates these actions within inhumane circumstances (but does not thereby exonerate them). The politics of conversion shuns the limelight—a limelight that solicits status seekers and ingratiates egomaniacs. Instead, it stays on the ground among the toiling everyday people, ushering forth humble freedom fighters—both followers and leaders—who have the audacity to take the nihilistic threat by the neck and turn back its deadly assaults.

The Evolution of Rap Music
Michael Eric Dyson

Trying to pinpoint the exact origin of rap is a tricky process that depends on when one acknowledges a particular cultural expression or product as rap. Rap can be traced back to the revolutionary verse of Gil Scott-Heron and the Last Poets, to Pigmeat Markham's "Here Come de Judge," and even to Bessie Smith's rapping to a beat in some of her blues. We can also cite ancient African oral traditions as the antecedents to various contemporary African-American cultural practices. In any case, the modern history of rap probably begins in 1979 with the rap song "Rapper's Delight," by the Sugarhill Gang. Although there were other (mostly underground) examples of rap, this record is regarded as the signal barrier breaker, birthing hip-hop and consolidating the infant art form's popularity. This first stage in a rap record production was characterized by rappers placing their rhythmic, repetitive speech over well-known (mostly R & B) black music hits. "Rapper's Delight" was rapped over the music to a song made by the popular seventies R & B group Chic, titled "Good Times." Although rap would later enhance its technical virtuosity through instrumentation, drum machines, and "sampling" existing records—thus making it creatively symbiotic—the first stage was benignly parasitic upon existing black music.

As rap grew, it was still limited to mostly inner-city neighborhoods and particularly its place of origin, New York City. Rap artists like Funky 4 Plus 1, Kool Moe Dee, Busy Bee, Afrika Bambaata, Cold Rush Brothers, Kurtis Blow, DJ Kool Hurk, and Grandmaster Melle Mel were experimenting with this developing musical genre. As it evolved, rap began to describe and analyze the social, economic, and political factors that led to its emergence and development: drug addiction, police brutality, teen pregnancy, and various forms of material deprivation. This new development was both expressed and precipitated by Kurtis Blow's "Those Are the Breaks" and by the most influential and important rap song to emerge in rap's early history, "The Message," by Grandmaster Flash and The Furious Five. The picture this song painted of inner-city life for black Americans—the hues of dark social misery and stains of profound urban catastrophe—screeched against the canvas of most suburban sensibilities:

> You'll grow up in the ghetto living second rate / And your eyes will sing a song of deep hate / The places you play and where you stay, / Looks like one great big alleyway / You'll admire all the number book takers / Thugs, pimps, and pushers, and the big money makers / Drivin' big cars, spendin' twenties and tens, And you want to grow up to be just like them / . . . It's like a jungle sometimes / It makes me wonder how I keep from goin' under.

"The Message," along with Flash's "New York, New York," pioneered the social awakening of rap into a form combining social protest, musical creation, and cultural expression.

As its fortunes slowly grew, rap was still viewed by the music industry as an epiphenomenal cultural activity that would cease as black youth became bored and moved on to another diversion, as they did with break-dancing and graffiti art. But the successes of the rap group Run-D.M.C. moved rap into a different sphere of artistic expression that signaled its increasing control of its own destiny. Run-D.M.C. is widely recognized as the progenitor of modern rap's creative integration of social commentary, diverse musical elements, and uncompromising cultural identification—an integration that pushed the music into the mainstream and secured its future as an American musical genre with an identifiable tradition. Run-D.M.C.'s stunning commercial and critical success almost single-handedly landed rap in the homes of many black and nonblack youths across America by producing the first rap album to be certified gold (five hundred thousand copies sold), the first rap song to be featured on the twenty-four-hour music video channel MTV, and the first rap album (1987's *Raising Hell*) to go triple platinum (3 million copies sold).

On *Raising Hell,* Run-D.M.C. showcased the sophisticated technical virtuosity of its DJ Jam Master Jay—the raw shrieks, scratches, glitches, and language of the street, plus the innovative and ingenious appropriation of hard-rock guitar riffs. In doing this, Run-D.M.C. symbolically and substantively wedded two traditions—the waning subversion of rock music and the rising, incendiary aesthetic of hip-hop music—to produce a provocative musical hybrid of fiery lyricism and potent critique. *Raising Hell* ended with the rap anthem, "Proud to Be Black," intoning its unabashed racial pride:

> Ya know I'm proud to be black ya'll, And that's a fact ya'll / . . . Now Harriet Tubman was born a slave, She was a tiny black woman when she was raised / She was livin'

to be givin', There's a lot that she gave /
There's not a slave in this day and age, I'm
proud to be black.

At the same time, rap, propelled by Run-D.M.C.'s epochal success, found
an arena in which to concentrate its subversive cultural didacticism aimed at
addressing racism, classism, social neglect, and urban pain: the rap concert,
where rappers are allowed to engage in ritualistic refusals of censored speech.
The rap concert also creates space for cultural resistance and personal agency,
loosing the strictures of the tyrannizing surveillance and demoralizing condemnation of mainstream society and encouraging relatively autonomous,
often enabling, forms of self-expression and cultural creativity.

However, Run-D.M.C.'s success, which greatly increased the visibility and
commercial appeal of rap music through record sales and rap concerts,
brought along another charge that has had a negative impact on rap's perception by the general public: the claim that rap expresses and causes violence.
Tipper Gore has repeatedly said that rap music appeals to "angry, disillusioned, unloved kids" and that it tells them it is "okay to beat people up." Violent incidents at rap concerts in Los Angeles, Pittsburgh, Cleveland, Atlanta,
Cincinnati, and New York City have only reinforced the popular perception
that rap is intimately linked to violent social behavior by mostly black and
Latino inner-city youth. Countless black parents, too, have had negative reactions to rap, and the black radio and media establishment, although not as
vocal as Gore, have voted on her side with their allocation of much less airplay
and print coverage to rap than is warranted by its impressive record sales.

Such reactions betray a shallow understanding of rap, which in many cases
results from people's unwillingness to listen to rap lyrics, many of which
counsel antiviolent and antidrug behavior among the youths who are their
avid audience. Many rappers have spoken directly against violence, such as
KRS-One in his "Stop the Violence." Another rap record produced by KRS-
One in 1989, the top-selling *Self-Destruction*, insists that violence predates rap
and speaks against escalating black-on-black crime, which erodes the social
and communal fabric of already debased black inner cities across America:

Well, today's topic is self-destruction, It
really ain't the rap audience that's buggin' /
It's one or two suckers, ignorant brothers,
Tryin' to rob and steal from one another / . . .
'Cause the way we live is positive. We don't
kill our relatives / . . . Back in the sixties our
brothers and sisters were hanged. How could
you gang-bang? / I never, ever ran from the
Ku Klux Klan, and I shouldn't have to run
from a black man, 'Cause that's / Self-
destruction, ya headed for self-destruction.

Despite such potent messages, many mainstream blacks and whites persist in categorically negative appraisals of rap, refusing to distinguish between enabling, productive rap messages and the social violence that exists in many inner-city communities and that is often reflected in rap songs. Of course, it is difficult for a culture that is serious about the maintenance of social arrangements, economic conditions, and political choices that create and reproduce poverty, racism, sexism, classism, and violence to display a significant appreciation for musical expressions that contest the existence of such problems in black and Latino communities.

Language of a Dancing Mind
Nobel Acceptance Speech 1993
Toni Morrison

"Once upon a time there was an old woman. Blind. Wise."

In the version I know the woman is the daughter of slaves, black, American, and lives alone in a small house outside of town. Her reputation for wisdom is without peer and without question. Among her people she is both the law and its transgression. The honor she is paid and the awe in which she is held reach beyond her neighborhood to places far away; to the city where the intelligence of rural prophets is the source of much amusement.

One day the woman is visited by some young people who seem to be bent on disproving her clairvoyance and showing her up for the fraud they believe she is. Their plan is simple: they enter her house and ask the one question the answer to which rides solely on her difference from them, a difference they regard as a profound disability: her blindness. They stand before her, and one of them says, "Old woman, I hold in my hand a bird. Tell me whether it is living or dead."

She does not answer, and the question is repeated. "Is the bird I am holding living or dead?"

Still she doesn't answer. She is blind and cannot see her visitors, let alone what is in their hands. She does not know their color, gender or homeland. She only knows their motive.

The old woman's silence is so long, the young people have trouble holding their laughter.

Finally she speaks and her voice is soft but stern. "I don't know," she says. "I don't know whether the bird you are holding is dead or alive, but what I do know is that it is in your hands. It is in your hands."

Her answer can be taken to mean: If it is dead, you have either found it that way or you have killed it. If it is alive, you can still kill it. Whether it is to stay alive, it is your decision. Whatever the case, it is your responsibility.

For parading their power and her helplessness, the young visitors are reprimanded, told they are responsible not only for the act of mockery but also for the small bundle of life sacrificed to achieve its aims. The blind woman shifts attention away from assertions of power to the instrument through which that power is exercised.

Speculation on what (other than its own frail body) that bird-in-the-hand might signify has always been attractive to me, but especially so now thinking, as I have been, about the work I do that has brought me to this company. So I choose to read the bird as language and the woman as a practiced writer. She is worried about how the language she dreams in, given to her at birth, is handled, put into service, even withheld from her for certain nefarious purposes. Being a writer she thinks of language partly as a system, partly as a living thing over which one has control, but mostly as agency—as an act with consequences. So the question the children put to her: "Is it living or dead?" is not unreal because she thinks of language as susceptible to death, erasure; certainly imperiled and salvageable only by an effort of the will. She believes that if the bird in the hands of her visitors is dead the custodians are responsible for the corpse. For her a dead language is not only one no longer spoken or written, it is unyielding language content to admire its own paralysis. Like statist language, censored and censoring. Ruthless in its policing duties, it has no desire or purpose other than maintaining the free range of its own narcotic narcissism, its own exclusivity and dominance. However moribund, it is not without effect for it actively thwarts the intellect, stalls conscience, suppresses human potential. Unreceptive to interrogation, it cannot form or tolerate new ideas, shape other thoughts, tell another story, fill baffling silences. Official language smitheryed to sanction ignorance and preserve privilege is a suit of armor polished to shocking glitter, a husk from which the knight departed long ago. Yet there it is: dumb, predatory, sentimental. Exciting reverence in schoolchildren, providing shelter for despots, summoning false memories of stability, harmony among the public.

She is convinced that when language dies, out of carelessness, disuse, indifference and absence of esteem, or killed by fiat, not only she herself, but all users and makers are accountable for its demise. In her country children have bitten their tongues off and use bullets instead to iterate the voice of speechlessness, of disabled and disabling language, of language adults have abandoned altogether as a device for grappling with meaning, providing guidance, or expressing love. But she knows tongue-suicide is not only the choice of children. It is common among the infantile heads of state and power merchants whose evacuated language leaves them with no access to what is left of their human instincts for they speak only to those who obey, or in order to force obedience.

The systematic looting of language can be recognized by the tendency of its users to forgo its nuanced, complex, mid-wifery properties for menace and subjugation. Oppressive language does more than represent violence; it is violence; does more than represent the limits of knowledge; it limits knowledge. Whether it is obscuring state language or the faux-language of mindless media; whether it is the proud but calcified language of the academy or the commodity driven language of science; whether it is the malign language of law-without-ethics, or language designed for the estrangement of minorities, hiding its racist plunder in its literary cheek—it must be rejected, altered and exposed. It is the language that drinks blood, laps vulnerabilities, tucks its fascist boots under crinolines of respectability and patriotism as it moves relentlessly toward the bottom line and the bottomed-out mind. Sexist language, racist language, theistic language—all are typical of the policing languages of mastery, and cannot, do not permit new knowledge or encourage the mutual exchange of ideas.

The old woman is keenly aware that no intellectual mercenary, nor insatiable dictator, no paid-for politician or demagogue; no counterfeit journalist would be persuaded by her thoughts. There is and will be rousing language to keep citizens armed and arming; slaughtered and slaughtering in the malls, court-houses, post offices, playgrounds, bedrooms and boulevards; stirring, memorializing language to mask the pity and waste of needless death. There will be more diplomatic language to countenance rape, torture, assassination. There is and will be more seductive, mutant language designed to throttle women, to pack their throats like paté-producing geese with their own unsayable, transgressive words; there will be more of the language of surveillance disguised as research; of politics and history calculated to render the suffering of millions mute; language glamorized to thrill the dissatisfied and bereft into assaulting their neighbors; arrogant pseudo-empirical language crafted to lock creative people into cages of inferiority and hopelessness.

Underneath the eloquence, the glamor, the scholarly associations, however stirring or seductive, the heart of such language is languishing, or perhaps not beating at all—if the bird is already dead.

She has thought about what could have been the intellectual history of any discipline if it had not insisted upon, or been forced into, the waste of time and life that rationalizations for and representations of dominance required— lethal discourses of exclusion blocking access to cognition for both the excluder and the excluded.

The conventional wisdom of the Tower of Babel story is that the collapse was a misfortune. That it was the distraction, or the weight of many languages that precipitated the tower's failed architecture. That one monolithic language would have expedited the building and heaven would have been reached. Whose heaven, she wonders? And what kind? Perhaps the achievement of Paradise was premature, a little hasty if no one could take the time to understand other languages, other views, other narratives period. Had they, the heaven they imagined might have been found at their feet. Complicated, demanding, yes, but a view of heaven as life; not heaven as post-life.

She would not want to leave her young visitors with the impression that language should be forced to stay alive merely to be. The vitality of language lies in its ability to limn the actual, imagined and possible lives of its speakers, readers, writers. Although its poise is sometimes in displacing experience it is not a substitute for it. It arcs toward the place where meaning may lie. When a

President of the United States thought about the graveyard his country had become, and said, "The world will little note nor long remember what we say here. But it will never forget what they did here," his simple words are exhilarating in their life-sustaining properties because they refused to encapsulate the reality of 600,000 dead men in a cataclysmic race war. Refusing to monumentalize, disdaining the "final word", the precise "summing up", acknowledging their "poor power to add or detract", his words signal deference to the uncapturabillty of the life it mourns. It is the deference that moves her, that recognition that language can never live up to life once and for all. Nor should it. Language can never "pin down" slavery, genocide, war. Nor should it yearn for the arrogance to be able to do so. Its force, its felicity is in its reach toward the ineffable.

Be it grand or slender, burrowing, blasting, or refusing to sanctify; whether it laughs out loud or is a cry without an alphabet, the choice word, the chosen silence, unmolested language surges toward knowledge, not its destruction. But who does not know of literature banned because it is interrogative; discredited because it is critical; erased because alternate? And how many are outraged by the thought of a self-ravaged tongue?

Word-work is sublime, she thinks, because it is generative; it makes meaning that secures our difference, our human difference—the way in which we are like no other life.

We die. That may be the meaning of life. But we do language. That may be the measure of our lives.

"Once upon a time, . . ." visitors ask an old woman a question. Who are they, these children? What did they make of that encounter? What did they hear in those final words: "The bird is in your hands"? A sentence that gestures towards possibility or one that drops a latch? Perhaps what the children heard was "It's not my problem. I am old, female, black, blind. What wisdom I have now is in knowing I cannot help you. The future of language is yours."

They stand there. Suppose nothing was in their hands? Suppose the visit was only a ruse, a trick to get to be spoken to, taken seriously as they have not been before? A chance to interrupt, to violate the adult world, its miasma of discourse about them, for them, but never to them? Urgent questions are at stake, including the one they have asked: "Is the bird we hold living or dead?" Perhaps the question meant: "Could someone tell us what is life? What is death?" No trick at all; no silliness. A straightforward question worthy of the attention of a wise one. An old one. And if the old and wise who have lived life and faced death cannot describe either, who can?

But she does not; she keeps her secret; her good opinion of herself; her gnomic pronouncements; her art without commitment. She keeps her distance, enforces it and retreats into the singularity of isolation, in sophisticated, privileged space.

Nothing, no word follows her declaration of transfer. That silence is deep, deeper than the meaning available in the words she has spoken. It shivers, this silence, and the children, annoyed, fill it with language invented on the spot.

"Is there no speech," they ask her, "no words you can give us that helps us break through your dossier of failures? Through the education you have just given us that is no education at all because we are paying close attention to what you have done as well as to what you have said? To the barrier you have erected between generosity and wisdom?

"We have no bird in our hands, living or dead. We have only you and our important question. Is the nothing in our hands something you could not bear to contemplate, to even guess? Don't you remember being young when language was magic without meaning? When what you could say, could not mean? When the invisible was what imagination strove to see? When questions and demands for answers burned so brightly you trembled with fury at not knowing?

"Do we have to begin consciousness with a battle heroines and heroes like you have already fought and lost leaving us with nothing in our hands except what you have imagined is there? Your answer is artful, but its artfulness embarrasses us and ought to embarrass you. Your answer is indecent in its self-congratulation. A made-for-television script that makes no sense if there is nothing in our hands.

"Why didn't you reach out, touch us with your soft fingers, delay the sound bite, the lesson, until you knew who we were? Did you so despise our trick, our modus operandi you could not see that we were baffled about how to get your attention? We are young. Unripe. We have heard all our short lives that we have to be responsible. What could that possibly mean in the catastrophe this world has become; where, as a poet said, "nothing needs to be exposed since it is already barefaced." Our inheritance is an affront. You want us to have your old, blank eyes and see only cruelty and mediocrity. Do you think we are stupid enough to perjure ourselves again and again with the fiction of nationhood? How dare you talk to us of duty when we stand waist deep in the toxin of your past?

"You trivialize us and trivialize the bird that is not in our hands. Is there no context for our lives? No song, no literature, no poem full of vitamins, no history connected to experience that you can pass along to help us start strong? You are an adult. The old one, the wise one. Stop thinking about saving your face. Think of our lives and tell us your particularized world. Make up a story. Narrative is radical, creating us at the very moment it is being created. We will not blame you if your reach exceeds your grasp; if love so ignites your words they go down in flames and nothing is left but their scald. Or if, with the reticence of a surgeon's hands, your words suture only the places where blood might flow. We know you can never do it properly—once and for all. Passion is never enough; neither is skill. But try. For our sake and yours forget your name in the street; tell us what the world has been to you in the dark places and in the light. Don't tell us what to believe, what to fear. Show us belief's wide skirt and the stitch that unravels fear's caul. You, old woman, blessed with blindness, can speak the language that tells us what only language can: how to see without pictures.

Language alone protects us from the scariness of things with no names. Language alone is meditation.

"Tell us what it is to be a woman so that we may know what it is to be a man. What moves at the margin. What it is to have no home in this place. To be set adrift from the one you knew. What it is to live at the edge of towns that cannot bear your company.

"Tell us about ships turned away from shorelines at Easter, placenta in a field. Tell us about a wagonload of slaves, how they sang so softly their breath was indistinguishable from the falling snow. How they knew from the hunch of the nearest shoulder that the next stop would be their last. How, with hands prayered in their sex, they thought of heat, then sun. Lifting their faces as though is was there for the taking. Turning as though there for the taking. They stop at an inn. The driver and his mate go in with the lamp leaving them humming in the dark. The horse's void steams into the snow beneath its hooves and its hiss and melt are the envy of the freezing slaves.

"The inn door opens: a girl and a boy step away from its light. They climb into the wagon bed. The boy will have a gun in three years, but now he carries a lamp and a jug of warm cider. They pass it from mouth to mouth. The girl offers bread, pieces of meat and something more: a glance into the eyes of the one she serves. One helping for each man, two for each woman. And a look. They look back. The next stop will be their last. But not this one. This one is warmed."

It's quiet again when the children finish speaking, until the woman breaks into the silence.

"Finally", she says, "I trust you now. I trust you with the bird that is not in your hands because you have truly caught it. Look. How lovely it is, this thing we have done—together."

The Task of Negro Womanhood
Elise Johnson McDougald

Throughout the years of history, woman has been the weathervane, the indicator, showing in which direction the wind of destiny blows. Her status and development have augured now calm and stability, now swift currents of progress. What then is to be said of the Negro woman of to-day, whose problems are of such import to her race?

A study of her contributions to any one community, throughout America, would illuminate the pathway being trod by her people. There is, however, an advantage in focusing upon the women of Harlem—modern city in the world's metropolis. Here, more than anywhere else, the Negro woman is free from the cruder handicaps of primitive household hardships and the grosser forms of sex and race subjugation. Here, she has considerable opportunity to measure her powers in the intellectual and industrial fields of the great city. The questions naturally arise: "What are her difficulties?" and, "How is she solving them?"

To answer these questions, one must have in mind not any one Negro woman, but rather a colorful pageant of individuals, each differently endowed. Like the red and yellow of the tiger-lily, the skin of one is brilliant against the star-lit darkness of a racial sister. From grace to strength, they vary in infinite degree, with traces of the race's history left in physical and mental outline on each. With a discerning mind, one catches the multiform charm, beauty and character of Negro women, and grasps the fact that their problems cannot be thought of in mass.

Because only a few have caught this vision, even in New York, the general attitude of mind causes the Negro woman serious difficulty. She is conscious that what is left of chivalry is not directed toward her. She realizes that the ideals of beauty, built up in the fine arts, have excluded her almost entirely. Instead, the grotesque Aunt Jemimas of the street-car advertisements, proclaim only an ability to serve, without grace of loveliness. Nor does the drama catch her finest spirit. She is most often used to provoke the mirthless laugh of ridicule; or to portray feminine viciousness or vulgarity not peculiar to

Negroes. This is the shadow over her. To a race naturally sunny comes the twi-light of self-doubt and a sense of personal inferiority. It cannot be denied that these are potent and detrimental influences, though not generally recognized because they are in the realm of the mental and spiritual. More apparent are the economic handicaps which follow her recent entrance into industry. It is con-ceded that she has special difficulties because of the poor working conditions and low wages of her men. It is not surprising that only the most determined women forge ahead to results other than mere survival. To the gifted, the zest of meeting a challenge is a compensating factor which often brings success. The few who do prove their mettle, stimulate one to a closer study of how this achievement is won under contemporary conditions.

Better to visualize the Negro woman at her job, our vision of a host of individ-uals must once more resolve itself into groups on the basis of activity. First, comes a very small leisure group—the wives and daughters of men who are in business, in the professions and a few well-paid personal service occupations. Second, a most active and progressive group, the women in business and the professions. Third, the many women in the trades and industry. Fourth, a group weighty in numbers struggling on in domestic service, with an even less fortunate fringe of casual workers, fluctuating with the economic temper of the times.

The first is a pleasing group to see. It is picked for outward beauty by Negro men with much the same feeling as other Americans of the same economic class. Keeping their women free to preside over the family, these women are affected by the problems of every wife and mother, but touched only faintly by their race's hardships. They do share acutely in the prevailing difficulty of finding competent household help. Negro wives find Negro maids unwilling generally to work in their own neighborhoods, for various reasons. They do not wish to work where there is a possibility of acquaintances coming into contact with them while they serve and they still harbor the misconception that Negroes of any sta-tion are unable to pay as much as persons of the other race. It is in these homes of comparative ease that we find the polite activities of social exclusiveness. The luxuries of well-appointed homes, modest motors, tennis, golf and country clubs, trips to Europe and California, make for social standing. The problem con-fronting the refined Negro family is to know others of the same achievement. The search for kindred spirits gradually grows less difficult; in the past it led to the custom of visiting all the large cities in order to know similar groups of cultured Negro people. In recent years, the more serious minded Negro woman's visit to Europe has been extended from months to years for the purpose of study and travel. The European success which meets this type of ambition is instanced in the conferring of the doctorate in philosophy upon a Negro woman, Dr. Anna J. Cooper, at the last commencement of the Sorbonne, Paris. Similarly, a score of Negro women are sojourning abroad in various countries for the spiritual relief and cultural stimulation afforded there.

A spirit of stress and struggles characterizes the second two groups. These women of business, profession and trade are the hub of the wheel of progress. Their burden is twofold. Many are wives and mothers whose husbands are insufficiently paid, or who have succumbed to social maladjustment and have abandoned their families. An appalling number are widows. They face the great problem of leaving home each day and at the same time trying to rear children in their spare time—this, too, in neighborhoods where rents are large, standards of dress and recreation high and costly, and social danger on the increase. One cannot resist the temptation to pause for a moment and pay tribute to these Negro mothers. And to call attention to the service she is rendering to the nation, in her struggle against great odds to educate and care for one group of the country's children. If the mothers of the race should ever be honored by state or federal legislation, the artist's imagination will find a more inspiring subject in the modern Negro mother—self-directed but as loyal and tender as the much extolled, yet pitiable black mammy of slavery days.

The great commercial life of New York City is only slightly touched by the Negro woman, of our second group. Negro business men offer her most of their work, but their number is limited. Outside of this field in Negro offices, custom is once more against her, and competition is keen for all. However, Negro girls are training and some are holding exceptional jobs. One of the professors in a New York college has had a young colored woman as secretary for the past three or four years. Another holds the head clerical position in an organization where reliable handling of detail and a sense of business ethics are essential. Quietly these women prove their worth, so that when a vacancy exists and there is a call, it is difficult to find even one competent colored secretary who is not employed. As a result of the opportunity in clerical work in the educational system of New York City, a number have qualified for such positions, one having been recently appointed to the office of a high school. In other departments, the civil service in New York City is no longer free from discrimination. The casual personal interview, that tenacious and retrogressive practice introduced into the federal administration during the World War, has spread and often nullifies the Negro woman's success in written tests. The successful young woman cited above was three times "turned down" as undesirable on the basis of the personal interview. In the great mercantile houses, the many young Negro girls who might be well suited to sales positions are barred from all but menial positions. Even so, one Negro woman, beginning as a uniformed maid in the shoe department of one of the largest stores, has pulled herself up to the position of "head of stock." One of the most prosperous monthly magazines of national circulation has for the head of its news service a Negro woman who rose from the position of stenographer. Her duties involve attendance upon staff conferences, executive supervision of her staff of white office workers, broadcasting and journalism of the highest order.

Yet in spite of the claims of justice and proved efficiency, telephone and insurance companies and other corporations which receive considerable patronage from Negroes deny them proportionate employment. Fortunately this is an era of changing customs. There is hope that a less selfish racial attitude will prevail. It is a heartening fact that there is an increasing number of Americans who will lend a hand in the game fight of the worthy.

Throughout the South, where businesses for Negro patronage are under the control of Negroes to a large extent, there are already many opportunities for Negro women. But, because of the nerve strain and spiritual drain of hostile social conditions in that section, Negro women are turning away from opportunities there to find a freer and fuller life in the North.

In the less crowded professional vocations, the outlook is more cheerful. In these fields, the Negro woman is dependent largely upon herself and her own race for work. In the legal, dental and medical professions, successful women practitioners have usually worked their way through college and are "managing" on the small fees that can be received from an under-paid public.

Social conditions in America are hardest upon the Negro because he is lowest in the economic scale. The tendency to force the Negro downward, gives rise to serious social problems and to a consequent demand for trained college women in the profession of social work. The need has been met with a response from young college women, anxious to devote their education and lives toward helping the submerged classes. Much of the social work has been pioneer in nature; the pay has been small, with little possibility of advancement. For, even in work among Negroes, the better paying positions are reserved for whites. The Negro college woman is doing her bit at a sacrifice, along such lines as these: as probation officers, investigators and police women in the correctional departments of the city; as Big Sisters attached to the Children's Court; as field workers and visitors for relief organizations, missions and churches; as secretaries for traveller's aid societies; in the many organizations devoted to preventative and educational medicine; in clinics and hospitals and as boys' and girls' welfare workers in recreation and industry.

In the profession of nursing, there are over three hundred in New York City. In the dark blue linen uniform of Henry Street Visiting Nurse Service, the Negro woman can be seen hurrying earnestly from house to house on her round of free relief to the needy. Again, she is in many other branches of public health nursing, in the public schools, milk stations and diet kitchens. The Negro woman is in the wards of two of the large city hospitals and clinics. After a score of years of service in one such institution, a Negro woman became superintendent of nurses in the war emergency. Deposed after the armistice, though eminently satisfactory, she retained connection with the training school as lecturer, for the inspiration she could be to "her girls." The growing need for the executive nurse is being successfully met as instanced by the supervisors in day nurseries and private sanitariums, financed and operated in Harlem entirely by Negroes. Throughout the South there is a clear and anxious call to nurses to carry the gospel of hygiene to the rural sections and to minister to the suffering not reached by organizations already in the communities. One social worker, in New York City, though a teacher by profession, is head of an organization whose program is to raise money for the payment of nurses to do the work described above. In other centers, West and South, the professional Negro nurse is supplanting the untrained woman attendant of former years.

In New York City, nearly three hundred women share in the good conditions obtaining there in the teaching profession. They measure up to the high pedagogical requirements of the city and state law, and are increasingly leaders in the community. In a city where the schools are not segregated, she is meeting with success among white as well as colored children in positions ranging from clerk in the elementary school on up through the graded ranks of teachers in the lower grades, of special subjects in the higher grades, in the junior high schools and in the senior high schools. One Negro woman is assistant principal in an elementary school where the other assistant and the principal are white men and the majority of the teachers white. Another Negro woman serves in the capacity of visiting teacher to several schools, calling upon both white and colored families and experiencing no difficulty in making social adjustments. Still another Negro woman is a vocational counsellor under the Board of Education, in a junior high school. She is advising children of both races as to future courses of study to pursue and as to the vocations in which tests prove them to be apt. This position, the result of pioneer work by another Negro woman, is unique in the school system of New York. . . .

With all these forces at work, true sex equality has not been approximated. The ratio of opportunity in the sex, social, economic and political spheres is about that which exists between white men and women. In the large, I would say that the Negro woman is the cultural equal of her man because she is generally kept in school longer. Negro boys, like white boys, are usually put to work to subsidize the family income. The growing economic independence of Negro working women is causing her to rebel against the domineering family attitude of the cruder working-class husband. The masses of Negro men are engaged in menial occupations throughout the working day. Their baffled and suppressed desires to determine their economic life are manifested in overbearing domination at home. Working mothers are unable to instill different ideals in the sons. Conditions change slowly. Nevertheless, education and opportunity are modifying the spirit of the younger Negro men. Trained in modern schools of thought, they begin to show a wholesome attitude of fellowship and freedom for their women. The challenge to young Negro womanhood is to see clearly this trend and grasp the proffered comradeship with sincerity. In this matter of sex equality, Negro women have contributed few outstanding militants, a notable instance being the historic Sojourner Truth. On the whole the Negro woman's feminist efforts are directed chiefly toward the realization of the equality of the races, the sex struggle assuming the subordinate place.

Obsessed with difficulties which might well compel individualism, the Negro woman has engaged in a considerable amount of organized action to meet group needs. She has evolved a federation of her clubs, embracing between eight and ten thousand women in New York state alone. The state federation is a part of the National Association of Colored Women, which, calling together the women from all parts of the country, engages itself in enterprises of general race interest. The national organization of colored women is now firmly established, and under the presidency of Mrs. Bethune is about to strive for conspicuous goals.

In New York City, many associations exist for social betterment, financed and operated by Negro women. One makes child welfare its name and special concern. Others, like the Utility Club, Utopia Neighborhood, Debutantes' League, Sempre Fidelius, etc., raise funds for old folks' homes, a shelter for delinquent girls and fresh-air camps for children. The Colored Women's Branch of the Y. W. C. A. and the women's organizations in the many churches as well as the beneficial lodges and associations, care for the needs of their members.

On the other hand, the educational welfare of the coming generation has become the chief concern of the national sororities of Negro college women. The first to be organized in the country, the *Alpha Kappa Alpha*, has a systematized, a continuous program of educational and vocational guidance for students of the high schools and colleges. The work of Lambda Chapter, which covers New York City and its suburbs, has been most effective in carrying out the national program. Each year, it gathers together between one and two hundred such students and gives the girls a chance to hear the life stories of Negro women, successful in various fields of endeavor. Recently a trained nurse told how, starting in the same schools as they, she had risen to the executive position in the Harlem Health Information Bureau. A commercial artist showed how real talent had overcome the color line. The graduate physician was a living example of the modern opportunities in the newer fields of medicine open to women. The vocations, as outlets for the creative instinct, became attractive under the persuasion of the musician, the dressmaker and the decorator. A recent graduate outlined her plans for meeting the many difficulties encountered in establishing a dental office and in building up a practice. A journalist spun the fascinating tale of her years of experience. The *Delta Sigma Theta* Sorority (national in scope) works along similar lines. Alpha Beta Chapter of New York City, during the current year, presented a young art student with a scholarship of $1,000 for study abroad. In such ways as these are the progressive and privileged groups of Negro women expressing their community and race consciousness.

We find the Negro woman, figuratively struck in the face daily by contempt from the world about her. Within her soul, she knows little of peace and happiness. But through it all, she is courageously standing erect, developing within herself the moral strength to rise above and conquer false attitudes. She is maintaining her natural beauty and charm and improving her mind and opportunity. She is measuring up to the needs of her family, community and race, and radiating a hope throughout the land.

The wind of the race's destiny stirs more briskly because of her striving.

Black English: The Counter Narrative of Toni Cade Bambara
Eleanor Traylor

Old Wife: *I'ma get my walkin shoes soon, Min, cause them haints fixing to beat on them drums with them cat bones and raise a rukus. So you just leave me here and I'll talk to you after while. I can't stand all that commotion them haints calling music . . .* (The Salt Eaters 62)

Min: *Old wife, what are you but a haint?*

Old Wife: *I'm a servant of the Lord, beggin your pardon.*

Min: *I know that. But you a haint. You dead ain't you?*

Old Wife: *There is no death in spirit, Min, I keep tellin you [that]. Why you so hard headed?* (SE 62)

> *You [just] rip them fancy clothes off, Min, and thrash out into them waters, churn up all them bones we dropped from the old ships, churn up all that brine from the salty deep where our tears sank, and you grab them chirren by the neck and bop'm a good one and drag'm on back to shore and fling'm down and jump to it, pumping and cussing, fussing and cracking they ribs if ya have to to let'm live, Min. Cause love won't let you let'm go.* (SE 62)

A sense of the wonderful—the pervasive atmosphere—informing the fictional universe of Toni Cade Bambara is achieved through a language alive with self-confidence as it invents

> *. . . new possibilities in formation*
> *new configurations to move with . . . (SE 293)*
> *the need for legend and fable,*
> *for the extraordinary so big,*
> *the courage to pursue . . . (SE 268)*

It is ever alert to and adept at testing its own trustworthiness:

> *. . . The dream is real, my friends.*
> *The failure to make it work is the unreality . . . (SE 126)*
> *It requires "exacting ceremonies," Min. (145)*

It points to the way it has forever existed as music, lore, saga, poetry, oratory, rhetoric; as a core of ideas and beliefs and values and literature (*Black English* 81) and humor and fun. It is the instrument of creation itself:

> *. . . And God said,*
> *I believe I'll make me a world . . .*
> *And God said: That's good! (Johnson 17)*

It signals pride when it records its transitions as it defied and continues to defy the muzzle since the time when it said,

> *. . . I must navigate my way through circumstance*
> *that will otherwise destroy me. (Equiano et passim)*
>
> *. . . I set out with a firm purpose to learn.*
> *(Douglass 275)*

It expresses impish glee when it recalls its willfulness—its vulnerable though intrepid impulse to fly in the face of conventional wisdom in order to insure posterity:

> *. . . Come down off dat gate post, you little sow,*
> *lookin' dem white folks dead in dey eye, dey gon*
> *lynch you yet, git in dis house. You hear me?*
> *(Hurston)*

Loving its amazing powers, this language connects two interacting worlds: *Aye* (the tangible and visible world of living beings) and *Orun* (its invisible companion, the ever present otherworld of spirits, ancestors, gods.) It conflates tenses to sound in a present moment the voices of the past and the prescient voices of the yet unborn. This language is "clairvoyant, clairfeelant, clairaudient, and clairdoent" (*SE et passim*). It is the stubborn, enduring, deeply textured language of Toni Cade Bambara, alias T.C.B., alias the swamp hag, alias the loa of the yellow flowers, alias Miz Hazel, alias the "she" who with her "Afrafemcentric"—co-conspirator—"shes" of literature and of film creates a language called *she:*

> *She [had] learned to read the auras of trees and stones and plants and neighbors . . . And studied the sun's corona, the jagged petals of magnetic colors . . . And then the threads that shimmered between wooden tables and flowers and children and candles and birds . . . She could dance their dance and match their beat and echo their pitch and know their frequency as if her own . . . She knew each way of being in the world and could welcome them home again open to wholeness.*
> *(SE 48)*

This she-language, confident of its self-chosen, life-saving, life-enhancing, corrective, and healing purpose understands everything there is to know about the arbitrariness of signs. The questions it asks are these: who is controlling the sign? Is some glib and hypocritical HUNCa Bubba or some mean-spirited self-deprecating Miz Turner breaking the heart of Little Hazel Elizabeth Deborah Parker or Little Luther—dashing their dreams and aspirations by wielding a sign reading grown-up-common-sense-wisdom: the ability to "mis-inform, mis-direct, smoke-out, screen out, black-out, confound, contain, intimidate?" (*BE* 78) Are the children of "Bovanne's" Miz Hazel under the sign of "we hipper than you" refusing "home-tongue proficiency" (*BE* 78) in favor of some "unattached," "unobliged," "psychically immature, spiritually impoverished, and intellectually undisciplined" (*SE* 133) hype?

These and similar questions regarding the nature of language had received by 1972 a stunning and rigorous response from Toni Cade Bambara in an essay called "Black English" published by *The Black Child Development Institute* in a collection called *Curriculum Approaches from a Black Perspective*. In that essay, she corroborates James Baldwin, following Max Weinreich's observation that people who raise powerful armies are said to speak a language; those who do not are said to speak a dialect. Many premises of twentieth century linguistics and semantics, of course, support this observation, but two in particular are the focus of Bambara's "Black English." One is that, in her words, "language is the single most important political institution in a culture" (78). The other is that language, as W.E.B. DuBois and other scholars laying the foundation for more recent thinkers knew it, is "a political institution that functions in the interest of the ruling class" (78). As she reminds us, the political way of looking at and speaking about language is "not the way schools approach language" (78). She continues:

> In school, we have focused on how language operates as grammar, diction, vocabulary. We have focused on language as noun (namer)

not on what or who is named or on who is doing the naming; we have focused on language as verb (generator of action or situation of being) not on what kind of action is being generated or on who or what is situated in what kind of state of being. In schools we do not emphasize the real function of language in our lives: how it operates in courts, in hospitals, in schools, in the media, how it operates to perpetuate a society, maintain a social order, to reflect biases, to transmit basic values. In schools we focus on vocabulary, diction and grammar, but not on the implications of words, not on the use to which words are put. (*BE* 78)

In her essay, she raises the question being aired in the National Media today: "What is Black English anyway?" (77) She muses: Is it "ghettoese, a sloppy variation of proper speech" . . . is it what many teachers, Black and non-Black describe it to be, slang, profanity; a language that demonstrates the intellectual deficiencies of Black folks, or that demonstrates perhaps sheer perversity on the part of the student . . . is it, as some parents describe it, "something shameful, disgraceful, the language of low-life, unambitious folk?" . . . or "among the pedagogues," ". . . those who get their Ph.D.'s hustling Black stuff—there is the notion that the whole issue can be summed up" [in a question]: "Are Black students bidialectal or bilingual? Bidialectal meaning that the language of the home is a variation of a standard. Bilingual meaning that Black English is a language . . . *foreign*, perhaps" (*BE* 77).

Old wife: It won the Nobel, didn't it, Min. Whatever dey call dem prizes.

Min: Please, old wife, remember that you are a haint.

Old Wife: Min, your brain is a sieve. I told you ain't no death. You just pull off dat red suit and bop em.

Black English, continues Miss Bambara, "The language of our music, poetry," stories, intellectual discourses "has been maintained through the usual methods, by traditional use. It has been kept alive by our caretakers and custodians—our writers, and teachers, and singers. It is reinforced by ideological maintenance where there is a cultural aggression on our language (which has nothing to do with illiteracy of any kind). This language has persisted at great odds," she says (*BE* 83).

In her short fictions, collected in *Gorilla My Love* (1972), the *Sea Scabirds Are Still Alive* (1977), in *The Salt Eaters* (1980), her novel, and in the stories collected in *Deep Sightings and Rescue Missions* just published by Louis Messiah and Toni Morrison, Toni Cade Bambara perfects a narrative mode and appropriates a language which writes against the language of another narrative mode. That other has been suggested by Toni Morrison and my students as a *master narrative,* a school, an overwhelming volume of literature, theory, argument, hypothesis and accepted belief. It is a school which, finally, betrays, abandons the teacher and plunges the student into the void of homelessness.

Countering this school, the language of Toni Cade Bambara constructs a universe of intelligence where foolishness—a fateful handicap—is laughed to derision; this narrative universe is a place where language—in the creation of "broad sympathy, a knowledge of the world that was and is and the relation of all of us to it," as W.E.B. DuBois put it,—loves itself. It is this language with its host of contributors that Miss Bambara calls *Black English.*

Works Cited

Bambara, Toni Cade. "Black English." *Curriculum Approaches from a Black Perspective.* Atlanta: Black Child Development Institute, 1972.

_____. *The Salt Eaters.* New York: Vintage, 1992.

Douglass, Frederick. *Narrative of the Life of Frederick Douglass, an American Slave, The Classic Slave Narratives.* Ed. Henry Louis Gates, Jr. New York: Penguin, 1987.

Equiano, Olaudah. *The Interesting Narrative of the Life of Olaudah Equiano, or Gustavus Vassa, the African. The Classic Slave Narratives.* Ed. Henry Louis Gates, Jr. New York: Penguin, 1987.

Hurston, Zora Neale. *Dust Tracks on a Road, an Autobiography.* 1st. ed. Philadelphia: Lippincott, 1942.

Johnson, James Weldon, "Creation." *God's Trombones.* New York: Viking, 1927.

Private School, Private Pain
Patricia Elam Ruff

Today's public schools, especially those in the District, are handicapped by budget crises, bulging classrooms, bureaucracies and violence. And so while many African American parents received fine public school educations themselves, more and more of them are beginning to realize that public education is not so fine for their children. In the words of Steven Wright, a history teacher who sent six of his seven children to private schools, "Public schools prepare students to graduate; private schools prepare them to be leaders of tomorrow." While public schools must pluck the weeds before they can tend to the garden, private schools can get right down to planting seeds and watching them grow.

The most beautiful gardens have all kinds of flowers, but that variety does not come naturally to private schools. In most, black students are still a tiny minority, and thus vulnerable to isolation, unreasonable scrutiny and scrambled identities. For black students, a private school education has a cost above and beyond the tuition. I paid that price when I integrated a private girls' school in Boston more than 30 years ago. Now I find my son and his black private school peers reliving much of my history.

I couldn't sleep the night before attending my 25th reunion at Winsor, the school where I was one of four black girls who broke the color bar. Ellen and Pam, two of my fellow trailblazers in Winsor's class of 1971, also had restless nights. None of us had been back to Winsor since graduation, and Pam and I had actually decided against attending the reunion until Ellen called with her idea of forming a panel to discuss our memories. Our panel would be entitled "Red, Black and White"; red and white being Winsor's school colors and black, of course, being us.

Seated in front of the mostly white audience, we black women begin reminiscing about penetrating the land of white privilege. In 1964, when we were 10 years old, Ellen and I entered Winsor's fifth grade. Pam came the next year. I tell our audience that most of our class did not know many black people, other than their maids and chauffeurs. Our new classmates would ask us questions they didn't dare ask their household help. "Can you wash your color off? Do you sing 'We Shall Overcome' at dinnertime?" We were unprepared for these queries and had no idea why we were being asked.

Those seated in front of us sit rapt and visibly moved. Unexpectedly, my eyes fill and I notice many in the audience are tearful, too.

Ellen remembers us taking the entrance exam in the school library with a group of white girls staring at us through glass windows. "Look at the black girls," she heard them say. "It was then," she notes, "that I knew what it was like to be an animal in a zoo." She rubs her hands together in her lap, gazing at a safe place on the wall in front of her.

Thirty years later, African American students in mostly white D.C.–area private schools say they, too, sometimes feel on display as they field questions about whether all of Southeast is a ghetto or how they wash their hair while it's braided. Although the number of black students in private schools has certainly grown since I was in school, for the past three years it has hovered between 9 percent and 20 percent, according to the Black Student Fund. The only local school that surpasses these numbers is the Newport School in Kensington, where more than 40 percent of its students are African American.

At many private schools, the numbers often translate into a single black student in a class—which renders that student, willing or not, a spokesman. "Last year we were talking about slavery and the teacher wanted me to speak for the whole race," says Asiatu Lawoyin, who is currently the only African American in the senior class at the Field School in Northwest Washington. "Then in history someone didn't understand the relationship between Martin Luther King, Malcolm X and Elijah Muhammad. The teacher asked me to explain it, and I asked, 'Why are you putting me on the spot?' But he forced me to answer the question."

Some black students fear that if they make a mistake, they embarrass not just themselves but their race; that makes the pressure, already intense in rigorous private schools, even more so. "There were times when I was scared to speak up, unless I was sure I had the right answer, for fear that I might reinforce negative stereotypes that blacks aren't as smart as whites," says Brandye Lee, a 1996 graduate of Sidwell Friends. Many African American parents told me that while their children's grades are fine, their evaluations indicate that they need to speak up more in class.

Black students' school experience becomes defined by their difference. Lee, who also attended the Potomac School in McLean, says that she felt alienated most of the time. "At Potomac I didn't fit in with white kids. They pretended I did until school dance time—there were no black boys so I didn't dance. I was constantly looking for acceptance among my white peers."

I remember frantically, sometimes painfully, trying to comb the coarseness out of my hair so it would hang down, like that of my classmates, straight and lank against my face. Later I rebelled against that ideal by wearing a large afro—and deciding to forgo college because it wasn't "relevant to my authentic blackness." (I took a year off after graduation during which I realized my blackness would be best authenticated by attending college.)

I see similar gropings for identity among the students I talk to now, including the shunning of their "blackness." Kui Price, who left the Bullis School in Potomac three years ago to return to public school, says that she "got caught up in going to [whites'] country clubs and bar mitzvahs. I was living their life. Every weekend was like a fantasy. I'd be really happy and then really disappointed when I went home because it wasn't the kind of house they had." At a recent dance at Madeira, students told me, the black boys would dance only with white girls.

Other black students decide that preserving their blackness means rejecting "white values"—such as ambition. Some black parents take their children out of public school to escape just that anti-achievement ethic, but it may end up being magnified at a predominantly white school, where black students feel compelled to assert their "realness," whether by not studying or hanging with their homeboys on the street.

In doing so, they are partly questing for acceptance from their public school peers. "In my Southeast neighborhood," Brandye Lee says, "I was constantly teased for 'sounding white' or 'acting white.'" Lee's family helped her stay balanced, but not all kids are so fortunate. Some consciously switch from school culture to neighborhood culture as soon as they get home.

I tell the reunion audience I don't have any memories of blatant racism, but there were always painful reminders of my separateness. When I, the only black student in my English class, was asked to read a passage from "Huckleberry Finn," I scanned the page to make sure there were no "Nigger Jims." But of course there was one, sitting at the end of the paragraph, pompous and taunting. I remember how fast my heart was beating, how I planned to skate across the words and render them inaudible, how desperately I didn't want to cry. But when I said those two words it was as if I were Nigger Jim and the whole class knew it.

Even though black children should be taught not to let racism hold them back or keep them from taking responsibility for their actions, black parents do a disservice if they don't prepare their children for racism. Kui was told that she had "nasty nigger hair" by a sixth-grade classmate when she was at Bullis.

Black students need to help each other through these times, but unfortunately, school administrations and white students sometimes disdain black students' efforts to comfort one another. Instead of understanding the healing it allows, white folk seem threatened by the self-segregation of African Americans. At Holton-Arms in Bethesda, which Lawoyin attended for three years, she says "when the black girls sat together at one table, the white girls would talk about us. But it was our one chance to be together and discuss what was going on. It was survival."

Black students need each other all the more because there are usually few black faculty members for them to turn to. Most private schools have 6 percent to 10 percent black faculty—an improvement over my school days, but still a discouraging statistic.

The parents and students I talked to suggest that some private schools seem to look for black teachers who check their blackness at the school door. While schools may be more comfortable with this kind of teacher, they need to realize that both black and white students would benefit from contact with grownups who do not try to play their blackness down or make it more palatable for white folk.

I met two African American teachers, Abe Wehmiller at Bullis and Brian King at Maret, who both sought careers in independent schools because they had no one they could relate to when they were in private school. These men, while obviously chock-full of knowledge, are also "keeping it real" and commanding respect from their students, black and white. "I taught a class with only one black student," King recalls, "and when we were studying slavery I could see the tears in his eyes. Years ago, at Georgetown Day, I was the boy. The difference was I was there for him."

Because of his own experience at an independent school, Wehmiller understands the importance of go-gos (dances featuring black go-go music) to black students at Bullis. "There was resistance [by the school administration] because of misconceptions about them attracting violence and hoodlums," he says. Wehmiller went to bat for the black students. "I explained . . . how important it was for the black kids who come into this other world every day to have an opportunity to feel like insiders for the first time, to share something from their world for once." The school agreed.

My school visits suggest to me that most schools are striving to change, and some are making tangible strides. Winsor now has 30 black students out of 399, and 11 black faculty and administrators out of 100. But I'd like to see every school follow Newport's lead and determine to have 50 percent African American enrollment, then do the same with the faculty. If private schools are truly creating future leaders, then their students must be prepared to overcome the racial divide rather than perpetuate it. Reflecting the general population isn't enough; our children need the strength of critical mass.

"Would you send your children to a school like Winsor?" someone at my reunion asks. Not like it was then, I tell them. Pam, Ellen and I all have children in private schools because we know the caliber of the education can't be matched, but we also know we have to work extra hard to keep our children grounded, happy and proud of who they are, and that we must stay active in their schools.

My mother is in the audience, and I see the pain etched in her face. She speaks, telling the audience who she is. "I felt I could take care of affirming the heritage. I didn't realize the pain would have such lasting effects, fueling rage and rebellion in Patricia. I don't know that I would make the same decision now. . . I hoped that my grandchildren would not be facing the same situation, but they are."

As a parent now, I understand that my parents felt a responsibility to provide the best education they could. And in some ways they succeeded: I breezed through college, learned how to write well, do thorough research and study in an organized fashion. And I learned not to be intimidated when I find myself in the minority, as I did in law school, graduate school and many other settings.

I know now that not only black students benefit from diverse education. As our panel wrapped up, a white former classmate rose. "I just want to say that you guys enriched our class. . . . You made our class aware. You guys stood up and said these things are bad and you changed things. You said white is not the only good color. Thank you," she says.

After the panel, other former classmates rush to me in tears, saying things like, "I'm so sorry if I said anything stupid to you back then." I tell them not to worry, it wasn't their fault, they didn't know any better.

But their parents and the school should have. As Barbara Patterson, president of the Black Student Fund, says, "Someone should be making sure that black children feel as good about their blackness as white children feel about their whiteness . . . the reality is that there's no tuition deduction for what's missing."

Faking the Funk:
The Middle Class Black Folks
of Prince George's County
Nathan McCall

When the sun is out and the weather is nice, about fifteen young bloods sometimes gather on the corner of Lake Arbor Way and Winged Foot Drive. Maybe in their late teens, they chill on that spot, rap casually, and slyly pass forty-ounce bottles of brew from hand to hand.

Of course, they sport the popular gangsta look and wear the standard street gear: knit skullcaps pulled over their shaved heads; bulky, unlaced brogans; and baggy sweatshirts flung over blue jeans that ride low—*real low*—on their butts.

In dress and manner, they could pass for a typical crew of young hustlers in Washington, D.C. And as you drive by, they even eye you warily, like leery drug dealers scoping for the Man. But cruising through there, you're struck by the realization that something's wrong with this picture. There's a major contradiction here. There's something that, well, just doesn't seem to make sense.

The discrepancy begins with the setting: The backdrop for the fellas is not boarded-up tenements, graffiti-marked walls, and urban blight. The backdrop is $250,000 homes with manicured lawns—houses that are sprinkled around a sprawling, well-tended community golf course and near jogging trails that circle a scenic, man-made lake.

In other words, this is not the rugged Chocolate City, where the gang bangers rule. This is Prince Georges County, a serene suburb of Washington. And the dudes hanging on the corner aren't desperate hoods trying to survive a hard-scrabble life; they're middle-class black kids with braces on their teeth. They're wanna-bes who are just acting out, pretending to be the gritty street warriors they see in D.C.

257

If you think *they're* a little confused, you should see their parents.

Their parents are the professional and business people who help make Prince Georges the richest majority-black county in the United States. By practically every barometer—income, education, and so on—used by our "social experts," they're the black crème de la crème. But like their children, they seem to be caught up in a bizarre identity crisis of some sort. And just like their offspring, their struggle is sometimes a pathetic sight.

In the normal scheme of things, the middle-class black people of Prince Georges County (everyone calls it P.G. for short) wouldn't be particularly noteworthy. In most ways, they're just typical Americans—or they're what we tend to think average Americans are: They're hardworking, honest folks who want the best for themselves and their families. They're good people—the kind of black folks that whites seem to get little exposure to.

But they are also something else. They are black America's crystal ball: Hailed by the media as a "national showcase for black achievement," P.G. is a scale model of what *is* and *is not* happening among the most promising African Americans in this splintered land. And the goings-on of brothers and sisters there offer some clues about the future, especially for the black poor, who are catching hell.

The middle-class blacks of Prince Georges County symbolize our greatest hope. They're part of a spontaneous, quietly budding movement that seems to be catching on everywhere. In suburbs surrounding cities such as Atlanta, Philadelphia, and Chicago, the movement consists of upwardly mobile blacks who have broken from the pattern of following white folks wherever they settle. Instead, these blacks have made a conscious decision to live among their own.

Unlike the movements of the past, which were in-your-face and on the streets, this one is more subtle and more instinctive. In fact, it's so low-key that you can become a part of it without even realizing it.

It happened that way for me several years ago, when my teenage son came to live with me in D.C. With my son so close by, the city worried me as never before: Too many people have become casualties of the crack epidemic or the out-of-control gangsterism that's made Washington seem like a war zone. So we did what lots of black folks have done: We left.

First, we moved in with my sister-in-law in a mostly white Virginia suburb. There, I faced the usual hassles that you encounter when living among whites: suspicious Caucasians whispering concerns to our landlord that we might bring down their property values or break into their houses and rip off their TVs.

Often when I left home for work at *The Washington Post*, I encountered so many wary whites on sidewalks and buses that I often was pissed off by the time I reached the office in downtown D.C. Disgusted, I decided to move someplace else, someplace where I could get away from paranoid whites.

That's when I heard about P.G. I was told that in some parts of the county, blacks had formed enclaves in peaceful communities as nice as you'll find anywhere. I went to a place called Mitchellville, looked around, and bought a townhouse right away.

Before blacks moved there in large numbers, Prince Georges County was one vast cow pasture run by white, beer-bellied good old boys. Blacks began moving in around the 1970s. Two decades later, the county of 750,000 had a black majority. In 1994, blacks showed off their new political might and elected the first black county executive ever to run the place.

Of course, there are working-class and even some poor areas in P.G., just like anywhere else, but the county is known mostly for the large concentration of well-off blacks who have settled there. The community where I now live, known as Lake Arbor, is surrounded by others very much like it—developments called Fort Washington, Kettering, Perrywood. These are sprawling, rustic neighborhoods where the median income is relatively high and the crime is low. A survey found that blacks with college degrees outnumber college-educated whites in P.G. County and that more blacks than whites live in households with earnings above fifty thousand dollars. P.G. has also become a magnet for local black celebrities. Former heavyweight champion Riddick Bowe, the writer Marita Golden, and several NBA basketball stars live there.

Any P.G. resident will tell you what it means to feel welcome in your community. Often, when I step out onto my deck and scan the woodsy landscape that fronts my neighborhood, the tranquillity of the place fills me with a deep sense of racial pride. My euphoria is prompted partly by the atmosphere, which is really nice: The townhouses where I live stand in the shadows of a lake, a golf course, and large houses. But more than that, the good feeling comes from the realization that this may be as close to heaven as I will ever get: I can travel for a couple of miles in any direction and see mostly black folks, mostly *my* people; I can step outdoors without worrying about being insulted by some arrogant white dude who thinks I'm after his wallet; I can stroll through my neighborhood without seeing some old, blue-haired white lady clutching her bags when she sees me. In fact, when I go outdoors, my neighbors are genuinely glad to see me. They wave and say a cheerful hello.

Driving through my neighborhood, you can't help being impressed. And if you're not careful, you can get *really* carried away and interpret the outward appearance of things as a promising sign that we black people are finally pulling ourselves together. As the theme song for the old sitcom *The Jeffersons* went, it looks like "we're movin' on up."

But as the young bloods who hang on that corner demonstrate, things aren't always what they appear to be. The truth is, some blacks in P.G. County are living what one of my neighbors called an illusion of success. Their houses are impressive and their cars look expensive, but few have any real wealth to speak of. Many are not even nigger rich, though some have learned, damned well, to act the part. Although they may *look* as though they have things together, many are just groping in the dark. A schoolteacher who moved there recently from Florida told me, "They seem to have lost their focus. They're just like ostriches with their heads in the sand."

What she meant is that among the "successful" blacks of P.G. and, by extension, middle-class blacks everywhere, many have failed the crucial commitment test: This crowd—my generation of college-trained blacks—came up in the world with some high expectations heaped on them. We are the people expected to form the "talented tenth" that W.E.B. Du Bois imagined; we rode the shoulders of our predecessors, the civil rights protesters who fought, and sometimes sacrificed their lives, to open doors for us. We were expected to use our skills and training to take the black struggle to the next level. For a long time, it was assumed that when we got our chance, we'd figure out a way to reach back and help those poor blacks who were left in the urban trenches to fend for themselves.

But if the prosperous blacks in P.G. County are any indication, the huddled poor masses may just have to wait awhile. The truth is, black America's middle class is a conflicted bunch of people who are still unsure of the power they wield. Right now, they can't save the poor—they're too preoccupied trying to figure out who *they* are.

Despite all the material signs of progress, there's no indication that the middle-class movement will spread beyond the thriving bounds of places like P.G. County and embrace those blacks most in need of our help.

For one thing, there's no concrete game plan at work here. This middle-class movement is not spearheaded by the NAACP or the National Urban League or even by some charismatic leader. There's no indication that the man or woman who will be the next Martin Luther King, Jr., or Malcolm X will spring from this bunch to lead the way. You get the feeling that the college-trained blacks with that kind of potential are too busy hustling the dollar, trying to make partner in some prominent white law firm.

"I think that too many of us are too tied to the system to be effective in the way that Martin and Malcolm were. Martin and Malcolm weren't beholden to the system," noted one friend, a lawyer who also lives in P.G.

The result is that the movement lacks direction. So the black people of Prince Georges County—and middle-class African Americans everywhere—are improvising; they're just taking the black struggle day by day.

As I wonder about my own role in helping the poor, I realize that the main question the black middle class faces is this: Beyond the quest for financial security and personal comfort, what, if anything, are we committed to? It's not that we don't have plenty of good, firsthand reasons to fight for the cause. A *Washington Post* story on the subject said, "Middle-class African Americans are more likely to feel they face racism than working-class and poor blacks. Nearly six in 10 middle-class blacks says they have experienced racism in the past 10 years and six in 10 say that they are concerned that they or a family member will face discrimination in the future."

The writer of the article, Kevin Merida, went on to say, "This unease comes at a time when many high-achieving blacks see their status threatened by corporate and government downsizing and their gains being challenged in the courts, in the political arena and in the theories of conservative scholars. As a result, though they are viewed within their race as having 'made it,' they are drawing closer politically to those who haven't."

Yet middle-class blacks clearly are not drawing closer to the black poor in other ways. Like cats curled up comfortably on a favorite rug, many of them live in what amounts to what the writer Sam Fulwood described as a "self-protective buppie cocoon, separate from poor blacks and all whites."

The blacks in Prince Georges seem to bear that out. If P.G. County is a symbol of success for the black middle class, for the poor it's also a discouraging sign of black flight. Of course, the term *black flight* makes many middle-class blacks cringe. In defense of themselves, some are quick to point out that theirs is not flight in the traditional sense of the word. (Blacks in P.G. want you to know that they're not so much running *from* something as running *to* something.)

Still, many middle-class blacks in P.G., and everywhere else, seem to be nagged by a deep sense of guilt about the notion that they've abandoned the poor. "I shouldn't feel guilty, because I didn't get a free ride," Bravitte Manley, a corporate lawyer, once told me. "But when you see blacks who are hopeless, you feel guilty, and you feel helpless because you don't know how to make the situation better. What most people do is try not to think about it because if you think about it, it's intellectually unjustifiable to say, *So what?*"

The guilt stems from the fact that for many African Americans who have come into their own in recent decades, economic success has been doubled-edged: It's brought them material comfort, but it's distanced them—physically and emotionally—from those for whom the mainstream remains out of reach.

In response, the so-called black underclass has created a defiant counterculture all its own. It has developed its own language, values, music, and—as ruthless as the drug trade may be—a self-sustaining industry. That counterculture has evolved so swiftly and furiously, and the devastation of poverty and violence in its wake is so far-reaching, that it's left the entire nation dumbfounded. The astonishing murder rate among blacks attests to this.

The result is that now, in the midst of one of the toughest challenges ever to our collective survival, middle-class and poor blacks have become terribly divided. This estrangement has crippled our struggle, which once had unity. "I've been disgusted with myself because I've become very class-conscious and very mainstream," a friend once confessed to me. "I don't feel personal guilt, but I do feel ashamed that many of us who have arrived have not banded together to help the underclass. I struggle with that."

In P.G. County, some folks try to relieve their guilty feelings by taking up social causes. But they don't seem like the kinds of folks who'd actually go to the ghetto and work in the trenches. They're more likely to scribble a check in arm's-length support of some worthy black cause. Or they'll turn to mentoring and other relatively risk-free activities to convince themselves that at least they're doing *something*.

It doesn't help matters that some middle-class blacks secretly relish their buppie status. For such folks, even charity is a status symbol. Jackie Woods, a friend who has lived in Philly, Chicago, and D.C., told me about a gathering she attended that could easily have passed for a scene in a Tom Wolfe novel: A group of well-to-do blacks got together in an elegant high-rise apartment, drinking wine and nibbling asparagus tips and lobster while planning fundraisers to help the homeless. "There were twenty-five people in the room, and everybody had on a thousand dollars worth of clothes," she said. "We were talking about helping the homeless, and there wasn't a homeless person in the room."

I truly believe that most middle-class blacks do want to help. Like me, they feel frustrated and so overwhelmed by the complex web of problems facing African Americans that they don't know where to begin. It's also true that virtually every element in America's black communities is pitching in. People in neighborhoods are taking to the streets to help the police fight crime. Civil rights groups are launching public relations campaigns to stop the violence. And churches, as usual, are doing their thing.

One battle cry that you hear more often now is the call for black suburbanites to return and help revive the cities they've abandoned. But the option of returning poses a serious practical problem: At a time when bystanders are often caught in the cross fire of gun battles, most people with a choice are understandably reluctant to place themselves and their families at risk. For many, it's plain foolish to go back when it's clear that the people there are fighting losing battles with drug lords armed with automatic weapons.

The issue of whether or not to return to the city is not just about establishing a physical presence. Unfortunately, some middle-class blacks also consider it necessary to distance themselves totally from the problems confronting us. In action, if not in philosophy, they subscribe to the view of Reverend Ike, the slick-haired, money-loving preacher who says, "The best thing you can do for the poor is not to become one of them."

So some middle-class blacks create their own strange existence, one that leaves them torn between two conflicting worlds: On the one hand, they're disillusioned by the racial realities of America, which hates blacks and the poor; on the other hand, they're still in love with the idea and the hope of achieving white folks' American dream. They're troubled by their loyalty—or lack of it—to less fortunate blacks, and yet for all their striving, for all the effort they've made to live among their own kind, the model of middle-class success that they pattern themselves on is lily-white.

Drive to Mitchellville Plaza, one of the many little shopping centers that have sprung up near upscale P.G. neighborhoods, and you'll see what I mean. You'll catch hints of chaotic lifestyles that reveal that some blacks haven't gotten as far away from the influence of whites as they may think they have. You'll see in their lifestyles a tangled mesh of contradictions and weird behaviors that are as confusing as the sight of bourgeois black kids hanging on a street corner, sucking brew.

A rush of activity flows through the shopping-center parking lot most evenings, when the professional blacks, returning from their oppressive jobs, zip to *this* shop or *that* store to pick up necessities. One by one, you see them rolling in, driving gleaming late-model Lexuses, Benzes, and Jeep Cherokees with disoriented-looking children strapped inside. Although they sport the trappings of prosperity, they don't seem happy. They look hurried and harried, tense—as uptight as the white people they emulate.

Every day, the frantic pattern at that shopping center repeats itself as predictably as the rising of the sun: After collecting their kids from day care and school, many parents stop first at the Blockbuster Video outlet and rent movies to baby-sit their children for the evening. From there, it's on to the McDonald's to pick up Happy Meals. Then, they head home, where the kids wolf down their high-cholesterol food and watch TV while Mama and Daddy collapse upstairs and try to catch their shortening breath.

It's success, white American style. It's blacks blindly caught up in the daily performance of what one writer in *The New Yorker* described as "the adrenaline surge that accompanies perhaps the fiercest desire of all these days—the desire to get ahead."

Although few would admit it, many of the blacks of P.G. County also pattern their lives on whites' lives in other, more subtle ways. When I first moved to the county, the complaint I heard most often was that expensive retailers, such as Macy's, Lord & Taylor, and other high-end businesses that follow white money everywhere had failed to open branches in P.G. I wondered whether those blacks really understood what they were saying: Without being aware of it, they were saying that they were upset that white retailers were refusing to come in and *exploit* them. They seemed to overlook the possibility that white racism could provide motivation for blacks to create their own businesses.

Fortunately, there is a sprinkling of black businesses operating in P.G. Black entrepreneurs recently opened BET SoundStage, an elaborate black-theme restaurant owned by Black Entertainment Television. And soul-food joints are springing up everywhere.

But for the most part, black business development in P.G. has followed the same pattern as it follows in poor neighborhoods: There's a glut of black barbershops and hair salons, and there's a black shopping mall nearby. (You can tell the black malls by the proliferation of stores that sell gold chains, beepers, and Payless shoes.)

Lots of nonblacks certainly have no problem recognizing the business potential in P.G. County. In recent years, as word has spread that there's black money to be had, a rainbow of other races has stormed into the county and set up businesses. There's a Jerry's Pizza place on Central Avenue, but it's not run by anybody named Jerry. It's owned and run by a group from Pakistan, who pooled their resources and bought the franchise. There's a carryout seafood joint, where you can buy crabs by the barrel. The place is named Homeboys, but the owner is white. At Kettering Plaza, there's a place called simply Beauty Barber. There, you can buy all kinds of special products for blacks—much of it adorned with the colors and symbols of African kinte cloth. You can buy nappy Afro wigs and hair products galore that come in tall bottles that say

MADE BY AFRICANS FOR AFRICANS. You can also buy products whose labels declare that they are manufactured by companies that are 100 PERCENT AFRICAN AMERICAN OWNED. But the store is run by Koreans.

"The Asians are like fleas on the back of a dog," one resentful friend complained. "You can't get rid of them. They follow black folks around, sucking blood, wherever they go."

There is a determination among the P.G. blacks to demand respect, especially from the foreigners who come to their communities and earn livelihoods off them. The problem is, their commitment to the struggle is often expressed in ways that are uniquely black bourgeois.

Once, they protested when Eddy's, a new Chinese takeout restaurant in Lake Arbor, refused to provide seats for customers waiting for their orders. The demonstration was cool, but it was hard to get fired up about it after seeing all those well-heeled folks out in front of the place in their monogrammed shirts and expensive suits, marching and waving protest signs.

On another occasion, they protested when the Giant Food store in Kettering Plaza placed magnetic detectors near the doors to catch shoplifters. One irate woman told me, "We wanted to let them know that blacks out *here* don't steal."

I went to the Giant and asked a black employee about the matter. He chuckled as if reflecting on the pretentious head trips that sometimes come with being black and middle-class. The employee told me that the store managers put up the detectors after learning that in the previous year, twenty thousand dollars worth of merchandise had walked out the door.

At some point, neighborhood activists who met with the management demanded that the "insulting" detectors be removed, but the management refused. "I guess they lost that battle," the store employee said.

"Yeah," I told him. "That's not the only battle they've lost."

Of course, it's also a status statement among some blacks in P.G. County to imitate white folks' obsession with protecting their property values. When it comes to that property, some blacks proved they can be as racist toward their people as some white folks are. In Perrywood, when too many young black boys and men began gathering at a basketball court, distressed "activists" encouraged the police to get aggressive with them. Just as they have harassed brothers in white areas, the police began randomly confronting young black men at the court, demanding that they show proof that they live in the neighborhood.

And dig this. Blacks in a section of P.G. called Woodmoor, where homes run around five hundred thousand dollars, campaigned successfully to get a new zip code because the old one associated them too closely with a place called Landover, where many lower-income blacks live.

For all the confusion among blacks in P.G. County, there is some cause for hope. Recently, a group of black churches banded together and launched a plan to form their own banks, which would extend loans to black businesses and home buyers, who routinely get turned down by white lenders.

The promise of that and other, similar efforts leads you to believe—or maybe you just *want* to believe—that the professional blacks of P.G. County are going to work things out. Like middle-class black folks everywhere, they *have* to work it out. Nothing less than the future of black America depends on it.

For the moment, though, it looks rough for the home team. It looks confusing, as conflicting as the notion of African Americans giving lip service to the need to support black life, then acting as if they valued their property more than human beings.

This contradiction has been apparent sometimes in the clumsy ways they've handled problems with young people in some P.G. County neighborhoods. In Lake Arbor, when ballplayers got a little rowdy at a playground court, community activists also did the white reactionary thing—they had the basketball rims taken down without providing a gym or some other alternative recreational outlet for the young.

And as for the young bloods who gather sometimes on the corner to shoot the breeze and drink their brew, they've been taken care of, too. They were ordered to take their confusion somewhere else.

Prison Abolition
Angela Davis

I was initially somewhat put off by the title of this collection, especially by what I interpreted to be its elitist implications. But Walter Mosley convinced me that this deliberately provocative title is meant to urge us to think about genius in essentially less elitist and more inclusive and collective ways. Well, that sounds all right to me. I will see what I can do to help summon up the collective genius of our community.

I want to focus on the prison-industrial complex and its very specific impact on black communities. I want to urge you to think very deeply about our reluctance to engage in serious discussions about the impact of jails and prisons on the black community. In particular, think about the fact that black women are being incorporated quietly into this complex, and consider how contemporary developments such as the disestablishment of the welfare system will escalate the feminization of prison populations.

Civic Death and the Objectification of Black Prisoners

How many of you, my black readers, know someone who is or was in jail or prison? Or perhaps I should ask, How many of you do not know anyone who has been touched in some way by the criminal justice system? Most of us have family or friends whose lives have already been claimed by jail or prison. When I asked these same questions twenty years ago, there were fewer than 200,000 people in prison, which at the time seemed an enormous number. Now the incarcerated population is about 1.5 million. Cousins of mine are currently doing time or previously did time in some of California's most notorious prisons. And I guess I have to say that I myself have been touched by the system as well.

With all of your connections to incarcerated black people, how does prison figure in your everyday conversations? Do you have discussions about prison experiences or prison life with members of your family, friends, and colleagues, or are your imprisoned friends and relatives treated as if they have somehow disappeared into a void that is at once so frightening and so shameful that you are unwilling to acknowledge its existence?

Of course, prison is a frightening phenomenon. When I was arrested many years ago—in 1970 I guess it was—something happened that taught me about the way people tend to treat those who are claimed by the penal system. A bunch of my friends went to my apartment and divided my stuff up among themselves. Afterwards, when I got out of jail, I would visit my friends' apartments, and see things that belonged to me. I think they thought that I was gone in a way, that somehow I had died as a result of having been claimed by the system. We often treat people in jail or prison as if they were dead or as if they had suffered a kind of civic death when they were sentenced. It is true that prisoners do suffer a civic death in that the vast numbers of people who have been convicted of felonies temporarily or permanently lose their right to vote. But we do not have to treat them the same way the system does. Unfortunately, prisoners suffer another kind of civic death at the hands of those of us in the "free world," which is what life out here is called by those who are on the other side. This second death is created by the collective silence with which we in the "free world" respond to their predicament.

Our collective amnesia vis-à-vis the imprisoned population is reminiscent of another amnesia—our historical tendency toward willed forgetfulness regarding slavery. We have inherited a fear of memories of slavery. It is as if to remember and acknowledge slavery would amount to our being consumed by it. As a matter of fact, in the popular black imagination, it is easier for us to construct ourselves as the children of Africa, as the sons and daughters of kings and queens, and thereby ignore the Middle Passage and centuries of enforced servitude in the Americas. Although some of us might indeed be the descendants of African royalty, most of us are probably the descendants of their subjects, the daughters and sons of African peasants or workers. Naturally, people would rather imagine themselves the progeny of nobility than the offspring of servants.

Important as it might be to affirm our connection to Africa, the Africa that is created in the popular imagination is not the historical Africa that our ancestors produced. Besides, the emphasis on Africa to the exclusion of the experience of slavery often reflects a very masculinist notion of black history, one which ignores the experiences and contributions of women. It is impossible to engage the history of slavery without acknowledging the part that women played in ensuring the survival and liberation of our communities.

I remember when Toni Morrison's *Beloved* and Sherley Williams's *Dessa Rose* were published. These novels asked us to imagine what it might have been like for black human beings, women as well as men, to have experienced slavery and to have constructed their own lives within the confines of that institution. Haile Gerima's film *Sankofa* poses the same question to us. Imagine life behind the walls, and fiercely challenge the tendency to turn hundreds of thousands of black people who inhabit the prisons into abstract versions of the "criminal," just as Toni Morrison's work challenged us to be self-critical of our habits of envisioning slave women and men as abstract versions of the "slave."

I recognize that restoring the personhood of black prisoners is a tall order, given the role popular culture plays today in criminalizing communities of color. Both mainstream reality-based police programs on television and the lyrics of black rap or hip-hop portray blacks as criminals. *America's Most Wanted* has actors re-creating crimes, including violent ones, in order to persuade viewers to join in what the narrator frequently refers to as the "manhunt." A show like *Cops*, on the other hand, is not just reality-based; it presents actual footage of pursuits and arrests. It is a frightening fact that such programs provide "entertainment" for millions of Americans. Of course, there is the argument that *America's Most Wanted* has resulted in the arrest of numerous fugitives, but in my mind these productions have one overarching impact and that is to further separate the presumably law-abiding citizens who are staring into the television from the "criminals" who are caught "in the act" on tape or as represented by actors. The entertainment industry thrives on glorified violence, which results in the desensitization of the viewing public to violent acts, blood, gore, and the like. Thus, Jane and Joe Q. Public who sit in their living rooms watching *Cops* and *America's Most Wanted* are not so much aghast at what they see as they are pacified, entertained by the action, and relieved that the streets are being made safe by "the law." This is a very complicated matter because "the law" includes the television program! But the most insidious effect of reality-based shows is that the myth of rampant crime is reinforced, and the repetitions of "criminals" that flash across the television screen become symbolic objects in the viewers' minds that then translate into fearful and racist responses to certain types of people, often people of color, who are criminalized by these representations. Finally, the specter of crime that is suggested by politicians and these sorts of television shows is, I think, always greater than the reality.

As for rap or hip-hop, in the weeks following the fatal drive-by shooting of the rapper Notorious B.I.G. (a.k.a. Biggie Smalls) in Los Angeles, the media reported speculation as to a possible connection between this senseless killing and the murder, by similar means, of Tupac Shakur in Las Vegas. Meanwhile, Tupac's friend and associate Shug Knight was given a nine-year sentence for violating his parole by allegedly getting into a fight just hours before Tupac's murder. Tupac had just been released from prison himself not long before he was killed. Biggie also had his own run-ins with the law from his days on the streets of Brooklyn.

I would not agree that rap music glamorizes prisons, or rather the prospect of spending time in prison. With all of the brothers who did or currently are doing time, I do not think any sane black man would glamorize the prison experience. But, at the same time, I think it is fair to say that to some degree the "gangsta" culture—for which Tupac, Biggie, and numerous other rappers (some, by their peers' standards, less "legitimately" than others) have been self-proclaimed spokesmen—does reinforce certain practices that tend to land people, namely young black men, in jails and prisons. Guns, violence, and to a lesser degree drugs are integral props for many rap acts, the lives of whose members have been shaped in part by an outlaw subculture that too often is the only access to "power" (guns, money) they can conceive.

This aspect of rap/hip-hop culture is unfortunate because the medium does have revolutionary potential, but it is merely a reflection of a larger society that, through its increasing disregard for what it considers the throw-away populations of the inner city, perpetuates the self-destructive activities in which those populations often engage. From the perspective of many an inner-city youth, however, the name of the game is survival, by whatever means necessary. Drugs are big business in the ghetto, and the violence that comes along with establishing, protecting, and expanding that business translates into power. But we are talking about power over the very people—youths, families, single mothers—who are struggling daily to have a chance of life beyond the boundaries of the ghetto. It is a very vicious cycle, indeed.

The problems do not begin with gangsta rappers, but these brothers certainly can become a part of the problem. By the same token, however, they can become part of the solution, and more and more of them are striving to do so. Ice-T is an excellent example of a brother who has maintained his "legitimacy" among his peers and his audience alike, while simultaneously doing some very important work to stop the violence and to address issues like unemployment. Also, I saw a public-service message on Fox during a break in *New York Undercover* in which Method Man was speaking out against violence. Mainstream hip-hop generation publications like *Vibe* are becoming more and more politicized, and there continue to be grassroots publications on urban culture that can serve to bring people together around important issues affecting young people of color.

I hope that, in the wake of Biggie's murder and the dialogue that followed, rappers from both coasts will renew their efforts not only to bring peace to the hip-hop community but to work for peace in the communities from which they hail, and for social justice in the larger society. With their access to the media, these brothers have a lot of power to speak to a lot of people. This is where hip-hop's revolutionary potential lies, for it can function as a tool to facilitate the subjectivity of its audience, which is largely objectified by the mainstream media. The important contributions of many women rappers who in their work have challenged misogyny are excellent examples of this process.

Black people must recognize that they may be reproducing the very ideologies that are used to dominate us. If we are not vigilant, black people can be persuaded to participate in the process of reproducing racism. Consider the fact that there are corporate criminals who are responsible for the deaths and maiming of thousands and thousands of people or for assaults on the environment, yet they end up perhaps paying only a fine. When we walk down the street, however, and see someone who could be one of those corporate executives in his three-piece suit, we are not frightened. We cannot imagine being afraid. Yet when we see a young black brother walking down the street, the fear immediately takes hold. There is very important work to be done, and part of that work is trying to regenerate among our people a sense of collective struggle. This is a challenge which must be met particularly by and among our youth. It is the young people who will generate these new movements, whom we can draw upon for sustenance, in order to nurture our courage, and develop the collective possibility of assuming radical positions. We have to become radical again.

Slavery and the Penal System: Powerful Analogies

Indeed, we can do much more to combat the prison-industrial complex which is ravishing our communities if we recognize its historical connection with slavery and look at the nineteenth-century abolitionist movement as an inspiration for a late twentieth-century abolitionist movement that will work to reduce and ultimately abolish the use of imprisonment as the main means of addressing (or rather not addressing) social problems that are rooted in racism and poverty. Moreover, we may be able to use historical similarities, parallels, and conjunctures in the activist work that we must do to foster the abolition of prisons. We have to do something. We have to figure out how we are going to persuade vast numbers of people to stand up and oppose the expansion of the prison-industrial complex.

In the rest of this essay, I want to elaborate on the historical connection between the institution of slavery and the institution of prisons. First, I will consider some of the structural similarities between slavery and the penal system. Second, I want to discuss further the relationship between slavery and prisons on an ideological level. This time I want to focus on how we have learned to think or avoid thinking about these institutions in a way that renders women especially invisible. Finally, I want to explore parallels between the historical social movement that helped to abolish slavery and a possible new mass movement calling for the disestablishment of the prison system as we know it today.

There were not many black people in prison during slavery. The system of slavery was in fact a system of incarceration because it constructed walls around those it enslaved and determined their possibilities of physical movement. (By this definition, the reservation system, which crowded large numbers of indigenous peoples, Native Americans, into confined spaces, was also a system of incarceration.) The slave codes strictly defined what black slaves could or could not do; they often did not permit them past the boundaries of the plantation or farm without written permission. Even the slaves' most private and sexual relationships were regulated by their masters.

Slavery, then, was its own prison. But as soon as slavery was abolished, the population of southern prisons became predominately black. Between 1874 and 1877, the black imprisonment rate went up 300 percent in Mississippi and Georgia. In some states, previously all-white prisons could hardly contain the influx of African Americans who were sentenced to hard labor for petty offenses—offenses as bogus as impudence or failing to look down at the street when passing a white person. It was during this period that the convict lease system emerged. Under this system, black people were arrested for the most negligible crimes and then were "leased out" to work on plantations and farms doing the same work from which they had just been liberated as a result of emancipation. Thus, the penitentiary system allowed for the continuation of slavery. The Thirteenth Amendment abolished involuntary servitude only for those who were not convicted of crimes.

The connection between slavery and the penal system is evident in the parallels between the representations of female slaves and their contemporary counterparts, our incarcerated sisters. I was in jail when I wrote my first article about slave women. It did not occur to me until much later that I was drawn to doing research on black women and slavery precisely because I was experiencing something very similar in 1970. I had engaged in a number of conversations by mail with people like George Jackson and others who at that time were very much influenced by the masculinist propaganda of the period. For example, the Moynihan report argued that the real problem in the black community was the matriarchal structure of our families. It was very clear to me that there was a connection between the way black women were being represented in the society and Daniel Patrick Moynihan's attempt to make them responsible for what he called "a tangled web of pathology" within the black community. So I decided to do research on slave women.

However, I was only allowed to have books in my cell that related to my case. I had been recognized as my own attorney. I had other attorneys as well, but I had argued that I should have the right to defend myself. I had to argue that the works I needed in order to do the article on women and slavery were required by me for the preparation of my case. Interestingly enough, it turned out that I did need those materials. Unaware of it at the time, I later recognized how important it was to talk about the intersection of gender and race in order to develop a compelling case.

I also discovered how few people acknowledged the fact that there were women slaves. People, scholars even, often assumed that, if there were women slaves, they were house slaves. There was also the popular myth that somehow or other black women slaves were in collusion with the white masters against black male slaves. (Regrettably, I think we may be experiencing some contemporary versions of this story.) Since that time, a number of really important historical studies, novels, and other literary works about black women and slavery have appeared, but it occurs to me now that there is a similarity between our historical tendency to render slave women invisible and the way we tend to talk about the penal system as if there were no women in prison.

In focusing on the relative invisibility of women prisoners, I am not calling for some kind of gender-based equality within regimes of incarceration. In September of 1996, I saw a picture in the *New York Times* of three women prisoners in Phoenix, Arizona. The photograph foregrounded their combat boots, which were linked together by chains, and the accompanying caption read "A Chain Gang of Women." The article said, "The nation's first female chain gang began work yesterday, picking up trash and pulling weeds in downtown Phoenix. The 15 women were chained at the ankles in groups of five." The article goes on to quote Sheriff Joe Arpaio: "I don't believe in discrimination in my jail system." He in essence claimed that he was combating gender discrimination by giving women the opportunity to work on chain gangs. Of course, that is ridiculous. But it says something about the way in which we have to guard against formulating issues within what I would call a framework of bourgeois democratic equal rights, because it creates as many problems as it solves, if not more. In a sense, a call for equal rights for women prisoners only reinforces the punishment industry.

Vast numbers of women, and black women in particular, are heading toward the prison system. The rate of increase in arrests, convictions, and imprisonment is much higher for women than for men. In absolute numbers, a much smaller cohort of women than of men is currently behind bars, but the rate of construction of prison space for women far outstrips that for men. Think about the historical trajectory. Think about what the prison population will be like ten or twenty years from now.

The feminization of the imprisoned population is partly the result of the disestablishment of the welfare system, which is prompting increasing numbers of women to participate in alternative economies, like the drug trade and the market for sexual services, which lead them directly into the criminal justice system and into prison. This is one of the most striking implications of Clinton's disestablishment of the welfare system. Moreover, there is a history of black women being locked away in mental institutions, rather than receiving the kind of treatment and/or assistance they need. With the disestablishment of mental institutions, prisons have become the repository for these women. Furthermore, because drug use is higher among women in black communities (the reasons behind this reality are too numerous to go into here), many black women are incarcerated when they should, in fact, have access to drug rehabilitation programs. (Of course, all sorts of preventive measures should be in place to keep people from reaching the point of drug abuse, but that is an entirely different conversation.)

The Prison-Industrial Complex

It is important for us to think about the penal system as a prison-industrial complex. I am not one to nostalgically invoke the sixties as others do, because I do not want to go back there—it was too crazy then. But I think we can learn from them some lessons that are useful for the work that we need to do today. There was a time, back in the sixties, when a few people used the term "military-industrial complex." I can remember the conscious efforts to politicize and educate people, on a popular level, about the concept; they succeeded to the point that the phrase became a term sisters and brothers used regardless of whether they were doing work within educational institutions like universities or in similar institutions like prisons.

I remember in the late 1960s, when black activists first began to do political work on behalf of political prisoners and then expanded their area of concern to include the prison system in general, there were perhaps 150,000 people in prison. In 1980, there were approximately 500,000 people in federal and state prisons and in local jails. Five hundred thousand, and that was quite a lot. In 1995, there were over 1.5 million people in prison. That represents a tripling of the incarcerated population in fifteen years. In addition to the 1.5 million people at present in prison, some 700,000 are on parole and 3 million on probation. So we are talking about 5.4 million people under the direct supervision of correctional systems. In 1980, the figure was 1.8 million. We obviously have a serious problem.

Compare the numbers of people who are incarcerated here with the numbers in other countries. Recently, I conducted a series of interviews with women imprisoned in the Netherlands, outside of Amsterdam. The percentages with respect to women of color were roughly the same there as here. Half the prison population consists of people of color from the former Dutch Caribbean and South American colonies; vast numbers of people from what is now the South American Republic of Surinam are in prison. But in the Netherlands there are 55 people per 100,000 in prison. In England there are a few more, 96 per 100,000. Do you know what the figure is for this country? Six hundred per 100,000! America's incarcerated population is the largest both proportionately and absolutely. America operates the largest prison-industrial complex in the world.

I refer to the "prison-*industrial* complex" because the prisons do not stand alone. The right-wing politicians who participate in the process of crimininalizing minority and poor populations are not the only ones with stakes in the continuation and growth of prisons. There are corporate stakeholders as well. Prison construction is the most profitable segment of the construction industry. Moreover, because of the deindustrialization of the U.S. economy and the movement of vast numbers of corporations to the Third World in search of cheap labor, many Americans have been left jobless. One of the reasons that so many people of color and poor people are in prison is that the deindustrialization of the economy has led to the creation of new economies and the expansion of some old ones—I have already mentioned the drug trade and the market for sexual services. At the same time, though, there are any number of communities that more than welcome prisons as a source of employment. Communities even compete with one another to be the site where new prisons will be constructed because prisons create a significant number of relatively good jobs for their residents.

Also to be factored into the equation are the privatization of prisons and the joint venture programs that make use of prison labor in a way that recapitulates the convict lease system, which represented the continuation of slavery through the prison system. In California, for example, a joint venture program invites corporations to come into the prisons and make use of prison labor on-site. This program is publicized in a brochure that essentially tells corporations, "There is a perfect labor force for you here." First, there is no need to worry about vacation benefits, health benefits, or any kind of benefits at all. Second, there are no child care problems. And then, of course, prison workers are not organized into unions and therefore have no collective autonomy; they can be used in the same way corporations attempt to use workers in so-called Third World countries. The trade union movement certainly ought to get involved in challenging the importation of jobs into prison.

Thus, the stakes are really much higher and more diverse than they might at first appear to be. We must begin to talk about the prison-industrial complex.

It is very clear that prisons have not solved any problems. They have not helped to eliminate the material conditions in poor communities and communities of color that create the trajectories that lead their members into the criminal justice system. The whole notion of prisoner rehabilitation has become obsolete. It has been replaced with a goal of punishment across the board. Educational opportunities are being cut. Prisoners are not even supposed to lift weights. The history of the prison system in this country reflects pendulum swings between policies of rehabilitation and reform, on the one hand, and policies of punishment and retribution, on the other. Reform does not work, because prisons cannot be reformed in a way that would assist them in rehabilitating human beings. How can you rehabilitate individuals when you do not allow them even a small measure of autonomy? How can you rehabilitate them when you do not treat them as human beings? Prisoners are told when to get up, when to brush their teeth, when to take a shower, and when to eat. Nearly every possible choice that one might make about one's life is taken from them. And how do you expect people to feel? I can remember how I felt after experiencing such control for sixteen months. It was really difficult to have to learn again how to make simple decisions. I can imagine what it must be like for someone who has been incarcerated for ten or twenty years. I do not think, even if we were pursuing it now, that rehabilitation would actually be possible in the prison environment. Perhaps it might work in community-based situations where small numbers of people live in houses, but not in huge institutions.

In order for any antiracist theory or practice to be successful, it must counter the widespread assumptions that prisons are here to stay and that we are powerless to affect their consumption of the social resources that ought to be directed toward education, health, housing, and other antipoverty initiatives. We can take inspiration from the fact that as eternal as the American system of slavery was assumed to be by its defenders, and those who profited from the labor of Africans, it nonetheless could be and indeed was abolished. Of course, northern industrialists recognized that wage labor could be much more profitable than slave labor; that was one of the reasons why the capitalists joined with the abolitionists against the slavocracy.

I went to the exhibition of artifacts from the *Henrietta Marie*, a British slave ship that sank in waters off the coast of Florida, when they were on display in Charlotte, North Carolina. The wreck was discovered in the 1970s. It is one of just three sunken slave ships discovered in America, and the only one in the world from which artifacts have been recovered. Among the artifacts I saw were shackles for children. It was very moving. But a ship like the *Henrietta*

Marie should serve as a reminder not only of the historical pain and suffering of slavery but also of the impermanence of the institution. I want us to imagine the possibility of future generations visiting prison museums. Imagine a time when these fortresses no longer occupy their present place in society.

I am sure you are asking yourselves, "What about the rapists and murderers?" That question always comes up. That is where our concern takes us when we think about abolishing prisons, isn't it? Be honest. Because we immediately worry about what will happen to the people who have committed horrendous crimes, it is possible for vast numbers of people who have not committed such crimes to be locked up and treated as less than human beings. The vast majority of women are in prison for what we call "victimless crimes" like prostitution, yet no one does anything about their incarceration, because of the specter of turning loose murderers and rapists. This ideological bind serves to support the expansion of the prison-industrial complex.

The idea of abolishing jails and prisons grows out of the belief that the social ills these institutions are supposed to address have roots outside of the individuals who are locked up and punished. I am not advocating that we do away with all correctional facilities and let violent offenders roam the streets. Perhaps we do need to lock up the murderers and the rapists, but these are not the only people in jails or prisons, yet the stereotype that they very nearly are causes many citizens to balk at the notion of prisoners' rights. Many people who commit violent crimes need psychological help, but these people should not be the basis for a discussion of abolition. Consider, rather, the many non-violent offenders, like drug abusers, whose crimes harm only themselves. We need to take the discussion to another level. If we talk only about violent offenders—the worst cases—there will never be any forward motion in the direction of prison abolition. Instead, we need to focus on creative dialogue around the possibility of abolishing jails and prisons as the knee-jerk response to every form of crime. We need to advocate such alternatives as community-based programs and the decriminalization of drugs and prostitution.

We must come up with some solutions. I do not have any answers, but I do know that we have to try to break down the ideological and material walls of the prison system. Everyone of you must ask yourself what you can do from where you are. I am appealing to all of you to become prison activists.

Many of us assume that activism involves a calling—that one is "called" to activism the way one is "called" to the ministry. For years and years, people asked me, "When were you called?" I tried to remember if I had experienced a moment of conversion, an epiphany. Was it this time? Was it that? No, it couldn't have happened then, because I was already active. Finally I realized that activism is not a vocation or a calling. It can be the way we live our lives. It was just how I learned to be in this world, how I learned to live my every-day life. Large numbers of movements in this country have emerged as a result of people's approaching activism in the same way, especially women. It is not a big deal. It is not anything extraordinary. It is not anything for which we seek or deserve applause or acknowledgment.

We have to begin to think about those of our sisters and brothers who are on the other side, and to figure out how we can prevent the expansion of the monstrous prison-industrial complex. All of us can do the work of dismantling this complex whether we are students, educators, artists, writers, or trade union members. If we do not manage to bring everyone into this campaign, increasing numbers of us will find ourselves on the other side.

Educating on Behalf of Black Public Health
Joycelyn Elders, M.D.

A System Delivering More Sick Care Than Health Care

Our society is sick. We know that it is sick. It has been sick for a long time, and it should not be sick. It should not be sick, because we have the technology, the resources, and the know-how, yet we lag behind many industrialized countries in terms of health. We have the best sick-care system in the world; you just have to be sick enough to get into it. The sicker you are, the better we doctor. The problem is we do not have a *health care* system. The United States is one of only two industrialized nations that do not have universal access to health care for all of their citizens. South Africa is the other, and it is working very hard to provide health care for all its people.

We have seen many changes take place in our health care system as we prepare to go into the twenty-first century. We have seen advances in medical technology. We have seen advances in biosynthetic hormone research. When I started doctoring, we used to get growth hormone from human pituitaries. Now it can be made biosynthetically, which is wonderful. We have lasers so powerful that we can read a license plate in Japan. Right in our own living rooms, we watched a war being fought in the Persian Gulf as it was happening.

Yet, our society is not able to prevent the consequences of tobacco smoking, to prevent teenage pregnancy, to immunize or even to feed all the children, or to prevent premature birth and premature mortality. Furthermore, we are still unable to prevent the spread of HIV disease or AIDS. We watched AIDS start out as a white gay male disease, and then spread from our two coasts to throughout our country. We watched it evolve from being a political football to being a disease. (For a while, it was not even allowed to be a disease.) We watched it when it was a fatal infection. Today AIDS has become for some a chronic disease that we are teaching people to live with, rather than to die from, which is a good thing. Yet, now we are watching it move through minority communities, among heterosexuals and particularly among black women. While African Americans make up 14 percent of our population, 59 percent of the women with HIV disease are black.

We have seen the cost of our health care system (or our sick-care system) go from 5.1 percent of our gross domestic product in 1960 to 14 percent in 1994. If the pattern continues, costs are projected to reach 19 percent by the year 2000. With expenditures of more than a trillion dollars, we spend more on health care than any other country, yet we do not have the best statistics when it comes to health. Even with regard to our best-off, our white women, we rank behind other industrialized countries.

The statistics concerning African Americans are staggering. I often say that if you take any negative statistic that you want and multiply it by two, you will come close to what the figure is for black Americans. Take infant mortality. In 1993, the infant mortality rate was 16.5 percent for black babies and 6.8 percent for white babies. The life expectancy of a black male child born in 1994 was 64.9 years, while that of a white male was 73.2 years; of a black female, 74.1 years; and of a white female, 79.6 years. When we consider some of the diseases that afflict Americans, we also see a wide variation by race. Blacks with cancer are thirty times more likely to die than whites with cancer. The black cancer rate is not higher; blacks just get into treatment later, and when they get into treatment, they may not get all of the services that others tend to get, or they may not know to ask for or demand the services they need.

When we consider our young black men, we find that their rate of death from homicide since 1985 has increased 39.5 percent. We are losing a very valuable part of our human resources. We know that unemployment is three times higher among black males than among white males. Blacks are twice as likely not to have insurance as whites. When we look at our young black women, we find that we are very often losing them to poverty, ignorance, and enslavement because of our failure to educate and our failure to get involved. "Well, Dr. Elders, what does that have to do with health?" I am asked. Health is more than the absence of disease. Health is about jobs and employment, education, the environment, and all of those things that go into making us healthy.

Finally, consider the fact that blacks seek health care from our black health care professionals. Of 261 million Americans, approximately 32–34 million are black or African American. But look at our representation in the health care professions. Blacks constitute only 3 percent of doctors, 5 percent of pharmacists, 4 percent of nurses, and 4 percent of dentists. That tells me that something is wrong and that we have got to do something about it.

We have a multiheaded dragon in our midst that for too long has been waging a domestic war on our young, our poor, our elderly, and our underserved. The faces of this dragon sometimes manifest themselves as poverty, the source of the most pervasive health problem we have in America. Sometimes they manifest themselves as diseases such as AIDS, sometimes as violence, and sometimes as racism, sexism, and classism. For too long our "isms" have pushed our young, our poor, and our minorities to the back of the social justice bus. I think it is time for us to ask the question "Do we feel that every American should have a right to health care?" In our society, we feel that every criminal has a right to a lawyer. Shouldn't we feel that every sick person has a right to a doctor?

If I Had It to Do All Over Again

Most of you know that I was your surgeon general, and I want to tell you that I loved being your surgeon general. I did the very best job that I knew how to do. I also want you to know that if I had it to do all over again, starting in the morning, I would do it exactly the same way. I feel I did it right the first time. I felt that the issues I was talking about were the issues that we need to talk about. They are issues that our community is facing every day. I was out there saying that we need to have health education as part of our school program. Let's educate young people about how to be healthy. Of course, that was misinterpreted, and it was said that I wanted to teach young people how to have sex. Well, we all know that nobody ever needs to teach anybody about how to have sex. God taught us how, so we do not need to be taught *how*; but we do need to be teaching young people how to be responsible, rather than sitting around trying to legislate their morals. That was what I was about.

When I was out there saying I wanted to prevent unplanned, unwanted pregnancies, of course, that was interpreted that I wanted women to have abortions. Well, you know, I tell people all the time I am not about promoting abortions. I have never been about abortions. I am about preventing unplanned, unwanted pregnancies. If you prevent unplanned, unwanted pregnancies, there is never a need for an abortion. I have never known any woman to need an abortion if she was not already pregnant. We need to deal with the real issues, rather than all of those side issues.

We get involved with all this blue smoke and mirrors. People out there talking about abortion do not have to deal with the problem of access to health care, for example. Let me talk about Arkansas and the South because I do not know about every place else. People in the South fought so hard, absolutely fought against desegregation and integration. They invoked all of these Bible verses that supposedly said that integration of the races was wrong and that children of different races should not go to school together. Well, these are the same people who are now fighting so hard and talking about the right to life. Think about whom they are fighting and whom they are hurting. Women who have had abortions for the most part are women who can afford them. If you have the green, you can get an abortion whenever you please. The only people the antiabortion forces really hurt are the young, the poor, and the ignorant. These abortion opponents say they want to help the little babies, but they do not want them to get welfare, they do not want them to get health care, and they do not want them to get any early childhood education. They want to make sure the babies endure and perpetuate another cycle of poverty, ignorance, and enslavement.

We have to step back and ask what the real issues are, what do we really need to be talking about. I have come to understand that the best way to reform welfare is to prevent the need for welfare. I have never known anybody you could pay to be poor, so let's be real. We need to be certain that we actually understand and know what is going on. Look at prison construction. We have built more prisons in the past ten years than schools. Can you believe that? The average cost of keeping one inmate in prison for one year is $35,000. I bet a prisoner could go to NYU for less than what we pay to send him or her to the penitentiary. We hear all this talk about family values. Let's talk about family values. If one genuinely believed in family values, one would support those institutions that support families, like those that assure secure jobs, safe schools, safe communities, and safe families. I think those are the things that we have to begin to speak about.

Most of you know that I once mentioned that I felt that we should study the legalization of drugs. I said *study* it! We spend $17 billion a year on a "war on drugs" that is failing. We need to know what we are doing. Of course, the administration said that it was not going to study the matter, and it rained all over me. But, as far as I am concerned, we need to know how to approach drugs. I did not say *legalize* drugs, but if that is an option, if we can do better to help our people by legalizing drugs, then as far as I am concerned, we should do what makes good sense and what makes for good public health. I essentially said let us look at all the options. Other countries are looking at other options. Our present policies have made Uncle Sam the world's biggest jailer. We have gone from fewer than 2,000 people in prisons or jails in 1970 to 1.5 million people by 1996. Sixty percent of all incarcerations are related to drugs, and you know who the incarcerated are. Young black men are fourteen times more likely to be incarcerated than any other group. We send whites to treatment programs and blacks to prison.

We have got to look for things we need to do to make a difference and stand up and fight for them. I know that we have had a lot of problems and a lot of adversity and diversity, but we cannot let that prevent us from healing, organizing, and moving forward. My brother tells me, "You've got fifteen to twenty years of schooling, and our mom only finished the eighth grade, but our mother sometimes uses a lot more sense than you do." Indeed, some of the things that my mom told me really helped me to survive. That is what parents give you, the Bible skills. There are four proverbs or sayings that my mom gave me that really helped when things got tough. The first thing she told me was "If you want to get out of the cotton patch, you've got to get something in your head." She meant you have got to get an education. Most people have never picked or chopped cotton, so you probably do not know anything about that, but I can tell you the prospect of working in the cotton fields was a real inducement to getting an education. Another thing that my mom told us was "You have to recognize the truth and speak out. The day you see the truth and cease to speak out is the day you begin to die." You can tell I am going to live a long time, because I am always speaking out. My mom also told us, "Always do your best; that's good enough." I rely on that one a lot. The fourth and final thing she said was "Don't ever throw away your tomorrows worrying about yesterday." When I got kicked out of public office, I had to say that to myself many times in order to be able to survive the ordeal.

I have thought about what I said many, many times since leaving the position of surgeon general, I want you to know that if I held the same job and were asked the very same question about masturbation that led to my departure in the same way today, I would give the same answer. I thought I gave a smart answer. I thought I gave a correct and proper answer to a question asked by a physician, of a physician. Nobody has ever had to teach children how to masturbate. Ninety percent of men say they masturbate, 80 percent of women say they masturbate, and the rest lie. We need to stop lying to children. We need to stop telling them that hair will grow on their hands if they masturbate, or that they will go crazy, or that they will go blind. We really need to begin to be honest and tell the truth. That is among the things I was fighting about. Dealing with and talking about the facts has never given anybody AIDS, and it has never gotten anybody pregnant. It is not all bad.

The Health Status of the Least-Well-Off among Us

We are facing many problems as we move into the twenty-first century, especially in terms of health and very especially in terms of minority health. If we fix health care for everybody and make it accessible to all people, we will have made health care accessible to the least of them.

Fifty percent of the causes of premature death are social and behavioral problems, like drug usage, risky sexual behavior, and alcohol consumption. Twenty percent are environmental, 20 percent are genetic, and only 10 percent are related to access to health care. Consider how our life expectancies have been extended by thirty years since 1900. Just think, every year our life expectancy increases one month. Every week it increases seven hours, and every day it increases fifteen minutes. If one gets past the age of fifty—that is, if one gets past the early years of life—then one will very likely live to a very ripe old age. Doctoring and all of our fancy technology have increased life expectancy only eleven years. The rest of the increase is attributable to the things you do for yourself, like maintaining good nutrition, not smoking, not drinking, not driving while drunk, not engaging in high-risk sexual behavior—in other words, avoiding the activities that relate to and cause premature death.

Much of the increase in life expectancy is related to things that we take for granted, like clean drinking water, putting screens on windows, and immunization. Immunizations, for example, have probably saved more children than anything we have ever done. Certainly there are side effects, but their incidence is very low. If we could get 90 percent or more of the population immunized, enough to get herd immunity, we would not have any problem. But if we allow parents to just decide indiscriminately who is going to be immunized, the percentages could drastically change, and we would start see-ing cases of polio, measles, and whooping cough. There is no question but that, if parents will not immunize children when they are babies, they will have to be immunized before they go to school. It would be much better if chil-dren were immunized on time. In some cases, children are not even allowed into day care unless they have been immunized.

We have to deal with the problem of poverty, especially as it regards our children. Thirty percent of the minority population is poor. If we look at chil-dren in general, we find that in 1970 one child in seven was poor; in 1990 it was one in five; and in 1992 it was one in four. If you look at minority children, the rate is one in two; 49 percent of minority children under six years of age are below the federal poverty line.

Children who are poor will be members of only one club in their lives. We call it the 5-H Club. 5-H children are hungry every night, though they live in the richest country in the world. Between 3 and 5 million American children go to bed hungry. 5-H children are healthless. Out of 261 million Americans, 43 million have no health insurance. Roughly 58 million people have no health insurance sometime during the year. Moreover, 133 million Americans have insurance with significant caps on coverage. That means that when their medical bills reach a certain amount, usually when they have contracted a bad disease and need health insurance the most, they lack sufficient coverage. Moreover, most of our health insurance is related to our jobs. When we get sick and lose our jobs, we often lose our health insurance. We have children who are homeless. When mothers are homeless, children are homeless. We have children who are hugless. We have children who find it easier to get drugs than hugs. We have children who are hopeless. When hope dies, moral decay cannot be far behind. So there you have it: hungry, healthless, homeless, hugless, and hopeless children. The members of the 5-H Club.

We, of course, have a tobacco industry that attacks our young every day. It daily recruits 3,000 young people to start smoking. According to Centers for Disease Control statistics, the overall rate of teenage smoking in 1995 was 34.5 percent. In a departure from the usual pattern, the rate of adolescent smoking is lower among blacks than among whites: 19.2 percent to 38.3 per-cent. (The rate for Hispanic youth, however, is 34 percent.) Smoking among young black males has increased (to 28 percent), though it is below the rate for whites and Hispanics. We do not really know why black adolescents smoke less. When I suggested that they don't have the money to buy cigarettes, I was told, "Dr. Elders, they've got money to buy everything else. Why don't they have the money to buy cigarettes?" We know that 90 percent of the people who smoke started before the age of nineteen, so if we can keep teens from smoking before they reach the age of nineteen, they will probably never smoke. We need to keep going whatever is working for black kids.

A major source of poverty, ignorance, and enslavement in our society is children becoming parents before they become adults. If we can get our arms around that problem, we can begin to deal with some of the other issues influencing health. More than one million teenagers become pregnant every year. Black teenagers are twice as likely as white teenagers to have a pregnancy before the age of twenty. But what many of us never talk about is that 84 percent of teenagers under fourteen who become pregnant were made pregnant by somebody in their own home. Eighty-four percent! That to me is a real problem. Seventy percent of the teenagers who become pregnant were abused at sometime in their life, and 70 percent of their abusers were adult men. I tried to get a law passed in Arkansas that would have required that any girl aged 14 or under who became pregnant be evaluated for possible sexual abuse. I did not say that these children had in fact been abused. I simply said that the matter should be evaluated or looked into. "Dr. Elders, what if she's lying?" How much lying can a girl fourteen and pregnant do? We know that there is a real possibility of statutory rape in such situations.

We are not talking about children having sex with children today. The Alan Guttmacher Institute, which has done wonderful research, tells us that more than 70 percent of the children born to teenagers are fathered by adult men, not teens, yet we do not make much of that. On the other hand, there was a story in the newspaper a while ago that really disturbed me. An eighteen-year-old man in Milwaukee got his fifteen-year-old girlfriend pregnant. He quit school to go to work in order to take care of his child, and the authorities wanted to prosecute him and send him to prison for forty years. Can you imagine? An eighteen-year-old and a fifteen-year-old. We want to punish children who are trying to be responsible. Yet, we do nothing about the abuse of adult men that results in the majority of teen pregnancies that we see going on out there in our society.

We spend more than $30 billion a year for public assistance, food stamps, and Medicaid for children born to children. Still, we do not want to spend $200 million for family planning for all the poor women in America. Roughly half of all pregnancies in the U.S. each year are unintended. We have the highest teenage pregnancy rate in the industrialized world—twice as high as England's and Canada's; ten times as high as Japan's. A single act of unprotected sex carries a 1 percent risk of HIV, a 30 percent risk of genital herpes, and a 50 percent risk of gonorrhea. That to me is a real problem.

Strategies That Might Make a Difference

So, what are some of the strategies that we must pursue if we are really going to make a difference? I think that we have to strengthen our personal health care system. The system we have now is not coherent, is not comprehensive, and is not cost-effective. It costs too much and delivers too little. We do not have choice; we only think we have choice. When employers pick the doctors they are going to use, we have to pick from what they've picked. The system is not equitable. It may be equitable if you have enough money to pay for it, but if you do not have the money, you have to go where you can. The system is certainly not universal.

We have to strengthen our public health system if we want to save our society. We have to deal with the three P's—poverty, population, and pollution. We are not doing very well with any one of them. We've got to make every child born in America a planned and wanted child. We know how, we have the resources, and we must make the commitment to get it done.

Nothing saves more money than keeping people healthy. One low-birth-weight baby can cost more than health education for an entire school system. We still prefer to keep people in prison, care for people after they contract AIDS, nurture low-birth-weight babies after they are born, and treat measles in children after they get the measles, rather than prevent any of this. We have to start thinking prevention. We have too much intervention.

I have often accused our churches of not doing the things they need to do. They have been moralizing from the pulpit and preaching to the choir. When I was state public health director, I did a lot of work with churches (though when I was in Washington I was called an atheist). The ministers said of the reforms I advocated, "Dr. Elders, it's just morally wrong." When they wanted to talk about what is morally wrong, I reminded them that it is morally wrong for children to be hungry, morally wrong for children to be cold, and morally wrong for children to be abused. The ministers saw what is happening in our society and never said anything about it. We take these hard lines with regard to some issues and say nothing about what is going on over here that is or ought to be equally disturbing. It is time for the churches to get out into the streets, get involved, and begin to make a real difference. They have the power, the prestige, and the position, and they need to use these to begin to make a difference, especially in our black communities.

We have got to educate, educate, educate. We've been making smart bombs, while Japan was making smart children. We have young people graduating from high school with shoes that light up when they walk and brains that go dead when they talk. We cannot keep a person healthy, if she or he is not educated. We've got to start early. We've been doing too little too late. Only 18 percent of poor children—those on Medicaid, the poorest of the poor—ever have any early childhood education. Eighteen percent! Almost 80 percent of other children, the nonpoor, get early childhood education. The nonpoor children don't have to go to Ms. Janes's Schoolhouse. They could get it right there at home. We've also got to have comprehensive health education in our schools from grades K through 12.

We have to educate parents. Parents are doing the best they can; they do not know any better. We have a lot of dysfunctional families. We have to teach those families how to be healthy. Just because the parents are ignorant does not mean that we must commit their children to the same fate. As a function of community life, we need to make a difference. We have to make services available to people wherever they are. Schools are a wonderful place. We have 50 million children in school every day. Why can't we take the services to where the children are? We have to offer all of our young people hope, hope for the future, if we are going to make a difference in our society.

So what is your role? What is your role as a black leader or as a white leader or as somebody who wants to make a difference for the twenty-first century? What should you be about? How can you make a difference? I think we all have to decide whether we want our society to fly up and soar with the eagles or whether we are going to continue to crawl with the snakes. We have to have leaders who are willing to lead. We have an awful lot of leaders who take a poll, find out which way the wind is blowing, and jump out in front. We have to begin to be real leaders, leaders who can make a difference in our society. We have to recognize the source of our power. You know, too many of our young black men carry their power in their pockets in the form of a weapon, as opposed to an education in their heads.

We have to educate, educate, educate. We've got to educate our communities, educate our schools, educate our teachers, educate everybody, so we can begin to do the things we must do to educate our politicians. I tell you they are educable, but they are slow learners. Just keep working on them. We've got to become aware of the problems, become advocates for solutions, and develop an action plan that is right for our country and right for our world.

We've got to make health services available, accessible, and affordable. Once we do what is right, all of our people will be able to get on board. You know, some of us could go out there and swim across the river, but many of us need a bridge to get across. We need to make sure that all of us will be able to get across. We've got to be dedicated to programs that support prevention, rather than just intervention. We have to empower people, and we empower people through education.

The Hip-Hop Nation
Whose Is It? In the End, Black Men Must Lead

Touré

I live in a country no map maker will ever respect. A place with its own language, culture and history. It is as much a nation as Italy or Zambia. A place my countrymen call the Hip-Hop Nation, purposefully invoking all of the jingoistic pride that nationalists throughout history have leaned on. Our path to nationhood has been paved by a handful of fathers: Muhammad Ali with his ceaseless bravado, Bob Marley with his truth-telling rebel music, Huey Newton with his bodacious political style, James Brown with his obsession with funk.

We are a nation with no precise date of origin, no physical land, no single chief. But if you live in the Hip-Hop Nation, if you are not merely a fan of the music but a daily imbiber of the culture, if you sprinkle your conversation with phrases like off the meter (for something that's great) or got me open (for something that gives an explosive positive emotional release), if you know why Dutch Masters make better blunts than Phillies (they're thinner), if you know at a glance why Allen Iverson is hip-hop and Grant Hill is not, if you feel the murders of Tupac Shakur and the Notorious B.I.G. in the 1997–98 civil war were assassinations (no other word fits), if you can say yes to all of these questions (and a yes to some doesn't count), then you know the Hip-Hop Nation is a place as real as America on a pre-Columbus atlas. It's there even though the rest of you ain't been there yet.

The Nation exists in any place where hip-hop music is being played or hip-hop attitude is being exuded. Once I went shopping for a Macintosh. The salesman, a wiry 20-something white guy, rattled on about Macs, then, looking at the rapper, or what we call an MC, on my T-shirt, said: "You like Nas? Did you hear him rhyme last night on the 'Stretch and Bobbito' show?" I felt as if my jaw had dropped. He had invoked a legendary hip-hop radio show broadcast once a week on college radio at 2 in the morning. It was as if we were secret agents, and he had uttered the code phrase that revealed him to be my contact. We stood for an hour talking MC's and DJ's, beats and flows, turning that staid computer store into an outpost of the Hip-Hop Nation.

The Nation's pioneers were a multiracial bunch—whites were among the early elite graffiti artists and Latinos were integral to the shaping of DJing and MCing, b-boying (break dancing) and general hip-hop style. Today's Nation makes brothers of men black, brown, yellow and white. But this world was built to worship urban black maleness: the way we speak, walk, dance, dress, think. We are revered by others, but our leadership is and will remain black. As it should.

We are a nation with our own gods and devils, traditions and laws (one of them is to not share them with outsiders), but there has never been and never will be a president of the Hip-Hop Nation. Like black America, we're close-knit yet still too fractious for one leader. Instead, a powerful senate charts our future. That senate is made up of our leading MC's, their every album and single a bill or referendum proposing linguistic, musical and topical directions for the culture. Is Compton a cool spot? Can Edie Brickell, an embodiment of American female whiteness, be the source for a sample? Is a thick countrified Southern accent something we want to hear? Is police brutality still a rallying point? Like a politician with polls and focus groups, an MC must carefully calibrate his musical message because once his music is released, the people vote with their dollars in the store and their butts in the club, ignoring certain MC's and returning them to private life while anointing others, granting them time on our giant national microphone.

Unlike rhythm-and-blues, hip-hop has a strong memoiristic impulse, meaning our senator-MC's speak about themselves, their neighborhoods, the people around them, playing autobiographer, reporter and oral historian. Telling the stories as they actually happened is what is meant by the catch phrase keeping it real. Outsiders laugh when that hallowed phrase is seemingly made hollow by obvious self-mythologizing—materialistic boasts that would be beyond even the Donald or tales of crimes that would be envied by a Gotti. But this bragging is merely people speaking of the people they dream of being, which, of course, is a reflection of the people they are.

How do you get into this senate? The answer is complex, involving both rhyming technique and force of personality. To be a great MC you must have a hypnotizing flow—a cadence and delivery that get inside the drum and bass patterns and create their own rhythm line. You must have a magnetic voice—it can be deliciously nasal like Q-Tip's, or delicate and sing-songy like Snoop Doggy Dogg's, or deep-toned like that of Rakim, who sounds as commanding as Moses—but it must be a compelling sound. And you must say rhymes with writerly details, up-to-the-minute slang, bold punch lines, witty metaphors and original political or sociological insights.

But, again like a politician, to be a great MC you must seem like an extension of the masses and, simultaneously, an extraordinary individual. There must be a certain down-homeness about you, a way of carrying yourself that replicates the way people in your home base feel about life. You must be the embodiment of your audience.

At the same time, you must seem greater than your audience. You must come across as supercool—an attitude based on toughness or sex appeal or intellect or bravado that inspires your listeners to say, I'd like to be you.

In the first decade and a half after the first hip-hop record was released in 1979, hip-hop was a national conversation—about urban poverty and police brutality, the proliferation of guns and the importance of safe sex, as well as the joy of a good party—in which the only speakers were black men.

In recent years that conversation has opened up. Hip-hop has become more democratic, cracking the monopoly that black men from New York and L.A. have long held over the Hip-Hop Nation senate.

Traditionally, hip-hop has been hypermodern, disdaining the surreal for gritty images of urban life. But Missy Elliott and her producer, Timbaland, have constructed a post-modern esthetic that manifests itself, on her latest album, *Da Real World,* in references to the sci-fi film *The Matrix* and videos in which Missy dresses as if she were in a scene from the 1982 movie *Blade Runner.* Her music also has a futuristic feel, from Timbaland's spare, propulsive beats filled with quirky sounds that evoke science-fiction to Missy's experiments with singing and rhyming, as well as using onomatopoeia in her rhymes. The duo have become part of the Nation's sonic vanguard, as well as door-openers for a new genre: hip-hop sci-fi.

Groups from the South Coast like GooDie Mob, Eightball and MJG and Outkast have also brought new perspectives. (The Hip-Hop Nation reconfigures American geography with a Saul Steinberg-like eye, maximizing cities where the most important hip-hop has come from, microscoping other places. When we speak of the East Coast, we mean the five boroughs of New York, Long Island, Westchester County, New Jersey and Philadelphia; by West Coast we mean Los Angeles, Compton, Long Beach, Vallejo and Oakland; and the region made up of Atlanta, New Orleans, Virginia, Miami and Memphis is called the South Coast.)

Outkast is a pair of Atlanta MC's, Dre (Andre Benjamin) and Big Boi (Antwan Patton), who are not new to many in the Hip-Hop Nation. But with the success of *Aquemini,* their third album, and months of touring as the opening act for Lauryn Hill, they are new to power within hip-hop. Their hip-hop mixes the cerebralness of New York rappers and the George Clinton-drenched funk favored out West with a particularly Southern musicality, soulfulness, twang-drenched rhymes and Baptist churchlike euphoric joy.

But the most polarizing and revolutionary new entry to the hip-hop senate is Eminem (born Marshall Mathers). There have been white MC's before him, but none have been as complex. Either they were clearly talentless (like Vanilla Ice) or they worshiped blackness (like MC Serch of 3rd Bass). Eminem is different. The fervency of fans, black and white, marveling at his skill and laughing at his jokes, has kept him in office, despite those offended by his whiny white-boy shock-jock shtick.

He is an original voice in the national conversation that is hip-hop because he speaks of the dysfunctionality of his white-trash world—his absentee father, his drugged-out mom, his daughter's hateful mother, his own morally bankrupt conscience. With Eminem the discussion turns to problems in the white community, or at least—because he is from a black neighborhood in Detroit—to the problems of whites in the black community. On a recent song (called "Busa Rhyme" from Missy's new album *Da Real World*) Eminem rhymes darkly: "I'm homicidal/ and suicidal/ with no friends/ holdin' a gun with no handle/ just a barrel at both ends." Finally someone has arrived to represent the Dylan Klebolds and Eric Harrises of America.

A rash of overprotectiveness within our nation keeps many fans from enjoying the hip-hop of a sneering white MC, but why shouldn't we welcome a frank discussion of white maladies into our homes when millions of white people allow our MC's into their homes to talk about our disorders every day?

The Hip-Hop Nation senate is swelling to include whites, women and Southerners, but don't expect that senate to become a true melting pot anytime soon. As long as upper-class white men stay in charge of the United States Senate, urban black men will remain our leading speakers. Hip-hop's history is long enough to grant us the maturity to open our world, but America is still white enough that we know we need our own oasis.

It all began with a few parties. Jams in New York city parks thrown by DJ's like Kool Here, Grandmaster Flash and Afrika Bambaataa. To your eyes it would've appeared to be a rapper in a public park, a DJ behind him, his cables plugged into the street lamp, the police not far away, waiting for just the right moment to shut it all down. But to us those parks were the center of a universe. The cops—or rather, five-oh (from the television series *Hawaii Five-O*)—were Satan. The music—James Brown, Sly Stone, Funkadelic and anything with a stone cold bass and drum rhythm you could rhyme over—breathed meaning and substance and soul into our bodies. It gave life. It was God.

From behind the turntables in his roped-off pulpit in the park, the DJ gave a rousing sermon sonically praising God's glory. Then up stepped the High Priest, the conduit between God and you—the MC. How crucial was he? In 1979, in its seminal song, "Rapper's Delight," the Sugar Hill Gang explained that even Superman was useless if he couldn't flow: "He may be able to fly all through the night/ But can he rock a party til the early light?"

A few years later, in the early 80's, a trickle of cassettes began appearing in urban mom-and-pop record stores like Skippy White's on Blue Hill Avenue in Mattapan Square in Boston. As a 12-year-old I would walk there from my father's office. Every other month or so a new hip-hop tape would arrive, direct from New York City: Run-DMC ... MC Shan ... the Fat Boys. A kid on an allowance could own all the hip-hop albums ever made. For all the force of the music, the culture was so small and precious you held it in your hands as delicately as a wounded bird.

In the mid-80's hip-hop won the nation's attention and was branded a fad that would soon die like disco. Hip-hoppers closed ranks, constructed a wall and instituted a siege mentality. We became like Jews, a tribe that knew how close extinction was and responded to every attack and affront, no matter how small, as if it were a potential death blow. Where Jews battle anti-Semitic attitudes and actions, we fought fans who are not orthodox and music not purely concerned with art. Where Jews hold holidays that celebrate specific legends, ancestors and miracles, hip-hoppers spoke of the old school with a holy reverence and urged new jacks to know their history. Our Zionism was the Hip-Hop Nation.

By the late 80's and early 90's mainstreaming had arrived bringing powerful gifts, as the devil always does. Now our music was broadcast on prime-time MTV, and our political views, via Chuck D and KRS-One, were heard on CNN and *Nightline*. Hip-hop, like jazz and rock-and-roll before it, had become the defining force of a generation. It was not going to die. The siege mentality subsided.

The guards at the gate were retired. The fan base grew, and the music diversified, which caused the fan base to grow larger still and the music to diversify further. But we continue to live in America, to suffer the daily assaults of racism. And our sanity continues to rely on having a place where the heroes look like us and play by our rules. As long as being a black man is a cross to bear and not a benediction, you can find me and my comrades locked inside one of those mass therapy sessions called a party, inside that tri-coastal support group called the Hip-Hop Nation.

Thoughts of Restitution
Randall Robinson

> Short of a revolution, the likelihood that blacks today will obtain direct payments in compensation for their subjugation as slaves before the Emancipation Proclamation, and their exploitation as quasi-citizens since, is no better than it was in 1866, when Thaddeus Stevens recognized that his bright hope of "forty acres and a mule" for every freedman had vanished "like the baseless fabric of a vision."
>
> [Derrick Bell]

If Bell is right that African Americans will not be compensated for the massive wrongs and social injuries inflicted upon them by their government, during and after slavery, then there is *no* chance that America can solve its racial problems—if solving these problems means, as I believe it must, closing the yawning economic gap between blacks and whites in this country. The gap was opened by the 246-year practice of slavery. It has been resolutely nurtured since in law and public behavior. It has now ossified. It is structural. Its framing beams are disguised only by the counterfeit manners of a hypocritical governing class.

For twelve years Nazi Germany inflicted horrors upon European Jews. And Germany paid. It paid Jews individually. It paid the state of Israel. For two and a half centuries, Europe and America inflicted unimaginable horrors upon Africa and its people. Europe not only paid nothing to Africa in compensation, but followed the slave trade with the remapping of Africa for further European economic exploitation. (European governments have yet even to accede to Africa's request for the return of Africa's art treasures looted along with its natural resources during the century-long colonial era.)

While President Lincoln supported a plan during the Civil War to compensate slave owners for their loss of "property," his successor, Andrew Johnson, vetoed legislation that would have provided compensation to ex-slaves.

Under the Southern Homestead Act, ex-slaves were given six months to purchase land at reasonably low rates without competition from white southerners and northern investors. But, owing to their destitution, few ex-slaves were able to take advantage of the homesteading program. The largest number that did were concentrated in Florida, numbering little more than three thousand. The soil was generally poor and unsuitable for farming purposes. In any case, the ex-slaves had no money on which to subsist for months while waiting for crops, or the scantest wherewithal to purchase the most elementary farming implements. The program failed. In sum, the United States government provided no compensation to the victims of slavery.

Perhaps I should say a bit here about why the question of reparations is critical to finding a solution to our race problems.

This question—and how blacks gather to pose it—is a good measure of our psychological readiness as a community to pull ourselves abreast here at home and around the world. I say this because no outside community can be more interested in solving our problems than we. Derrick Bell suggested in his review of Bittker's book *[The Case for Black Reparations]* that the white power structure would never support reparations because to do so would operate against its interests. I believe Bell is right in that view. The initiative must come from blacks, broadly, widely, implacably.

But what exactly will black enthusiasm, or lack thereof, measure? There is no linear solution to any of our problems, for our problems are not merely technical in nature. By now, after 380 years of unrelenting psychological abuse, the biggest part of our problem is inside us: in how we have come to see ourselves, in our damaged capacity to validate a course for ourselves without outside approval.

The issue here is not whether or not we can, or will, win reparations. The issue rather is whether we will fight for reparations, because we have decided for ourselves that they are our due. In 1915, into the sharp teeth of southern Jim Crow hostility, Cornelius J. Jones filed a lawsuit against the United States Department of the Treasury in an attempt to recover sixty-eight million dollars for former slaves. He argued that, through a federal tax placed on raw cotton, the federal government had benefited financially from the sale of cotton that slave labor had produced, and for which the black men, women, and children who had produced the cotton had not been paid. Jones's was a straightforward proposition. The monetary value of slaves' labor, which he estimated to be sixty-eight million dollars, had been appropriated by the United States government. A debt existed. It had to be paid to the, by then, ex-slaves or their heirs.

Where was the money?

A federal appeals court held that the United States could not be sued without its consent and dismissed the so-called Cotton Tax case. But the court never addressed Cornelius J. Jones's question about the federal government's appropriation of property—the labor of blacks who had worked the cotton fields—that had never been compensated.

Let me try to drive the point home here: through keloids of suffering, through coarse veils of damaged self-belief, lost direction, misplaced compass, sh—faced resignation, racial transmutation, black people worked long, hard, killing days, years, centuries—and they were never *paid*. The value of their labor went into others' pockets—plantation owners, northern entrepreneurs, state treasuries, the United States government.

Where was the money?

Where *is* the money?

There is a debt here.

I know of no statute of limitations either legally or morally that would extinguish it. Financial quantities are nearly as indestructible as matter. Take away here, add there, interest compounding annually, over the years, over the whole of the twentieth century.

Where is the money?

Jews have asked this question of countries and banks and corporations and collectors and any who had been discovered at the end of the slimy line holding in secret places the gold, the art, the money that was the rightful property of European Jews before the Nazi terror. Jews have demanded what was their due and received a fair measure of it.

Clearly, how blacks respond to the challenge surrounding the simple demand for restitution will say a lot more about us *and do a lot more for us* than the demand itself would suggest. We would show ourselves to be responding as any normal people would to victimization were we to assert collectively in our demands for restitution that, for 246 years and with the complicity of the United States government, hundreds of millions of black people endured unimaginable cruelties—kidnapping, sale as livestock, deaths in the millions during terror-filled sea voyages, backbreaking toil, beatings, rapes, castrations, maimings, murders. We would begin a healing of our psyches were the most public case made that whole peoples lost religions, languages, customs, histories, cultures, children, mothers, fathers. It would make us more forgiving of ourselves, more self-approving, more self-understanding to see, *really see*, that on three continents and a string of islands, survivors had little choice but to piece together whole new cultures from the rubble shards of what theirs had once been. And they were never made whole. And never compensated. Not one red cent.

Left behind to gasp for self-regard in the vicious psychological wake of slavery are history's orphans played by the brave black shells of their ancient forebears, people so badly damaged that they cannot *see* the damage, or how their government may have been partly, if not largely, responsible for the disabling injury that by now has come to seem normal and unattributable.

Until America's white ruling class accepts the fact that the book never closes on massive unredressed social wrongs, America can have no future as one people. Questions must be raised, to American private, as well as, public institutions. Which American families and institutions, for instance, were endowed in perpetuity by the commerce of slavery? And how do we square things with slavery's modern victims from whom all natural endowments were stolen? What is a fair measure of restitution for this, the most important of all American human rights abuses?

Latinegras
Desired Women—Undesirable Mothers, Daughters, Sisters, and Wives

Marta I. Cruz-Janzen

Latinegras are Latinas of obvious black ancestry and undeniable ties to Africa, women whose ancestral mothers were abducted from the rich lands that cradled them to become and bear slaves, endure the lust of their masters, and nurture other women's children. They are the mothers of generations stripped of their identity and rich heritage that should have been their legacy. Latinegras are women who cannot escape the many layers of racism, sexism, and inhumanity that have marked their existence. Painters, poets, singers, and writers have exalted their beauty, loyalty, and strength, but centuries of open assaults and rapes have also turned them into concubines, prostitutes, and undesirable mothers, daughters, sisters, and wives.

Latinegras are marked by a cruel, racialized history because of the shades of their skin, the colors and shapes of their eyes, and the textures and hues of their hair. They are the darkest *negras, morenas,* and *prietas,* the brown and golden *cholas* and *mulatas,* and the wheat-colored *trigueñas.* They are the light-skinned *jabás* with black features and the *grifas* with white looks but whose hair defiantly announces their ancestry. They are the Spanish-looking *criollas,* and the *pardas* and *zambas* who carry indigenous blood.

Latinegras represent the mirrors that most Latinos would like to shatter because they reflect the blackness Latinos don't want to see in themselves.[1] I am a Latinegra, born to a world that denies my humanity as a black person, a woman, and a Latina; born to a world where other Latinos reject me and deny my existence even though I share their heritage. As Lillian Comas-Díaz writes, the combination of race, ethnicity, and gender makes Latinegras a "minority within a minority."[2] Racism and sexism have been with me all my life. I was raised in Puerto Rico during the 1950s and 1960s, and lived on and off in the

United States during the 1970s and 1980s. Today, I still live in both worlds, and most of the gender and race themes I grew up with remain. This essay is my personal and historical narrative of the intersection of racism and sexism that has defined my life and that of other Latinegras.

Somos Una Raza Pura/Pura Rebelde (We Are A Pure Race/Pure Rebel)

"Aquí, el que no tiene inga, tiene mandinga. El que no tiene congo, tiene carabalí. ¿Y pa'los que no saben ná, tu abuela a'onde está?" This popular expression reveals what most Latinos throughout Latin America, and particularly in the Caribbean, know but wish to hide. It attests to the broad racial mixing that exists as well as to its denial. It states: "Here, those who don't have Inga, have Mandinga. Those who don't have Congo, have Carabali. And those who claim not to know, where's your grandma at?" The Ingas, or Incas, were indigenous Indians. Mandingas and Congos were Africans. Carabalis were runaway slaves, both African and indigenous Indians, feared for their rebelliousness. The question, "Where is your grandmother at?" publicly mocks the hypocrisy of white-looking persons who conceal their blackness and deny their ancestral black mothers.

Such expressions permeated my childhood and revealed the many contradictions of my world. Growing up biracial in Puerto Rico, I became aware of Latino racism at a very young age. As the child of a white Puerto Rican mother, whose family counted their drops of pure Spanish blood and resented our dark presence, and a very prieto (dark black) Puerto Rican father, I became aware of the social and economic gulf that prevails within this purportedly harmonious, integrated society. My paternal grandparents were educated, considered middle-class, and lived in a white neighborhood of paved streets and nice homes. Theirs was a neat wooden house with electricity, indoor plumbing, and a telephone. A large concrete balcony and front fence were decorated with ornamental wrought iron. Grandma kept a beautiful front flower garden. They were the only blacks in the neighborhood, always conscious of their neighbors' watchful and critical eyes. We were careful never to set foot outside the house unless we were impeccably groomed. In contrast, the rest of my father's family lived in a predominantly black slum on the outskirts of town. In that neighborhood, everyone was *puro prieto* (pure black). The dirt streets, the dilapidated houses, the numerous domestic and farm animals running loose, and the lack of electricity and sanitary facilities unequivocally punctuated the differences.

My siblings and I were raised in predominantly white neighborhoods and moved back and forth between two realities that seemed worlds apart. I do not recall a time when both sides of the family got together. Teachers and other adults in the community openly commented to me and my siblings that my mother had disgraced her family by marrying a black man while my father had elevated himself and his family by marrying a white woman. It was then that I learned how identity labels reveal the rancor of white Latinos toward Latinos of obviously nonwhite heritage. White Latinos are light-skinned Latinos who are usually the product of racial mixing, who profess white racial purity, and who are usually accepted as white ("social white"). While my father's family called me trigu(ñ)a, signifying a "step up" from being black, my mother's called me negra (black) and mulata, signifying a step down from being white. On one side of the family we were *negros finos* (refined blacks), while on the other side we were *una pena* (a disgrace, sorrow, and shame). Both sides of the family continually judged our looks; whoever had the most clearly defined white features was considered good-looking. I was constantly reminded to pinch my nose each day so it would lose its roundness and be sharper like those of my brothers and sisters. My younger sister was openly praised for her long flowing hair while I was pitied for my *greñas* (long mane of tangly hair). I felt fortunate, though, that at least it was long and not considered *ceretas* (short and knotty, like raisins).

When I was four my father took me to my first day of school. Later, when my mother came to pick me up and I jumped up happy to see her, my teacher exclaimed, "That can't be your mother. That woman is white." Sadly I realized for the first time that I was not like my mother or a lot of other people around me, including classmates and teachers. I recall holding hands with my parents, thereafter comparing skin colors, seeing that I was not like either one of them. Anxiously I realized that our different skin colors would always be an issue. I recall the cruel taunts of classmates, adults, and even teachers who called me *negativo*, meaning photo negative, because, while I resembled my mother, they joked that we were opposites. They often called me *Perlina* (pearly white), referring to a bleaching detergent with the picture of black children dressed in white on the label. Peers teased that I was *una mosca en un vaso de leche* (a fly in a glass of milk) because I stood out among them. They also teased that my father was *retinto* (double-dyed black) and *moyeto*, meaning black and ugly. I was reminded repeatedly that my destiny could have been crueler. At least I was not pura prieta. At best I was *mejorando la raza* (improving the race). It was my duty to maintain and promote that improvement. These and other abuses made me sad not to be like my mother but quite relieved not to be like my father.

In retrospect, I realize that having a white mother was an asset. Our mother was easily accepted in the community, whereas our father was not. As public ambassador of the family, Mami dealt with neighbors and negotiated many opportunities for us, especially at school. She always managed to place us with the advanced students. I learned that a black mother would not have been very powerful because Latinegras have been socialized, through generations, to accept their inferiority to all men and whites. As occupants of the lowest rungs on the social ladder, they are looked down upon, expected to be docile, subservient, uneducated, and ignorant. I always sensed others' resentment toward Papi (Father), especially by white men. Latino men challenge each other's machismo constantly, even in unspoken ways, and the authority of a black man is not accepted on equal terms. They commented to me that Papi thought himself *parao* (uppity), *presumío* (presumptuous), and *alzao* (elevated) because he married a white woman. The presence of an educated, successful, and very dark black man was threatening and simply not welcomed. I dreaded my father's presence in public because he didn't elicit the warmest of responses and was only superficially treated with respect. Behind his back, peers, teachers, neighbors, and other adults called him *negro come coco* (coconut-eating black man) an expression alluding to a popular cartoon that depicted a very dark monkey eating coconuts on a palm tree. It was clear to me that they were mocking my father for marrying a white woman.

When we moved to the United States mainland in the 1960s, concerned Latino friends advised me to emphasize my Latinness and to downplay my African traits to avoid being confused with African Americans. Some teachers advised that I might as well be black because I would be treated like one by white Latinos and mainstream white Americans. They felt that I should prepare myself for what inevitably awaited me. Fearful, I deliberately spoke with a Spanish accent even though schools kept placing me in speech courses; I learned to use a fan gracefully, and wore my hair long and straight. Many Latinos overtly distanced themselves from me by calling me morena (Moorish black), a derisive term reserved for dark-skinned blacks, especially African Americans.

Time has passed, but the realities of such racism remain constant. Two years ago a Latino educator in Colorado told me that I was not one of them: "Hispanics are from Spain. You are not Hispanic. Everyone knows you're black." At a Latino meeting where I raised concerns about the educational needs of African American children, I was addressed with contempt: "You ought to know; you're black like them." A Latina friend explained, "Some Hispanics here don't want to see you as one of them because you represent everything they do not want to be. They see you as a black person, and they don't want to be black. They want you to stop saying you're like them."

Prior to 1976, persons from Latin America in the United States were referred to as Latinos. Then the term "Hispanic" was introduced, purportedly to classify all persons from Spain, Latin America, and their compatriots and descendants within the United States. "Hispanic" has come under intense criticism as a label that exalts and promotes whiteness by focusing on the Spanish-speaking white European Spaniard as the ideal "Hispanic."[3] Hispanic connotes a homogeneous race and dilutes the black, Indian, and mestizo combinations that comprise this group of people. The term "Latino" also represents European Spaniards but is more inclusive of those Latin Americans who speak Spanish than those who do not.

In the United States blacks are usually identified as African American, and they are often considered the racialized group most discriminated against.[4] For

Latinos, to be black in the United States is a perceived liability.[5] Regardless of skin color and physical appearance, in the United States one drop of nonwhite blood makes the person 100 percent nonwhite, while in Latin America one drop of white blood makes the person whiter, or at least no longer black or Indian.[6] In Latin America "racial impurity" can be "cleansed" and "expunged" in ascending stages; in the United States racial "impurity" designates the person and his or her future generations as unfit and undesirable.[7] In a society where "color supersedes ethnicity and culture,"[8] black Latinos in the United States find themselves identified as African Americans by both whites and Latinos.[9] The more Latinos become immersed in the racial ideology of the United States, the sharper and more unyielding the black/white dichotomy becomes, and the more powerful is their need and desire to free themselves of any and all vestiges of African ancestry.[10] Many Latinegros try to deny their blackness and identify themselves as Hispanic like their European compatriots.

Two years ago at a conference in California I got on an elevator with two Latinas who, upon seeing me, switched their conversation from English to Spanish. When I asked them a question in flawless Spanish, they seemed surprised and remarked, "You don't look Latina!" They attempted to conceal their embarrassment and explained their surprise by telling me, *"Nosotros tenemos personas como usted en nuestro país"* (We [Latino whites] have persons like you [Latino blacks] in our own country). Since few black Latinos from Latin American countries besides Puerto Rico are financially or legally able to migrate to the United States, these Latinas assumed that I was African American, which simultaneously meant that I could not be Latina like them. I found their explanation neither comforting nor flattering as it clearly asserted their differences and distance from all Latinegros and me. It reaffirmed my belief that Latinos in the United States prefer to deny my legitimate group membership. Their subtle, yet powerful, implication asserts that Latinegros are not true compatriots in their respective countries or in the United States. Within their native countries and within Latino groups in the United States, Latinegros live as "foreigners of both locations."[11] "You don't look Latina/o [or Hispanic]" is something Latinegros hear often not only from white Americans but from other Latinos as well. It is another example of how Latinegros' ethnicity is repudiated.[12]

In the face of such repudiation the term Latinegro has been gaining currency among Latinos of African ancestry for several decades. The term emerged closely linked to the Civil Rights Movement of the 1960s and has become an empowering affirmation of Latinegros' legitimacy as Latinos. The term represents indisputable proof that not only have blacks not disappeared from the Americas but they also demand their integral place among all Latinos.

Upon entering Cornell University in 1968, I tried joining several Latino student organizations. When that failed, I tried to establish a club for Puerto Ricans. It became apparent that Puerto Ricans from the island and those from the United States mainland did not view themselves in the same way. Puerto

Ricans from the island did not want to be perceived as black and rejected me as well as mainland Puerto Ricans, quite shamelessly. In contrast, Puerto Ricans from the United States mainland saw their strength through unity with African American students. Many flaunted even the minutest African heritage with Afro hairstyles and African clothing. I severed ties with most Latinos from Latin America, including Puerto Rico, and sought out the African and African American communities. I styled my hair in an Afro and began wearing African clothes. I found myself in a constant struggle to find my identity. I felt obliged to prove my blackness to other African Americans, even when they looked just like me. I was the victim of jokes because my hair would not stay up, and, called "flat-top" and "lame-fro." I tried all sorts of styling chemicals; I even wore hairpieces and wigs. Finally, I cut my hair as short as possible. Repeatedly, African Americans told me that I must be ashamed of my African heritage because I tried to conceal it by claiming to be Latina and speaking Spanish. They insisted that blacks were foremost a single people, regardless of where they found themselves or what languages they spoke. I was accused of thinking myself superior, on one hand, and mocked as inferior for being impure and carrying the "blood of the Devil," on the other. I grew ashamed of my white heritage, prevented my mother from visiting me on campus, and worked hard to keep a dark tan. Eventually I stopped visiting Puerto Rico; I married an African American who planned to live in Africa, and I thought of adopting a traditional African name.

The culmination of my search for a legitimizing identity came when I visited Africa, "the homeland." Ironically, the search that took me halfway across the world brought me right back home. What began as a journey to establish my identity proved instead to be a dead end—I was not, nor could I ever be, an African: I was a Latinegra living among Africans in Africa. I further confirmed that I was not an African American. I had never felt so distant from my physical and psychological center. While in Africa, I could not celebrate the return to my roots because of a persistent fear of not knowing where I really belonged. I mourned the loss of all I had known myself to be, longed for the place that truly felt like home, and I resented the people who would not allow me to share a Latino home with them. The anger and frustration within me erupted, and I swore never again to allow others to tell me what I was or was not. I came back determined to claim and uphold a legitimate and rightful sense of self.

Today, I affirm proudly that I am a Latinegra whose African ancestors were brutally extracted from a distant place and time and experienced historical realities no African who stayed behind could have ever fathomed. I am a Latinegra, a black Latina whose African heritage stands as an indelible stamp on my life. I am a Latinegra who will no longer accept the rejection and scorn of others, especially from those Latinos who share my origins.

No Hay Moros En La Costa
(There Are No Moors [Blacks] On The Coast)

Many Mexican Americans have told me over the years that there are no blacks in Mexico. I puzzled over this, and, although I often suspected some individuals of having African heritage, I believed that there were no blacks in Mexico until I visited. I was quite surprised to meet obvious Latinegros in Guadalajara and other large cities. They openly welcomed me and told me about the many Latinegros throughout Mexico and the blatant hostility and racism against them. Nevertheless, Argentines, Mexicans, and other Latinos often state that blacks either no longer exist or are not a visible force in their nations and societies.[13] Many Latinos still have African bloodlines. Most Latin American countries do not maintain demographic data segregated by race, but it has been estimated, for example, that as many as 75 percent of the population of Mexico, Cuba, and Puerto Rico have African heritage.[14] Throughout Spain, across the Caribbean, from Mexico and all the way down to Argentina, Spaniards took great numbers of Africans. Although most blacks were brought as slaves, many were free.[15] In most Latin American countries, Africans rapidly comprised a significant portion of the total population. In many Latin American countries, Africans were rapidly assimilated through interracial unions, but dark-skinned Latinegros are still visible.[16]

I have come to the realization that Latino racism, throughout Latin America, Spain, and the United States, begins with the negation of the black presence in history. Whites in Latin America, and wherever African and indigenous slavery existed, have been responsible for writing history. Historical amnesia across Latin America, reflected in census counts and historical accounts have systematically minimized or completely obliterated the presence and contributions of blacks. The darker the Latino, the greater the oppression of his or her existence and linkages to other Latinos.[17] Several authors make accusations of historical and systematic obliteration of the existence of Latinegros across Latin America. Even today, *blanqueamiento* (whitening of the race) remains the key to personal and national advancement, while darkening of the race is "blamed for everything from poverty and underdevelopment to the whole sorry history" of all Latin America and the Caribbean.[18] Many Latinos struggle with acceptance of their own blackness while accusing and mocking each other for having black ancestry. Few publications ever comment on Mexican muralist Diego Rivera's African heritage.

While proclaiming racial democracy and integration, most Latin American countries simultaneously institute and maintain social, economic, and political structures that continue to disenfranchise their African and indigenous populations. Even Brazil, which openly recognizes many racial gradations with accepted terms for each, and other countries like Cuba, the Dominican Republic, Mexico, and Puerto Rico do not count their black or interracial populations.

This has enabled them to diminish and conceal the African influence and even the existence of very dark-skinned Latinegros, who remain on the margins of society. A tour of any one of these countries reveals that socioeconomic status and implied "fluid" racial classifications are very much racial in nature. The social, economic, and political isolation of blacks has contributed to the invisibility of Latinegros in these countries.

Many Latin American countries endorse policies of *negritud* (negritude or blackness), *mestizaje* (racial mixing), and blanqueamiento (whitening). French-speaking Haiti, for example, where the majority of the population is black, is the only Latin American nation to endorse open policies of *negritud*, or affirmation of a black identity.[19] Negritude is the affirmation of a black heritage grounded in the unique historical antecedents of the nation. It promotes black racial pride with increased economic, political, and social linkages to other African nations and all global black populations.

Mestizaje represents an interracial heritage manifest in white and indigenous unions. Many Spanish-speaking Latin American countries, and significantly Mexico, call themselves nations of mestizos but forget their African bloodlines. Even Latin American scholars endorse the doctrine of two "worlds," the Spanish and the indigenous, meeting on American soil.[20] The concept of mestizaje sheds light on the historical rejection of Latinegros within most Latino cultures. Many Latinos, aware of their interracial heritage, may admit to their indigenous legacy, the mestizo, but few will admit to a black ancestor. The black/African identity becomes suppressed, the words negro and moreno become equated with dark-skinned indigenous Indians, and national motherhood is presented through indigenous women. Mestizo, therefore, becomes the acceptable identity. My father's birth certificate defines him as mestizo even though both of his parents, my grandparents, are puros prietos.

The policies of blanquemiento, prevalent in most Latin American countries, blatantly promote complete commitment to the elimination of all nonwhite ancestral traces, particularly those who are African/black. Blanqueamiento affirms the perceived superiority of whites coupled with the perceived inferiority of all others, with blacks and indigenous persons at the bottom. This doctrine endorses racial mixing aimed at whitening the national populace. It endorses concealment and denial of blackness. It promotes the infusion of new white bloodlines through immigration from European nations, while it encourages emigration of blacks and persons of apparent racial mixing and restricts black immigration. Several African American acquaintances, even some married to native Mexican citizens, have tried to migrate to Mexico but have been denied permanent resident and/or citizen status.[21]

While it could be argued that education confers social mobility and greater status to Latin Americans of black and indigenous heritage, it cannot be denied that being, or becoming, anything other than black is preferable. Puerto Ricans, Dominicans, and Cubans, groups known for their apparent African ancestry, often joke, "There are more Indians today than when Columbus arrived."

The most blatant manifestation of Latino racism is denial. Many Latin Americans have even proclaimed the myth of racial integration and harmony along with the primacy of cultural identity over race. Indeed, many Latinos claim that their native countries or communities in the United States do not perceive race and racism as issues of concern. According to the North American Congress on Latin America, *The Black Americas, 1492–1992, Report on the Americas*, the "pervasive litanies" of Latin American color blindness and racial democracies belie the reality that "blatant discrimination continues to plague" the descendants of the millions of African slaves brought to the Americas.[22] Indeed, George Andrews Reid further asserts that racial inequality is endemic in Latin America.[23]

Madre Patria (Mother Country)

I wanted to be the Virgin Mary for the community Christmas celebration when I was in third grade in Puerto Rico. A teacher quickly informed me that the mother of Christ could not be black. A girl with blond hair and blue eyes was selected for the role, and I was a shepherd. In middle school, also in Puerto Rico, for a school play I was assigned the role of a house servant. Only children of black heritage played the slaves and servants. A white student with a painted face portrayed the only significant black character; all the other characters were white. I learned then that nonwhites could not represent the nation's greatness but could only serve as servants and slaves to the great white leaders. The strongly gendered nature of many Latino cultures, particularly those directly derived from Spain, add other enduring and significant contradictions to the Latinegra experience. Whereas my Spanish heritage taught me that women are weak and dependent, my African heritage taught me that women are strong and self-reliant. African women flourished in spite of the despair of their lives to emerge as enduring forces of cohesion and cultural transmission. My grandmother would often remind us that we were *negros finos y orugullosos* (refined [lightened] and proud blacks). As proud as she was of our racial mixing she was equally insistent that we know our heritage. Regularly, she shared stories of our "accomplished" ancestors, especially those with education, economic well being, and social integration within the white world.

Mothers are important in Latino cultures and are visible proof of matrilineal racial lines that cannot be concealed. Motherhood is also a paramount value within doctrines of nationalism, patriotism, and racialism endorsed by most Latino nations. Many countries around the world, including the United States and most in Latin America, revere motherhood and honor women's roles as creators and nurturers of the nations' past, present, and future. These national ideologies merge the powerful concepts of nationalism and patriotism with womanhood and motherhood to create a icon that defines and portrays these nations as inclusive of heritage both internally and to the outside world.

In Spanish, country of origin becomes *madre patria*, combining female and male symbolism. Literally, *madre patria* becomes mother of the fatherland and, ultimately, mother of the nation. In this context, nationalism and patriotism, without diminishing national patriarchy, legitimize women as bearers and nurturers of powerful men and nations. A complete national identity requires a mother. However, this powerful national icon cannot be the black/African woman. The Latinegra cannot be the representative of the national icon of motherhood because of what she historically represents to the nation—slavery and misogyny.[24]

Cada Oveja Con Su Pareja (Every Sheep With Its Partner)

A middle school teacher, who was also a family friend, punished a white classmate for dating a puro prieto. The school threatened to inform her parents whom she was going out with, and they were certain to be outraged. I recall sitting in the classroom after school with my inconsolable friend and the teacher, a so-called friend of my parents', debating the unfairness and hypocrisy of the situation. The teacher warned, *"Cada oveja con su pareja,"* an admonition that interracial marriages are frowned upon even by the Catholic Church. We are all *"ovejas de Dios"* (God's sheep), she preached, but I felt this superficial social acceptance merely concealed deeply ingrained racial prejudices and rejection.

Family lines and marriage are significant in a culture that has historically included extended families as well as genealogical and cultural connections through *compadrazgo*, or the joining of families through oaths of honor, loyalty, and support. While often unspoken, it is understood that the presence of blacks within a family drastically reduces its options in life. Options are very limited for Latinegros/as. There exists a sociocultural glass ceiling for Latinegros, and particularly for Latinegras. General cultural devaluation of females sets Latinegras additionally at risk. Because of the greater status and patriarchal authority bestowed on all males, regardless of race or social status, Latino cultures are more forgiving of blackness in males.[25]

Educational and career opportunities for Latinegros remain limited. In many Latino countries most Latinegros do not have access to a secondary school education or college. Many Latinegros, and particularly Latinegras, see education, even a limited one, as the only way out of a cruel, predetermined path. Although most lack financial resources and reside in areas with poorly staffed and funded schools, those who can pursue an education do so in part to avoid the most humbling servile jobs. Most dark-skinned persons work in menial low-paying jobs; positions that require a "good appearance" or contact with the public such as receptionists, bank tellers, or secretaries tend to be closed to them. Lighter-skinned Latinegros have better opportunities because they are favored over the darker-skinned ones.

While one of the few options available for Latinegras seeking an education and career is teaching, Mami did not want us to be teachers because in Puerto Rico, as in other Latin American countries, black teachers tend to be assigned to rural schools as opposed to city schools.[26] Rural populations tend to be poorer and have greater racial mixing.[27] Nevertheless, Mami emphasized education and prohibited my sisters and me from doing any service-oriented work, even baby-sitting, outside of our immediate family and close friends. I always found it odd that as my girlfriends grew older their household responsibilities increased, caring for younger siblings, cooking, and laundering; our mother, on the contrary, did not teach my sisters and me many household skills. Today, I understand that she planned it that way. It remains the practice to keep Latinegras, especially educated ones, out of sight and out of mind as it is still believed that an educated Latinegra is, unquestionably, *buscando pa'rriba* (searching to move up) by marrying a white man. Stories of pregnant Latinegras abandoned by white men abound, and Mami did not want her daughters distant and alone in a very dangerous world.

In addition to a proper education, Latinegras must also find a proper marriage situation. I often overheard my mother's relatives asking, "*¿Y cómo las vas a casar?*" (How are you going to get them married?). Clearly, getting us *bien casadas* (properly married) was problematic. Apparently this was not as great a concern with my brothers. Within many Latino groups, it is more acceptable and less threatening to marry a Latinegro than a Latinegra. If a Latinegra is dark-skinned, she is less socially acceptable and is considered more likely to bring the family down.[28] Properly married meant not only getting us legally married, but also married to an acceptable and upwardly mobile family. Parents prefer that sons and daughters marry "light."[29] I was constantly reminded of my responsibility, my duty, to continue the family *echando pa'lante* (moving ahead) by marrying someone lighter, hopefully someone white. In many Latin American countries white Europeans, including U.S. mainstream white Americans, have always been highly admired, and marriage to them is encouraged. To marry a white person, especially a Spaniard, European, or white American, is *dando pa'rriba* (moving up); to marry a darker person is *dañar la raza* (damaging to the race).

Although black women are coveted sexually, they are rejected as acceptable wives—the darker the skin color and apparent Negroid features, the less acceptable the women.[30] Brown-skinned mulatas and wheat-colored trigueñas are feared within white social circles because of their white racial bloodlines. Although viewed as lesser wives and mothers than white women, mulatas are nevertheless perceived as better marriage partners than black women. It is shameful enough to admit to a black concubine in the family, but to actually bring a black woman into the family through the sanctity of marriage is an unbearable public nightmare to many whites. Latinegras thus represent a real threat to the family's purity and public *honra* (honor).

"Social" whites also fear Latinegras because of *requintamiento*, or the appearance of apparent African traits that can manifest themselves in the fifth and subsequent generations. Literally translated, *requinto* refers to a return in the fifth generation. Whites with known or suspected black bloodlines fear having children with other mulattos for this reason. Racial mixing, even remote, may *requintar* in their children, grandchildren, or great-grandchildren if they marry other nonwhite Latinos.[31] *Requinto* is a pejorative term for persons who are sometimes jeered as *mulatos blancos* (white mulattos), people whose parents look white but have passed on detectable African features to their children. Families that bear a requinto are ridiculed as *tapujos* (lies) and *chayotes*, after a fruit, white inside and out, with a rough and prickly surface, said to resemble requintos *"con los pelos paraos"* (with hairs standing up). This is a cruel reminder that whiteness inside and out can still fail to hide blackness.

Many light-skinned Latinos attempt to conceal their nonwhite ancestors. For this reason, Latino cultures are deeply immersed in secrets. What is not stated is the fear that open discussions about race and racism may unveil personal and family mysteries. Another popular expression, *"Hasta en el mantel más fino cae la mancha* (The stain falls even on the finest tablecloth),"* underlies the common fear that la mancha spares no one. A number of stories I hear from other Latinegras confirm the extent of this fear. A twenty-six-year-old Latinegra I know confessed that white Latino men did not consider her attractive enough to date openly.[32] She reported that they would be her friend; they would have a clandestine affair; but open courtship and marriage was out of the question. Within her family, this Latinegra lived a different life from her mother, a "very white-looking" Mexican. Her mother was accepted as a Mexican American, while she was not. Latinos in her community constantly reminded her that she was not one of them: "I was looked down upon because I thought I was Mexican. They'd make fun of my hair. My skin is too dark. The boys especially, they'd let me know they didn't think I was attractive." She added: "The Mexican girls were really mean—evil. They would let me know verbally that I wasn't Mexican like them." Further, this Latinegra explained her willful refusal to learn Spanish because, as a Spanish-speaker, she feared the Latino community's even crueler repudiation.[33]

This year I was told by a twenty-two-year-old Puerto Rican Latinegra, whose father is a white Latino and whose mother is a black Latino, that her paternal family still refuses to accept her parent's marriage and children. The family discord reached the point that forced her parents to move to the United States. She added, visibly pained, that her lighter-skinned siblings are accepted "just a little bit more."

In addition, a twenty-six-year-old white Latina of Mexican American ancestry recently told me that her family did not approve of her engagement to an African American. Her family did not approve of her having dark-skinned children, particularly African American, and felt publicly dishonored and humiliated. In her words, her family had worked hard to "be white," or "as white [white American] as possible." To marry another Latino was acceptable but not as good as marrying a white American. Marrying a Latinegro was "stepping down." Marriage to an African American was the "worst that could be done," definitively "going beneath" herself and lowering the status of the entire family.

In contrast, when a Latinegra marries well, there is no end to the family's happiness. Two years ago I attended the wedding of a young Latinegra of Panamanian and Colombian parents to a mainstream white American. Her parents held an elaborate, very public, and expensive wedding to proclaim their daughter and family's good marriage and fortune. They could not wait to see the *precioso* (beautiful), *blanquito* (white) grandchildren they were going to have. Last year I attended the wedding of a twenty-four-year-old white Mexican American woman to a Spaniard from Madrid. The woman's family was very proud, and her parents began to plan their first trip to Spain to see the madre patria. Ironically, this family had ancestors in Mexico but none they could name in Spain. Last month a Latina colleague chose to spend several months in Spain. When asked why not a visit to a Latin American country, her response was a contemptuous, "What for? I haven't lost anything there." As I walked through campus recently, I met a Latinegra who told me that her brother had gone to Africa to "find his roots," upsetting the entire family. It seems some things never change.

Rejection of black Latinos by their own compatriots has intensified over the years, in Latin America as in the United States.[34] Latinegros know the reason: Africa is alive in all Latinos; the African blood that runs through my veins also runs deeply through the veins of all Latinos everywhere. Africa's blood clamors in the Spanish flamenco, resonates in the Mexican corrida, palpitates in Mexico's *La Bamba*, and laments in the Argentinian tango. It is alive in Diego Rivera's paintings. It calls to us in today's popular salsa sounds from the Caribbean. Just as earth is mother to us all, Africa is Latinos' other mother, *la querida* (mistress), *la concubina* (concubine), the exploited black woman, the mother of children whose patrimony cannot be denied. All Latinos, but especially Latinegras, must recognize racism as a source of oppression in their lives. Awareness is the first step in any personal change, and only through awareness can Latinegras develop the consciousness and subjectivity they will need to claim social, economic, and political empowerment.

Notes

1. Lillian Comas-Díaz, "LatiNegra: Mental Health Issues of African Latinas," in *The Multiracial Experience: Racial Borders as the New Frontier*, ed. Maria P. Root (Thousand Oaks CA: Sage Publications, 1996): 167–90.

2. Comas-Díaz, "LatiNegra," 169.

3. Jack D. Forbes, "The Hispanic Spin: Party Politics and Governmental Manipulation of Ethnic Identity," *Latin American Perspectives* 19:3 (1992): 59–78.

4. Toni Morrison, "On the Backs of Blacks," *Time*, December 2, 1993, Special Issue: *The New Face of America: How Immigrants are Shaping the World's First Multicultural Society*, 57; and Roberto Santiago, "Negro is a Spanish Word: The Issue of Racism Bedevils White and Black Hispanics," *Denver Post, Vista*, July 7, 1991, 6–7, 20. Morrison and Santiago discuss the perceived inferiority of African Americans by other groups in the United States. Santiago explains how Latinos, including Latinegros, scoff at being associated with African Americans, particularly African Americans who openly assert their ties to Africa.

5. Delina D. Pryce, "Black Latina," *Hispanic*, March 1999, 56.

6. F. James Davis, *Who is Black? One Nation's Definition* (University Park: The Pennsylvania State University Press, 1998); Lillian Comas-Díaz, "LatiNegra," 171.

7. Marta I. Cruz-Janzen, "Y Tu Abuela A'Onde Está?" *Sage Race Relations Abstracts* 26:2 (2001): 7–24.

8. Comas-Díaz, "LatiNegra," 180.

9. Gabriel Escobar, "Dominicans Assimilate in Black and White," *The Washington Post*, May 14, 1999, A2; and Mirta Ojito, "Best Friends, Worlds Apart," *The New York Times*, June 5, 2000, A1, A16–7.

10. Roberto Santiago, "Negro is a Spanish Word," 6.

11. Escobar, "Dominicans Assimilate in Black and White," 2.

12. Comas-Díaz, "LatiNegra," 168.

13. For more information about the systematic obliteration of the existence and contributions of Latinegros across Latin America, see George Andrews Reid, *Blacks and Whites in Sao Paulo, Brazil, 1888–1988* (Madison: University of Wisconsin Press, 1991); North American Congress on Latin America (NACLA), *The Black Americas, 1492–1992: Report on the Americas* (New York: NACLA, 1992); and Winthrop Wright, *Café con Leche: Race, Class, and National Image in Venezuela* (Austin: University of Texas Press, 1990).

14. Jameelah S. Muhammad, "Mexico," *No Longer Invisible: Afro-Latin Americans Today* (London: Minority Rights Publications, 1995), 163–80.

15. See Jalil Sued Badillo and Angel López Cantor, *Puerto Rico Negro* (Puerto Rico: Editorial Cultural, 1986) for further discussion of the presence of free blacks who came to the America as entrepreneurs, merchants, contracted free servants, or to join conquerors in their greedy expeditions and exploits for lands, riches, and slaves among the indigenous populations.

16. Minority Rights Group, eds., *No Longer Invisible: Afro-Latin Americans Today* (London: Minority Rights Publications, 1995).

17. Minority Rights Group, *No Longer Invisible.*

18. NACLA, *The Black Americas, 1492–1992,* 15.

19. NACLA, *The Black Americas, 1492–1992,* 18.

20. The doctrine of "two worlds," is discussed in NACLA, *The Black Americas, 1492–1992,* 15; and Muhammad, "Mexico," 176.

21. Muhammad, "Mexico," 170. Former dictator Porfirio Diaz banned immigration of people of African descent and encouraged immigration of European peoples, promising them jobs and economic stability. Although it is publicly proclaimed that such policies are no longer enforced, they are commonly practiced unofficially.

22. NACLA, *The Black Americas, 1492–1992,* 15.

23. George Andrews Reid, *The Afro-Argentines of Buenos Aires, 1800–1900* (Madison: University of Wisconsin Press, 1980).

24. Comas-Díaz, "LatiNegra," 171.

25. Comas-Díaz, "LatiNegra," 173.

26. Isabelo Zeñón Cruz, *Narciso Descubre su Traser: El Negro en la Cultural Puertorriqueña* (Utuado, Puerto Rico: Editorial Furidi, 1974).

27. Marta Cruz-Janzen, "Racial Amnesia, Avoidance, and Denial: Race and Racism Among Puerto Ricans," unpublished manuscript. This article discusses the creation of today's mountain people, *jíbaros.* Indigenous people and black slaves escaped to the mountain jungles where they could not be reached. They intermarried to create a highly diverse cultural group. As agricultural workers, they are often displaced from their source of income and must migrate to the U.S. mainland in search of work.

28. Comas-Díaz, "LatiNegra," 173.

29. Escobar, "Dominicans Assimilate in Black and White," 5.

30. Comas-Díaz, "LatiNegra," 186.

31. Cruz-Janzen, "Y Tu Abuela A'Onde Está?" 21.

32. Marta I. Cruz-Janzen, "Curriculum and the Self-Concept of Biethnic and Biracial Persons" (Ph.D diss., University of Denver, 1997), 167.

33. Cruz-Janzen, "Curriculum and the Self-Concept of Biethnic and Biracial Persons," 170.

34. Cruz-Janzen, "Y Tu Abuela A'Onde Está?" 23; Santiago, "Negro is a Spanish Word," 6; and Morrison, "On the Backs of Blacks," 57.

20/20 Hindsight
Jay Ford

Born in a middle class African-American family on the upper west side of Manhattan, I have spent most of my life chasing the (white) American dream. Absorbing the rhetoric brewed by the media, school curricula, and, more important, my teachers, I was graduated from high school with the goal of travelling to Europe, achieving a college degree, becoming a corporate lawyer and, eventually, marrying a spouse who would be most likely white or a light-skinned black. We would have two homes and probably three children. This was my rough sketch of my future, one with which I was satisfied. I would be a success and this was very important because I clearly represent what W.E.B. Du Bois coined as the "talented tenth." Therefore, I had a responsibility to my people to succeed, to vanquish the disabilities associated with my color and earn my place in white America, my America.

In starting off on my journey to success, I met my first obstacle as I neared the end of my sophomore year in college. The student body had taken over the administration building in hopes of persuading the University to divest monies invested in corporations in South Africa. A meeting between the students and the administration had been arranged during which the administration had thoroughly explained its position on divestment. Now it was the students' turn to respond. As student after student approached the microphone, explaining what he/she believed to be the most important reasons for disinvesting, an unsettling feeling began to overwhelm me. Although all of the explanations were more than legitimate reasons to disinvest, none of them had touched my personal reasons for protesting the University's position on divestment.

When it was my turn, I did not actually know what I wanted to say, but I was determined to say something. "My name is Julius J. Ford. I am an Afro-American. Inherent in my title is the word African, meaning "of Africa." My ancestry is from Africa. Africans are therefore my people, my history. So as long as you continue to oppress my people through violence or investment or silence, you oppress me. And as long as you oppress me, I will fight you! I will fight you!" As I returned to my seat, my friend leaned over, patted me on the back and said, "That was great, I never really knew you felt that way." I turned to him and said, "Neither did I."

It was this event that made me question myself. How could I be satisfied with my sketch of success when it had no background or depth? Why had I not felt this strongly about Africa or Africans before? Why was I more attracted to women who possessed European features (straight hair, light skin, thin nose) than those who possessed African features? Why did I feel that Europe was so great and Africa so primitive? Why did I choose to call myself an African-American when I knew virtually nothing about Africa? These questions would trouble my soul for the remainder of the year. In fact, they would push me to apply to a student exchange program in East Africa, Kenya.

Called "An Experiment in International Living," the program would offer me travel throughout the country, during which time I would live in both rural and urban areas, in both huts and hotels, for approximately four months from February through mid-May, 1989. I would be equipped with two academic directors with numerous university and government contacts and ensured a variety of learning opportunities, as I would stay with native families and be allowed to venture off on my own.

Even though this program seemingly presented an optimum opportunity to find answers to all my pending questions, I was still apprehensive about my decision to go. But, perhaps if there was one specific incident that canceled any wavering on my part, it was that Friday afternoon at drama class. On Fridays, I taught drama to about twenty 9–14-year-old kids from predominantly black families with low incomes at a community center about twenty minutes from my college. On this particular day I had decided to ask the class what they thought about my taking a trip to Africa. They shot off these responses: "Why would you want to go to Africa to get even blacker than you are now?", "Why don't you take a trip somewhere nice like Paris, London, Rome?", "But they say in Africa every one is backwards, they can't teach you anything," "People are so black and ugly there." And, although some of the comments from the children were said specifically to make the other children laugh, many of them were exemplifications of how our educational system and other forms of external social propaganda affect a black child's mind.

When I first arrived in Kenya, we stayed in its capital city, Nairobi. Surprisingly enough, my first impression of Nairobi was that it was just like any American city: skyscrapers, movie theatres, discos, and crime. In fact, I was a bit disappointed, feeling that I had travelled fifteen hours in a Pan Am jet just to come back to New York City. But upon more detailed observation, I realized that this city was quite different from any other I had visited before. This city was black and, when I say black, I'm not talking your coffee-colored Atlanta, Oakland, Harlem black people. I mean black! I mean when you were small and used to play games and chose to embarrass the darkest kid on the block by calling him "midnight," "shadow," and "teeth black."

But the lesson to be learned in Nairobi was that all shades of black were equally attractive and the small children did not penalize attractiveness according to shade of skin, or length of hair, or size of nose. Furthermore, being in a black city, knowing I was in a mostly black country that sits on a predominantly black continent, enhanced my confidence and hence my actions. For the first time in my life I felt as though I could do anything, fit in anywhere, be welcomed by everyone because of my color. This was the feeling I had often assumed blacks felt during the Twenties, the period of the Harlem Renaissance. It was wonderful! I would go for days without being aware of my color. It did not seem to matter.

It was only a few weeks into the program, however, when I began to notice social insecurities developing within my peer group (of twenty-four I was the only black). As many as half a dozen of the other students declared that they had begun to view black children as more beautiful than white, that black women and black features were more pleasing to the eye than white ones. Others simply segregated themselves from the black society as much as possible, refusing to stay with families without another white person present. Perhaps, then, inherent in the role of minority come feelings of inferiority, a certain lack of confidence, insecurity.

Because there is much tribalism in Kenya, the first title I had to drop was African-American. When people around me refer to themselves as Masai or Kikuyu as opposed to Kenyan or East African, then how could I refer to myself as an African? Furthermore, the language I spoke, my values, morals and education were not African. So this put me in an awkward position. No one could question my ancestry as African because of my color, so I enjoyed most benefits of majority status. Yet, to many Kenyans, I was much more similar to a white American than an African so there was a wide gap between us.

It was here I realized that to be an accepted descendant of Africa I had a lot of work to do. I needed to learn a new language and a new culture. I needed to assimilate, and I figured that that shouldn't be too hard as I had twenty years of experience in that in the United States. But, the difference between my American and Kenyan assimilations is that in Kenya it seemed to be welcomed if not encouraged by the majority. The more knowledge I attained of Kenya and the more I left my English at home and spoke Swahili or another tribal language, the more cultural doors opened to me. For example, as I became increasingly familiar with Gidiam tribal customs and my use of Kiswahili improved, I was able to travel along the coast for days never worrying about food or lodging. I was often given the opportunity to sit and discuss with elders, and take part in tribal ceremonies and had responsibilities bestowed on me by elder men, *Mzees,* or my temporary *Mama.* In fact, toward the end of my trip, when travelling alone, it was often difficult for me to convince people that I was African-American. They would tell me, "*Una toka Africa qwa sababo una weza kusema Kiswahili na una fambamu Africa life*" (You are from Africa because you are able to speak Kiswahili and you understand African life). The more I learned, the more comfortable I was with the title African-American.

I also took more pride in myself. Here it was important to learn that the black empowerment was not from sheer numbers, it was from the fact that the blacks in Africa possess a communal sense of self, a shared past that is to never be forgotten, that has passed through generations, and is used as a reference for modern-day experiences. An exemplification of this concept is the way in which Kenyans and Africans in general treat their elderly. In Kenya you are told that you never grow to equal your parents' authority or knowledge. Your elders will forever be your elders and respected as such. In Kenya, elderly people are cherished, not forgotten.

As we visited small villages in the areas of Kisumu, Nakru, and on the coast, villages which by American standards were far below the poverty line, we were welcomed with feasts of foods, drinks, people and music. To them we were guests paying them the honor of visitation. Even on a more individual level, most Kenyan families were extraordinarily hospitable. To be welcomed into a stranger's home and be offered food, wine, and a bed for an unlimited number of days is shocking to Americans and even more so to a New Yorker.

This humanistic view was very difficult to adapt to because it affected every level of Kenyan society. For example, Kenyans have a very limited concept of personal space (but in a country with a population growth rate of 4.3 percent that is quite understandable). So it was often difficult for me to discover that my four newly acquired brothers were also my newly acquired bedmates, to change money at the bank while the people behind me were looking over my shoulder examining my passport and money exchange papers, and, to learn not to tell your family that you would like to be left alone because crazy people stay by themselves.

Also, Americans are lost outside of a linear society. We are taught from kindergarten to stay in line. Order for us is symbolically represented by the line, and we therefore choose to see all other forms of non-linear collective activity as chaotic. Kenyans, however, do not have this same view of order. They choose to mass together, aggressively seeking out their desires and bringing new meaning to the words "organized chaos." Mobs catch buses, herds are seen at ticket counters, and, unfortunately, until your adjustment period is complete, you stand apart from the chaos, "jaw dropped," staring at the stampede of people. As a result, you do not obtain a ticket or get on the bus.

This conception of order plus the Kenyan view of personal space make for exciting moments in the public sphere. For example, there is a type of Kenyan public transportation called *matatus*. Matatus are small privately owned minivans that serve as buses for local citizens. To ride a matatu is like taking the most crowded New York City subway car during rush hour, placing that car on Broadway, and allowing a taxicab driver to control the wheel. Matatus do not actually stop at designated bus stops; in fact, they do not actually stop at all. Instead, they simply slow down and those who need to get off push and shove their way to the front of the van and jump out. And as for those who wish to board, they simply chase the matatu down and shove and push their way onto the van. As with circus clown cars, there is always room for one more.

Another linear concept I was introduced to was time. In rural areas there would sometimes be days when we would have no activities planned. It was at these moments when I would curse my directors for poor planning. But I was soon to learn that doing nothing was not necessarily wasted time. This time to think, relax, conversationalize was most important for a peaceful state of mind. I finally understood that it is not imperative even in America to eat breakfast, read the paper in the street while you are running to the subway, or to work two jobs just to pay off your life insurance bill. Here there was not "so much to do and so little time"; here there was a great deal to do but also the belief that that which is supposed to get done will get done in time.

For example, during the last month of my stay in Kenya I visited a small farm in Kisumu Kaubu, Uganda, with a woman and her three sons. I was only to stay for a day and one night. I had come to visit just prior to the time the rains were expected, so I had assumed that the family was going to spend very little time relaxing with me because it was imperative that the soil and seeds for the year be prepared for the rains which could come at any moment.

However, once I arrived, we did very little field work. We talked instead—about the history of her people, about America, and about American perceptions of Kenya. Of course this was hard work since their English was very limited and my Swahili is fair at best. And as the day crept on to the night, I asked her how she could afford to give her attentions to me when the threat of the rains could come at any day now. "*Pole Pole, bwana,*" she replied (We have not neglected our work to the fields. We have only delayed our work so to welcome our new son, who by joining us will ease our workload). I then asked her, "But, Mama, it is already 11:00 and I leave tomorrow at 9:00." She replied, "Don't worry, bwana, we start to work the cattle (plow) at 2:00 A.M. Good night."

It seemed as though Kenyan culture chose to be humanistic rather than materialistic. The value placed on human life and interaction is much greater than in the States. To shake hands, to share a meal or even your home with a foreigner is an honor, not a burden. And, for you as a guest to turn down that hand, meal, or bed is an insult. How wonderfully strange to travel to a foreign land where people who can hardly understand what language you speak are ready to take you home and make you part of the family. They wouldn't last too long in New York, I thought.

In most places in Kenya, it was common knowledge for one to know his/her environment. People could name the types of trees along the roads, tell you animals indigenous to the area, and explain which types of soil were best for growing specific crops. They could tell you the staple foods of different parts of Kenya *or* even the U.S. In fact, their world geography was superior to that of most American college students. Access to information, whether at home or in schools, was a privilege to be appreciated by those involved and then passed down to younger generations orally. I wonder why I did not feel this way. My country offers more educational opportunities than any other in the world and yet seldom are these opportunities fully exploited. American students go to school, but they do not go to learn. They go to get A's and move up economically. They go to play the game, the educational game of success that I like to refer to as DT (Diploma Training), a process that verifies one's intelligence by certificate as opposed to action or common sense.

Furthermore, along with this overwhelming appreciation for knowledge, Kenyans show reverence for everyday simplicities which we in America take for granted: the appreciation for candlelight, running water, a toilet with a seat cover, a long hot shower every day. Learning to live is to stay in Kenya and survive with twenty-three other people living mostly off rain water, sleeping in huts, and eating many fruits and vegetables with only the occasional beef meal. I felt as though Kenya taught me a new dimension of life, a rebirth of sorts. It put objectives, time, goals, values into a new perspective. It did not tell me, "Please be aware of how much water you use because a drought warning is in effect." It gave me a gallon of water and told me to drink and bathe for an undetermined period. It did not tell me of the beauties of nature, rather it revealed them to me by greeting me in the morning with the sights of Mt. Kenya, Kilimanjaro, and Lake Victoria. I saw no need for National Geographic or wildlife television, for when it wanted to introduce me to animals, a monkey, leopard, or family of raccoons would become my fellow pedestrians. There was no urge to tell me of the paradox of zoos when it could show me national parks with hundreds of acres of land.

In Kenya I felt more free than I have ever felt before. The only thing holding me captive was the earth which would grow the food, the sky which would quench the earth of its thirst, and the sun which would warm and help all things to grow. But these masters were sure to give back all that you have put in. When you worked hard, your rewards were great and if you chose to relax so would your crop and cattle. And with a give-and-take relationship like this, one learns that it is okay to take time, time for others, for oneself, time to enjoy and appreciate all that life and earth offer. Some choose to call this type of relationship religion, a covenant with the Lord and her divinity (sky, earth, and animals and I will not deny that there was a strong sense of God or Allah or Sa or Buddha).

A forest burning to the ground germinates the soil, allowing new life to grow. The omnipotence of nature—floods, lightning, hurricanes, earthquakes, the beauty of a cheetah or giraffe running, an open field, the sky, the mountains, the sea—is overwhelming and foreign to me living so long in a concrete jungle. When all of this engulfed me and I took the time to embrace it, I became convinced that there exists a master craftsperson of this creation, that there exists a God.

Kenya has more than (just) given me a new perception of the world; Kenya has widened my world view. I now realize that there are other significant cultures in the world besides a western one. I no longer think of the world in First, Second, and Third World terms. There are aspects of Kenyan values which should be regarded as more First World than American: humanistic sentiments, importance of family, pride of ancestry, appreciation and respect for other peoples' differences.

Also, whereas I ventured off to Kenya to learn about a new culture and its new people, I found that most of the more important discoveries and evaluations were about myself. Upon leaving Kenya I feel that I have grown more confident about my African-Americanness, my perceptions of the world around me, and my expectation of 21/21 vision and beyond. I do not believe I could have gone anywhere else on earth and been as personally challenged.

Paths to Glory: They Marched on Washington to Change America; Home Again, They Saw They'd Changed Themselves, Too
Wil Haygood

Sometimes the day seems as if it only happened in grainy newsreels. Swooping camera shots and heads bobbing in the sun. A great many folk carried little hand fans, the kind you saw in church on summer Sundays.

Now, with laws passed and walls down, it seems to recede even further. So many of the feet that marched in the nation's capital 40 years ago today are gone. There were the known, movie stars and singers, and the unknown, homemakers, factory workers, bricklayers.

Each step that day was a step away from the past. It was the day the word "march" took on muscle, the day it got frozen in those swooping camera moments. It would be uttered like Selma, like Birmingham: "the March." In one velvety and shimmering moment, the nation changed.

So many obits have been written since then. Folded over and tucked into Bibles. And how did those who got there get there? Folded over into history now themselves. Just what were they walking away from?

A quarter of a million people were there that day. Among them, three Ohio souls as joyful as anyone else. As unknown as anyone else. Linked by the day, the place, the march.

Otis Moss was a young minister from Cincinnati. He had met the Rev. Martin Luther King Jr. and followed him into the movement.

Gladys Howard was a housewife. There was so much she didn't know about her own history. About what haunted her husband. So she stepped into her high heels and went to Washington.

Reuben "Bobby" Maxey was not yet out of his teenage years. He had been raised in Mississippi by his grandfather, a man who had seen former slaves and the men who murdered the young Emmett Till.

The boy had to beg money to ride the bus that would take him to the nation's capital. He needed 25 bucks. He went looking for the door of the haunted man.

Elyria is an old industrial town 23 miles west of Cleveland. Runaway slaves once hid out in this terrain, as well as in nearby Oberlin. The Midwestern milieu would become renowned in later years from the writings of novelist Sherwood Anderson, who lived in Elyria from 1906 to 1913 and wrote of desperation in the region. Anderson's writing career evoked people who led desperate lives.

Many blacks arrived here during the last century's Great Migration from the South. Dreaming themselves away—long before any epic speech in the nation's capital—by train, bus, automobile.

One of them was Reuben Maxey. "My father got killed when I was 4, victim of a cafe shootout in Glen Allan, Mississippi," says Reuben, sitting on the back deck of his home in Elyria.

His grandfather, Joseph "Papa" Maxey, was a builder. The two would go together to watch barnstorming Negro League baseball teams, boy and grandfather, rooting into the twilight. The grandfather talked about reading, always reading. He took out subscriptions to the Chicago Defender and the Pittsburgh Courier, popular Negro publications that brought the North right into the South. "They mailed them to a shoe shop on Washington Avenue in Greenville [Miss.], and he would pick them up there," Maxey says of his grandfather.

His grandfather took him to business meetings (segregated) and to National Baptist conventions with big-shot ministers, gliding around hotel lobbies, sleeping in the motels that catered to Negroes. He couldn't take Reuben, however, to the trial of the men accused of the murder of that chubby-faced kid in Mississippi in 1955 by the name of Emmett Till. He told young Reuben it was too dangerous. So Papa Maxey went alone. Till, visiting Mississippi from Chicago, had whistled—so goes the legend—at a white woman in a store in small Money, Miss. The two white men charged with the murder would be acquitted by an all-white jury. "He came back and told me you could hear a pin drop in that courtroom," Maxey says of his grandfather.

In 1959 Reuben left Mississippi for Elyria. He was 15 years old. His mother was already there. Elyria was starkly different, beginning with the high school: "It was integrated."

In 1963 Maxey graduated from high school. He started hearing rumblings about a march in Washington. Some locals were going to charter a bus. Maxey found out the cost of the trip: $25. It was a princely sum for a recent high school graduate, and he simply did not have it. But "I knew it was my destiny to go," he says. "My grandfather had prepared me. And I felt like I would be representing all of Glen Allan, Mississippi."

There was one Negro lawyer in Elyria. His name was John Howard. He had an office on Main Street. Maxey gathered his nerve and strode down the avenue. Then he climbed the steps to talk to a man who wouldn't be going himself to Washington. If he left, there would not be a Negro lawyer in town, and no telling what Negro man or woman might need his services that day.

As long as hands are writing, it will be a story worth writing about:

The Kennedy administration was bothered by the planned march, how it would yank the nation's attention to the issue of civil rights. (Kennedy had depended on Southern Democrats to get him elected.)

The military was put on alert in the nation's capital, for fear of rioting. Plainclothes officers were given instructions to infiltrate as best they could. (They were hardly difficult to spot: Mostly white men, short hair, sunglasses, suit and tie even in the hot weather.)

Across America, especially in the South, the "Colored Only" signs hadn't yet become anyone's collector's items. There were still people alive who had known individuals born into slavery.

The year 1963 was notable for something else: It marked the centennial of the end of American slavery.

Some of those responsible for planning the march—Bayard Rustin, A. Philip Randolph—were old war horses of the civil rights movement. (Randolph had tried to launch such a march in the early 1940s.) King was a young war horse: a mere 34 years old. To everyone who met him, though, he seemed old beyond his years.

Just three months earlier, in May of '63, King, not long from a stay in a Birmingham jail, had swooped through Cleveland. Ten thousand came out to see him. Absent Negro royalty in Hollywood, the ministers in America—Adam Clayton Powell, Gardner Taylor, King—walked as stars right along with Negro jazz musicians, boxers and ballplayers. King's presence in Cleveland had required a police escort.

Not far away, the hours were ticking away in the little town of Elyria. A boy from Mississippi wanted to hit the road.

And a lawyer's wife had her back to one world and her suitcase swinging toward another.

Gladys Mackenzie grew up in Cleveland with her mother, father and seven siblings. Although Cleveland was a city with a charged racial history, she might as well have been living in a cocoon. And the cocoon was nice: the '40s and '50s sailed right by, rather lovely, as she remembers them. "I grew up in a house where chivalry ran rampant," she says.

The boys in her home were required to pull out the chairs for their sisters. Her father—never mind he tended boilers—had the habits of an English dandy. "My dad always kissed the back of my hand."

Her mother insisted on good manners and elegant dress. Gladys Mackenzie never knew about having things thrown at her, epithets or otherwise, because of the color of her skin. "My mother was so protective. I got taken to school and picked up from school."

She got tossed into the real world with her first marriage. She found herself soon enough with four children and trying to make an unhappy marriage work. "We'd break up, get back together for a couple of years," she says of her first husband. "Break up again." Finally came the divorce.

One day in 1949, at the courthouse—she was there to get a certified copy of her divorce—she pulled a cigarette from her pack. A lighter flicked a flame into her view. "The light for my cigarette came, and I followed the arm up to see where it came from and it was him," she says of John Howard.

Howard had actually seen Gladys around Cleveland before meeting her. He told friends he had never seen a woman so beautiful. Her beauty may have discouraged him in the beginning. She confesses as much: "He was afraid to approach me because he thought I was too haughty," says Gladys. Never mind she was a divorcee with four children. Love is its own mystery and Howard fell in love. "I told him I will never, ever get married again," she says. "He said, 'Oh yes you will.' "

They married in 1951.

Gladys Howard didn't consider herself anyone's version of a social activist. "I never heard such things, about lynchings and whatnot." But she started to pick up hints of another world from her new husband.

In fact, there was something about John Howard that worried his wife. To her he seemed haunted. "He would talk about the South, and about not being able to eat where white people ate. He couldn't stay in the same hotels with whites. He said the only time he really felt free was during a trip to Canada."

John Howard was born in 1923 in Elyria. He was a three-sport star athlete in high school. He would later recall that as a youth there were local restaurants where he couldn't "peek in the door." He went to college at Florida A&M in Tallahassee, graduating in 1945. He talked to Gladys about the segregation there—"about rooms he couldn't go in because there were white people in there," she says. He would go on to graduate from the Law School of Franklin University in Columbus.

A few years after they married, the couple left Cleveland and moved to Howard's home town to open a law office. "We found some old furniture," she recalls. "I scrubbed the floors."

He was the sole black lawyer in Elyria.

"When I moved here it was one of the most prejudiced places. They didn't even have a black garbage man," says Gladys.

Oddly enough, a lot of his clients—Howard's practice was mostly family law—were white. "Lots of times white people came to John because they didn't want their business in the streets," says Gladys.

When news of the planned March on Washington hit Elyria, Gladys Howard just knew she was going to go. "I didn't have sense enough to be nervous." So there she stood on departure day in the parking lot shared by Second Baptist Church and Mount Nebo Primitive Baptist Church, just above the Black River.

The bus smelled of perfume and freshly baked food. There were colorful folded blankets. The ride was quiet, pregnant with something no one could quite put into words. They were riding away from the past and toward the unknown. There was a rest stop in Breezewood, Pa. Then another stop, just before Washington. "They made the men get off the bus," recalls Gladys, "so the ladies could change clothes." Gladys told herself she wasn't going to be changing clothes on anybody's bus. She'd wait till Washington.

The planning for the march went right up to the last minute, and there were fears it might not happen at all. When word came down that it would, the Rev. Otis Moss gathered with his congregants in Cincinnati. Then he flew on ahead. So few Negroes flying in the air at that time. He was a long way from a childhood touched by death and uncertainty.

Moss was born in La Grange, Ga. "My mother died when I was 4," he is saying, an hour after delivering a Sunday morning sermon at his current church, Mount Zion Baptist in Cleveland. "At one point she was a country schoolteacher. My father was a sharecropper and also worked on the WPA [Works Progress Administration]. He was killed in an automobile accident when I was 16."

A lady who saw him crying over his father's death offered a roof, a home, and he accepted. Upon graduation from high school, he enrolled at Morehouse College in Atlanta. He worked one summer in Detroit after his freshman year to earn money for his second year in school. But it wasn't enough. He called Dr. Benjamin Mays, the head of Morehouse. "I had $208. Dr. Mays said, 'Take what you have and come on back to school. We'll see what we can do.'"

In 1955—a year away from graduation—Moss went to the National Baptist Convention in Memphis. It was the first time he saw King.

"He had just received his PhD from Boston University," Moss recalls of King. "That was really something else. Dr. Mays had been celebrating that on the Morehouse campus. We had heard about this young minister—Class of '48. The main theme of the convention, however, was Emmett Till. Every preacher had a sermon talking about it."

Powell, the Harlem minister and congressman, was the speaker at Moss's commencement in 1956. "Go from here with a sense of mission," Powell told the grads. "Martin Luther King is waiting on you to come march with him."

"Some of us," Moss says of the call to march, "took it literally."

By 1961, he had his own church in Cincinnati, and a position as one of King's lieutenants in the Southern Christian Leadership Conference. In Cincinnati he marched, led pickets, got arrested: A dues-paying, King man.

Reuben Maxey had gotten two $10 bills and a $5 bill. "I folded it up in my pocket," he says. Then he walked over to Second Baptist, headquarters for the marchers. "I told them I wanted to go." He handed over the money. "They put me on the list to go."

His mother's boyfriend, a man named Henry, drove him back to the church late on the afternoon of Aug. 27.

Maxey looked around and spotted his aunt, Ruby Jones. He didn't know she'd be on the bus. She was in her sixties and participated in an activity not talked about then in polite company in Elyria: She ran the numbers. Now Ruby Jones wanted to march.

He spotted Myrtle Stiles, who was sitting there with her son and two foster children. Myrtle Stiles did "day" work—which meant she cleaned and scrubbed for families in town. She also raised foster children. "It wasn't the richest kind of work," recalls her daughter, Barbara Paige. Hardworking Myrtle Stiles wanted to march.

The quiet of the bus ride didn't surprise Maxey. "Nothing like this had ever happened before."

And then they were there. They yawned and spread their arms and looked all around. It was Aug. 28, 1963. "I got off the bus and started searching for people from Mississippi," says Maxey. It was as if he thought they might appear like apparitions out of his boyhood. There were so many people, but he couldn't find a Mississippian.

He had enough money to buy himself a hamburger for breakfast. His head kept swiveling. "I had never been around that many people at one time. I just started to walk."

Otis Moss was in another part of the crowd. "It was an unusual thing that happened," he recalls. "Without any direction, the crowd just moved out toward the Lincoln Memorial."

Gladys Howard, having been unwilling to change clothes on the bus, made a beeline to a Washington hotel. "When I stepped into the elevator in the hotel," she says, "there was Sammy Davis Jr. and Harry Belafonte. I can remember what I was wearing. All orange. And my high heels."

She reconnected with the Elyria crowd. She started walking and she thought about her history, her Negro history ("I didn't know about such a thing") and her American history and why her husband could have such haunted looks on his face sometimes.

The placards echoed the determination: "WE MARCH FOR JOBS FOR ALL NOW." "WE DEMAND DECENT HOUSING NOW." "WE MARCH FOR INTEGRATED SCHOOLS NOW."

"The speeches were all great," recalls Howard. "But you know what really got to me? Peter, Paul and Mary singing 'Blowin' in the Wind.' The crowd was just going wild. Oh my. Whoooo."

An old lady, sitting in an Elyria restaurant, is singing a Bob Dylan song she heard 40 years ago on a stretch of pavement in the nation's capital.

> Yes, how many years can some people exist
> Before they're allowed to be free?
> Yes, how many years can a man turn his head
> Pretending he just doesn't see?
> The answer, my friend, is blowin' in the wind.

When the speeches started rolling, Maxey couldn't move. Then came King's words: "It stood you still," he says. "It still rings. You just knew and felt it was something special."

When it was over, King and the old war horses went over to the White House. Reuben Maxey and Myrtle Stiles and Gladys Howard and Ruby Jones went on back home, to Elyria.

They rode through the night and, when they alighted from the bus, Elyria hadn't changed one bit. And yet everything had changed.

"You just felt different," says Gladys Howard. "It seemed like 'we' could now do anything."

In the past she had never talked of "we." But now she had a history, a husband who could talk about things he had seen in the South and go stone silent, and she now knew better why. "I just didn't know before."

But now things were blowin' in the wind. Gladys Howard went home to her husband, the sole Negro lawyer in town. The man who had pulled $25 from his pocket and handed it to a young boy who dreamed of making a trip. "He never said one word to me," recalls Maxey.

When Maxey got home, he had a phone call to make to his grandfather. "I said, 'Papa Maxey, I just got back from the march.' He said, 'That's wonderful. I'm sorry I couldn't have been there with you.' I said, 'Papa, I marched for myself and I marched for you.' "

This is what stands out in the memory of a 59-year-old man sitting in his back yard on a beautiful afternoon with Sunday dinner in the oven: He had climbed on a bus 40 years ago and looked around, front to back, looked at the white bus driver, looked front to back again, and began searching for a seat. There was freedom in his stride. As if the very air on the bus were scented with it: "I realized that you could sit anywhere you wanted to sit."

The Venus Hip Hop and the Pink Ghetto

Negotiating Spaces for Women

Imani Perry

It seemed to happen suddenly. Every time one turned on BET (Black Entertainment Television) or MTV, one encountered a disturbing music video: Black men rapped surrounded by dozens of black and Latina women dressed in bathing suits, or scantily clad in some other fashion. Video after video proved the same, each one more objectifying than the former. Some took place in strip clubs, some at the pool, at the beach, or in hotel rooms, but the recurrent theme was dozens of half-naked women. The confluence of cultural trends leading to this moment merits more extended scholarly attention than it will receive here, but, in short, it occurred as pornography became increasingly mainstreamed and alluded to in objectifying shows such as *Baywatch*, as the tech boom gave rise to a celebration of consumption and widespread wealth, and as hip hop continued its pattern of shifting dominant foci—from political consciousness to social realism to gangsterism to humor to in this moment, a hedonist conspicuous consumption previously largely associated with Miami Bass music.

The sexist message embraced here proves complex. Its attack on black female identity is multifaceted. First, and most obviously, the women are commodified. They appear in the videos quite explicitly as property, not unlike the luxury cars, Rolex watches, and platinum and diamond medallions also featured. The male stars of the videos do not have access to these legions of women because of charisma or sexual prowess, but rather because they are able to "buy" them due to their wealth. The message is not, "I am a Don Juan," but instead, "I am rich and these are my spoils." Not only are the women commodified, but sex as a whole is.

Moreover the women are often presented as vacuous, doing nothing in the videos but swaying around seductively. Often, they avert their eyes from the camera, allowing the viewer to have a voyeuristic relationship to them. Or they look at the camera, eyes fixed in seductive invitation, mouth slightly open. Any signs of thought, humor, irony, intelligence, anger, or any other emotion, prove extremely rare. Even the manner in which the women dance signals cultural destruction. Black American dance is discursive in that sexuality is usually combined with humor, and that the body is used to converse with other moving bodies. Yet the women who appear in these videos usually dance in a two-dimensional fashion, in a derivative but nonintellectual version of black dance more reminiscent of symbols of pornographic male sexual fantasy than the ritual, conversational, and sexual traditions of black dance. Despite all the gyrations of the video models, their uninterested, wet-lipped languor stands in sharp contrast to (for example) the highly sexualized booty dancing of the Deep South, which features polyrhythmic rear end movement, innuendo, and sexual bravado.

This use of black women in the music videos of male hip hop artists often makes very clear reference to the culture of strip clubs and pornography. Women dance around poles, and porn actresses and exotic dancers are often the stars of the videos, bringing the movement-based symbols of their trades with them. The introduction of porn symbols into music videos is consistent with a larger movement that began in the late 1990s, in which pornographic imagery, discourses, and themes began to enter American popular culture. Powerful examples may be found in the *Howard Stern Show,* E! Entertainment Television, and daytime talk shows. Porn film stars attain mainstream celebrity, exotic dancers are routine talk show guests, and the public face of lesbianism becomes not a matter of the sexual preference of women, but of the sexual consumption and fantasy life of men. The videos discussed here make for an appropriate companion piece to this wider trend. While the music videos are male-centered in that they assume a heterosexual male viewer who will appreciate the images of sexually available young women, it is clear that young women watch them as well. The messages such videos send to young women are instructions on how to be sexy and how to look in order to capture the attention of men with wealth and charisma. Magazines geared toward young women have given instructions on how women should participate in their own objectification for decades, but never before has a genre completely centralized black women in this process.[1]

The beauty ideal for black women presented in these videos is as impossible to achieve as the waif-thin models in *Vogue* magazine are for white women. There is a preference for lighter-complexioned women of color, with long and straight or loosely curled hair. Hair that hangs slick against the head when wet as the model emerges out of a swimming pool (a common video image) is at a premium too. Neither natural tightly curled hair nor most coarse relaxed hair becomes slick, shining, and smooth when wet. It is a beauty ideal that contrasts sharply to the real hair of most black women. When brown-skinned or dark-skinned women appear in the videos, they always have hair that falls well below shoulder length, despite the fact that the average length of black women's natural hair in the United States today is four to six inches, according to Barry Fletcher.[2]

Camera shots linger on very specific types of bodies. The videos have assimilated the African American ideal of a large rotund behind, but the video ideal also features a very small waist, large breasts, and slim shapely legs and arms. Often, while the camera features the faces of lighter-complexioned women, it will linger on the behinds of darker women, implying the same thing as the early 1990s refrain from Sir Mix-A-Lot's "Baby Got Back," "L.A. face with an Oakland booty."[3] That is, the ideal features a "high-status" face combined with a highly sexualized body read by the viewer as the body of a poor or working-class woman.[4] Color is aligned with class, and women are created or valued by how many fantasy elements have been pieced together in their bodies.

While one might argue that the celebration of the rotund behind signals an appreciation of black women's bodies, the image taken as a whole indicates how difficult a beauty ideal this proves to attain for anyone. A small percentage of women, even black women, have such Jessica Rabbit proportions. As journalist Tomika Anderson wrote for *Essence* magazine, "In movies, rap songs and on television, we're told that the attractive, desirable and sexy ladies are the ones with 'junk in their trunks.' And even though this might seem ridiculous, some of us actually listen to (and care about) these obviously misogynistic subliminal messages—just as we are affected by racialized issues like hair texture and skin tone."[5]

Americans have reacted with surprise to abundant social scientific data showing that black girls comprise the social group that scores highest on self-esteem assessments and that they tend to have much better body images than white girls. While these differences in esteem and body image are to a large extent attributable to cultural differences, with black girls having been socialized to see beauty in strong personality characteristics and grooming rather than in particular body types, I believe the media plays a role as well. White girls find themselves inundated with images of beauty impossible for most to attain: sheets of blond hair, waif-thin bodies, large breasts, no cellulite, small but round features, and high cheekbones. Over the years, black women have remained relatively absent from public images of beauty, an exclusion which may have saved black girls from aspiring to impossible ideals. But with the recent explosion of objectified and highly idealized images of black women in music videos, it is quite possible that the body images and even self-esteem of black girls will begin to drop, particularly as they move into adolescence and their bodies come under scrutiny. Many of the music videos feature neighborhood scenes including children. In them, little black girls are beautiful. They laugh, smile, play double Dutch, and more. They are full of personality, and they emerge as cultural celebrations with their hair plaited, twisted, or curled and adorned with colorful ribbons to match their outfits in characteristic black girl grooming style. And yet the adult women generally remain two-dimensional and robbed of personality. Is this what puberty is supposed to hold for these girls?

A Feminist Response?

In such troubling moments, we should all look for a gender-critical voice—in the world, in ourselves. Where do we find a response to this phenomenon that will compellingly argue against such characterizations of black women, where do we find a hip hop feminism? Hip hop has seen a feminist presence since the 1980s in such figures as Salt-N-Pepa, Queen Latifah, and MC Lyte, and hip hop feminism continues to exist despite the widespread objectification of black female bodies. We can find numerous examples of feminist and antisexist songs in hip hop and hip hop soul. Mary J. Blige, Lauryn Hill, Destiny's Child, Missy Elliot, Erykah Badu, and others each have their individual manner of representing black female identity and self-definition.

Alicia Keys, one of the crop of singer-songwriters who fit into the hip hop nation, presents an image that contrasts sharply with the video models. The classically trained pianist who has claimed Biggie Smalls and Jay-Z among her music influences appeared in her first music video for the song "Fallin' " in a manner both stylish and sexy but decidedly not self-exploiting. Her hair in cornrows, wearing a leather jacket and fedora, she sings with visible bluesy emotion. She describes repeatedly falling in love with a man who is not good for her. In the music video, Keys travels by bus to visit the man in prison. This element figures as an important signifier of hip hop sensibilities, as rap music is the one art form that consistently engages with the crisis of black imprisonment and considers imprisoned people as part of its community. As Keys rides in the bus, she gazes at women prisoners working in a field outside the window. They sing the refrain to the song, "I keep on fallin', in and out, of love with you/I never loved someone the way I love you."[6] The women on the bus riding to visit men in prison mirror the women outside of the bus, who are prison laborers. This visual duality comments on the often overlooked problem of black female imprisonment in conversations about the rise of American imprisonment and black imprisonment in particular. It makes reference to two issues facing black women. One is that many black women are the mates of imprisoned men. The second is that many black women wind up in prison because they unwittingly or naively became involved with men participating in illegal activities.[7] The video poignantly alludes to these social ills with a close-up of a stone-faced woman in prison clothing with a single tear rolling down her cheek. Although, like Badu, Keys frequently appeared on her first albums to be narratively enmeshed in a "stand by your man" ethos that propped up male-centered heteronormativity, both of their voices and images offer dramatic feminist moments notable for their departure from objectifying and exploitative depictions.

Singer-songwriter India Arie offers another critical example of a black feminist space in the hip hop world. A young brown-skinned and dread-locked woman, she burst on the music scene with her song and companion music video "Video" which criticize the image of women in videos. In the refrain she sings, "I'm not your average girl from a video/My body's not built like a supermodel but/I've learned to love myself unconditionally/because I am a queen."[8]

Similar lyrics assert that value is found in intelligence and integrity rather than expensive clothes, liquor, and firearms. The video celebrates Arie who smiles and dances and pokes fun at the process of selecting girls for music videos. She rides her bicycle into the sunshine with her guitar strapped across her shoulder. Arie refuses to condemn artists who present a sexy image but has stated that she will not wear a skirt above calf length on stage and that she will do nothing that will embarrass her family. Musically, while her sound is folksy soul, she does understand her work as being related to hip hop. "I'm trying to blend acoustic and hip-hop elements," she explains. "I used the most acoustic-sounding drum samples, to have something loud enough to compete with other records, but to keep the realistic, softer feel."[9] Arie understands her work as inflected with hip hop sensibilities, more than with the music's compositional elements. She says: "I don't define hip-hop the way a record company would. The thread that runs though both my music and hip-hop is that it's a very precise expression of my way of life. It's like blues; it's very real and honest output of emotion into a song. Because of that legacy, my generation now has an opportunity to candidly state our opinions. That's what my album is about. I just wanna be me."[10]

Arie's definition of hip hop as honest self-expression is true to the ideology at the heart of the genre at its beginnings, a concept that multitudes of hip hop artists continue to profess to. Yet that element of hip hop stands in tension with the process of celebrity creation. The "honest" words in hip hop exist in a swamp of image making. It does not suffice to examine the clear and simple feminist presences in hip hop; we must consider the murkier ones as well. When it comes to feminist messages, often the words and language of a hip hop song may have feminist content, but the visual image may be implicated in the subjugation of black women. Unlike the individualistic and expressive visuals we have of Arie, Keys, Jill Scott, or Missy Elliot, other artists are often marketed in a manner quite similar to the way in which objectified video models are presented.

Tensions Between Texts

Wholesome young stars like Arie and Keys present both strong and respectable images of black womanhood, yet those women who are "sexy" in particular have a much more difficult time carving out a feminist space for themselves. In an earlier piece, "It's My Thang and I'll Swing It the Way that I Feel: Sexual Subjectivity and Black Women Rappers," I argued for the existence of a feminist space in hip hop in which women articulated sexual subjectivity and desire.[11] While I still do believe this is possible, I find it more difficult to achieve now. When the women articulating subjectivity are increasingly presented in visual media as objects rather than subjects, as they are now, their statement to the world is ambiguous at best, and, at worst, the feminist message of their work will become undermined. Joan Morgan reflects on the tension that this presents in her work, which details the conflicts facing a woman with a feminist identity and the erotics of a hip hop market culture: "Am I no longer down for the cause if I admit that while total gender equality is an interesting intellectual concept, it doesn't do a damn thing for me erotically. That, truth be told, men with too many feminist sensibilities have never made my panties wet, at least not like that reformed thug nigga who can make even the most chauvinistic 'wassup baby' feel like a sweet wet tongue darting in and out of your ear."[12] The question is whether the appeal to the erotics of male desire proves too strong to still make the sexy female MC a voice "for the cause."

A musical artist occupies a multitextual space in popular culture. Lyrics, interviews, music, and videos together create a collage, often finely planned, from which an audience is supposed to form impressions. But the texts may conflict with one another. Lil' Kim, the much discussed, critiqued, and condemned nasty-talking bad girl of hip hop, is a master of shock appeal. Her outfits often expose her breasts, her nipples covered by sequined pasties color-coordinated with the rest of her attire. Despite Kim's visual and lyrical vulgarity, many of her critics admit to finding her endearing. Her interviewers know her as sweet-natured and generous. But Lil' Kim stands as a contradiction because while she interviews as a vulnerable and sweet woman, she raps with the hardness adored by her fans. She has an impressive aggressive sexual presence, and she has often articulated a sexual subjectivity through words, along with an in-your-face camera presence. However, as Kim has developed as an entertainer, it has become clear that her image is complicit in the oppressive language of American cinematography in regard to women's sexuality. She has adopted a Pamela-Anderson-in-brown-skin aesthetic, calling on pornographic tropes but losing the subversiveness sometimes apparent in her early career. Andre Leon Talley of *Vogue* magazine noted her transformation from an "around the way girl" with a flat chest, big behind, and jet black (or green, or blue) weave to the celebrity Kim who shows off breast implants and shakes her long blond hair.[13] In her videos, the camera angles exploit her sexuality. In the video for the song "How Many Licks," she appears as a Barbie-type doll, her body parts welded together in a factory. The video stands as an apt metaphor for her self-commodification and use of white female beauty ideals. The video closes off its own possibilities. The doll factory image might have operated as a tongue-in-cheek criticism of image making or white female beauty ideals, but, instead the video functions as a serious vehicle for Kim to be constructed as beautiful and seductive with blond hair and blue eyes. To be a doll in American popular culture is to be perfect, and she will satisfy many male fantasies as many times as she is replicated. Over several years, Kim has become defined more by her participation in codes of pornographic descriptions of women than by her challenging of concepts of respectability or her explicit sexuality.

It is a delicate balance, but it is important to distinguish between sexual explicitness and internalized sexism. While many who have debated the image of female sexuality have put "explicit" and "self-objectifying" on one side and "respectable" and "covered-up" on the other, I find this a flawed means of categorization. The nature of sexual explicitness proves important to consider, and will become more so as more nuanced images will emerge. There is a creative possibility for liberatory explicitness because it may expand the confines of what women are allowed to say and do. We just need to refer to the history of blues music—one full of raunchy, irreverent, and transgressive women artists—for examples. Yet the overwhelming prevalence of the Madonna/whore dichotomy in American culture means that any woman who uses explicit language or images in her creative expression is in danger of being symbolically cast into the role of whore regardless of what liberatory intentions she may have, particularly if she does not have complete control over her image.

Let us turn to other examples to further explore the tensions between text and visual image in women's hip hop. Eve has emerged as one of the strongest feminist voices in hip hop today. She rhymes against domestic violence and for women's self-definition and self-reliance. She encourages women to hold men in their lives accountable for disrespectful or less-than-loving behavior. Yet the politics of Eve's image are conflicted. She has appeared in music videos for songs on which she has collaborated with male hip hop artists, videos filled with the stock legions of objectified video models. On the one hand, Eve's provocative dress validates the idea of attractiveness exemplified by the models. But the rapper is also distinguished from these women because she is the star. She appears dignified and expressive, while they do not. Her distinction from the other women supports their objectification. She is the exception that makes the rule, and it is her exceptionalism that allows her to have a voice. Similar dynamics have appeared in videos featuring hip hop singer Lil' Mo. In fact, a number of women hip hop artists who claim to be the only woman in their crews, to be the only one who can hang with the fellas, through their exceptionalism make arguments that justify the subjugation of other women, even the majority of women.

Moreover, both Eve and Lil' Kim often speak of the sexual power they have as deriving from their physical attractiveness to men. It is therefore a power granted by male desire, rather than a statement of the power of female sexual desire. While neither artist has completely abandoned the language of empowering female subjectivity in her music, any emphasis on power granted through conventional attractiveness in this media language limits the feminist potential of the music. In one of the songs in which Eve most explicitly expresses desire, "Gotta Man," the desire is rooted in the man's ability to dominate. She describes him as "the only thug in the hood who is wild enough to tame me,"[14] and therefore she is "the shrew," willingly stripped of her defiant power by a sexual union. Instead of using her aggressive tongue to challenge prevailing sexist sexual paradigms, she affirms them by saying that she simply needs a man stronger than most, stronger than she, to bring everything back to normal.

The tensions present in hip hop through the interplay of the visual and the linguistic, and the intertextuality of each medium, are various. Even Lauryn Hill, often seen as the redeemer of hip hop due to her dignified, intellectually challenging, and spiritual lyricism has a complicated image. As a member of the Fugees, she often dressed casually in baggy yet interesting clothes thoroughly rooted in hip hop style. It seems no accident that she became a celebrity, gracing the covers of British *GQ*, *Harper's Bazaar,* and numerous other magazines, when her sartorial presentation changed. Her skirts got shorter and tighter, her cleavage more pronounced, and her dreadlocks longer. When she began to sport an alternative style that nevertheless garnered mainstream acceptability, she was courted by high-end designers like Armani. As Lauryn's image became more easily absorbable into the language of American beauty culture, her celebrity grew. She even appeared on the cover of *Sophisticates Black Hair Magazine*, a black beauty guide that usually relegates natural hair to a couple of small pictures of women with curly afros or afro weaves, while the vast majority of its photos show women with long straight weaves and relaxers. The hip hop artist was certainly one of the few *Sophisticates* cover models ever to have natural hair, and the only with locks. (Interestingly, the silhouette of the locks was molded into the shape of shoulder-length relaxed hair.) In the issue of British *GQ* that featured Lauryn as a cover model, journalist Sanjiv writes, "She could be every woman in a way Chaka Khan could only sing about—the decade's biggest new soul arrival with the looks of a supermodel and Hollywood knocking at her door."[15]

In September of 1999, Lauryn appeared on the cover of *Harper's Bazaar*. The article inside discussed her community service projects, and the cover celebrated her model-like beauty. Of course, the cover had something subversive to it. Dark-skinned and kinky-haired Lauryn Hill was beautiful, and the image was ironic. Her locks were styled into the shape of a Farah Fawcett flip, a tongue-in-cheek hybridization at once referencing the seventies heyday of unprocessed afro hair and that era's symbol of white female beauty, Farah Fawcett. The hybrid cover proves analogous to the diverse elements used in the creation of the new in hip hop. Nevertheless, it is important to note that Lauryn became widely attractive when her silhouette—thin body and big hair—matched that of mainstream beauty. So even as the artist has been treated as the symbol of black women's dignity and intelligence in hip hop (and rightfully so given her brilliant lyricism), she too found herself pulled into the sexist world of image making. Although she has made some public appearances since cutting off her long hair, getting rid of the makeup, and returning to baggy clothes, publicity about her has noticeably dropped.[16]

In contrast to Lauryn Hill, Erykah Badu has remained unapologetically committed to the drama of her neo-Afrocentric stylings in her image making, and she therefore has only achieved limited mainstream beauty acceptance. After she shaved her head, doffed her enormous head wrap, and wore a dress shaped like a ball gown (although in reality it was a deconstructed, rough textured "warrior princess," as she called it, work of art), Joan Rivers named her the best-dressed attendee at the 2000 Grammy Awards. Yet she also, rather than simply complimenting her dress or style, said that this was the best Badu had ever looked and that she was an extremely beautiful woman. Rivers appeared to insinuate that the singer was receiving recognition for coming closer to looking "as beautiful as she really is," not for truly being the best dressed. A 2001 *Vogue* article discussed Badu in the context of how ugliness could prove beautiful and how fine the line between the beauty and ugliness was, making reference to her unusual attire, again a sign of how disturbing the beauty industry finds her unwillingness to fit into standard paradigms of female presentation, even as her large hazel eyes and high cheekbones undeniable appeal to individuals in that industry.

I used the examples of Lil' Kim, Eve, Lauryn Hill, and Erykah Badu—all very distinct artists—to draw attention to the kinds of tensions that might exist between a feminist content in hip hop lyrics and the visual image of the artist. I hope these examples encourage readers, as viewers and listeners of popular culture, to become attuned to the multitextual character of the music world and to read as many layers of the media as possible.

The Colonizer and Colonized

In her essay "Language and the Writer," novelist and cultural critic Torsi Cade Bambara reminds us that "the creative imagination has been colonized. The global screen has been colonized. And the audience—readers and viewers—is in bondage to an industry. It has the money, the will, the muscle, and the propaganda machine oiled up to keep us all locked up in a delusional system—as to even what America is."[17] Musical artists are cultural actors, but those backed by record labels are hardly independent actors. In music videos and photo layouts, they exist within what Cade Bambara has described as a colonized space, particularly in regard to race and gender. In a context in which a short, tight dress and a camera rolling up the body, lingering on behinds and breasts, holds particular power with regard to gender and personal value, we must ask how powerful words can be that intend to contradict such objectification. How subversive are revolutionary words in a colonized visual world full of traditional gender messages?

Notes

1. The most prominent black women's magazines, *Essence* and *Honey*, as well as *Girl*, geared toward a multicultural audience of adolescent girls, all have an explicitly feminist agenda. Readers of these magazines are not offered articles about how to seduce men or how to appear sexy, the typical fare of such publications as *Cosmopolitan*, YM, and *Glamour*.

2. Barry Fletcher, *Why Black Women are Losing their Hair* (New York: Unity Publishing, 2000), ii.

3. Sir Mix-A-Lot, "Baby Got Back," (Mix a Lot Records 1993).

4. There are many hip hop lyrics that identify the voluptuous body with women who live in housing projects or who come from the hood. Additionally, the assumption that lighter-complexioned black women are of a higher socioeconomic status, or have greater sexual desirability, constitutes a longstanding aspect of black American culture. Although this cultural phenomenon was challenged in the late civil rights era, it flourishes in the images that appear in many television shows, movies, books, and in the tendency of black male celebrities and athletes to choose very light-complexioned spouses if they marry black women.

5. Tomika Anderson, "Nothing Butt the Truth," *Essence*, November 2001, 116.

6. Alicia Keys, "Fallin' " *Songs in A Minor* (BMG/J, 2001).

7. President Clinton pardoned Kendra Smith, the most famous representative of this population, who spent years in prison as the result of her boyfriend's crimes.

8. India Arie, "Video," *Acoustic Soul* (Motown, 2001).

9. India Arie, interview, available at http://ww.mtv.com.

10. Ibid.

11. Imani Perry, "It's My Thang and I'll Swing It the Way that I Feel: Sexual Subjectivity and Black Women Rappers," in *Race, Class, and Gender in the Media,* ed. Gaul Dines and Jean M. Humez (Thousand Oaks, CA: Sage Press, 1994).

12. Joan Morgan, *When Chickenheads Come Home to Roost: My Life as a Hip-Hop Feminist* (New York: Simon and Schuster, 1999).

13. Andre Leon Talley, "Style Fax," *Vogue* November 1999, 18.

14. Eve, "Gotta Man," *RuffRyders* (Interscope, 2000).

15. Sanjiv, "Queen of the Hill: Lauryn Fugee Finds Her Voice," GQ (UK), October 1998, 188.

16. At the time of the publication of this book. I have found no interviews or articles addressing the reason for Lauryn Hill's second transformation, but it will be interesting to see if she understands it as a rejection of the way in which she was styled in order to be palatable to a widespread audience.

17. Toni Cade Bambara, "Language and the Writer," in *Deep Sightings and Rescue Missions: Fiction, Essays, and Conversations,* ed. Toni Morrison. (New York: Pantheon, 1996), 140.

Gangsta Culture
bell hooks

. . . Young beautiful brilliant black power male militants were the first black leftists to loudly call out the evils of capitalism. And during that call they unmasked wage slavery, naming it for what it was. Yet at the end of the day a black man needed money to live. If he was not going to get it working for the man, it could come from hustling his own people. Black power militants, having learned from Dr. King and Malcolm X how to call out the truth of capitalist-based materialism, identified it as gangsta culture. Patriarchal manhood was the theory and gangsta culture was its ultimate practice. No wonder then that black males of all ages living the protestant work ethic, submitting in the racist white world, envy the lowdown hustlers in the black communities who are not slaves to white power. As one young gang member put it, "working was considered weak."

Black men of all classes have come to see the market-driven capitalist society we are living in as a modern Babylon without rules, without any meaningful structure of law and order as a world where "gangsta culture" is the norm. Powerful patriarchal players (mostly white but now and then men of color) in mainstream corporate or high-paying government jobs do their own version of the gangsta culture game; they just do not get caught or when they do they know how to play so they do not end up in jail for life or on death row. This is the big stage most black male hustlers want to perform on, but they rarely get a chance because they lack the educational preparation needed. Or their lust for easy money that comes quick and fast does them in: soul murder by greed. In his book *The Envy of the World: On Being a Black Man in America*, Ellis Cose deliberately downplays the impact of racially based exploitation on black men's lives. To make his point that black men, and not systems of domination (which he suggests they should be able to transcend with the right values), are the problem, he must exclude any discussion of work, of joblessness.

Cose comes close to a discussion of work when he writes about young black male investment in gangsta culture but he never really highlights black male thinking about jobs and careers. When discussing the lure of the "street" he makes the important point that the street often seduces bright young males attracting them to a life of hustling, of selling drugs. Cose contends: "The lure of drug money for young inner-city boys is so strong because it offers such huge rewards to those who otherwise would have very little." He quotes a former drug dealer who puts it this way: "I came from poverty and I wanted nice things and money and everything. . . . I quit high school and . . . I just got caught up. . . . It was like, 'I'm eighteen. I want my money now.' " The grandiose sense of entitlement to money that this black male felt is part of the seduction package of patriarchal masculinity.

Every day black males face a culture that tells them that they can never really achieve enough money or power to set them free from racist white tyranny in the work world. Mass media schools the young in the values of patriarchal masculinity. On mass media screens today, whether television or movies, mainstream work is usually portrayed as irrelevant, money is god, and the outlaw guy who breaks the rules prevails. Contrary to the notion that black males are lured by the streets, mass media in patriarchal culture has already prepared them to seek themselves in the streets, to find their manhood in the streets, by the time they are six years old. Propaganda works best when the male mind is young and not yet schooled in the art of critical thinking. Few studies examine the link between black male fascination with gangsta culture and early childhood consumption of unchecked television and movies that glamorize brute patriarchal maleness. A biased imperialist white-supremacist patriarchal mass media teaches young black males that the street will be their only home. And it lets mainstream black males know that they are just an arrest away from being on the street. This media teaches young black males that the patriarchal man is a predator, that only the strong and the violent survive.

This is what the young black power males believed. It is why so many of them are dead. Gangsta culture is the essence of patriarchal masculinity. Popular culture tells young black males that only the predator will survive. Cleaver explains the message in *Soul on Ice:* "In a culture that secretly subscribes to the piratical ethic of 'every man for himself'—the social Darwinism of 'survival of the fittest' being far from dead, manifesting itself in our ratrace political system of competing parties, in our dog-eat-dog economic system of profit and loss, and in our adversary system of justice where truth is secondary to the skill and connections of the advocate—the logical culmination of this ethic, on a person-to-person level, is that the weak are seen as the natural and just prey of the strong." This is the ethic lots of boys in our society learn from mass media, but black boys, way too many of them fatherless, take it to heart.

Prisons in our nation are full of intelligent capable black men who could have accomplished their goals of making money in a responsible legitimate way but who commit crimes for small amounts of money because they cannot delay gratification. Locked down, utterly disenfranchised, black men in prison are in a place where critical reflection and education for critical consciousness could occur (as was the case for Malcolm X), but more often than not it is a place where patriarchal maleness is reinforced. Gangsta culture is even more glamorized in our nation's prisons because they are the modern jungle where only the strong survive. This is the epitome of the dog-eat-dog Darwinian universe Cleaver describes. Movies represent the caged black male as strong and powerful (this is the ultimate false consciousness) and yet these images are part of the propaganda that seduce and entice black male audiences of all classes. Black boys from privileged classes learn from this same media to envy the manhood of those who relish their roles as predators, who are eager to kill and be killed in their quest to get the money, to get on top.

In his memoir *The Ice Opinion*, rapper and actor Ice T talks about the lure of crime as a way to make easy money. Describing crime as "like any other job" he calls attention to the fact that most young black men have no problem with committing crimes if it gets them money. He makes the point that it is not only money that attracts black males to criminal activity, that "there's definitely something sexy about crime" because "it takes a lot of courage to fuck the system." There is rarely anything sexy about paid labor. Often black males choose crime to avoid the hierarchy in the workforce that places them on the bottom. As Ice T explains: "Crime is an equal-opportunity employer. It never discriminates. Anybody can enter the field. You don't need a college education. You don't need a G.E.D. You don't have to be any special color. You don't need white people to like you. You're self-employed. As a result, criminals are very independent people. They don't like to take orders. That's why they get into this business. There are no applications to fill out, no special dress codes. . . . There's a degree of freedom in being a criminal." Of course Ice T's cool description of crime seems rather pathetic when stacked against the large number of black males who are incarcerated, many of them for life, for "easy money" crimes that gained them less than a hundred dollars. The fantasy of easy money is pushed in popular culture by movies. It is pushed by state-supported lotteries. And part of the seduction is making individuals, especially men, feel that they deserve money they have not earned.

Of course there are lots of black males out in the world making money by legitimate and illegitimate means and they are still trapped in the pain of patriarchal masculinity. Unlike the world of responsible legitimate work, which, when not exploitative, can be humanizing, the world of money making, of greed, always dehumanizes. Hence the reality that black males who have "made it" in the mainstream often see their lives as empty and meaningless. They may be as nihilistic as their disenfranchised underclass poor black brothers. Both may turn to addiction as a way to ease the pain.

Very few black men of any class in this nation feel they are doing work they find meaningful, work that gives them a sense of purpose. Although there are more black male academics than ever before in our nation, even among the highest paid there is a lack of job satisfaction. Work satisfies black males more when it is not perceived to be the location of patriarchal manhood but rather when it is the site of meaningful social interaction as well as fulfilling labor.

There has been a resurgence of black-owned businesses in the nineties precisely because many black male entrepreneurs find that racism abounds in work arenas to such a grave extent that even jobs they liked were still made unbearably stressful. Owning one's own business and being the boss has allowed individual black men to find dignity in labor.

Hedonistic materialist consumerism with its overemphasis on having money to waste has been a central cause of the demoralization among working men of all races. Responsible middle-class black men who embody all that is best about the Protestant work ethic find that work satisfies best when it is not placed at the center of one's evaluation of manhood or selfhood but rather when it is seen simply as one aspect of a holistic life. At times an individual black male may be somewhat dissatisfied with his job and yet still feel it is worthwhile to endure this dissatisfaction because of the substantive ways he uses his wages to create a more meaningful life. This holds true for working black men across class. Throughout my life, I have been inspired by the example of my father. Working within a racist system where he was often treated disrespectfully by unenlightened white people, he still managed to have standards of excellence that governed his job performance. He, along with my mom, taught all his children the importance of commitment to work and giving your best at any job.

Despite these lessons our brother K. has been, throughout his life, lured by easy money. Lucky, in that his attempts to participate in gangsta culture happened early enough in his life to push him in other directions in midlife, he is still struggling to find a career path that will provide greater satisfaction for the soul. Like so many black males in our culture, he wants to make lots of money. Though he has a responsible well-paying job, his ability to be proud of where he is and what he has accomplished is often diminished by fantasies of having more. When he focuses his energies on doing more, rather than having more, his life satisfaction increases.

During the periods of his life when he was unemployed K. did spend his time working on self-development. Many black males in our culture face joblessness at some point in their lives. For some unemployment may be their lot for months, for others years. Patriarchal masculinity, which says that if a man is not a worker he is nothing, assaults the self-esteem of any man who absorbs this thinking. Often black males reject this way of thinking about work. This rejection is a positive gesture, but they often do not replace this rejection of the patriarchal norm with a constructive alternative.

Given the state of work in our nation, a future where widespread joblessness, downsizing, and reduction in wages is becoming more normal, all men, and black men in particular, are in need of alternative visions of work. Throughout their history in the United States decolonized black men have found those alternatives. Significantly, they see unemployment as time to nurture creativity and self-awareness. Not making money opened the space for them to rethink investment in materialism; it changed their perspectives.

They engaged in a paradigm shift. Martin Luther King, Jr., in his critique of materialism, describes this shift as a "revolution of values." King invited black men and all men to "work within the framework of democracy to bring about a better distribution of wealth" using "powerful economic resources to eliminate poverty from the earth." Enlightened individual black men who make no money or not enough money have learned to turn away from the marketplace and turn toward being—finding out who they are, what they feel, and what they want out of life within and beyond the world of money. Even though they have not chosen "leisure" time, they have managed to use it productively. In his 1966 anti-war speech at Berkeley, Stokely Carmichael offered this utopian vision: "The society we seek to build among black people is not a capitalistic one. It is a society in which the spirit of community and of humanistic love prevail." Imagine the revolution of values and actions that would occur if black men were collectively committed to creating love and building community.

Until a progressive vision of productive unemployment can be shared with black men collectively, intervening on the patriarchal assumption that equates unemployment with loss of value as well as challenging the materialist assumption that you are what you can buy, most black men (like many of their white counterparts among the poor and disenfranchised) will continue to confront a work world and a culture of joblessness that demoralizes and dehumanizes the spirit. Black male material survival will be ensured only as they turn away from fantasies of wealth and the notion that money will solve all problems and make everything better, and turn toward the reality of sharing resources, reconceptualizing work, and using leisure for the practice of self-actualization.

Putting Poverty in Museums
Muhammad Yunus

In 2000, all the nations of the world gathered at the United Nations head-quarters in New York City and declared their determination to achieve eight important goals by 2015, including the reduction of poverty by half. It was a daring declaration. Not every nation will achieve the goals by 2015, but many will. Their success will bring us to the threshold of another bold decision—to end poverty on the planet once and for all. It can be done if we believe it can be done and act on our belief.

Once poverty is gone, we'll need to build museums to display its horrors to future generations. They'll wonder why poverty continued so long in human society—how a few people could live in luxury while billions dwelt in misery, deprivation, and despair.

Each nation will have to choose its own target date for building a national poverty museum. The initiative could come from government, foundations, NGOs, political parties, or any other section of society. Civil society groups and students may form a citizens' committee to build the national poverty museum by a specific future date. This date will express a desire and a commitment to eradicate poverty in the country within a specific period. Fixing a date can build the national will and energize the nation to put plans into action to make it happen.

But does this sound real? Can we really have poverty in the museums?

Why not? We have the technology. We have the resources. All we need is the will to do it and to put the necessary institutions and policies in place. I have tried in this book to explain what steps are needed to create a safe world without poverty. In this final chapter, I'll present some ideas relating to how individuals and organizations can actively participate in building the world that we would all like to create.

A Better World Starts with Imagination

The world in which we live is changing faster and faster. It is particularly true in the realms of economic development and technology.

As recently as the 1960s, all developing countries looked almost the same: massive poverty, rampant disease, periodic extreme economic crises, high population growth, low levels of education and health care, low economic growth, absence of infrastructure, and so on. There seemed little basis for optimism. But in the next thirty-five years, the economic map changed dramatically. Taiwan, South Korea, and Singapore joined the ranks of the developed countries. The economies of China, India, Malaysia, Thailand, and Vietnam began growing very fast. In the past eighteen years, the poverty rate in Vietnam has fallen from 58 percent to 20 percent. Globalization, despite its shortcomings, is producing changes around the world that could not even be imagined a generation ago.

We can always make educated guesses about what the future holds for the nations of the developing world. But past experience shows that, when countries are ripe for change, they can improve far faster than our educated guesses suggest. In particular, dramatic changes in technology are driving today's ultra-rapid rate of change. In the past, it took entire generations for social and political changes to impact people's thinking. Now new ideas can spread across the globe not in years but in months, even days, even seconds.

This is good news and also bad news. Improvements in technology, advances in democracy, and new problem-solving techniques can spread faster than ever, bringing benefits to millions of people. But we can create disasters very fast, too. If we are lucky enough to have a great leader in a major country of the world, people around the globe can benefit from his leadership immediately. If we are unlucky and have a bad leader in a highly influential country, the whole world may suffer from turmoil, economic dislocation, and war. Soundness of governance, global as well as national, is more important in today's fast-moving, interconnected world than ever before.

Today's rapid pace of change makes it crucial that we, as individual citizens, have a clear idea as to where we want our world to go. If we hope to find and stay on the right course, we must agree on the basic features of the world we want to create. And we must think big, as big as we dare to imagine—lest we waste the unprecedented opportunities that the world is offering us. Let us dream the wildest possible dreams and then pursue them.

Let me give a wish list of my dream world that I would like to see emerge by 2050. These are my dreams, but I hope that many of my dreams will coincide with yours. I am sure I would love many of the dreams on your list so much that I would make them my dreams too. Here is my list:

- There will be no poor people, no beggars, no homeless people, no street children anywhere in the world. Every country will have its own poverty museum. The global poverty museum will be located in the country that is the last to come out of poverty.

- There will be no passports and no visas for anybody anywhere in the world. All people will be truly global citizens of equal status.

- There will be no war, no war preparations, and no military establishment to fight wars. There will be no nuclear weapons or any other weapons of mass destruction.

- There will be no more incurable diseases, from cancer to AIDS, anywhere in the world. Disease will become a very rare phenomenon subject to immediate and effective treatment. High-quality healthcare will be available to everyone. Infant mortality and maternal mortality will be things of the past.

- There will be a global education system accessible to all from anywhere in the world. All children will experience fun and excitement in learning and growing up. All children will grow up as caring and sharing persons, believing that their own development should be consistent with the development of others in the world.

- The global economic system will encourage individuals, businesses, and institutions to share their prosperity and participate actively in bringing prosperity to others, making income inequality an irrelevant issue. "Unemployment" and "welfare" will be unheard of.

- Social business will be a substantial part of the business world.

- There will be only one global currency. Coins and paper currency will be gone.

- Technology will be available with which all secret bank accounts and transactions of politicians, government officials, business people, intelligence agencies, underworld organizations, and terrorist groups can be easily detected and monitored.

- State-of-the art financial services of every kind will be available to every person in the world.

- All people will be committed to maintaining a sustainable lifestyle based on appropriate technologies. Sun, water, and wind will be the main sources of power.

- Humans will be able to forecast earthquakes, cyclones, tsunamis, and other natural disasters precisely and in plenty of time to minimize damage and loss of life.

- There will be no discrimination of any kind, whether based on race, color, religion, gender, sexual orientation, political belief, language, culture, or any other factor.

- There will be no need of paper and therefore no need to cut down trees. There will be biodegradable reusable synthetic papers, in cases where "paper" is absolutely needed.

- Basic connectivity will be wireless and nearly costless.

- Everybody will read and hear everything in his own language. Technology will make it possible for a person to speak, read, and write in his own language while the listener will hear and the reader will read the message in his own language. Software and gadgets will translate simultaneously as one speaks or downloads any text. One will be able to watch any TV channel from anywhere and hear the words in his own language.

- All cultures, ethnic groups, and religions will flourish to their full beauty and creativity, contributing to the magnificent unified orchestra of human society.

- All people will enjoy an environment of continuous innovation, restructuring of institutions, and revisiting of concepts and ideas.

- All peoples will share a world of peace, harmony, and friendship devoted to expanding the frontiers of human potential.

These are all achievable goals if we work at them. I believe that, as we proceed through the future, it will be easier and easier to get closer to our dreams. The difficult part is making up our minds now. As more of us can agree on what we want to achieve, the quicker we can reach our goals. We tend to be so busy with our everyday work and enjoying our lives that we forget to look through the windows of our lives to find out where we are right now in our journey, and take time off to reflect where we wish to go ultimately. Once we know where we want to go, getting there will be so much easier.

Each of us should draw up a wish list of our own—to reflect on what kind of world we would like to see when we retire. Once it is done, we should hang it on our walls to remind us daily whether we are getting closer to the destination.

Then we should insist that the drivers of our societies—the political leaders, academic experts, religious teachers, and corporate executives—take us where we want to go. Remember, we each have only one life to live; we must live it our way, and the choice of destination should be ours.

This process of imagining a future world of our liking is a major missing element in our education system. We prepare our students for jobs and careers, but we don't teach them to think as individuals about what kind of world they would like to create. Every high school and university ought to include a course focused on just this exercise. Each student will be asked to prepare a wish list and then to explain to the class why he wants the things he wants. Other students may endorse his ideas, offer better alternatives, or challenge him. Then the students will go on to discuss how to create the dream world they imagine, what they can do to make it happen, what the barriers are, and how partnerships and organizations, concepts, frameworks, and action plans can be created to promote the goal. The course would be fun, and, more important, it would be a great preparation for an exciting journey.

Practical Steps toward the Dream-World of the Future

Dreaming about a better world is fun. But what can individuals do to help bring that world closer to reality? One practical step is to create a small organization to realize part of the goal—something I call a "social action forum."

A social action forum can be as small as three people who band together to address a single, manageable, local problem. If others want to join, that is fine, too. But if you feel comfortable with three, don't try to expand the number. You can give your forum an interesting, funny, bold, innovative name, or simply name it after your members: Cathy, Kushal, and Lee's Social Action Forum, the Jobra Social Action Forum, the Midas Touch Social Action Forum, or any other name you like.

Once you've started your forum, define your action plan for this year. Keep it simple. It may be to help one unemployed person, a homeless person, or a beggar to find an income-earning activity and begin the climb out of poverty. Select the poor person you want to help, sit down with him or her to learn about his or her problem with earning an income—then find a solution for it.

I am planning to create a website where you can register your social action forum. On the website, you can describe your plan for the year, record your thoughts, mention the frustrations and excitements of your work, show the progress you are making, and display pictures relating to your project. It takes no special expertise, credentials, or resources to start a forum; all you need is the willingness and initiative to make a difference. If at the end of each year you submit an annual report on your forum and submit a new plan for the next year, your forum's registration will be extended for the coming year. At any time, anybody can visit the website of all the active forums and get in touch with them.

A social action forum can be built around any number of local problems and opportunities. Is there an abandoned lot in your neighborhood where garbage is piling up and disease is spreading? Start a forum for neighborhood improvement to transform the lot for some interesting purpose—a community garden, a playground, a recycling center, introducing something new in your neighborhood school, or anything else.

If you live in a developing country, the action program for your forum may be built around helping a beggar find a job or self-employment, getting a dropout to go back to school, helping a sick person find medical attention, or improving the sanitation or the water quality in your village.

Some social action forums may remain small but continue to do significant work. Others may grow bigger and bigger, and some may even become successful social businesses. An idea from one forum may inspire other forums to replicate the idea. A few forums may grow into major programs with the potential to transform entire nations. Some forums can have a global impact by developing innovative ideas to address a serious problem.

Aside from launching a social action forum, there are many steps that individuals can take to help promote the social-business idea. If you are a teacher or administrator at a school, college, or university, you could help launch a course to teach young business people about social business. If you are a member of a faith or civic group, you could help arrange a series of lectures, meetings, or conferences about opportunities for social business in your community. If you help to oversee or manage investment funds for a school, a pension fund, a faith organization, or any other institution, you can propose that a part of those resources be set aside to invest in social businesses. And, of course, if you are a business executive, you can explain to your CEO or board of directors the value of creating a social business and propose to create a social business by investing a part of the company profit with the consent of the shareholders.

Probably the most challenging and important aspect of this endeavor is likely to be designing social businesses. It will require all our creativity and imagination to come up with excellent business ideas that effectively address critical social objectives. One way to generate social-business ideas will be to hold business design competitions. Any organization or person can sponsor such a competition—a school, a foundation, a chamber of commerce, a corporation, an NGO, a church group, a civic group, an investment or venture capital fund, and so on. A social action forum could enter a competition or start a competition of its own.

I can picture local, regional, and even global competitions, with hundreds or thousands of participants vying to create the most practical, ambitious, and exciting concepts for social businesses. Prizes for the best business designs could include investing funding to finance the projects, or connections to social investors, social venture-capital providers, and lenders who might be interested in partnering to build the new businesses. All the proposals submitted could be published on the Internet to inspire the designers in the subsequent competitions or to provide ideas for entrepreneurs who want to start social businesses.

I have been promoting this idea of a social-business competition for the past several years, and now the Taiwanese magazine *Business Weekly* has actually announced such a competition. It has raised $1.5 million to provide seed money for the top ten submissions, which will be announced in November 2007. I am absolutely delighted about this initiative and look forward to attending the event at which the prizes will be presented.

New Frontiers for Foundations

Philanthropic institutions—especially the foundations launched by successful leaders in business—will find social business an especially appealing concept.

Throughout the twentieth century, foundations created by the premier entrepreneurs of the industrial age—John D. Rockefeller, Henry Ford, Andrew Carnegie—provided support for many of the world's most important charitable projects. In recent years, philanthropy has achieved new levels of visibility through the activities of some of the newest and largest foundations. In 2000, the founder of Microsoft and his wife launched the Bill and Melinda Gates Foundation, whose current endowment (March 2007) stands at $33.4 billion, the largest sum ever given to create a charitable foundation. Then, in June 2006, Warren Buffett, along with Gates among the three richest persons in the world (Mexican telecom mogul Carlos Slim Helú is the other), announced a plan to donate $37 billion from his personal fortune to the Gates Foundation, the largest single charitable gift in world history.

I believe the philanthropists of the future will be strongly drawn to social business. Because most major donors come from the business world, they will immediately understand that the social-business dollar is much more powerful than the charity dollar. Whereas the charity dollar can be used only once, the social-business dollar recycles itself again and again, *ad infinitum*, to deliver benefits to more and more people. Furthermore, philanthropists will be attracted to the idea of social business because it will allow them to leverage their business experience to tackle some of the world's most serious problems.

If Warren Buffett had asked for my advice, I would have advised him to use part of his money to create a social business whose mission would be to provide affordable, high-quality health insurance to the 47 million Americans without it. If Buffett himself—a business genius with decades of experience in the insurance industry—were involved in designing this social business, anybody can easily guess the outcome: The company would achieve a resounding success, and Buffett would be remembered in the history of American health care.

An End to Poverty

As understanding of social business spreads, and as more and more people take up the call to create social businesses, we can move closer and closer to achieving the ultimate goal: To relegate poverty, once and for all, to poverty museums.

Impossible? Not at all. There was a time when certain infectious diseases were thought to be unstoppable. They killed millions of people every year, and many people assumed they were an unchanging part of the human condition. Now, thanks to human creativity, scientific breakthroughs, and determined efforts by public health workers, some of those diseases have been virtually wiped out. The only way scientists can study them now is by examining samples of the microbes in carefully guarded laboratories. Why not strive to do the same with the disease of poverty?

This should be an objective to which people in every village, town, region, and country in the world commit themselves. It simply takes a few people to say, "Let's pledge to work together until the last poor person in our village has been lifted out of poverty." It takes a few more to make the same pledge about a city or county or local district. As this objective is achieved in one locality after another, the time will eventually come when the only way our children or grandchildren can understand what poverty *used* to be like will be by visiting the poverty museums.

When we look back at human history, it is clear that we get what we want—or what we fail to refuse. If we are *not* achieving something, it is because we have not put our minds to it. We are accepting psychological limitations that prevent us from doing what we claim we want.

At this moment, we accept the idea that we will always have poor people among us, that poverty is part of human destiny. The fact that we accept this notion is precisely *why* we continue to have the poor. If we firmly believe that poverty is unacceptable—that it should have no place in a civilized human society—then we will build appropriate institutions and policies to create a poverty-free world.

Poverty exists because we've built our philosophical framework on assumptions that underestimate human capacities. We've designed concepts that are too narrow—our concept of business (which makes profit the *only* viable human motive), our concept of credit-worthiness (which automatically eliminates the poor), our concept of entrepreneurship (which ignores the creativity of the majority of people), and our concept of employment (which relegates humans to passive receptacles rather than active creators). And we've developed institutions that are half-complete at best—like our banking and economic systems, which ignore half the world. Poverty exists because of these intellectual failures rather than because of any lack of capability on the part of people.

All human beings have the inner capacity not only to care for themselves but also to contribute to increasing the well-being of the world as whole. Some get the chance to explore their potential to some degree. But many never get any opportunity to unwrap this wonderful gift they were born with. They die with their gifts unexplored, and the world is deprived of all they could have done.

My work with Grameen Bank has brought me into close touch with the poorest of the poor. This experience has given me an unshakable faith in the creativity of human beings. None of them is born to suffer the misery of hunger and poverty. Each one of those who suffer this misery has the potential to be as successful a human being as anybody else in this world.

It is possible to eliminate poverty from our world because it is not natural to human beings—it is artificially imposed on them. Let's dedicate ourselves to bringing an end to it at the earliest possible date, and putting poverty in the museums once and for all.

Late Bloomers
Why Do We Equate Genius with Precocity?
Malcolm Gladwell

Ben Fountain was an associate in the real-estate practice at the Dallas offices of Akin, Gump, Strauss, Hauer & Feld, just a few years out of law school, when he decided he wanted to write fiction. The only thing Fountain had ever published was a law-review article. His literary training consisted of a handful of creative-writing classes in college. He had tried to write when he came home at night from work, but usually he was too tired to do much. He decided to quit his job.

"I was tremendously apprehensive," Fountain recalls. "I felt like I'd stepped off a cliff and I didn't know if the parachute was going to open. Nobody wants to waste their life, and I was doing well at the practice of law. I could have had a good career. And my parents were very proud of me—my dad was so proud of me. . . . It was crazy."

He began his new life on a February morning—a Monday. He sat down at his kitchen table at 7:30 A.M. He made a plan. Every day, he would write until lunchtime. Then he would lie down on the floor for twenty minutes to rest his mind. Then he would return to work for a few more hours. He was a lawyer. He had discipline. "I figured out very early on that if I didn't get my writing done I felt terrible. So I always got my writing done. I treated it like a job. I did not procrastinate." His first story was about a stockbroker who uses inside information and crosses a moral line. It was sixty pages long and took him three months to write. When he finished that story, he went back to work and wrote another—and then another.

In his first year, Fountain sold two stories. He gained confidence. He wrote a novel. He decided it wasn't very good, and he ended up putting it in a drawer. Then came what he describes as his dark period, when he adjusted his expectations and started again. He got a short story published in *Harper's*. A New York literary agent saw it and signed him up. He put

355

together a collection of short stories titled "Brief Encounters with Che Guevara," and Ecco, a HarperCollins imprint, published it. The reviews were sensational. The *Times Book Review* called it "heartbreaking." It won the Hemingway Foundation/PEN award. It was named a No. 1 Book Sense Pick. It made major regional best-seller lists, was named one of the best books of the year by the San Francisco *Chronicle*, the Chicago *Tribune*, and *Kirkus Reviews,* and drew comparisons to Graham Greene, Evelyn Waugh, Robert Stone, and John le Carré.

Ben Fountain's rise sounds like a familiar story: the young man from the provinces suddenly takes the literary world by storm. But Ben Fountain's success was far from sudden. He quit his job at Akin, Gump in 1988. For every story he published in those early years, he had at least thirty rejections. The novel that he put away in a drawer took him four years. The dark period lasted for the entire second half of the nineteen-nineties. His breakthrough with "Brief Encounters" came in 2006, eighteen years after he first sat down to write at his kitchen table. The "young" writer from the provinces took the literary world by storm at the age of forty-eight.

Genius, in the popular conception, is inextricably tied up with precocity—doing something truly creative, we're inclined to think, requires the freshness and exuberance and energy of youth. Orson Welles made his masterpiece, "Citizen Kane," at twenty-five. Herman Melville wrote a book a year through his late twenties, culminating, at age thirty-two, with "Moby-Dick." Mozart wrote his breakthrough Piano Concerto No. 9 in E-Flat-Major at the age of twenty-one. In some creative forms, like lyric poetry, the importance of precocity has hardened into an iron law. How old was T. S. Eliot when he wrote "The Love Song of J. Alfred Prufrock" ("I grow old . . . I grow old")? Twenty-three. "Poets peak young," the creativity researcher James Kaufman maintains. Mihály Csíkszentmihályi, the author of "Flow," agrees: "The most creative lyric verse is believed to be that written by the young." According to the Harvard psychologist Howard Gardner, a leading authority on creativity, "Lyric poetry is a domain where talent is discovered early, burns brightly, and then peters out at an early age."

A few years ago, an economist at the University of Chicago named David Galenson decided to find out whether this assumption about creativity was true. He looked through forty-seven major poetry anthologies published since 1980 and counted the poems that appear most frequently. Some people, of course, would quarrel with the notion that literary merit can be quantified. But Galenson simply wanted to poll a broad cross-section of literary scholars about which poems they felt were the most important in the American canon. The top eleven are, in order, T. S. Eliot's "Prufrock," Robert Lowell's "Skunk Hour," Robert Frost's "Stopping by Woods on a Snowy Evening," William Carlos Williams's "Red Wheelbarrow," Elizabeth Bishop's "The Fish," Ezra Pound's "The River Merchant's Wife," Sylvia Plath's "Daddy," Pound's "In a Station of the Metro," Frost's "Mending Wall," Wallace Stevens's "The Snow Man," and Williams's "The Dance." Those eleven were composed at the ages of twenty-three, forty-one, forty-eight, forty, twenty-nine, thirty, thirty, twenty-eight, thirty-eight, forty-two, and fifty-nine, respectively. There is no evidence, Galenson concluded, for the notion that lyric poetry is a young person's game. Some poets do their best work at the beginning of their careers. Others do their best work decades later. Forty-two per cent of Frost's anthologized poems were written after the age of fifty. For Williams, it's forty-four percent. For Stevens, it's forty-nine percent.

The same was true of film, Galenson points out in his study "Old Masters and Young Geniuses: The Two Life Cycles of Artistic Creativity." Yes, there was Orson Welles, peaking as a director at twenty-five. But then there was Alfred Hitchcock, who made "Dial M for Murder," "Rear Window," "To Catch a Thief," "The Trouble with Harry," "Vertigo," "North by Northwest," and "Psycho"— one of the greatest runs by a director in history—between his fifty-fourth and sixty-first birthdays. Mark Twain published "Adventures of Huckleberry Finn" at forty-nine. Daniel Defoe wrote "Robinson Crusoe" at fifty-eight.

The examples that Galenson could not get out of his head, however, were Picasso and Cézanne. He was an art lover, and he knew their stories well. Picasso was the incandescent prodigy. His career as a serious artist began with a masterpiece, "Evocation: The Burial of Casagemas," produced at age twenty. In short order, he painted many of the greatest works of his career—including "Les Demoiselles d'Avignon," at the age of twenty-six. Picasso fit our usual ideas about genius perfectly.

Cézanne didn't. If you go to the Cézanne room at the Musée d'Orsay, in Paris—the finest collection of Cézannes in the world—the array of masterpieces you'll find along the back wall were all painted at the end of his career. Galenson did a simple economic analysis, tabulating the prices paid at auction for paintings by Picasso and Cézanne with the ages at which they created those works. A painting done by Picasso in his mid-twenties was worth, he found, an average of four times as much as a painting done in his sixties. For Cézanne, the opposite was true. The paintings he created in his mid-sixties were valued fifteen times as highly as the paintings he created as a young man. The freshness, exuberance, and energy of youth did little for Cézanne. He was a late bloomer—and for some reason in our accounting of genius and creativity we have forgotten to make sense of the Cézannes of the world.

The first day that Ben Fountain sat down to write at his kitchen table went well. He knew how the story about the stockbroker was supposed to start. But the second day, he says, he "completely freaked out." He didn't know how to describe things. He felt as if he were back in first grade. He didn't have a fully formed vision, waiting to be emptied onto the page. "I had to create a mental image of a building, a room, a façade, haircut, clothes—just really basic things," he says. "I realized I didn't have the facility to put those into words. I started going out and buying visual dictionaries, architectural dictionaries, and going to school on those."

He began to collect articles about things he was interested in, and before long he realized that he had developed a fascination with Haiti. "The Haiti file just kept getting bigger and bigger," Fountain says. "And I thought, O.K., here's my novel. For a month or two I said I really don't need to go there, I can imagine everything. But after a couple of months I thought, Yeah, you've got to go there, and so I went, in April or May of '91."

He spoke little French, let alone Haitian Creole. He had never been abroad. Nor did he know anyone in Haiti. "I got to the hotel, walked up the stairs, and there was this guy standing at the top of the stairs," Fountain recalls. "He said, 'My name is Pierre. You need a guide.' I said, 'You're sure as hell right, I do.' He was a very genuine person, and he realized pretty quickly I didn't want to go see the girls, I didn't want drugs, I didn't want any of that other stuff," Fountain went on. "And then it was, *boom*, 'I can take you there. I can take you to this person.' "

Fountain was riveted by Haiti. "It's like a laboratory, almost," he says. "Everything that's gone on in the last five hundred years—colonialism, race, power, politics, ecological disasters—it's all there in very concentrated form. And also I just felt, viscerally, pretty comfortable there." He made more trips to Haiti, sometimes for a week, sometimes for two weeks. He made friends. He invited them to visit him in Dallas. ("You haven't lived until you've had Haitians stay in your house," Fountain says.) "I mean, I was involved. I couldn't just walk away. There's this very nonrational, nonlinear part of the whole process. I had a pretty specific time era that I was writing about, and certain things that I needed to know. But there were other things I didn't really need to know. I met a fellow who was with Save the Children, and he was on the Central Plateau, which takes about twelve hours to get to on a bus, and I had no reason to go there. But I went up there. Suffered on that bus, and ate dust. It was a hard trip, but it was a glorious trip. It had nothing to do with the book, but it wasn't wasted knowledge."

In "Brief Encounters with Che Guevara," four of the stories are about Haiti, and they are the strongest in the collection. They feel like Haiti; they feel as if they've been written from the inside looking out, not the outside looking in. "After the novel was done, I don't know, I just felt like there was more for me, and I could keep going, keep going deeper there," Fountain recalls. "Always there's something—always something—here for me. How many times have I been? At least thirty times."

Prodigies like Picasso, Galenson argues, rarely engage in that kind of open-ended exploration. They tend to be "conceptual," Galenson says, in the sense that they start with a clear idea of where they want to go, and then they execute it. "I can hardly understand the importance given to the word 'research,' " Picasso once said in an interview with the artist Marius de Zayas. "In my opinion, to search means nothing in painting. To find is the thing." He continued, "The several manners I have used in my art must not be considered as an evolution or as steps toward an unknown ideal of painting. . . . I have never made trials or experiments."

But late bloomers, Galenson says, tend to work the other way around. Their approach is experimental. "Their goals are imprecise, so their procedure is tentative and incremental," Galenson writes in "Old Masters and Young Geniuses," and he goes on:

The imprecision of their goals means that these artists rarely feel they have succeeded, and their careers are consequently often dominated by the pursuit of a single objective. These artists repeat themselves, painting the same subject many times, and gradually changing its treatment in an experimental process of trial and error. Each work leads to the next, and none is generally privileged over others, so experimental painters rarely make specific preparatory sketches or plans for a painting. They consider the production of a painting as a process of searching, in which they aim to discover the image in the course of making it; they typically believe that learning is a more important goal than making finished paintings. Experimental artists build their skills gradually over the course of their careers, improving their work slowly over long periods. These artists are perfectionists and are typically plagued by frustration at their inability to achieve their goal.

Where Picasso wanted to find, not search, Cézanne said the opposite: "I seek in painting."

An experimental innovator *would* go back to Haiti thirty times. That's how that kind of mind figures out what it wants to do. When Cézanne was painting a portrait of the critic Gustave Geffroy, he made him endure eighty sittings, over three months, before announcing the project a failure. (The result is one of that string of masterpieces in the Musée d'Orsay.) When Cézanne painted his dealer, Ambrose Vollard, he made Vollard arrive at eight in the morning and sit on a rickety platform until eleven-thirty, without a break, on a hundred and fifty occasions—before abandoning the portrait. He would paint a scene, then repaint it, then paint it again. He was notorious for slashing his canvases to pieces in fits of frustration.

Mark Twain was the same way. Galenson quotes the literary critic Franklin Rogers on Twain's trial-and-error method: "His routine procedure seems to have been to start a novel with some structural plan which ordinarily soon proved defective, whereupon he would cast about for a new plot which would overcome the difficulty, rewrite what he had already written, and then push on until some new defect forced him to repeat the process once again." Twain fiddled and despaired and revised and gave up on "Huckleberry Finn" so many times that the book took him nearly a decade to complete. The Cézannes of the world bloom late not as a result of some defect in character, or

distraction, or lack of ambition, but because the kind of creativity that proceeds through trial and error necessarily takes a long time to come to fruition.

One of the best stories in "Brief Encounters" is called "Near-Extinct Birds of
the Central Cordillera." It's about an ornithologist taken hostage by the FARC
guerrillas of Colombia. Like so much of Fountain's work, it reads with an easy
grace. But there was nothing easy or graceful about its creation. "I struggled
with that story," Fountain says. "I always try to do too much. I mean, I probably wrote five hundred pages of it in various incarnations." Fountain is at
work right now on a novel. It was supposed to come out this year. It's late.

Galenson's idea that creativity can be divided into these types—conceptual
and experimental—has a number of important implications. For example, we
sometimes think of late bloomers as late starters. They don't realize they're
good at something until they're fifty, so of course they achieve late in life. But
that's not quite right. Cézanne was painting almost as early as Picasso was. We
also sometimes think of them as artists who are *discovered* late; the world is just
slow to appreciate their gifts. In both cases, the assumption is that the prodigy
and the late bloomer are fundamentally the same, and that late blooming is
simply genius under conditions of market failure. What Galenson's argument
suggests is something else—that late bloomers bloom late because they simply
aren't much good until late in their careers.

"All these qualities of his inner vision were continually hampered and
obstructed by Cézanne's incapacity to give sufficient verisimilitude to the per-
sonae of his drama," the great English art critic Roger Fry wrote of the early
Cézanne. "With all his rare endowments, he happened to lack the compara-
tively common gift of illustration, the gift that any draughtsman for the illus-
trated papers learns in a school of commercial art; whereas, to realize such
visions as Cézanne's required this gift in high degree." In other words, the
young Cézanne couldn't draw. Of "The Banquet," which Cézanne painted at
thirty-one, Fry writes, "It is no use to deny that Cézanne has made a very poor
job of it." Fry goes on, "More happily endowed and more integral personalities have been able to express themselves harmoniously from the very first.
But such rich, complex, and conflicting natures as Cézanne's require a long
period of fermentation." Cézanne was trying something so elusive that he
couldn't master it until he'd spent decades practicing.

This is the vexing lesson of Fountain's long attempt to get noticed by the literary world. On the road to great achievement, the late bloomer will resemble
a failure: while the late bloomer is revising and despairing and changing
course and slashing canvases to ribbons after months or years, what he or she
produces will look like the kind of thing produced by the artist who will never
bloom at all. Prodigies are easy. They advertise their genius from the get-go.
Late bloomers are hard. They require forbearance and blind faith. (Let's just be
thankful that Cézanne didn't have a guidance counsellor in high school who
looked at his primitive sketches and told him to try accounting.) Whenever we
find a late bloomer, we can't but wonder how many others like him or her we

have thwarted because we prematurely judged their talents. But we also have to accept that there's nothing we can do about it. How can we ever know which of the failures will end up blooming?

Not long after meeting Ben Fountain, I went to see the novelist Jonathan Safran Foer, the author of the 2002 best-seller "Everything Is Illuminated." Fountain is a graying man, slight and modest, who looks, in the words of a friend of his, like a "golf pro from Augusta, Georgia." Foer is in his early thirties and looks barely old enough to drink. Fountain has a softness to him, as if years of struggle have worn away whatever sharp edges he once had. Foer gives the impression that if you touched him while he was in full conversational flight you would get an electric shock.

"I came to writing really by the back door," Foer said. "My wife is a writer, and she grew up keeping journals—you know, parents said, 'Lights out, time for bed,' and she had a little flashlight under the covers, reading books. I don't think I *read* a book until much later than other people. I just wasn't interested in it."

Foer went to Princeton and took a creative-writing class in his freshman year with Joyce Carol Oates. It was, he explains, "sort of on a whim, maybe out of a sense that I should have a diverse course load." He'd never written a story before. "I didn't really think anything of it, to be honest, but halfway through the semester I arrived to class early one day, and she said, 'Oh, I'm glad I have this chance to talk to you. I'm a fan of your writing.' And it was a *real* revelation for me."

Oates told him that he had the most important of writerly qualities, which was energy. He had been writing fifteen pages a week for that class, an entire story for each seminar. "Why does a dam with a crack in it leak so much?" he said, with a laugh. "There was just something in me, there was like a pressure."

As a sophomore, he took another creative-writing class. During the following summer, he went to Europe. He wanted to find the village in Ukraine where his grandfather had come from. After the trip, he went to Prague. There he read Kafka, as any literary undergraduate would, and sat down at his computer.

"I was just writing," he said. "I didn't know that I was writing until it was happening. I didn't go with the intention of writing a book. I wrote three hundred pages in ten weeks. I *really* wrote. I'd never done it like that."

It was a novel about a boy named Jonathan Safran Foer who visits the village in Ukraine where his grandfather had come from. Those three hundred pages were the first draft of "Everything Is Illuminated"—the exquisite and extraordinary novel that established Foer as one of the most distinctive literary voices of his generation. He was nineteen years old.

Foer began to talk about the other way of writing books, where you painstakingly honed your craft, over years and years. "I couldn't do that," he said. He seemed puzzled by it. It was clear that he had no understanding of how being an experimental innovator would work. "I mean, imagine if the craft you're trying to learn is to be an original. How could you learn the craft of being an original?"

He began to describe his visit to Ukraine. "I went to the shtetl where my family came from. It's called Trachimbrod, the name I use in the book. It's a real place. But you know what's funny? It's the single piece of research that made its way into the book." He wrote the first sentence, and he was proud of it, and then he went back and forth in his mind about where to go next. "I spent the first week just having this debate with myself about what to do with this first sentence. And once I made the decision, I felt liberated to just create—and it was very explosive after that."

If you read "Everything Is Illuminated," you end up with the same feeling you get when you read "Brief Encounters with Che Guevara"—the sense of transport you experience when a work of literature draws you into its own world. Both are works of art. It's just that, as artists, Fountain and Foer could not be less alike. Fountain went to Haiti thirty times. Foer went to Trachimbrod just once. "I mean, it was nothing," Foer said. "I had absolutely no experience there at all. It was just a springboard for my book. It was like an empty swimming pool that had to be filled up." Total time spent getting inspiration for his novel: three days.

Ben Fountain did not make the decision to quit the law and become a writer all by himself. He is married and has a family. He met his wife, Sharon, when they were both in law school at Duke. When he was doing real-estate work at Akin, Gump, she was on the partner track in the tax practice at Thompson & Knight. The two actually worked in the same building in downtown Dallas. They got married in 1985, and had a son in April of 1987. Sharie, as Fountain calls her, took four months of maternity leave before returning to work. She made partner by the end of that year.

"We had our son in a day care downtown," she recalls. "We would drive in together, one of us would take him to day care, the other one would go to work. One of us would pick him up, and then, somewhere around eight o'clock at night, we would have him bathed, in bed, and then we hadn't even eaten yet, and we'd be looking at each other, going, 'This is just the beginning.'" She made a face. "That went on for maybe a month or two, and Ben's like, 'I don't know how people do this.' We both agreed that continuing at that pace was probably going to make us all miserable. Ben said to me, 'Do you want to stay home?' Well, I was pretty happy in my job, and he wasn't, so as far as I was concerned it didn't make any sense for me to stay home. And I didn't have anything besides practicing law that I really wanted to do, and he did. So I said, 'Look, can we do this in a way that we can still have some day care and so you can write?' And so we did that."

Ben could start writing at seven-thirty in the morning because Sharie took their son to day care. He stopped working in the afternoon because that was when he had to pick him up, and then he did the shopping and the household chores. In 1989, they had a second child, a daughter. Fountain was a full-fledged North Dallas stay-at-home dad.

"When Ben first did this, we talked about the fact that it might not work, and we talked about, generally, 'When will we know that it really isn't working?' and I'd say, 'Well, give it ten years,' " Sharie recalled. To her, ten years didn't seem unreasonable. "It takes a while to decide whether you like something or not," she says. And when ten years became twelve and then fourteen and then sixteen, and the kids were off in high school, she stood by him, because, even during that long stretch when Ben had nothing published at all, she was confident that he was getting better. She was fine with the trips to Haiti, too. "I can't imagine writing a novel about a place you haven't at least tried to visit," she says. She even went with him once, and on the way into town from the airport there were people burning tires in the middle of the road.

"I was making pretty decent money, and we didn't need two incomes," Sharie went on. She has a calm, unflappable quality about her. "I mean, it would have been nice, but we could live on one."

Sharie was Ben's wife. But she was also—to borrow a term from long ago—his patron. That word has a condescending edge to it today, because we think it far more appropriate for artists (and everyone else for that matter) to be supported by the marketplace. But the marketplace works only for people like Jonathan Safran Foer, whose art emerges, fully realized, at the beginning of their career, or Picasso, whose talent was so blindingly obvious that an art dealer offered him a hundred-and-fifty-franc-a-month stipend the minute he got to Paris, at age twenty. If you are the type of creative mind that starts without a plan, and has to experiment and learn by doing, you need someone to see you through the long and difficult time it takes for your art to reach its true level.

This is what is so instructive about any biography of Cézanne. Accounts of his life start out being about Cézanne, and then quickly turn into the story of Cézanne's circle. First and foremost is always his best friend from childhood, the writer Émile Zola, who convinces the awkward misfit from the provinces to come to Paris, and who serves as his guardian and protector and coach through the long, lean years.

Here is Zola, already in Paris, in a letter to the young Cézanne back in Provence. Note the tone, more paternal than fraternal:

> You ask me an odd question. Of course one can work here, as anywhere else, if one has the will. Paris offers, further, an advantage you can't find elsewhere: the museums in which you can study the old masters from 11 to 4. This is how you must divide your time. From 6 to 11 you go to a studio to paint from

> a live model; you have lunch, then from 12 to
> 4 you copy, in the Louvre or the Luxembourg,
> whatever masterpiece you like. That will
> make up nine hours of work. I think that
> ought to be enough.

Zola goes on, detailing exactly how Cézanne could manage financially on a monthly stipend of a hundred and twenty-five francs:

> I'll reckon out for you what you should
> spend. A room at 20 francs a month; lunch at
> 18 sous and dinner at 22, which makes two
> francs a day, or 60 francs a month. . . . Then
> you have the studio to pay for: the Atelier Su-
> isse, one of the least expensive, charges, I
> think, 10 francs. Add 10 francs for canvas,
> brushes, colors; that makes 100. So you'll
> have 25 francs left for laundry, light, the thou-
> sand little needs that turn up.

Camille Pissarro was the next critical figure in Cézanne's life. It was Pissarro who took Cézanne under his wing and taught him how to be a painter. For years, there would be periods in which they went off into the country and worked side by side.

Then there was Ambrose Vollard, the sponsor of Cézanne's first one-man show, at the age of fifty-six. At the urging of Pissarro, Renoir, Degas, and Monet, Vollard hunted down Cézanne in Aix. He spotted a still-life in a tree, where it had been flung by Cézanne in disgust. He poked around the town, putting the word out that he was in the market for Cézanne's canvases. In "Lost Earth: A Life of Cézanne," the biographer Philip Callow writes about what happened next:

> Before long someone appeared at his hotel
> with an object wrapped in a cloth. He sold the
> picture for 150 francs, which inspired him to
> trot back to his house with the dealer to in-
> spect several more magnificent Cézannes.
> Vollard paid a thousand francs for the job lot,
> then on the way out was nearly hit on the
> head by a canvas that had been overlooked,
> dropped out the window by the man's wife.
> All the pictures had been gathering dust, half
> buried in a pile of junk in the attic.

All this came before Vollard agreed to sit a hundred and fifty times, from eight in the morning to eleven-thirty, without a break, for a picture that

Cézanne disgustedly abandoned. Once, Vollard recounted in his memoir, he fell asleep, and toppled off the makeshift platform. Cézanne berated him, incensed: "Does an apple move?" This is called friendship.

Finally, there was Cézanne's father, the banker Louis-Auguste. From the time Cézanne first left Aix, at the age of twenty-two, Louis-Auguste paid his bills, even when Cézanne gave every indication of being nothing more than a failed dilettante. But for Zola, Cézanne would have remained an unhappy banker's son in Provence; but for Pissarro, he would never have learned how to paint; but for Vollard (at the urging of Pissarro, Renoir, Degas, and Monet), his canvases would have rotted away in some attic; and, but for his father, Cézanne's long apprenticeship would have been a financial impossibility. That is an extraordinary list of patrons. The first three—Zola, Pissarro, and Vollard—would have been famous even if Cézanne never existed, and the fourth was an unusually gifted entrepreneur who left Cézanne four hundred thousand francs when he died. Cézanne didn't just have help. He had a dream team in his corner.

This is the final lesson of the late bloomer: his or her success is highly contingent on the efforts of others. In biographies of Cézanne, Louis-Auguste invariably comes across as a kind of grumpy philistine, who didn't appreciate his son's genius. But Louis-Auguste didn't have to support Cézanne all those years. He would have been within his rights to make his son get a real job, just as Sharie might well have said no to her husband's repeated trips to the chaos of Haiti. She could have argued that she had some right to the life style of her profession and status—that she deserved to drive a BMW, which is what power couples in North Dallas drive, instead of a Honda Accord, which is what she settled for.

But she believed in her husband's art, or perhaps, more simply, she believed in her husband, the same way Zola and Pissarro and Vollard and—in his own, querulous way—Louis-Auguste must have believed in Cézanne. Late bloomers' stories are invariably love stories, and this may be why we have such difficulty with them. We'd like to think that mundane matters like loyalty, steadfastness, and the willingness to keep writing checks to support what looks like failure have nothing to do with something as rarefied as genius. But sometimes genius is anything but rarefied; sometimes it's just the thing that emerges after twenty years of working at your kitchen table.

"Sharie never once brought up money, not once—never," Fountain said. She was sitting next to him, and he looked at her in a way that made it plain that he understood how much of the credit for "Brief Encounters" belonged to his wife. His eyes welled up with tears. "I never felt any pressure from her," he said. "Not even covert, not even implied."

A Just and Lasting Peace
Acceptance Speech of Nobel Peace Prize, 2009
Barack H. Obama

Your Majesties, Your Royal Highnesses, distinguished members of the Norwegian Nobel Committee, citizens of America, and citizens of the world:

I receive this honor with deep gratitude and great humility. It is an award that speaks to our highest aspirations—that for all the cruelty and hardship of our world, we are not mere prisoners of fate. Our actions matter, and can bend history in the direction of justice.

And yet I would be remiss if I did not acknowledge the considerable controversy that your generous decision has generated. (Laughter.) In part, this is because I am at the beginning, and not the end, of my labors on the world stage. Compared to some of the giants of history who've received this prize—Schweitzer and King; Marshall and Mandela—my accomplishments are slight. And then there are the men and women around the world who have been jailed and beaten in the pursuit of justice; those who toil in humanitarian organizations to relieve suffering; the unrecognized millions whose quiet acts of courage and compassion inspire even the most hardened cynics. I cannot argue with those who find these men and women—some known, some obscure to all but those they help—to be far more deserving of this honor than I.

But perhaps the most profound issue surrounding my receipt of this prize is the fact that I am the Commander-in-Chief of the military of a nation in the midst of two wars. One of these wars is winding down. The other is a conflict that America did not seek; one in which we are joined by 42 other countries—including Norway—in an effort to defend ourselves and all nations from further attacks.

Still, we are at war, and I'm responsible for the deployment of thousands of young Americans to battle in a distant land. Some will kill, and some will be killed. And so I come here with an acute sense of the costs of armed conflict—filled with difficult questions about the relationship between war and peace, and our effort to replace one with the other.

Now these questions are not new. War, in one form or another, appeared with the first man. At the dawn of history, its morality was not questioned; it was simply a fact, like drought or disease—the manner in which tribes and then civilizations sought power and settled their differences.

And over time, as codes of law sought to control violence within groups, so did philosophers and clerics and statesmen seek to regulate the destructive power of war. The concept of a "just war" emerged, suggesting that war is justified only when certain conditions were met: if it is waged as a last resort or in self-defense; if the force used is proportional; and if, whenever possible, civilians are spared from violence.

Of course, we know that for most of history, this concept of "just war" was rarely observed. The capacity of human beings to think up new ways to kill one another proved inexhaustible, as did our capacity to exempt from mercy those who look different or pray to a different God. Wars between armies gave way to wars between nations—total wars in which the distinction between combatant and civilian became blurred. In the span of 30 years, such carnage would twice engulf this continent. And while it's hard to conceive of a cause more just than the defeat of the Third Reich and the Axis powers, World War II was a conflict in which the total number of civilians who died exceeded the number of soldiers who perished.

In the wake of such destruction, and with the advent of the nuclear age, it became clear to victor and vanquished alike that the world needed institutions to prevent another world war. And so, a quarter century after the United States Senate rejected the League of Nations—an idea for which Woodrow Wilson received this prize—America led the world in constructing an architecture to keep the peace: a Marshall Plan and a United Nations, mechanisms to govern the waging of war, treaties to protect human rights, prevent genocide, restrict the most dangerous weapons.

In many ways, these efforts succeeded. Yes, terrible wars have been fought, and atrocities committed. But there has been no Third World War. The Cold War ended with jubilant crowds dismantling a wall. Commerce has stitched much of the world together. Billions have been lifted from poverty. The ideals of liberty and self-determination, equality and the rule of law have haltingly advanced. We are the heirs of the fortitude and foresight of generations past, and it is a legacy for which my own country is rightfully proud.

And yet, a decade into a new century, this old architecture is buckling under the weight of new threats. The world may no longer shudder at the prospect of war between two nuclear superpowers, but proliferation may increase the risk of catastrophe. Terrorism has long been a tactic, but modern technology allows a few small men with outsized rage to murder innocents on a horrific scale.

Moreover, wars between nations have increasingly given way to wars within nations. The resurgence of ethnic or sectarian conflicts; the growth of secessionist movements, insurgencies, and failed states—all these things have increasingly trapped civilians in unending chaos. In today's wars, many more civilians are killed than soldiers; the seeds of future conflict are sown, economies are wrecked, civil societies torn asunder, refugees amassed, children scarred.

I do not bring with me today a definitive solution to the problems of war. What I do know is that meeting these challenges will require the same vision, hard work, and persistence of those men and women who acted so boldly decades ago. And it will require us to think in new ways about the notions of just war and the imperatives of a just peace.

We must begin by acknowledging the hard truth: We will not eradicate violent conflict in our lifetimes. There will be times when nations—acting individually or in concert—will find the use of force not only necessary but morally justified.

I make this statement mindful of what Martin Luther King Jr. said in this same ceremony years ago: "Violence never brings permanent peace. It solves no social problem: it merely creates new and more complicated ones." As someone who stands here as a direct consequence of Dr. King's life work, I am living testimony to the moral force of non-violence. I know there's nothing weak—nothing passive—nothing naïve—in the creed and lives of Gandhi and King.

But as a head of state sworn to protect and defend my nation, I cannot be guided by their examples alone. I face the world as it is, and cannot stand idle in the face of threats to the American people. For make no mistake: Evil does exist in the world. A non-violent movement could not have halted Hitler's armies. Negotiations cannot convince al Qaeda's leaders to lay down their arms. To say that force may sometimes be necessary is not a call to cynicism—it is a recognition of history; the imperfections of man and the limits of reason.

I raise this point, I begin with this point because in many countries there is a deep ambivalence about military action today, no matter what the cause. And at times, this is joined by a reflexive suspicion of America, the world's sole military superpower.

But the world must remember that it was not simply international institutions—not just treaties and declarations—that brought stability to a post-World War II world. Whatever mistakes we have made, the plain fact is this: The United States of America has helped underwrite global security for more than six decades with the blood of our citizens and the strength of our arms. The service and sacrifice of our men and women in uniform has promoted peace and prosperity from Germany to Korea, and enabled democracy to take hold in places like the Balkans. We have borne this burden not because we seek to impose our will. We have done so out of enlightened self-interest—because we seek a better future for our children and grandchildren, and we believe that their lives will be better if others' children and grandchildren can live in freedom and prosperity.

So yes, the instruments of war do have a role to play in preserving the peace. And yet this truth must coexist with another—that no matter how justified, war promises human tragedy. The soldier's courage and sacrifice is full of glory, expressing devotion to country, to cause, to comrades in arms. But war itself is never glorious, and we must never trumpet it as such.

So part of our challenge is reconciling these two seemingly irreconcilable truths—that war is sometimes necessary, and war at some level is an expression of human folly. Concretely, we must direct our effort to the task that President Kennedy called for long ago. "Let us focus," he said, "on a more practical, more attainable peace, based not on a sudden revolution in human nature but on a gradual evolution in human institutions." A gradual evolution of human institutions.

What might this evolution look like? What might these practical steps be?

To begin with, I believe that all nations—strong and weak alike—must adhere to standards that govern the use of force. I—like any head of state—reserve the right to act unilaterally if necessary to defend my nation. Nevertheless, I am convinced that adhering to standards, international standards, strengthens those who do, and isolates and weakens those who don't.

The world rallied around America after the 9/11 attacks, and continues to support our efforts in Afghanistan, because of the horror of those senseless attacks and the recognized principle of self-defense. Likewise, the world recognized the need to confront Saddam Hussein when he invaded Kuwait—a consensus that sent a clear message to all about the cost of aggression.

Furthermore, America—in fact, no nation—can insist that others follow the rules of the road if we refuse to follow them ourselves. For when we don't, our actions appear arbitrary and undercut the legitimacy of future interventions, no matter how justified.

And this becomes particularly important when the purpose of military action extends beyond self-defense or the defense of one nation against an aggressor. More and more, we all confront difficult questions about how to prevent the slaughter of civilians by their own government, or to stop a civil war whose violence and suffering can engulf an entire region.

I believe that force can be justified on humanitarian grounds, as it was in the Balkans, or in other places that have been scarred by war. Inaction tears at our conscience and can lead to more costly intervention later. That's why all responsible nations must embrace the role that militaries with a clear mandate can play to keep the peace.

America's commitment to global security will never waver. But in a world in which threats are more diffuse, and missions more complex, America cannot act alone. America alone cannot secure the peace. This is true in Afghanistan. This is true in failed states like Somalia, where terrorism and piracy is joined by famine and human suffering. And sadly, it will continue to be true in unstable regions for years to come.

The leaders and soldiers of NATO countries, and other friends and allies, demonstrate this truth through the capacity and courage they've shown in Afghanistan. But in many countries, there is a disconnect between the efforts of those who serve and the ambivalence of the broader public. I understand why war is not popular, but I also know this: The belief that peace is desirable is rarely enough to achieve it. Peace requires responsibility. Peace entails sacrifice. That's why NATO continues to be indispensable. That's why we must strengthen U.N. and regional peacekeeping, and not leave the task to a few countries. That's why we honor those who return home from peacekeeping and training abroad to Oslo and Rome; to Ottawa and Sydney; to Dhaka and Kigali—we honor them not as makers of war, but of wagers—but as wagers of peace.

Let me make one final point about the use of force. Even as we make difficult decisions about going to war, we must also think clearly about how we fight it. The Nobel Committee recognized this truth in awarding its first prize for peace to Henry Dunant—the founder of the Red Cross, and a driving force behind the Geneva Conventions.

Where force is necessary, we have a moral and strategic interest in binding ourselves to certain rules of conduct. And even as we confront a vicious adversary that abides by no rules, I believe the United States of America must remain a standard bearer in the conduct of war. That is what makes us different from those whom we fight. That is a source of our strength. That is why I prohibited torture. That is why I ordered the prison at Guantanamo Bay closed. And that is why I have reaffirmed America's commitment to abide by the Geneva Conventions. We lose ourselves when we compromise the very ideals that we fight to defend. And we honor—we honor those ideals by upholding them not when it's easy, but when it is hard.

I have spoken at some length to the question that must weigh on our minds and our hearts as we choose to wage war. But let me now turn to our effort to avoid such tragic choices, and speak of three ways that we can build a just and lasting peace.

First, in dealing with those nations that break rules and laws, I believe that we must develop alternatives to violence that are tough enough to actually change behavior—for if we want a lasting peace, then the words of the international community must mean something. Those regimes that break the rules must be held accountable. Sanctions must exact a real price. Intransigence must be met with increased pressure—and such pressure exists only when the world stands together as one.

One urgent example is the effort to prevent the spread of nuclear weapons, and to seek a world without them. In the middle of the last century, nations agreed to be bound by a treaty whose bargain is clear: All will have access to peaceful nuclear power; those without nuclear weapons will forsake them; and those with nuclear weapons will work towards disarmament. I am committed to upholding this treaty. It is a centerpiece of my foreign policy. And I'm working with President Medvedev to reduce America and Russia's nuclear stockpiles.

But it is also incumbent upon all of us to insist that nations like Iran and North Korea do not game the system. Those who claim to respect international law cannot avert their eyes when those laws are flouted. Those who care for their own security cannot ignore the danger of an arms race in the Middle East or East Asia. Those who seek peace cannot stand idly by as nations arm themselves for nuclear war.

The same principle applies to those who violate international laws by brutalizing their own people. When there is genocide in Darfur, systematic rape in Congo, repression in Burma—there must be consequences. Yes, there will be engagement; yes, there will be diplomacy—but there must be consequences when those things fail. And the closer we stand together, the less likely we will be faced with the choice between armed intervention and complicity in oppression.

This brings me to a second point—the nature of the peace that we seek. For peace is not merely the absence of visible conflict. Only a just peace based on the inherent rights and dignity of every individual can truly be lasting.

It was this insight that drove drafters of the Universal Declaration of Human Rights after the Second World War. In the wake of devastation, they recognized that if human rights are not protected, peace is a hollow promise.

And yet too often, these words are ignored. For some countries, the failure to uphold human rights is excused by the false suggestion that these are somehow Western principles, foreign to local cultures or stages of a nation's development. And within America, there has long been a tension between those who describe themselves as realists or idealists—a tension that suggests a stark choice between the narrow pursuit of interests or an endless campaign to impose our values around the world.

I reject these choices. I believe that peace is unstable where citizens are denied the right to speak freely or worship as they please; choose their own leaders or assemble without fear. Pent-up grievances fester, and the suppression of tribal and religious identity can lead to violence. We also know that the opposite is true. Only when Europe became free did it finally find peace. America has never fought a war against a democracy, and our closest friends are governments that protect the rights of their citizens. No matter how callously defined, neither America's interests—nor the world's—are served by the denial of human aspirations.

So even as we respect the unique culture and traditions of different countries, America will always be a voice for those aspirations that are universal. We will bear witness to the quiet dignity of reformers like Aung Sang Suu Kyi; to the bravery of Zimbabweans who cast their ballots in the face of beatings; to the hundreds of thousands who have marched silently through the streets of Iran. It is telling that the leaders of these governments fear the aspirations of their own people more than the power of any other nation. And it is the responsibility of all free people and free nations to make clear that these movements—these movements of hope and history—they have us on their side.

Let me also say this: The promotion of human rights cannot be about exhortation alone. At times, it must be coupled with painstaking diplomacy. I know that engagement with repressive regimes lacks the satisfying purity of indignation. But I also know that sanctions without outreach—condemnation without discussion—can carry forward only a crippling status quo. No repressive regime can move down a new path unless it has the choice of an open door.

In light of the Cultural Revolution's horrors, Nixon's meeting with Mao appeared inexcusable—and yet it surely helped set China on a path where millions of its citizens have been lifted from poverty and connected to open societies. Pope John Paul's engagement with Poland created space not just for the Catholic Church, but for labor leaders like Lech Walesa. Ronald Reagan's efforts on arms control and embrace of perestroika not only improved relations with the Soviet Union, but empowered dissidents throughout Eastern Europe. There's no simple formula here. But we must try as best we can to balance isolation and engagement, pressure and incentives, so that human rights and dignity are advanced over time.

Third, a just peace includes not only civil and political rights—it must encompass economic security and opportunity. For true peace is not just freedom from fear, but freedom from want.

It is undoubtedly true that development rarely takes root without security; it is also true that security does not exist where human beings do not have access to enough food, or clean water, or the medicine and shelter they need to survive. It does not exist where children can't aspire to a decent education or a job that supports a family. The absence of hope can rot a society from within.

And that's why helping farmers feed their own people—or nations educate their children and care for the sick—is not mere charity. It's also why the world must come together to confront climate change. There is little scientific dispute that if we do nothing, we will face more drought, more famine, more mass displacement—all of which will fuel more conflict for decades. For this reason, it is not merely scientists and environmental activists who call for swift and forceful action—it's military leaders in my own country and others who understand our common security hangs in the balance.

Agreements among nations. Strong institutions. Support for human rights. Investments in development. All these are vital ingredients in bringing about the evolution that President Kennedy spoke about. And yet, I do not believe that we will have the will, the determination, the staying power, to complete this work without something more—and that's the continued expansion of our moral imagination; an insistence that there's something irreducible that we all share.

As the world grows smaller, you might think it would be easier for human beings to recognize how similar we are; to understand that we're all basically seeking the same things; that we all hope for the chance to live out our lives with some measure of happiness and fulfillment for ourselves and our families.

And yet somehow, given the dizzying pace of globalization, the cultural leveling of modernity, it perhaps comes as no surprise that people fear the loss of what they cherish in their particular identities—their race, their tribe, and perhaps most powerfully their religion. In some places, this fear has led to conflict. At times, it even feels like we're moving backwards. We see it in the Middle East, as the conflict between Arabs and Jews seems to harden. We see it in nations that are torn asunder by tribal lines.

And most dangerously, we see it in the way that religion is used to justify the murder of innocents by those who have distorted and defiled the great religion of Islam, and who attacked my country from Afghanistan. These extremists are not the first to kill in the name of God; the cruelties of the Crusades are amply recorded. But they remind us that no Holy War can ever be a just war. For if you truly believe that you are carrying out divine will, then there is no need for restraint—no need to spare the pregnant mother, or the medic, or the Red Cross worker, or even a person of one's own faith. Such a warped view of religion is not just incompatible with the concept of peace, but I believe it's incompatible with the very purpose of faith—for the one rule that lies at the heart of every major religion is that we do unto others as we would have them do unto us.

Adhering to this law of love has always been the core struggle of human nature. For we are fallible. We make mistakes, and fall victim to the temptations of pride, and power, and sometimes evil. Even those of us with the best of intentions will at times fail to right the wrongs before us.

But we do not have to think that human nature is perfect for us to still believe that the human condition can be perfected. We do not have to live in an idealized world to still reach for those ideals that will make it a better place. The non-violence practiced by men like Gandhi and King may not have been practical or possible in every circumstance, but the love that they preached—their fundamental faith in human progress—that must always be the North Star that guides us on our journey.

For if we lose that faith—if we dismiss it as silly or naïve; if we divorce it from the decisions that we make on issues of war and peace—then we lose what's best about humanity. We lose our sense of possibility. We lose our moral compass.

Like generations have before us, we must reject that future. As Dr. King said at this occasion so many years ago, "I refuse to accept despair as the final response to the ambiguities of history. I refuse to accept the idea that the 'isness' of man's present condition makes him morally incapable of reaching up for the eternal 'oughtness' that forever confronts him."

Let us reach for the world that ought to be—that spark of the divine that still stirs within each of our souls.

Somewhere today, in the here and now, in the world as it is, a soldier sees he's outgunned, but stands firm to keep the peace. Somewhere today, in this world, a young protestor awaits the brutality of her government, but has the courage to march on. Somewhere today, a mother facing punishing poverty still takes the time to teach her child, scrapes together what few coins she has to send that child to school—because she believes that a cruel world still has a place for that child's dreams.

Let us live by their example. We can acknowledge that oppression will always be with us, and still strive for justice. We can admit the intractability of depravation, and still strive for dignity. Clear-eyed, we can understand that there will be war, and still strive for peace. We can do that—for that is the story of human progress; that's the hope of all the world; and at this moment of challenge, that must be our work here on Earth.

Thank you very much.

Echoes of T.V.'s First Lady:
Michelle Obama's Last True Cultural Antecedent Is 'Cosby's' Clair Huxtable
Robin Givhan

So far, the first lady has chosen to be a food bank volunteer with an outsize entourage and an education activist with the largest soapbox imaginable. But Michelle Obama also fills a role that is not of her choosing but that may, in fact, be the most influential: She serves as a symbol of middle-class progress, feminist achievement, affirmative-action success and individual style.

And she has done all this on the world stage . . . while being black.

Time and again, observers grasp for adjectives to describe Obama's combination of professional accomplishment and soccer-mom maternalism. It's no wonder so many eye her with awe and disbelief. Or why a minority still view her with suspicion. There have been few broad cultural precedents for what she represents.

Historically, television has been more progressive than reality, preparing a society for the moment when what only existed in the shadows surges into the spotlight. From "Soap" to "Will & Grace," TV helped people envision gay couples living picket-fence lives. "Maude" and daytime soap operas raised the topic of abortion before it became a political wedge issue. Television made the case for the first female commander in chief. And popular culture has more than once suggested that the idea of an African American president wasn't so far-fetched. But it rarely introduced viewers to anyone like Michelle Obama.

The last similarly accomplished and wholesome black woman to enter the homes of TV audiences—both black and white, in small towns and big cities — was Clair Huxtable, the matriarch of "The Cosby Show." It is a cultural comparison more apt than the one made to Jackie Kennedy, which is rooted in little more than the two first ladies being mothers of young children and their affection for sleeveless dresses.

Television, in particular, speaks to viewers intimately, in the privacy of their homes, building long-term relationships and weaving complicated narratives. People discuss the lives of TV characters—from soap opera stars to reality-show contestants—with the kind of emotional empathy normally saved for family members. Syndication allows characters to live forever and connect to multiple generations, whether it is the blended family of "The Brady Bunch" or the codependent New Yorkers on "Seinfeld."

Even as viewing habits have become more fragmented through cable and DVRs, TV still serves as a lingua franca. It can gently and affably prod disparate groups toward greater tolerance and acceptance. TV builds kinship.

But most of the prominent portrayals of black women on television are men in corpulent drag (Madea), strutting tarts ("The Real Housewives of Atlanta") or emotionless law enforcement officers (Lt. Anita Van Buren of "Law & Order"). In its most enlightened moments, popular culture presents black women as strident taskmaster with the heart of gold—see Dr. Miranda Bailey of "Grey's Anatomy."

In a recent essay for the Nation, Columbia law professor Patricia Williams shared her frustrations about popular culture's failure to present more images of the sort that Obama reflects. Black women—and women of color, in general—still are dogged by the tropes that have haunted them for generations, she wrote. But instead of images such as Mammy and Prissy from "Gone With the Wind," contemporary women must deal with "the adventures of Flavor Flav and Strom Thurmond" as well as "depictions from Don Imus and the minstrelsy of Tyler Perry."

"Where, for heaven's sake, is a picture of black femininity (in particular, that of darker-skinned, non-tragic femininity) that might signify beauty, chic, elegance, vulnerability, sophistication?"

Where are the images that celebrate the educated black woman? "The jurisprudence of the entire 20th century was about black people trying to get into school," Williams said in a telephone interview. "That's invisible." Niche media have tried to showcase the black professional class—from the stories of uplift in Ebony magazine to "Harlem Heights," a reality show about 20-something buppies that debuted this spring on BET, a rarity on a black-oriented cable network often criticized by viewers for pandering to the worst stereotypes of African Americans. There have been shows that have spoken knowingly to a predominantly black audience, such as "Living Single" and "Girlfriends." "Soul Food" and "Lincoln Heights" address the small segmented audiences of cable.

Only Audra McDonald's character on ABC's "Private Practice"—a divorced, stylish doctor with a young daughter, a vibrant social life and a healthy relationship with her ex-husband—really reflects a generation of black women with advanced degrees, solid self-esteem and no anger issues.

But TV audiences have to go back to "The Cosby Show" to find a close fac-simile to what Obama represents both professionally and personally, and that's going back more than 17 years. Clair Huxtable—the stylish mother, wife and lawyer—remains a lonely figure in popular culture.

"The Cosby Show," a sitcom about a black American family with five chil-dren, a lawyer-mom played by Phylicia Rashad and comedian Bill Cosby as the doctor-dad, ran from 1984 to 1992. Inspired by Cosby's monologues on child-rearing, the show was an anomaly when it premiered in the wake of TV series such as "Sanford and Son," "Good Times" and "The Jeffersons," which told the stories of down-and-out black Americans and upwardly mobile ones with equal parts slapstick and buffoonery.

"The Cosby Show" was doggedly upper-middle class in its sensibility. Every detail, from the choice of artwork in the Huxtable living room to the use of jazz in its opening credits to references to historically black colleges, spoke of the "Talented Tenth," a functional, culturally proud segment of the African American community that did not make the evening news.

In its first season, "The Cosby Show" finished third in the ratings. For the next four seasons, it was the top-rated series on television. Over the course of its run, it revived the situation-comedy format, resuscitated a flailing NBC, sparked conversations about race and made Cosby into America's dad.

Author Susan Fales-Hill, 46, began her career on the show as an apprentice and then a writer. Later, she became executive producer and head writer for the spinoff series "A Different World," about life on a fictional, historically black college campus through which viewers could see work-study students and trust-fund babies.

"There's something that happens when you validate the existence of some-one by visually representing them," she says. "What people see, they believe."

And what they do not see on a regular basis, they assume to be rare or even nonexistent.

Fales-Hill could write from her own experience. She is the biracial daughter of actress Josephine Premice, a contemporary of Diahann Carroll and Lena Horne. She is a published author and comes from a background of private schools.

During her time on "Cosby," Fales-Hill remembers people telling her that families like the one on the show didn't exist, but her rejoinder was her per-sonal story. "I had people tell me this is like a white family," Fales-Hill recalls. "But 'Cosby' brought the dirty secret of America—the black bourgeoisie—out of the closet."

When "Cosby" went off the air, the lesson Hollywood took was not that sto-ries about functional black professionals can have broad appeal. It was that Bill Cosby has broad appeal, that stand-up comics could sustain entire sitcoms and that situation comedies can draw large audiences. "The Cosby Show" opened the door for "Grace Under Fire," "Home Improvement," "The Fresh Prince of Bel-Air," "Cybill" and "Roseanne." And Cosby went on to star in another self-named comedy, which ran from 1996 to 2000. (And once again, Rashad played his wife, although the role was a modest one.)

By the end of the millennium, white, angst-ridden yuppies and white, wacky singles were dominating the airwaves. "Survivor" debuted in 2000 to launch the reality-show juggernaut. And women like Fales-Hill largely vanished from popular culture.

"There's a generation with very little exposure to the black professional class, and they stand in amazement," Fales-Hill says. "People say, 'You're so articulate.' And it's because I can string a sentence together!"

In a culture in which every white woman is presumed to be Everywoman until proven out of the mainstream, Obama has brought the normalcy of black women into the broader social consciousness. All it took were her two Ivy League degrees, a six-figure boardroom salary, a Norman Rockwell family, soccer-mom bona fides and an ability to dress herself without the aid of an entourage.

In many ways, the first lady has made people see—really see—black women for the first time. For example, when a black model appeared on the May cover of Vogue, news articles credited the "Obama effect," ignoring the concerted lobbying by fashion industry activists that began long before Barack Obama was even a presidential contender.

The role of style in defining the first lady might easily be dismissed as a distraction from more substantive issues. But Williams says the fan magazine breathlessness is significant because "it implies a kind of parity we really needed."

Enthusiasm over glossy-magazine beauty as defined by a darker-skinned black woman has to be seen against the backdrop of history, when black women's appearance was used as a tool of oppression. High culture rhapsodized in love sonnets about ivory complexions, flaxen hair and ruby lips. And today, black women still mostly surface as sidebars in beauty stories.

"Somewhere in the core of it is the question of whether black really is beautiful," Williams says. "That's why I think it's not about superficiality. It's a precarious moment. Only a minute ago, she was Angela Davis."

In the NAACP's most recent report on diversity on television, the civil rights organization noted in December that "it is hard to draw any positive conclusions." And in particular, it pointed to "The Hills" and "Gossip Girls," which are aimed at a youth market. Viewers in their teens and 20s live in a more diverse society than their parents did. But little had changed since what the NAACP called the "whiteout" years of shows such as "Friends" and "Seinfeld"—and more recently "Sex and the City" and "Lipstick Jungle"—which were situated in the melting pot of New York City but seemed to exist in a parallel, nearly all-white universe.

Hollywood producer Mara Brock Akil was a regular "Sex and the City" viewer. "They were able to show women as layered and flawed—and spending obscene amounts of money on accessories—and still empowered and smart women," Akil says. "I related to it, but I longed to see myself physically validated, which they rarely did."

Akil, 39, grew up middle class in the Baldwin Hills neighborhood of Los Angeles and in Kansas City, Mo. But unlike television viewers who find themselves disappointed by network offerings and can only blog about it, Akil had the ability to alter the landscape.

So she created "Girlfriends." It debuted in 2000 on UPN, a new network that was aggressively courting a black audience. Among black women, it was appointment television. The ongoing saga of Joan (Tracee Ellis Ross) and her trio of friends gave professional, stylish black women a voice on television.

"I almost felt like a documentarian," Akil says. "I wanted people to know what's on our mind."

The show talked about romance and work, and it poked fun at the assumptions about black culture vs. white. Joan, for example, was a huge fan of Celine Dion—because Akil is—as well as more soulful singers such as India.Arie.

"I also wanted to combat a stereotype on TV that black women are either the sister-girl or the asexual judge with no life. I can be fearless at work, but I can also be stupid over a guy. I can be all those things at once. I wanted to show how fashionable we are. The fashion and the femininity, I really wanted to talk about that," Akil says. "My agenda was to speak to the widest audience possible, but I knew the core would be the African American audience."

"Girlfriends" ran for eight seasons—eventually moving to CW. In that time, it was a favorite at the BET Honors and the NAACP Image Awards, winning at least five times. It was nominated for only one prime-time Emmy—in 2003, for cinematography. It lost to "Will & Grace."

The show didn't have the broad cultural impact of "The Cosby Show," which, during its eight-year run, won virtually every award possible except a Nobel prize. No other show about the professional black class has made the inroads that "Cosby" did. None of pop culture's most enduring archetypes of funny, smart, professional, pretty women—from Mary Richards to Murphy Brown to Carrie Bradshaw—have been black.

And Clair Huxtable, despite Rashad's successes on Broadway, is now most often seen by middle America as the latest Jenny Craig spokeswoman touting her weight loss.

Balm:
Styling Her Daughters' Hair Each Morning, She was Attending to Something Deeper Than a Beauty Ritual

Lonnae O'Neal Parker

Soon now, these days will be gone from me.

As I settle myself on the couch, my 11-year-old daughter, Savannah, brings me her hair basket: comb, water bottle, hair grease, barrettes. She plants herself on the floor, squarely between my knees, and I begin my work. There's the everyday hair-doing, but wash day takes more time, and slowly I separate the thick, kinky tangle growing from her head. I rub in a dollop of grease—Kemi Oyl or root stimulator lotion, but mostly just dark blue Ultra Sheen (I like the standards)—to make the hair obedient, and part it into sections, clipping each firmly to her head.

My hands are slower and gentler now than they were when she was younger and I was younger, with a career to chase, and an older daughter who had her own head of hair for me to do, and another baby yet to come.

Sometimes, if I was pressed for time, I could get by with a few surface brush strokes and a liberal application of gel to make the girls passably presentable, but it took 20 minutes of work to make them look special. Twenty minutes to make them feel pretty so that neighbors would comment on the straightness of their parts. Twenty minutes to be reassured that I'd sent my children into the world making clear that they were valued and loved. Twenty minutes. Every day. Minimum. Apiece. For me to feel assuaged that if one day, please, God, no, they suddenly disappeared, I could persuade the 24-hour cable networks that my girls really were worthy enough to be news—because, after all, black mothers can't recall a time where missing black women and children got national media attention.

Back then, when I craved only sleep, my children's tears—because there is an unassailable physical hurt to the pulling and detangling of black girl hair—often left me unmoved or impatient, or sometimes mingled with my own tired tears. Because, like my mother before me, I had so many other things to attend to.

My mother, a Chicago schoolteacher for 33 years, combed my hair and my sister's hair for 35 minutes every morning in her slip so as not to get hair grease on her work clothes. She reminds me of how much those mornings used to hurt. "You'd want to turn around and look at me with all this woe on your face so that maybe I would stop," Momma remembers. "But, you know, I couldn't stop, because you had to have your hair combed." And she had to get to work. And every two weeks, when she washed my hair, "it would be all over your head, like you had an afro the size of a small umbrella and that had to be pulled back down in something I could reasonably deal with."

Years ago, it was easy to lose sight that this ritual, this touching of my children every day, had an expiration date. But now ours is close.

I begin at the nape of Savannah's neck and make my first row of two-strand twists small and precise. The style is much like the one that first daughter 11-year-old Malia Obama wore last year on her first day of school in Washington, and this summer in Rome and at Martha's Vineyard. For us, children favored by the sun, whose natural kinks want nothing more than to stand at attention all over our heads, this hair thing between mothers and daughters goes back to the beginning, and I wonder if Malia's momma washes and twists her hair on Sunday afternoons, too. Or if the first lady knows how quickly this time with our girls slips away. Probably not. When our oldests are still young, we think they'll stay that way forever.

With more than an hour of parting and twisting ahead, and no place for either of us to go, Savvy and I talk. She wants to know if she can go to school for fashion design and if I like the name Harlowe for a girl. She tells me how she's the guitarist for "Black Dragon," the rock band she's formed with Nia and Alexis, although she can't play guitar, and how none of the Goosebumps books are scary, but "in terms of creepiness," "Chicken, Chicken" is worse than "Ghost Beach." She says she started reading "The Diary of Anne Frank" and that it made her angry that the Jews had to give the Nazis their bikes.

Such is the nature of hair space in my house; it is a time for rumination and a time for prattle.

"Mommy, I don't want you to call me Savvy anymore. My new name is Sav Sav," Savannah announced to me one day. "And I don't want you to call me Savannahsaurus Rex. My new nickname is Sav Sav Rex."

Sometimes, over barrettes and tonics, we go deep.

It was hair time on the green couch when my oldest daughter, Sydney, then 5, came to the realization that she was different from the girls on the commercials; that her hair would never reach for her waist. "Even when I get older?" She cried; I cried; her godmother, Dana, cried.

It is, for little black girls, that "For Whom the Bell Tolls" moment when Miss Clairol comes for you. When you are just old enough to realize what the culture prizes as beautiful and just old enough to know that you aren't it. Non-black mothers whose daughters have ample thighs or flat chests or who fret about the shape of their eyes doubtless know the moment. But black people are the only ones in the world with black people hair, so our daughter's pain is ours alone. It is a moment when even a mother's love is not nearly enough comfort, but it's the only balm we have.

Savannah, whose hair is longer and curlier than Sydney's, was more resigned in her hair epiphany. She wondered why hers was so kinky. As the children's book says, we are "Happy to Be Nappy," I tried to explain to her cheerfully, but Savannah was skeptical. Nappy hair is hard to comb, she said, and wondered why she should be happy that her hair was hard to comb. "But okay, whatever."

"Did they have color television when you where a kid?" Savannah asks, breaking my reverie. I murmur affirmations as I twist. I chime in when appropriate or, under the guise of detangling, rhythmically knead my fingertips in her scalp until her eyelids start to fall. My daughter is right there on the brink of growing up, already showing signs of the woman she'll become. Her legs are longer now, and her T-shirts no longer lay flat against her ribs. My features are becoming more pronounced in her face. I keep rubbing, prolonging our time as I listen to her words or her sweet, untroubled silence.

As it happened with her sister before her, I will lose this intimacy with my last daughter to friends and parties and, worst of all, to boys and, eventually, men and children; to people who will come to mean more to her everyday life than I ever will again. I have been such a harried mother with Savannah, so distracted by the constant demands of husband and career and other children, and now, just as I'm looking up, my youngest daughter is almost beyond the old rituals. So I rub her scalp for the times I combed her hair hard, for the times I rushed through her kinks too quickly, for the times I yelled when I wish I had whispered. For the time I spanked her harder than I meant to for erasing an hour-long interview I had typed on my computer. I grease her hair and rub her scalp.

Let this be the hand she remembers.

In little more than an hour, our time is over. Savannah scarcely gives me a moment to admire her, this luminous little girl poised for adolescence, all mine for just seconds before she's off to find her soccer ball, her friend Pearl and the whole wide rest of her world.

It's okay, I console myself. Her sister still kisses me every night and sometimes asks me to roll her hair, so I know I won't lose this connection with Savannah altogether. Our time together will merely change. I lie across the couch, weary from my labor, and my own eyelids grow heavy. Savannah comes back to retrieve something and pauses. She lays a blanket across my length and gently tucks the ends under my sides.

Drifting off to sleep, I smile. Even without a comb in my hand, I think these days will never really be gone from me.

Love All God's Children, Straight or Gay
Desmond Tutu

Hate has no place in the house of God. No one should be excluded from our love, our compassion or our concern because of race or gender, faith or ethnicity—or because of their sexual orientation. Nor should anyone be excluded from health care on any of these grounds. In my country of South Africa, we struggled for years against the evil system of apartheid that divided human beings, children of the same God, by racial classification and then denied many of them fundamental human rights. We knew this was wrong. Thankfully, the world supported us in our struggle for freedom and dignity.

It is time to stand up against another wrong.

Gay, lesbian, bisexual and transgendered people are part of so many families. They are part of the human family. They are part of God's family. And of course they are part of the African family. But a wave of hate is spreading across my beloved continent. People are again being denied their fundamental rights and freedoms. Men have been falsely charged and imprisoned in Senegal, and health services for these men and their community have suffered. In Malawi, men have been jailed and humiliated for expressing their partnerships with other men. Just this month, mobs in Mtwapa Township, Kenya, attacked men they suspected of being gay. Kenyan religious leaders, I am ashamed to say, threatened an HIV clinic there for providing counseling services to all members of that community, because the clerics wanted gay men excluded.

Uganda's parliament is debating legislation that would make homosexuality punishable by life imprisonment, and more discriminatory legislation has been debated in Rwanda and Burundi.

These are terrible backward steps for human rights in Africa.

Our lesbian and gay brothers and sisters across Africa are living in fear.

And they are living in hiding—away from care, away from the protection the state should offer to every citizen and away from health care in the AIDS era, when all of us, especially Africans, need access to essential HIV services.

That this pandering to intolerance is being done by politicians looking for scapegoats for their failures is not surprising. But it is a great wrong. An even larger offense is that it is being done in the name of God. Show me where Christ said "Love thy fellow man, except for the gay ones." Gay people, too, are made in my God's image. I would never worship a homophobic God.

"But they are sinners," I hear the preachers and politicians say. "They are choosing a life of sin for which they must be punished." My scientist and medical friends that have shared with me a reality that so many gay people have confirmed, I now know it in my heart to be true. No one chooses to be gay. Sexual orientation, like skin color, is another feature of our diversity as a human family. Isn't it amazing that we are all made in God's image, and yet there is so much diversity among his people? Does God love his dark- or his light-skinned children less? The brave more than the timid? And does any of us know the mind of God so well that we can decide for him who is included, and who is excluded, from the circle of his love?

The wave of hate must stop. Politicians who profit from exploiting this hate, from fanning it, must not be tempted by this easy way to profit from fear and misunderstanding. And my fellow clerics, of all faiths, must stand up for the principles of universal dignity and fellowship. Exclusion is never the way forward on our shared paths to freedom and justice.